The 1945 Detroit Tigers

The 1945 Detroit Tigers

Nine Old Men and One Young Left Arm Win It All

BURGE CARMON SMITH

McFarland & Company, Inc., Publishers

Jefferson, North Carolina, and London

LIBRARY OF CONGRESS CATALOGUING-IN-PUBLICATION DATA

Smith, Burge Carmon.
   The 1945 Detroit Tigers : nine old men and one young left
arm win it all / Burge Carmon Smith.
     p.   cm.
   Includes bibliographical references and index.

   ISBN 978-0-7864-4196-9
   softcover : 50# alkaline paper ∞

   1. Detroit Tigers (Baseball team)—History—20th century.
2. World Series (Baseball) (1945)   I. Title.   II. Title: Nineteen
forty-five Detroit Tigers.
   GV875.D6S62   2010
   796.357'640977434—dc22   2010009797

British Library cataloguing data are available

Cover photograph: Hal Newhouser (AP photo); background ©2010
Shutterstock

Manufactured in the United States of America

McFarland & Company, Inc., Publishers
  Box 611, Jefferson, North Carolina 28640
   www.mcfarlandpub.com

In memory of
Dalton Roy "Tony" Filter,
a great Dutch Hill and
St. John's sandlot buddy

Table of Contents

Preface and Acknowledgments

When I first sat down with Dr. John Childrey, late in 2001, to discuss the possibility of an advanced degree at Florida Atlantic University through their employee program, I had little interest in being accepted into their liberal arts program. I was 67 years old and retired from a 39-year career of coaching and teaching. During that time, to balance our family budget, I worked as a senior clerk at Florida Atlantic University's information desk in Davie, Florida. I didn't have the desire to put myself through another degree program. But as we talked and others began to encourage me, such as Dr. Childrey and Dr. Mark Rose, I became stimulated enough by their support to begin making the effort.

In addition to those wonderful professors, I am also greatly thankful to Professor Kitty Oliver and Dr. Cliff McCue for their diligence as members of the committee that critically reviewed the work for my degree. Other large motivators were the suggestions and the friendship of Dr. Robert Heppler from the adjacent Broward County Community Junior College (BCC) campus. All of these educators helped make my degree possible, and I owe a large amount of gratitude to all of them.

When I chose the Detroit Tigers and the World Series of 1945 as my main project, I was following a passion for the Tigers and the game of baseball that I had nurtured from childhood. The last year of passage from one era to another was 1945. The history attached to 1945 in and outside of baseball was fascinating to me. Before taking Professor Oliver's class concerning oral history, I decided to interview as many of the living members of that 1945 Detroit team as possible.

After reading an article on Red Borom, a utility infielder for Detroit in 1945, I went about trying to contact him. When I found him in Dallas he accepted my interview request. Red and his friends were wonderful hosts. I conducted and taped my first interview with him in Richardson, Texas. Red opened some doors for me to speak with other living team members, and soon I was talking face to face with a number of my boyhood heroes throughout the country.

I owe the Detroit Tiger Club thanks for helping me contact several players

1

whose addresses were unknown to me at that time. Most of these players were in their late seventies and eighties, and a few in their nineties. All of them, despite their advanced age, were wonderful hosts and grand conversationalists. They granted me an ample amount of their time to tape, discuss and give me their opinions about their experiences. I was moved by their openness as well as their concern for the fans of the game and the history of their era. In addition to Red Borom, I offer heartfelt thanks to Virgil Trucks, Jimmy Outlaw, John McHale, and George Kell (with Philadelphia in 1945), Billy Pierce, Les Mueller, Ed Mierkowicz, and Del Baker Jr., whose father had been a manager of the Tigers and in 1945 was a coach for the Red Sox. I also am in debt to two high school teammates: Jerry Turner, whose interview unfortunately would not fit the time frame for my topic but hopefully will be used in the future; and Jim Terpeney, a high school baseball teammate and friend, whose support has been greatly appreciated.

After unexpectedly moving back to Texas, I decided to take the material I used for my project paper and attempt to put it together for a book. This took me into a deeper look at the Tigers' 1945 season and the World Series of that year.

For helping throughout this period of struggle, I heartily give my appreciation, gratitude, and eternal thanks to the Rev. Dr. Richard Dinda, Concordia University professor emeritus, whose language expertise and knowledge was a substantial factor in this work. His patience and friendship throughout the years have been invaluable to me.

Many of the resource materials for the project were made available to me through the combined Broward Community Junior College/Florida Atlantic University Library in Davie, Florida; the Milwaukee Public Library; the Hall of Fame Library in Cooperstown, New York; the Public Library in Adrian, Michigan; the Waxahachie Museum in Waxahachie, Texas; and the Society for American Baseball Research (SABR).

I need to acknowledge and give thanks to my friend John Bosch for his labors in photo shop and for giving me of his precious time. I also should give credit to the Sun City Computer Staff, especially Mose Blaine for mentoring me through several challenging projects. I thank my nephew Christopher Deibert for printing and vacuum packaging my original copy for a first mailing to various book companies.

Finally, I thank my wonderful wife, Beverly Jane for all of her understanding, patience, help, love and tolerance during my work on this project.

Introduction:
1945 — A Watershed Year

An eleven-year-old, as most of us know, lives in the present. At eleven years old I firmly believed that 1945 saw the best that baseball had to offer. The greatest players, the most exciting games — and certainly the best team of all time. This was the year the Detroit Tigers beat the Chicago Cubs in the World Series. I was too young to be drafted, but I was just the right age to follow my beloved Tigers inning by inning as they inched their way to the American League pennant and finally to the world championship.

I did sense, however, that something was missing. I lived in Adrian, Michigan, a town of about 20,000. Twenty or thirty minutes of walking could get me just about anywhere in town. I could see the women going about their errands walking to the grocery stores, working on the lawns and gardens of their homes, hanging out the wash on the line, and young children, of which I was one, playing in the neighborhoods, streets, and parks, or walking back and forth to school. There were older men shuffling to and from work in the factories with their lunch pails underneath their arms, but what I didn't see were the hardy young men who were yesterday's high school athletes and town heroes strutting around town. This was the empty space, the missing element everyone had felt since December 7, 1941.

World War II removed these young men from their communities and had swallowed them up in squads and companies. The family next door, for instance, the Kirsches, had three sons: Dick was in Germany; Bill was on some South Pacific atoll; and Joe was finishing high school, about to enlist in the service. He would soon leave for basic training. There were numerous families like the Kirsches with empty places at the supper table. The gold-star banners that hung in windows throughout many neighborhoods within the nation bore witness to the ultimate sacrifices American households made during this war.

It was a time when people needed recreation and levity to maintain sanity, and the one great recreational outlet of that day was played on manicured diamond fields, in vacant lots, and even on the neighborhood streets. I thought

3

everyone had an opinion about baseball. I believed that people were reading about it, listening to it on the radio, and discussing it daily at work and at home. If people didn't talk about anything else, they talked about baseball. They followed the standings in each league, discussed the box scores and knew about the players, coaches and managers not only of their favorite team but of all sixteen major league squads.

My neighborhood was German-American, but boys at the fairgrounds where we played baseball were from a number of ethnic backgrounds and from other neighborhoods. They would find their way to the empty spaces at the fairgrounds to play on makeshift diamonds, using paper, wood and stone for bases, home plate and the pitcher's rubber. Sometimes there were as many as eighteen or twenty boys and then other times as few as two, three or four, playing pepper, home-run derby or flys and grounders, but we played day in and day out during the summer months before the grounds opened up for the fair later in the year. The Detroit Tigers was just about everyone's team. As we threw, hit, fielded and ran the bases, visions of Greenberg, Cullenbine, Mayo, Cramer, Newhouser, Trout, and other Tiger members flashed through our minds. The fairgrounds became Briggs Stadium. The fantasy and passion of youth put us into our own make-believe world. It was a passion that helped us to forget the rest of the world of 1945 for a while.

The ethnic environment and culture from which we descended really belonged more to our grandparents than to us, the third generation of Americans. Many of the moms and dads were busy making a living working side by side with people from various walks of life, conscious of their background, but living with much more tolerance than their parents. They instilled some of that magnanimity and impartiality into their children. As we ran, threw, hit and competed against each other, it was as Americans. The question wasn't so much what you were or what you looked like or what you said you could do, but how you could play this game and what type of attitude you displayed in playing it.

Things changed: money was made and money was lost, times were good or they became bad, wars appeared and disappeared, people grew up and people died, but baseball was always there as the one constant democratizing activity that affected our young lives.

We made our own rules, supplied our own equipment for the unsupervised scrimmages, and settled arguments among ourselves. There was no adult supervision, just kids playing baseball. As we grew into young men and adults, some of us continued to play with high school teams, in recreational leagues, on American Legion teams, or later, perhaps, amateur recreational leagues, semi-pro baseball, even college baseball and in a few rare cases on professional teams. The better maintained diamonds in town were great to play on, but places like the fairgrounds were always available to practice skills.

In the American League, the era was highlighted by a one-armed player in St. Louis and a 4-F southpaw pitcher from Detroit. Professional baseball had suffered a huge loss of talented young men to the war effort. In fact, there was significant discussion about curtailing it during the war. The president and Congress, however, permitted the game to continue in order to preserve some semblance of normalcy on the home front during the conflict. Baseball reflected our country's work force, her lifestyle and her hopes.

The game was part of the transition connecting the Depression era to a foundation being laid for a new American society that would emerge after World War II. It was the last bridge in baseball from the old era of absolutist ownership, submissive player contracts, and racial and ethnic class divisions.

The best baseball had to offer that year, the World Champion Detroit Tigers, is the subject of my research, and the search starts for me as an eleven-year-old Tiger fan. I'm just a sandlot kid, who spent summer afternoons and early evenings

Roger "Doc" Cramer (artwork ©1997 John Phillips, Perry, Georgia).

playing, talking, and reading baseball. The bond that kids form connecting them to athletic heroes was especially strong in my life. I lived in a world torn by war, hardship, and economic difficulties; heroes were important in such times.

The 1945 Tiger Scorecard

Name	Age	Birthplace	Ht.	Wt.	B	T	Nickname	Position
Benton, Alton	34	Noble, OK	6' 04"	206	R	R	Big Al	Pitcher
Bridges, Thomas	38	Gordonsville, TN	5' 10"	155	R	R	Tommy	Pitcher
Caster, George	36	Holton, GA	6' 01"	192	R	R		Pitcher
Eaton, Zebelon	25	Cooleemee, NC	5' 11"	175	R	R	Zeb	Pitcher
Houtteman, Arthur	18	Detroit, MI	6' 01"	183	R	R	Art	Pitcher
Mueller, Leslie C.	26	Belleville, IL	6' 03"	190	R	R	Les	Pitcher
Newhouser, Harold	24	Detroit, MI	6' 02"	182	L	L	Hal, Hurricane Hal, Prince Hal	Pitcher
Overmire, Frank	26	Moline, MI	5' 07"	162	R	L	Stubby	Pitcher
Pierce, Walter W.	18	Detroit, MI	5' 10"	142	L	L	Billy	Pitcher
Tobin, James	32	Oakland, CA	6'	195	R	R	Jim, Abba Dabba	Pitcher
Trout, Paul H.	30	Terre Haute, IN	6' 01"	195	R	R	Dizzy	Pitcher
Trucks, Virgil O.	26	Birmingham, AL	5' 11"	195	R	R	Fire	Pitcher
Wilson, Walter	29	Glenn, GA	6' 04"	185	L	R		Pitcher
Miller, James	32	Celeste, TX	5' 11"	215	R	R	Hack	Catcher
Richards, Paul R.	36	Waxahachie, TX	6' 02"	182	R	R		Catcher
Swift, Robert	29	Salina, KS	5' 11"	185	R	R	Bob	Catcher
Borom, Edward	28	Spartanburg, SC	5' 11"	180	L	R	Red	Infielder

Name	*Age*	*Birthplace*	*Ht.*	*Wt.*	*B*	*T*	*Nickname*	*Position*
Hoover, Robert	29	Brawley, CA	5' 11"	175	R	R		Infielder
Maier, Robert P.	30	Dunellen, NJ	5' 09"	180	R	R	Bob	Infielder
Mayo, Edward J.	32	Holyoke, MA	5' 11"	180	L	R	Hot Shot	Infielder
Webb, James L.	33	Meridian, MS	5' 09"	150	R	R	Skeeter	Infielder
York, Rudolph P.	32	Ragland, AL	6' 01"	209	R	R	Big Chief	Infielder
Cramer, Roger	40	Beach Haven, NJ	6' 02"	185	L	R	Doc, Flit	Outfielder
Cullenbine, Roy	30	Nashville, TN	6'	188	B	R		Outfielder
Greenberg, Henry Benjamin	34	New York, NY	6' 03½"	205	R	R	Hammering Hank, Hankus Pankus, Big Stick, Hank	Outfielder
Hostetler, Charles Cloyd	40	McClellandtown, PA	6'	175	L	R	Chuck	Outfielder
McHale, John J.	24	Detroit, MI	6'	200	L	R		Outfielder
Mierkowicz, Edward F.	21	Wyandotte, MI	6' 04"	205	R	R	Butch	Outfielder
Outlaw, James P.	32	Orme, TN	5' 08"	165	R	R	Runt	Outfielder/ Infielder

Manager: Steve O'Neill; Scout: A.J. (Wish) Egan
Coach: Art Mills; Scout: Bruce Connatser
Traveling Sec'y: Clair J, Berry; Scout: Dan Crowley
Trainer: Dr. Raymond D. Forsyth; Scout: Ed Katalinas
Owner: Walter Owen Briggs; Scout: Frank Shellenback; Scout: Al Vincent

(Names based on 1945 World Series roster. Missing are those who played during season but for one reason or the other were not on the series eligibility roster.)

1

Sunday, September 30, 1945

"'If I get a chance,' he said, 'in this inning, I think I've got this pitcher figured out in what he is doing.' When Hank knew what pitch was coming there was nobody that could keep the ball in the ball park...."

John McHale

I pulled a list from the back pocket of my jeans and stared at it intently. I always had an agenda, and today's order of business listed three items for my attention. Item one was a one-word entry that simply said, "Church." It was the Lord's Day, and even if I wanted to skip, I knew Mom would insist otherwise. I knew it was a waste of time to debate a topic that was not debatable. That item would stay on the list.

Item two was debatable. The word "movie" accelerated my fantasies and imagination with a mixture of great curiosity and anticipation. The Family Theatre was showing the latest B-western cowboy film. Charles Starrett, alias "The Durango Kid," was starring in this weekend's attraction, *Both Barrels Blazing*. However, the movie conflicted with my timetable, because item three was circled twice. The words "Tiger Game" highlighted this list.

It was the first game of a double-header in St. Louis. The Tigers were playing the Browns, and if the Detroit squad won just one of the two games, they would win the American League pennant. The year before, I had become a fan of the Tigers. The last week of that 1944 season Detroit split a series with the last-place Washington Senators, but the Browns swept the Yankees four straight to take the pennant. The state of Michigan was shocked. I had a lot of company feeling the pain of defeat. I wasn't sure I wanted to experience that feeling again. To listen or not to listen to the game became a dilemma. Just how much did that game mean to me as compared to the movie? I wanted to do both. Perhaps the weather would delay the game for awhile. St. Louis, the game site, was suffering through nine days of rain. The city was deluged, and rain fell throughout a large area of the Midwest, including my small town. The heavy portion of the storm seemed to be taking a respite. I mulled over the situation trying to figure out what to do.

Meanwhile, in St. Louis, the Tigers' utility infielder, Edward Jones "Red" Borom, was checking the grounds of Sportsman's Park. The infield was a morass in its tenth straight day of rain. Sportsman's Park, on Grand between Dodier and St. Louis Avenue, was one of the poorer major league fields. The two St. Louis teams shared the same field. When the Cardinals played on the road, the Browns played at home; and when the Browns were on the road, the Cardinals played at home. Because the field was in constant use, it never received the necessary maintenance. Looking out from the dugout, Red muttered, to no one in particular, "Lousy infield."

Red's versatility in playing three different infield positions made him a valuable member of the Tigers bench. Before he entered the service, Red had been a career "journeyman" player, bouncing around minor league southern towns and semi-pro associations. He had been discharged from the Army when he was 27 in March of 1944, and his thoughts of professional ball were vanishing with his increasing age. But since the war started, international hostilities had taken so many of the former major league players that Red found himself typecast as a "wartime ballplayer." He was an excellent infielder who could go deep into the hole for grounders, a left-handed hitter who sprayed hits to all fields, and an exceptional bunter, with the speed to beat out the bunt and to steal bases.

The Tigers, like the rest of the major league teams in 1945, were desperate for decent players to replace drafted veterans. When Red returned from the service he was ready to settle down to factory work and play for the plant team. An old Detroit pitcher, Red Phillips, related Borom's baseball history back to Detroit's general manager, Jack Zeller. Zeller signed Red as well as his friend, Chuck Hostetler, whose baseball history was similar to Borom's, and in 1945 both were utility players for a veteran Tiger team.

Because the double-header in St. Louis would determine the pennant, organized baseball was trying to play despite the bad weather. Washington had a Cinderella season that year. Cellar-dwellers in 1944, they trailed the Tiger squad by two games and could tie for the flag, should the Browns sweep the twin bill. Baseball had made plans for a playoff in Detroit if the Browns prevailed. The Senators had completed their season and now had to sit back and sweat out the Browns-Tigers double-header. This situation had been created because the owner of the Washington team, Clark Griffith, had contracted to rent the Senators' facilities to the Redskin football team to play their first home game during the last week of the baseball season.

The rain also played a part in deciding the league champion. If both games were rained out, they would not be replayed due to wartime rules and travel restrictions. This would let Detroit claim the flag.[1]

The press had been giving organized baseball a difficult time about wartime players and the poorer standard of play that had grown worse with each war year. The writers couldn't wait for the veterans to return from the war. They already had mentioned the metaphor, the "Umbrella Champions," that they would tag the Tigers with if they backed into the pennant instead of winning it on the field.[2]

The Senators sent their starting pitchers to Detroit to rest up for a possible playoff, and the rest of the Washington squad was waiting at Griffith Stadium in D.C. listening to the radio and ready to board the first train to Detroit should the Tigers fail.

Hank Greenberg, Detroit's star outfielder, had some serious thoughts about the Senators. He wrote in his autobiography, "They had played a lot of dirty tricks on me over the years, like Jake Powell running into me for no reason at all and breaking my wrist, and that catcher telling Jimmy Foxx the pitches so he could tie me for the league home-run title in 1935. And Joe Kuhel, the former White Sox player with whom I once had a fight, was now the Senators' first baseman." Greenberg would have a certain amount of satisfaction if Detroit could wrap up the flag in St. Louis.

But the weather was another story. It rained continuously the day of the game. The game was delayed for fifty minutes due to bad weather. Lyall Smith, a reporter for the *Detroit Free Press*, wrote, "Armies with mops and brooms tried to soak up the water. By the time the game began, there weren't many people at the ballpark."[3]

The game would begin despite the terrible cold and damp. The temperature registered fifty-seven degrees while the mist and fog engulfed the stadium from the start to the end, and rain fell continuously throughout the contest. Players waddled around in the mud. The contest had been delayed for almost an hour. If it were not for the importance that this game held, it would never have been played. The St. Louis management, however, wanted the game in the books as much as Detroit wanted to play and win it on the field. The critical eye of Washington owner Clark Griffith could be felt all the way from the nation's capital, and no one wanted to explain to him any reason that this game shouldn't have been played.

The conference with the umpires and the managers broke up, and despite the rain, the delay, and the condition of the field, the plate umpire, Charley Berry, bent over, cleaned off home plate as best he could, and shouted, "Play ball!" The Tigers' quest to play for the flag had a green light.

The St. Louis squad started "Nels" Potter on the mound. His best pitch was a screwball that broke in and down to a right-handed hitter. The last time he faced the Tigers he had shut them out in their own ball park.

Potter continued to show his mastery over Detroit by sailing right through their lineup for three quick outs in the first inning. As the Browns trotted off the field to bat in the bottom of the first, they watched the Tiger hurler, Virgil Oliver "Fire" Trucks, toe the pitching rubber for his warm-up tosses. This was the first time since 1943 that Trucks had been able to look down the path towards home plate from a major league mound.

In 1943 Trucks was one of the most promising young hurlers in the Tigers' den. He had just been discharged from the U.S. Navy, and the Detroit manager, Steve O'Neill, decided to give him this important start. He wanted to hold his more experienced veteran pitchers back in case he needed them for game two or a play-off game with the Senators.

The Browns had other ideas. Their second baseman, Gutteridge, cracked a double off Trucks, and immediately the next hitter, Finney, singled, scoring Gutteridge from second base. The Tigers were behind in a jiffy, 1–0. Almost as if he had read the nervous minds of his teammates, Trucks took hold of the situation and retired the next three batters in order. Borom and his teammates stirred uncomfortably on the bench.

Trucks held firm, and in the top of the fifth the Tigers unsheathed their claws. Potter lost his focus and walked Trucks. Shortstop Skeeter Webb singled, and second baseman Eddie "Hot-Shot" Mayo followed with another single, sending Trucks across home with the tying run. The Tiger bench came alive, but Potter put down the uprising. Trucks kept the Browns at bay through the bottom of the fifth. Then the Detroit outfit drew blood again in the top of the sixth as Potter's wildness allowed two walks. Catcher Paul Richards responded with a clean hit to left field, and outfielder Roy Cullenbine trotted across home for the lead run. A smile came across Red's face on the bench as he thought, "Wouldn't it be something to be in the World Series?"

Meanwhile, back in Michigan, I had completed two of the three items from my Sunday agenda. I had chosen the movie, hoping to get a two-for-one entertainment outing for the afternoon. I was betting the game had started late because of the weather. When the movie ended I headed for the theater lobby and saw the overcast skies which were threatening rain again. I lifted my collar over my neck, pulled down my cap to secure it, and bolted out into the drizzle that fell softly from the skies. I started to sprint east towards my neighborhood, Dutch Hill. I was eager to get home, out of the rain, and listen to the radio, so I ran awhile, and walked awhile, and ran some more. As I ran and walked I started to feel guilty about choosing the movie.

The Tigers had one of the oldest rosters in the majors in 1945. They averaged a season lineup age of 32, but their experience seemed to work well for them. It was in this era that newspapermen referred to players as either "too gray or too grassy green" to be considered major leaguers. The phrase was lifted from a popular 1944 song called "They're Either Too Young or Too Old."[4]

I disagreed with the print media. I believed Detroit had a great defense, led by a pitching staff that featured Hal Newhouser and Dizzy Trout, two of the best pitchers in all of baseball. They also featured an offense that was capable of putting up multiple scores in one inning. Veteran Roy Cullenbine, an outfield acquisition from Cleveland in the early part of the season, was having a career season. Former veteran players Hank Greenberg, Al Benton, Les Mueller, Red Borom, Walt Wilson and Tommy Bridges all had made their way back from Uncle Sam's armed forces and were making contributions to the pennant drive.

My access to this world of information beyond Adrian were the papers and the radio. The radio was a technology that brought reality to my imagination. As I listened to unknown voices that I could only put a face to with my own imagination, I heard of events happening in faraway places. The radio had to have been invented especially for baseball. The little box on the refrigerator had changed my understanding of our American scene.

The voice from the radio transported me and other listening fans to the ballpark. Detroit's announcer, Harry Heilmann, gave play by play that always put me right in the middle of the action.

In St. Louis, the thoughts Borom had of being in the World Series began to fade like some unreachable dream. Trucks had weakened in the bottom of the sixth inning. He gave up a double and a walk with one out and O'Neill replaced him with the ace of the staff, Newhouser. "Prince Hal," a 24-game winner, was the force that pitched the Tigers into contention. He struck out Byrnes, the first hitter he faced, and then induced McQuinn to fly to center, ending the inning.

Newhouser, however, was an arm-weary pitcher, and he started to struggle the next inning. St. Louis tied the game with a double by Moore and a single from the bat of slugger Vern Stephens. The game was now Newhouser's to win or lose. He worked his way out of the seventh without allowing any more runs but the game was in jeopardy.

In the top of the eighth the Tigers lost their growl and left two runners stranded when Greenberg got caught napping at third base and was picked off. Then the Browns treated the Prince badly in the bottom of the eighth. Finney singled, McQuinn ripped a blow off the right field screen and the lead run crossed the plate for St. Louis. Newhouser then focused hard and retired the next three hitters, but when Detroit entered their dugout for the ninth they were down by a run. By now I had completed my journey home from the movies.

On the front porch of 1013 East Maple Avenue, I wiped my feet on the mat, and just as I put my hand on the doorknob I heard a familiar voice. "You're late, Smitty!" I immediately recognized the voice of my neighbor, Mr. Kirsch, who had stuck his head out of his door. I started biting my fingernails, and at the same time I yelled to him, "What's the score?" He removed the pipe from his mouth and said with an encouraging smile, "We're losing three to two, in the top of the ninth, but the Browns just walked Doc Cramer to load the bases, and Greenberg is coming to the plate!" A sudden surge of heat shot through me. The opportunity to win the pennant was within one bat swing from the mighty Greenberg.

I was practically airborne as I flew into the house and headed for the radio on top of the refrigerator, or as we still called it, the icebox. I whipped the small kitchen chair around in front of the radio and tuned in the game. I nervously wrapped my legs around the chair and began to gnaw on the chair's wooden back, much to the annoyance of my sister Carol, my mother, and Grossmutter Edith, who were all having a light supper at the kitchen table.

Carol stared at me with her mouth agape, and Grossmutter spoke harshly in German. Mother raised her voice towards me, saying, "Get your mouth off that chair right now!" I complied, but I returned the fire towards Grossmutter and said, "Mein Grossmutter, Mom said we speak English, not German, because we are Americans." Mom interrupted before Grossmutter could speak and said, "That will be enough of that. One more time and that radio will go off." I quickly closed my mouth and then the voice of Heilmann seemed to fill the room.

Heilmann's broadcast was not live. He was doing the "wire." Those sitting in the booth in St. Louis telegraphed him, and Harry, in Detroit, would do his own version of the play, just a notch behind the action, for his audience. I loved to listen to Heilmann and his stories. When Detroit played at home, Harry would allow the mike to dangle by its cord from the booth during an exciting play, and the noise from the ballpark would be heard throughout the room. He would fall silent and let the crowd become the main event with their cheering. Then after a moment he would resume play by play with the words, "That, listeners, is the sound of baseball!" Today there was no stadium noise to send chills up my spine; just Harry's voice.

A lot had taken place before I tuned in the radio. The weather had held attendance down to 5,582 customers, and not many of those remained to watch as the weather became worse. The park was becoming a hollow cathedral. O'Neill looked to the bench for a pinch hitter to hit in place of Newhouser to start the top of the ninth. He picked Harvey "Hub" Walker.

At 39 years of age, Hub Walker was typical of the term "wartime player." This would be his last season. He was used primarily as a pinch hitter, but his average was anemic, with only two hits in twenty-two trips to the plate during the season. O'Neill, however, was having a magical season, making decisions that seemed risky to his critics, but he succeeded with his instincts, much to the wonderment of all.

Hub planted his back foot and drove the right-hander's pitch cleanly into straightaway center field for a single. Skeeter Webb dropped down a sacrifice bunt onto the wet turf and Hub dug for second. First baseman McQuinn fielded the bunt, but in his attempt to throw out the lead runner his toss was off-line. Umpire Joe Rue called Hub safe at second over the strong protests of the Browns, who stormed futilely around Umpire Rue. Walker was no speedster, and O'Neill went to his bench calling for Borom to run for Hub. The rain increased and continued to fall, but there was no chance anyone was going to call the game now. Detroit had runners on first and second with no one out.

The Browns rode both the umpires and the Tigers from the bench with comments that Detroit should cut the umpires in for a full share of the series money.[5] Second baseman Mayo stepped in and dropped another beautifully executed bunt down the muddy third base line.

Borom rocketed towards third base and Webb headed for second. Red was conscious of the running surface and he hit the ground hard with an aggressive slide. He was safe at third, as Skeeter was at second.

Borom explained: "The rain fell off of my Old English-D cap, and my feet were muddy from just standing by second base. When Mayo dropped a bunt down third, I ran with everything I had in me to beat a possible thrown ball to third. As I slid into third, the wetness of the field sent me sliding past the base. Swinging my body to the bag, I grabbed it with both hands. I was a muddy redhead, but I was safe at third."

The Browns had but one play and that was on Mayo at first base. Mayo did his job. Now with one out, the Tigers had runners in perfect position to take the lead with a decent hit from the next Tiger hitter, center-fielder Roger "Doc" Cramer.

Cramer, a typical gray-bearded product of this time, had reached his 40th birthday that summer, but he was still a dangerous hitter. Behind him in the on-deck circle was Greenberg, the slugger, who had returned from the Army to spur the Tigers on in the race for the pennant.

The Browns had a decision to make. Should they pitch to the contact hitter who had speed, even at 40, or take a chance on the slower slugger who might be prone to hit into a double play? Luke Sewell, the Browns' manager, decided to walk Cramer and go for the double play.

By now my kitchen had become very quiet.

During the course of the game Greenberg had studied the St. Louis pitcher very carefully. Before Hank went to the on-deck circle in the top of the ninth he sat down on the bench next to two young rookies, John McHale and Eddie Mierkowicz.

McHale remembered the conversation:

> Mierkowicz and I were sitting together on the bench. Hank came over to us, grabbed his bat and sat down next to us. "If I get a chance," he said, "in this inning, I think I've got this pitcher figured out in what he is doing." When Hank knew what pitch was coming there was nobody that could keep the ball in the ball park. I believe it was Potter who was pitching for the Browns. Hank said, "If he stops at the top of his cap that will be his screwball or off speed pitch; if he goes to the back of his neck when he winds up, that's his fastball." The rain was coming down and it just turned to our advantage that Hank was the next hitter. Hank stepped in and he had Potter all figured out.

Greenberg discarded the hunk of bone which he had been using to harden his bat and strolled to the plate.[6] The slugger, 6'3", 210 lbs., stepped into the batters' box, reached his bat across the plate and positioned himself to hit. Red stood by third base with the rain falling on him. His feet and uniform were even muddier now from his slide. As he stood on the saturated ground he recalled thinking, "My cap seems to weigh a pound and a half."

Potter whipped the first pitch toward the plate and Greenberg took the pitch for ball one. Then, just before the second pitch, Potter's right hand went right to the bill of his cap. Heilmann's voice described the action: "Potter delivers the pitch, [pause] Greenberg swings, [another pause] IT'S TROUBLE, [a pause] TROUBLE, TROUBLE, [another pause] IT'S A HOME RUN!"

Borom remembered Hank's connection: "About the third pitch [second pitch] he hit a towering fly ball down the left-field line. I was standing on base. I wasn't about to leave until I knew it was a fair ball. It was fair by less than two feet. That was the way we won the pennant."

Red watched the ball soar toward the left-field marker. It was very close to the foul line, but it was called a fair ball. Greenberg had just busted a grand-slam homer. The photographer who took the picture of Red scoring the first of four runs caught him with his foot still airborne headed in the direction of home plate and Umpire Berry's eagle eye watching to make sure he touched the plate. The smile on Red's face was visible despite the mud and rain that surrounded him.

One by one they crossed the plate until Hank touched the plate for Detroit's sixth run. The whole Detroit bench poured out of the dugout to greet him. Red leaped up, grabbed his neck, and planted a kiss on his cheek.[7] Behind him was Hostetler, who did the same. Before Hank could get out of his teammates' clutches, he was being given slaps to his back, handshakes, shoves and hugs. The deliriously crazy mob from the Tiger bench surrounded and mobbed him while two players rode his back to the dugout.[8]

Greenberg, in his book, described the event this way:

> I guess that was my biggest thrill of all: what was going through my mind as I was rounding the bases is that only a few months before, I was in India, wondering if the war would ever end, and now the war was actually over, and not only that, but I'd just hit a pennant-winning grand-slam home run. I wasn't sure whether I was awake or dreaming.... We won the game, and the pennant, and all the players charged the field when I reached home plate. They pounded me on the back and carried on like I was a hero. There was almost nobody in the stands to pay attention, and there were few newspapermen. Just the ballplayers giving me a hero's welcome. When we returned to Detroit there were thousands of people at the train station giving me a big hand, but the best part of that home run was hearing later what the Senator players said. "Goddamn that dirty Jew bastard, he beat us again." They were calling me all kind of names, and now they had to pack up and go home, while we were going to the World Series.

In the bottom of the ninth, "Big Al" Benton was sent to the mound to protect the three-run lead. With one out and a Brown runner on base, he induced the next hitter to hit a ground ball to third baseman Jimmy Outlaw, who turned it into a slick double play, 5-4-3, Outlaw to Mayo to York. The Tigers had just put the pennant in their pocket.

Hank Greenberg hit the pennant-winning grand-slam homer (Brace Photo).

The second game started well after four o'clock, but was halted after half an inning. Just before five o'clock, darkness fell on the park and it became impossible to play any further. The game was called due to inclement weather. Detroit's rousing season ended and its win-loss percentage for the year was logged in at .575. That was the lowest percentage to win a championship in major league history for either league.

The players scurried back to the lockers. Umpire Berry caught up with Red Borom and flipped him a new baseball: "Have the boys sign this for me, will you, Red?" When Red came back to return the ball, it dawned on him that this was probably the first signed baseball of the new American League Champions and his name was on it.

The Browns resented losing the game but had to respect Greenberg's homer. It was a wallop. Third baseman Clary, in Peter Golenbock's book *The Spirit of St Louis: A History of the St. Louis Cardinals and Browns*, said: "We were leading in the ninth when Greenberg hit a home run off of Potter with the bases loaded in St. Louis. It was pouring down rain, and he hit that thing plumb over that hot dog stand in left field. You got to go like hell to drive one through there. To hit it over the back of the left-field bleachers you gotta power it, and it was pouring down rain. Greenberg hit it, and won it for them that year."

The Browns' second baseman Gutteridge added: "He hit the ball to left field, and we thought it was foul, but the umpire called it fair. All hell broke loose. We had a big argument. Everybody out in left field, the fans, was pointing foul. Everybody thought it was foul, but if you look in the book now, it's fair! We resented that very much, because we wanted to beat them."

John McHale commented: "All I remember was that the umpire signaled fair and gave the signal for a home run. It was very bad weather and the umpires did a good job of keeping the game going. They didn't want to call the game, and we didn't want them to call it because the score would have reverted back to the St. Louis victory. We were very happy to have won the American League pennant and there was a celebration in the clubhouse."

Third baseman Jimmy Outlaw said: "We felt like Hank would do something. After he hit the ball he didn't want to run. He was trying to watch it. Oh, we met him at the plate. We figured we had it in our pocket then, all the way to the World Series."

Starting pitcher Trucks voiced his experience: "O'Neill told me to go ahead and take a shower.... I didn't see Hank's grand slam, but I was listening to it on the radio in the clubhouse and I knew what was going on. That was a happy occasion for all of us."

Greenberg replied to a question about the type of pitch he hit, saying, "It was a screwball I hit and it was right down the middle." Tiger owner Walter O. Briggs called within a matter of seconds after the flag was settled and gave firm orders for a large celebration on the Tigers' "Victory Special." He was

Red Borom scores, Umpire Berry watches closely, and Skeeter Webb jogs towards home plate (courtesy E.J. Borom).

blunt and said he wanted it to be a good one for the players as he would be disappointed if it wasn't. Needless to say, he wasn't disappointed.[9]

Pitcher Les Mueller spoke of that day:

OH, GOD...! It was huge. I'll never forget it. Yeah, it was a great moment because you knew ... the World Series was coming up ... it was quite a trip going back to Detroit. A lot of celebrating. I will never forget while at the railway station waiting to get on the train to get back to Detroit. You remember in those days they had these big things with the steel wheels that they would pack the baggage onto to put on the train ... one of them came by and who was laying on it but York, the Tigers' first baseman, and he was completely out. That was funny. I mean everybody seen him there ... absolutely out, lying on that luggage rack. Everybody was in a great mood and everyone had a drink or two, I am sure. Yep, it was a great time.

York was feeling gratified and perhaps a little overwhelmed at being part of the American League pennant champions.

Rookie Mierkowicz remembers Rudy's exuberant behavior:

Well, that homer was the pennant. First we got something to eat, and then we went to the train station. I remember one incident there. You know, of course, when you win a pennant everyone is drinking ... and Rudy York was a little rouser. He drank a little more than he should. He and Povich [the Washington newspaper sportswriter] didn't like each other from the beginning, you know. Povich had written something

Greenberg and mates: Mierkowicz, Hoover, and Borom celebrate the winning home run in the dugout (courtesy E.J. Borom).

about Rudy earlier in the year that he didn't like. Rudy got to feeling pretty good and he almost threw Povich off the train.... You know, Greenberg roomed with Rudy. O'Neill had roomed them together. He hoped Hank would cool him off, because Rudy did drink a lot. He drank that whiskey and that Indian in him got out. Greenberg came over to him and pulled him off of Povich and he was a life saver."

Rudy sauntered through the car and grabbed Billy Pierce. He shook his hand and wouldn't let go. Pierce related: "He had a grip on my hand and he was a strong, strong guy. He told me how we were going to beat those Cubs and said, 'Listen to me.' I finally said, 'Rudy, let go of my hand or I won't be able to fit it into my glove.'"

As the squad boarded the train, Borom parked his tired body into a seat and pondered for a moment. "A World Champion, I could be a part of a World Championship." It was a heady thought for a worn old minor leaguer.

One player after another, including O'Neill, found the sportswriter who had dubbed the squad the possible umbrella champions. They backed him into a room on the Victory Special train and demanded to know: "Well, did we back into it like everybody was saying?"[10] It seemed the phrase had them upset for days and they were happy to have proved that they could win like champions on the field.

O'Neill left no doubt that Newhouser would start the series opener. Someone asked him if he would pitch his southpaw ace three times against the Cubs.

"What do you mean, three times?" yelled the hot-shot second baseman of the Tigers, Eddie Mayo. "How can we use Hal three times? We are going to take those Cubs four straight." O'Neill, with his ever-present cigar handy, chuckled, "If you got a pitcher like that boy you use him. You would have thought those guys were playing for the pennant instead of us. As a matter of fact, we should not even have had to play under the conditions we did."[11] But somehow play it they did and Greenberg hit the jackpot. Newhouser was extremely happy about the Greenberg smack that gave him his 25th victory of the year, but he said his left shoulder hurt him with every pitch he made.

As the evening train roared back to Detroit, Lyall Smith reported: "On the train back to Detroit the players and the writers covering them enjoyed a marathon party, a wild scene that lasted all night. Drinks, food, music ... we had it all. It was one of the wildest parties I'd ever seen. Paul Trout picked up the check beforehand. I thought that was something — a player buying for sportswriters. The next day Trout walked up to me and whispered, 'Let me have fifty, will you? I blew my entire roll last night.'"[12]

In Adrian, whatever doubts I might have had about this 1945 team could now be put to rest. From that time on I was a believer and a fan of the Old English D.

2

Historical Background

"Labor loved the Tigers, but fought with Briggs, tooth and nail."
Author

Judge Kenesaw Mountain Landis, named after the Civil War battlefield where his father had been wounded, received his appointment to the bench from President Theodore Roosevelt in 1905. Because of a judgment of nearly thirty million dollars against Standard Oil of Indiana, he had developed a reputation as a tough but fair judge.

When the White Sox were found guilty of throwing the 1919 World Series, the baseball club owners turned to Landis for help to regain the trust of a skeptical public. They created the office of Commissioner of Baseball, and when Landis demanded absolute power in governing professional baseball, the owners of baseball allowed him to control it with complete authority. More than once those owners questioned their decision of giving one man that authority during Landis's reign from 1920 to 1944, for he was his own person; he ruled more often in favor of players than of owners, and he ruled with an iron hand.

Because he was not obligated to any higher power, Landis decided judgment with but one thought in his mind: what benefits baseball? Gambling was bad for baseball, and Landis came down with a heavy fist against gambling and gamblers inside the game. Baseball quickly became trustworthy again.[1]

Just about this time, along came Babe Ruth. George Herman Ruth was transformed from a starting pitcher to a full-time player. Traded from Boston to the New York squad, the Yankee outfielder began to shatter home run records. No one in the history of the game had hit as many and hit them as far as this robust athlete of the 1920s. Ruth changed a pitcher's game to a hitter's game. The fans loved Ruth and his home runs. A new enthusiasm for baseball blossomed in the 1920s: Landis saved baseball's reputation and Ruth's home runs generated new interest in the game. Baseball not only became healthy, it became lusty, hearty, and vigorous. Landis guided the game through the

20

"Roaring Twenties" and the Depression era, and was still the autocratic commissioner when the attack on Pearl Harbor plunged the United States into World War II.

In Michigan the '30s had been harsh, and the city of Detroit was struggling to keep its economy afloat along with all the cities in the country.

The '20s and the '30s were the era of Frank Navin and Walter O. Briggs for the Tigers. These owners were typical of baseball owners of that time. Navin was always tight with a dollar in dealing with his players. That type of attitude among owners had played a large part in the Black Sox scandal. The Black Sox alibis about the fix were centered on the claim that they were grossly underpaid. Both Detroit owners were representative of the late 19th and early 20th century views concerning labor,

Frank Navin, early owner of the Detroit Tigers (National Baseball Hall of Fame Library, Cooperstown, New York).

race and ownership. Navin and Briggs, however, were two of Landis's biggest supporters. They realized ownership could not structure itself without greed ruining the game. Because the game itself was in jeopardy it was urgent that an outside power should keep ownership and labor in line.

Frank Navin was a product of Adrian, Michigan. He was a lawyer and a bookkeeper for Sam Angus, an insurance broker, who headed a syndicate that owned the Tigers. Navin invested in Tiger stock in 1903 with $5,000 he had supposedly won in a poker game, hence the nickname "Poker Face" Navin.[2] After Angus sold out to William Yawkey, Navin stayed on, and for $40,000 in 1907 he became half owner of the team. Yawkey became a silent partner and let Navin run the team. When Yawkey died in 1919, Navin became sole owner. Detroit won five pennants and one world championship under his leadership. His guidance ushered in the Tigers' golden age and turned Detroit into a great baseball town.

The depression, however, and Navin's love of owning and gambling on racehorses, depleted his fortune. Gone were the days of Cobb, Crawford, Mullin,

Jennings, Veach, and Heilmann, as well as the three American League pennants of 1907–09. Navin needed to turn a mediocre depression team into a winner if he wanted to control the club financially. In 1933 the Tigers came off their sixth losing season in a row.

Navin had looked around professional baseball for someone who might be the savior he needed. He thought that Ruth as a player-manager would help the gate. He made the offer to Ruth, who was ending his active playing career after the 1933 season. The offer came at a bad time for Ruth. He was scheduled for a Hawaii vacation in Honolulu, where he had some exhibitions arranged, and he wanted to meet Navin after he returned. Navin told him he needed an answer before he left. Ruth left for his vacation without giving Navin an answer and Navin was miffed.

At this time Connie Mack was having financial problems with the Philadelphia Athletics. His American League teams of 1929, '30 and '31 were American League pennant winners and his '29 and '30 squads were World Series champions. But he began to dismantle his club because of his need for cash. He wanted a lot of money for his catcher, Mickey Cochrane, who was an excellent player and an outstanding leader of men. Navin believed Cochrane was what he needed. From his catching position on the field Cochrane directed Mack's champions like a quarterback in football. He was the spark plug of the team, and pushed his teammates to excel. Navin believed he would be a playing manager that would lift his team to a championship season.

Mr. Mack's asking price of $100,000 was big money. Navin couldn't afford such an exorbitant amount, so he went to his partner Walter O. Briggs.[3]

Mr. Briggs, an auto industrialist, along with a fellow businessman, John Kelsey, had each bought a 25 percent share of the Detroit club in 1920. By 1927 Briggs had bought Kelsey's 25 percent share upon Kelsey's death, making him an equal partner with Navin. Mr. Briggs had always been a Tiger fan, stretching back to the days of Ty Cobb.

Briggs, like Yawkey, left the business of baseball to Navin while he ran his own auto-body business, where he made a fortune. He thought if Cochrane was successful he would be a bargain for $100,000. He was. The investment paid off handsomely with two American League pennants in 1934 and 1935 and a World Series flag in 1935. That success turned the city of Detroit into a baseball-crazy town. Navin's glory, however, was short-lived. He suffered a fatal heart attack when he was thrown from a horse a month after the 1935 World Series. Briggs then became the sole owner of the Detroit baseball team.

Walter Owen Briggs started Briggs Manufacturing in 1909 and built it into the world's largest independent producer of automobile bodies.[4] He supported a number of charitable acts for the city of Detroit, not the least of which was the building and remodeling of Navin Field, which became known as Briggs Stadium. The park was considered as "the state of the art" for that time. In 1948 he installed the finest lighting system in baseball, and that, too, became the talk of the big leagues. Like other wealthy owners, he didn't necessarily look to make a profit from the club; and even though he did very well he looked upon his team more as a representative of the city of Detroit and its people. He was generous in backing the city and the state of Michigan with financial gifts for the cultural and economic good of its communities and inhabitants, such as Detroit's symphony orchestra and the Detroit Zoological Gardens. He funded the building of an athletic field and a field house for Michigan State Normal College (now Eastern Michigan University) in Ypsilanti, Michigan.

Typical of many business leaders at that time he was a "robber baron" and his contributions and wealth were created by those who labored long and hard for him. He did what he thought he needed to do to keep his company profitable and grew wealthy through the labor of his workers. This was not unusual for his generation, and he wasn't alone in the style he used to manage his business. These were not the days of established unions and racial equality. Detroit's boiling pot of multicultural, racial and ethnic diversity had little tolerance or discipline. There was real human suffering going on within the labor class, especially during the depression years. This pressure would eventually build into an explosive racial and class predicament.

The evening of June 20, 1943, with a series of altercations between white sailors and young African Americans on the Belle Isle Bridge, a racial clash took place. It came during the war years, just at the time when the country counted most on Detroit's industrial output and the need for cooperative conditions. Amidst rumors that a white woman had been raped by an African American, countered with another rumor that an African American woman and her baby had been thrown over the side of the bridge, the city exploded into an uncontrollable war zone. The Tigers were in town waiting to start a series with the Cleveland team. Ballplayers were told to stay in their homes or their hotel. A few of the curious ignored the warning and adventurously wandered out onto the streets. One of them, Doc Cramer, observed a dangerous scene when a Detroit policeman shot and killed a sniper in Cramer's presence. Five thousand troops were imported into the city to restore order, which they did, but the reputation loss for the city was huge. Briggs called off the regularly scheduled game for the following day and rescheduled a double-header on June 23. He had the city and government officials station 300 armed soldiers throughout the stadium. Briggs's prejudices were quite strong and were further aggravated during this era of internal strife.[5] Baseball conducted business as usual during this time without drawing itself into the social issues of the United States. Both whites and blacks, however, were affected by the prevailing attitude.

In the late '30s and early '40s Detroit found itself in a number of bloody labor-management uprisings. W.O. Briggs was right in the middle of many of these disputes with labor. Labor loved the Tigers, but fought with Briggs, tooth and nail.

In his own mind Briggs believed he had done the workers a favor by keeping the auto body plant open despite the declining sales. At times he had paid workers in scrip with the thought that it would be good for their families because they wouldn't waste money and deprive their families. It was a very nineteenth-century, paternalistic managerial and manufacturing attitude that he displayed, and it was an attitude that was wearing out its welcome.

That belief system had become the foundation block in building industrial America with cheap labor, but it also denied the common man a decent slice of the American pie, keeping him in near slavery to the industrial and large entrepreneurial companies.

Baseball had its own special chain that linked its workers to economic slavery. The "reserve clause" in a player's contract shackled players to the clubs with no hope of being able to direct their own future. This was a reflection of the common working laborer in factories and construction at this time, because they lived with the economic burden in most manual laboring jobs that doomed them to a lifetime of labor status with little pay or opportunity.[6]

The racial beliefs of that time eventually turned Detroit into one of the most explosive cities in the world. Baseball itself was pure white, with one notable exception. The exception was an unwritten agreement that allowed teams to use players on their clubs who were not from the United States. The Washington club and the Philadelphia Athletics used Cuban participants during this period. No one protested this arrangement. In fact, there was no written rule in baseball that said a club couldn't use African Americans. When questioned about African American players, Landis stated there is no formal policy against the signing of Negro players; each team was free to do as it wished.[7] The owners just chose to ignore black players. African American communities had their own professional teams. To interfere with those owners would not be "ethical" in the eyes of the white owners. Such sentiments prevented integration.

The professional African American leagues teemed with baseball talent. Detroit had a great Negro team called the Detroit Stars. A Hall of Fame player on the Stars team was an outfielder named Norman "Turkey" Stearnes. Despite his talent, no scout spoke to him about playing for the Tigers. The irony of that scenario was that many of the Stars were employed at the Briggs Manufacturing Company. Stearns never played major league baseball but was recognized as a Negro League star and entered Cooperstown in July of 2000.[8]

It wasn't until Branch Rickey broke the barrier with Jackie Robinson in October of 1945, by signing him to a Dodger contact, that baseball pioneered a foundation for civil rights in America.

The racial element wasn't the only social problem in the country. An anti-ethnic atmosphere also was prevalent. The common epithets of "wop," "dago," "kraut," "hun," "polack," "kike," "mick," etc., were not uncommon in most American communities, including Detroit.

Strong men in American industry and religion targeted the Jewish population of Detroit into the '30s. Henry Ford promoted a booklet called *The International Jew*, which accused Jews of wanting to take over capitalism and replace the Christian community's influence in public life. He published anti–Jewish material for distribution out of his offices in Dearborn, Michigan.[9]

From the Roman Catholic pulpit the bitter racist sermons of the "Radio Priest," Father Charles Coughlin, were preached, and these broadcasts were heard nationwide on Sundays. The Jewish communities were shocked with what seemed to be pro–Nazi propaganda from an influential priest in a major United States city.[10]

Then, along came Hank Greenberg, who stepped into a dangerous anti–Semitic atmosphere. Greenberg was destined to become a Jewish-American icon, whether he wanted to be an icon or not. His hard work and athletic abilities were recognized by the writers and gave self-esteem and hope to the Jewish population not only in Detroit, but throughout the nation.

Criminal organizations gained footholds throughout the urban sections of America. Detroit had its Jewish Purple Gang in the mid-thirties. The Mafia then, very smoothly, replaced them without missing a beat. Many gang members, like the rest of Detroit's population, were Tiger fans.[11]

Minor league baseball suffered during this period because of the conflict within baseball concerning a professional relationship that bordered between independence and complete dependency of the minors on the parent major league clubs.

Branch Rickey, a complex man, but a baseball genius whose methods often contradicted his outward religious manner, developed a feeder system for his team. There were those that loved Rickey and those that hated and distrusted him. No matter what side of Rickey baseball people believed, and everyone respected his ability, few trusted him. His contribution during this time was the expansion of the farm system. When he joined the St. Louis Cardinals in 1917 his team had neither talent nor the money to purchase top-notch players. It was here that he developed his thoughts about signing players all over the country and farming them out to be developed, taught and trained in the minor league system. He knew this would be a long-term investment but when it paid off in a few years he would keep the best and either trade or sell the others as a surplus. By 1926 his idea worked well enough to make the Cardinals a World Series winner. He had a farm system. He went on to sign hundreds of players through tryout camps and a well-developed scouting system. Then he found places in minor league baseball for them. Some were owned by the parent major league club, but a number were not, and many minor league teams had undisclosed financial relationships with major clubs. Most of the players had no chance to play in the majors, but filled a void to keep the minors afloat during hard times. When players were replaced by incoming talent, they were cut loose with no opportunities to continue their careers. Owners hid many of the good players in the minors and kept them from other major league teams by illegal agreements with different minor league clubs.

Minor league baseball was a rough life. Signing a contract to play professional baseball was risky because of the confusion surrounding the ownership of the contract. The travel was difficult. There were no superhighways during that time, no air travel to speak of, even very little train travel for the minor system. The buses, cars and trucks they did use were always subject to breakdowns and repairs. The pay was just enough to keep one alive. The equipment was second-rate and scarce. The competition was fierce and injuries frequent. The players, hooked on the hope of an uncertain dream, had little chance of succeeding. The system worked well for major owners. Minor and major league baseball clubs were all well stocked with good players.

Landis despised the farm system. He could see what it was doing to the future of the young men who would grow old in it and then be discarded. The cheating within the system that made the connection between the majors and the minors was rampant and the judge had a problem with anyone who broke his rules. The commissioner cracked down on the Cleveland Indians, the St. Louis Cardinals, and eventually the Detroit Tigers. By the time he finished, he had sent a strong message to those inside baseball. At first the judge thought Rickey's little empire would self-destruct, but he was wrong. Rickey's system worked well as long as the owners could hide from or sidestep the judge. As players began to be dealt from club to club, their status known only to the parent club, the Cardinals, Rickey's team, prospered. Rickey was so successful that other teams attempted to copy his program. When clubs and general managers started to revise their old systems and copy the Cardinals they ran the risk of drawing Landis's wrath.

Landis confronted Rickey, who defended his program as a solution to the economic times that had made entrepreneurship a dangerous proposition. Landis bided his time and eventually a situation arose that Landis used against stocking illegal players. In the spring of 1937, Tommy Henrich of the Cleveland Indians' minor league farm team in Zanesville, Ohio, was shuttled to Monessen, Pennsylvania, then to New Orleans, where he hit .346 with 100 runs batted in. He became a hot prospect. By the end of the year his contract was moved to Milwaukee, another Indian farm club. The rumors were that Cleveland would trade him to the Browns. The trouble was no one could figure out who owned him, Milwaukee or Cleveland. The only one Henrich felt he could trust was the commissioner of baseball, so he wrote him a letter.

When Landis was advised, he came to the conclusion that Henrich's status had been covered up to benefit Cleveland, and that by moving him around in the minors that year they had prevented his advancement to a major league club. Landis declared that Henrich's rights had been violated and made him a free agent. He also barred the Indians from bidding for Henrich's services. Nine of the 16 major clubs went after him. Henrich signed with the Yanks for $25,000, a rich sum for that day. Henrich used the office of the commissioner to achieve his purpose. Landis appreciated his candid approach and the decision to allow the authority of the office to take its course. This sent a signal to the owners and administrators. The competitive bargaining for a player's services revealed a peek at what the future was to hold.

By 1938, Landis was ready to deal with "Rickeyism." The judge chose the Cedar Rapids case to warn Mr. Rickey. It came to light that the Cardinals were running two farm systems, one legitimate, but the other illegitimate, involving the patronage of the Class A Western League's Cedar Rapids club. The Cedar Rapids-St. Louis connection involved four different Class D leagues and the Cards had multiple farm teams in each league. The unspoken gentleman's agreement with St. Louis made for a complex situation that benefited the Cardinals. Landis found against Rickey and freed seventy-four players. The players' value was $200,000. One of them was a slick-fielding but light-hitting shortstop named James "Skeeter" Webb. In 1945 he helped to support the Tigers' defensive infield.

As tough as the judge was on Rickey, the farm system had suffered but a slight bump in the road. Within two years the Cards had 32 farm clubs and working agreements with eight more. Six hundred players were in their system in a web known only to them.[12] By early 1940 Landis looked at the Detroit farm system designed by general manager Jack Zeller. He had been using Beaumont, Texas, as a team that had agreements with a number of minor league teams. Landis destroyed the Tigers' farm system. He left them with just seventy-eight players, thirty-five of whom were on the major league roster.[13] When the dust settled, Detroit lost $500,000 worth of highly skilled athletes and paid $47,250[14] to fifteen players in fines. This system, however, was the beginning of a new economics of baseball. The ownership saw a way in the depression, with the reserve clause in players' contracts, to move players in a progressive method to the big leagues. The surplus would allow the minor leagues to be a teaching ground that aided the parent clubs. As World War II engulfed the country, that system was constrained to an extent, but was in place and ready to resume full power after the war. The link that kept the game alive during the war years was the product of that prewar system. It became part of the social mix within baseball that had its effect on the game and its workers. The factors of economics, labor disputes, criminal activities, and finally war put a face upon a part of America's social scene.

The judge died on November 26, 1944. The 1945 season started without a commissioner.[15] In April of 1945, baseball elected the former Governor of Kentucky, Senator A.B. "Happy" Chandler, to the post.[16] When the 1945 season ended Rickey signed Jackie Robinson, and by 1951 Chandler was refused another term by the owners. This decision broke the absolute power of future commissioners, and within ten years baseball reflected a much different look.[17] But the 1945 season was a unique year of transformation in baseball.

3

Players of That Time

"They had that old pea-gravel, and boom-boom, they sounded like machine guns when you drove and kicked up the gravel."

E.J. "Red" Borom

The players of the '30s and '40s were tough, independent, and willing to fight to keep their jobs; there were many times they played with injuries or sickness. They could hardly believe they were being paid to play a game they loved, while so many in the country were out of work. The competition was fierce.[1]

Many of the issues of management-labor relations, racial equality, player opportunity, etc., went on hold when America entered World War II. The problems didn't go away, but Major League Baseball had to address the issue of survival during this period, and whatever social issues surfaced had to wait while America put all its resources into winning the war.[2]

The players that played in the thirties either laid down their uniforms for Uncle Sam's "monkey suit" during World War II, or went to work in one of the many industrial plants for the war effort. Those that were too old for the draft, but still retained enough skill to play professional baseball, continued playing, and kept the game alive during the war. Many played past their prime and were considered the graybeards of the era. Some of the elderly who were famous from the depression era and played into the war years were Mel Ott, Ben Chapman, Paul Derringer, Joe Medwick, and Roger Cramer.[3]

Another group in the system was the youngsters who were not eligible for the draft. Many, such as Joe Nuxhall, Tommy Brown, Billy Pierce and Art Houtteman, received the opportunity to play in the majors at a very young age, but were labeled green as grass.[4]

The last group included those who were designated 4-F and were physically unable to serve their country. These were players like Hal Newhouser, Marty Marion, Ted Wilks, and Russ Christopher, who in spite of their physical limitations became talented, seasoned veterans and contributed leadership to their teams.[5]

Red Borom dumps and drags a bunt at Briggs Stadium in Detroit during the 1945 season (courtesy E.J. "Red" Borom).

The 1945 Tiger players were subject to the economic difficulties and the new type of farm systems that developed during the depression. They felt the winds and clouds of the coming war that threatened western civilization. These players had been shaped by organized baseball and its times during the late "roaring" 1920s, the severe depression years of the 1930s, and now the uncertain days of World War II. During those years baseball, its owners and players were guided by the firm hand of Landis.

Players both loved him and feared Landis. Virgil Trucks said of him: "[Organized baseball] brought Landis in and that is when they curbed the Black Sox [gambling] scandal.... You got to have a man who has an iron fist like Landis did, and you're not very likely to find another man like Landis. I never met Mr. Landis, but I liked him. Oh, he ruled with an iron fist as long as he was commissioner. I think 'Happy' Chandler was just about like him. He was a good commissioner. But the owners didn't like him because he was close to the ballplayers."

Reserve outfielder Ed Mierkowicz stated: "I read about Landis. I believed him to be a strict man, because of the 1934 World Series with Detroit and St.

Louis. The Cardinals' 'Ducky' Medwick dove into third base and tried to hurt the Tigers' third baseman Owens. The fans thought Medwick was a little rough and pelted him with fruit and garbage.... The game was held up, and Landis just took Medwick out of the ball game. I wish we had a commissioner like that now. He was the ballplayers' friend."

Pitcher Les Mueller had this to say about the judge:

I think a good example is when he [Landis] declared a lot of those fellows free agents. He stopped something that was getting worse all the time. That was one of the few times that a player got some help. I wish he would have freed me. I was at Henderson at that time. We had a pitcher, Steve Roushnock was his name, and he was declared a free agent. He was picked up by the Dodgers, but he never pitched much in the big leagues after that. I thought Landis was a good commissioner. He would always say: "If you got a problem don't go to them [management]. Come to me." I think they need a man that runs things with a firm hand.

There was little recourse for a player who was dissatisfied with his position in the game. Labor unions were still struggling to establish themselves in the business and factory communities of our country. The only recourse for labor in baseball was the commissioner himself. His opinion would reign supreme and, although his door was open, he could be a difficult man in arbitration for either side. It was not unusual for baseball owners to make under-the-table deals with each other and to hide their methods of doing business with the commissioner.

The judge had the respect of the players. Leo Durocher said, "He would tell the players, 'Don't worry about them. They're not out to help you. You know where your friend is. Right here, I'm your man.'"

Elden Auker, the old Tiger pitcher, spoke of him this way: "We all knew the judge. When he'd come to Detroit, he'd always come in our clubhouse. We all knew him and we all respected him. I think we all feared him.... But he was a great man.... Just a regular common old shoe.... Kinda grumpy guy, but had a great sense of humor, great sense of humor. He loved baseball, and he was a protector, and we knew it.... He was the judge. He had our respect. The best thing that happened to baseball. I wish we had him today.... And he might appear at most any game. You never knew.... He used to come to Detroit regularly. He was affiliated with the game, and he kept his eye on it."[6]

A newspaper article stated that Detroit bought Virgil Trucks's contract for $100, implying that the Tigers had received a bargain.

Starting pitcher Virgil Trucks:

Yes ... but they paid more than that. I signed two contracts.... They had signed me in 1938, the first of the season ... they didn't have room for me on their minor clubs. They wanted me to stay in Birmingham and play semi-ball. But I went to a little Alabama town called Shawmut, in the Textile League, and played there ... won ten and lost none. I became a pitcher. Detroit signed me as an outfielder and gave me $100, but I would come in and relieve once in a while because I could throw hard. This catcher with the Shawmut club made a pitcher out of me.

Andalusia was in the Alabama-Florida League. Local people like doctors, merchants, lawyers that wanted to invest in it owned the minor league teams. Doctor Grisham called me in Birmingham and asked if I would come to Andalusia. They won the first half of the league and Union Springs won the second half.... So he said, "We will give you $35 and pay your expenses down and back to Birmingham." I go and I pitch the opening game. We won 5–0. It gets down to the final game and I pitch a shutout. So they give the players an outing at Ft. Walton Beach. They paid expenses and the owners of the club were having a poker game. I never played in a poker game. Every once in awhile a chip would fall off the table and I would pick it up, and they said, "Stick it in your pocket." I didn't know what it was good for. You couldn't eat it. When the game ended I had two bulging pockets of chips. I said, "What do I do with these?" And they said, "Give them to that guy; he will take care of it." I said, "OK." ... I dumped them all out on his table. I started walking away and he said, "Wait a minute, you got money coming." I thought he was going to pay me for the games I pitched. He counted them up and it was eighty dollars' worth of chips. He said, "Well, here is your money." I said, "Look, that isn't all. I am supposed to have transportation money." He said, "Well, you get that in the office." ... Man, I was rich. Later on I saw what was happening, but didn't realize it at the time. When we got back to Andalusia the owner said, "We want you to come up to the office and we will give you your money." I said, "You already gave me some." He said, "That is just a gift." So I went up to the office and he said, "That will be seventy-five dollars, thirty-five per game." I started to leave and they said, "Wait a minute, would you be interested in signing with us for five hundred?" I thought that was great. I never seen five hundred dollars in my life. I hadn't even seen the hundred dollars my dad got because he had to sign the contract [with Detroit]. If I'm going to get five hundred dollars I'm going to take it. They gave me a five-hundred-dollar check and I signed.

So now comes spring training and I am getting a contract from Andalusia and I am getting one from Detroit to go to Beaumont. I thought they would put me in jail. I don't know what to do. I decided to go back up to the Cotton Mill League. I asked Bob James, the manager of Lanett, if I could come and play on his team. "Sure, I'd love to have you," he said. I didn't have to work, free room and board, and I would make about seventy-five dollars a week. I said, "I'll be there." We had spring training and those other clubs were sending me contracts and I was sending them back saying they weren't paying enough money. The contracts were ample. There were league rules that you couldn't pay only so much money. Five people up there couldn't make more than seventy-five dollars a month, and a Beaumont player could only make two hundred dollars a month. It wasn't a question of money, but I can't sign two contracts.

Finally Paul Richards and the Atlanta Crackers came through there for the spring training games and I pitched against them. I pitched six innings and shut them out. Paul was outside the stadium when I came out. He had a flat tire on his vehicle and he was fixing it.... He said, "Do you belong to anybody?" and I said, "Not really." He said, "Well, if you do, just tell me and I will try to make a deal for you." I told him Detroit.

We were getting ready to open the season, so was that cotton mill town, and so was the class D team in Andalusia. Yam Yaryan, who had played with Chicago at one time, was the manager. He called me and I told him, "Yam, it isn't enough money, I'm not coming until I get what I want." After that conversation I went to James. I told him what had happened. He said, "No problem. I'll tell you who you belong to, in about two hours." I went back and he told me I belong to Andalusia. I said, "Why? I signed with Detroit first." He said, "Judge Brown said [Detroit] pigeonholed your contract and Andalusia sent it in right away. That made you the property of Andalusia." Yam called again the next day and said, "I'm coming to get you." And I said, "Fine," because I knew I could go, but I said, "There's one thing, that is not enough money." He said, "I can't give you more than that." I said, "Well, I am not going to come if you don't give me more and I want one hundred twenty-five dollars a month." He said, "OK, I will give it to you, but you will have to take fifty under the table." I said, "As long as I get the one hundred twenty-five dollars." I pitched the opening game and won 5–0. Eddie Groosetree, the Detroit scout, who had signed me for Detroit, was in the stands. Andalusia sold my contract back to Detroit for ten thousand dollars. I had a great year.

Trucks was one of many prospects whom parent clubs shuttled and moved here and there to cover future prospects. This time the cover-up backfired and cost Detroit ten thousand dollars instead of one hundred dollars.

The minors were no picnic. Red Borom shares some memories:

Well, I speak to these guys nowadays and tell them what the minor leagues were like in my day, and what they compensated us. They don't understand. We got one dollar and twenty-five cents meal money for one day. A lot of the guys were playing for seventy, eighty, or ninety dollars a month. We would go over to three towns in Arkansas and Mississippi. You had to ferry the Mississippi River. They don't know anything about that. It's just totally different.

I enjoyed the train. It was a real joy to get on a train after you had been riding the school buses. They weren't comfortable buses; all straight-back seats. Back in those days ... they didn't have those freeways. In Mississippi they had pea-gravel roads and old headlights on the vehicles that used to sit on the bumper; everybody in Mississippi had a canvas bag and loaded it with cotton and put them on the bumper, tied them over the lights in the daytime, so the cars coming toward them wouldn't break their headlights from the flying gravel they kicked up. The windshields had thick plastic. Some guy was made a millionaire in a hurry putting them over the windshields. Every windshield in Mississippi was cracked. They didn't have paved roads. They had that old pea gravel, and BOOM-BOOM, they sounded like machine guns when you drove and kicked up the gravel. The cars and the buses would be all beat up and you would be traveling a lot.

Every time you would go to Arkansas you had to cross the river, and you played one hundred and forty games in 120 days with double-headers every Sunday. There was no air conditioning, and the heat down South made life miserable. The players changed bed sheets every thirty minutes or so. They would soak them in water to cool down. The heat, the lack of sleep, the day-in and day-out physical difficulties of traveling, and playing that many games in a row made the minors a rough proposition. As far as injuries were concerned, unless something was broken badly, we just ignored the discomfort and played through it.

This was also a gangster era. Landis took a very disapproving view of associating with gangsters. He chastised Cub catcher Gabby Hartnett for having his picture taken with Al Capone at the park.[7] He rid baseball of several players who had been known to gamble and who been associated with gangsters. He kept his eye on all of them. He suspended the new Phillies owner William D. Cox on November 23, 1943, for gambling on his club to win.[8] During his reign Landis suspended sixteen baseball people involved with breaking his rules. Not one of them could or did return to the game in any capacity.

Yet gangsters showed up and associated with players. The Tigers were no exception. Del Baker Jr. recalls his father, Del Baker Sr., who was a Tiger coach and later a Detroit manager, speaking about the gangs:

> The only story about the Tigers that I remembered in that era is there was a gang in Detroit called the Purple Gang. They had become friendly with Detroit ballplayers.
> My Dad told me that one of the Purple Gang said to him, "Del, we know that you shop at a certain grocery store and I would stay away from that store for another week." That grocery store, a few days later, was blown up.... You can allow your imagination to run wild, but they would forewarn ballplayers not to be in a certain area at a certain time. It's kind of interesting. They were good friends of Greenberg and that whole Detroit team. They went to all of the games because of their acquaintances with the players ... and they were nice enough to tell them to stay away from certain areas.

Landis was aware of crime connections and stressed that under no circumstances should a player associate with gamblers. A gambling connection could ruin baseball because of the lack of trust the public would have. That is why even today there are no exceptions to the rule that is posted in every professional league locker room prohibiting gambling and associating with those who do. As strong and as clear as Landis was, players still formed friendships with questionable characters.

The Tigers' mighty slugger Greenberg had a loose connection. When he entered the service he had decided not to play ball for any camp team, but to tend strictly to the business of being a soldier. When he was stationed at Fort Custer in Michigan, one of the Purple Gang members contacted him about playing in a game against the prisoners' team in Jackson. The man's brother was incarcerated there for life. By the mid-thirties the Purple Gang had all but disappeared from the scene. They had been captured, killed or put in prison. He told Greenberg it would mean a lot to him to consider it. Greenberg played at the Jackson prison and played for the home team. He hit a home run that day over the wall, about 500 feet from home plate. The prisoners gasped at the hit and then came the cry from the bleachers of "I'LL GO GET IT!"[9]

Another problem not discussed seriously was race. George Kell played for Mack's Athletics during the mid-forties and remembered a puzzle that he couldn't figure out.

> Bobby Estalella was a Cuban ballplayer and I remember making a remark and somebody told me I better keep my mouth shut. Bobby was a black Cuban. I said, "If he can play, why can't the blacks in America play?" The Washington club also had two or three black Cubans that played major league baseball, but the American black ballplayer couldn't play. It just didn't seem right to me. If you were a black Cuban and a citizen of Cuba you could play, or Puerto Rico, or any of those countries....
> One day a fly ball was hit into left field and Estalella misplayed it. It cost "Bobo" Newsom, our pitcher, a couple of runs. I was with Philadelphia then and when we came back into the dugout Bobo got all over Estalella. He was just eating him alive.

Mr. Mack got up and said, "That is enough of that now, just stop it!" Bobo told Mr. Mack, "Just tell him to catch the damn ball!" Mr. Mack said, "Look, you just pitch and let him play left field!" Newsom said, "Well, the hell with you, Mr. Mack!" Mr. Mack never uttered an oath in his life and he said to him, "Well, horse feathers to you, Mr. Newsom!" That was the closest he ever came to letting out an oath while I was around him. Then he went back and sat down.

The teams Estalella played for always publicly promoted him as a Cuban player, but he was obviously a person that displayed prominent black-African facial skin and bone characteristics. Players and writers had no doubt that he was as much African as Cuban. The *Washington Post* sportswriter Shirley Povich would dodge the issue by referring to him as "swarthy" when he was playing for the Senators.

The exclusion and treatment in baseball of African Americans continued as an unwritten and unbroken rule until Rickey and Commissioner Chandler forced the issue after the 1945 season. Baseball was the passion of America; it was American to be part of baseball as a fan or a player. As the poet Whitman said, "It is our game." The "Black Sox" scandal and the depression didn't stop the game and neither did two world wars. The war gave it a unique twist. How does one play the game without quality players? The comment of 40-year-old Tiger outfielder Doc Cramer was, "I don't care what they say or write, it is still the major leagues."

4

1945 Spring Training

"Spring training then was a lot different than it is now. You had to get yourself in shape.... The theory was, if you couldn't learn how to do it in the minor leagues, they weren't going to teach you too much in the major leagues."

John McHale

Mention spring training to fans and their thoughts immediately rush to sunny Florida and its balmy breezes or to the desert southwest and its winter warmth. In Chicago the fans' thoughts might drift to Catalina Island, located off the California coast, and dream of the Cubs training in a Hawaiian atmosphere during the blustery March winds and snows of Chicago. Not so in 1945. Wartime travel restrictions wouldn't allow such a luxury. The Detroit squad found itself in not-so-balmy Evansville, Indiana.

When the war began in 1941, baseball thought it would have to close down for the duration. President Roosevelt, however, gave Judge Landis his Green Light letter, which allowed play to continue for the morale of the nation.[1]

The judge, a patriotic American, accommodated the government in many ways. Requested by the head of the Office of Defense, Joseph B. Eastman, to have baseball economize its travel and comply with the gas rationing laws, Landis went beyond Eastman's expectations. He set up a plan designed to save five million "man miles" a year with the railroads. He stated the majors would maintain their normal 154-game schedule, but each team would visit its rivals three rather than four times annually. And then he restricted pre-season games by dictating that all clubs hold spring training sites north of the Ohio and Potomac Rivers. The exception were the Browns and Cardinals, who could train anywhere in Missouri. This was the Landis-Eastman Line, concocted by the judge without the owners' approval, and it was an example of his dictatorship over ownership.[2]

The Tigers were organizing as fast as possible. The road secretary for the Detroit Tigers, Clair Berry, informed players in the Detroit area that they would

Bill Pierce, Tiger rookie, 1945 (courtesy Dr. Paul Rogers).

leave the city for Evansville by March 15. Neal Conway, the groundskeeper of Briggs Stadium, arranged to leave the first week in March to put the facility at Evansville in shape. Manager O'Neill planned to meet with General Manager Zeller to check out the details for the pre-season and arrive in Evansville by March 5.[3]

By 1945, victory for the Allies was a foregone conclusion, but the war was well into its fourth year, and it was obvious that it was still not finished and would drag on. The government had demanded so much sacrifice in manpower to bring the war to a conclusion that baseball, despite the 1942 Green Light letter, had concerns about finishing the season due to the lack of personnel. Organized baseball was barely hanging on. The owners of the clubs pondered if they could play at all during this pivotal year.

On the home front, baseball was popular as ever. Even the smallest towns had some kind of team. In large cities, civic recreational programs fostered leagues involving youngsters twelve through eighteen years of age. Detroit had its "Baseball Federation" for amateur play in its city parks.

Billy Pierce remembered his Detroit sandlot days:

> Everything was different; it was a community. We organized our own sandlot teams that played in this federation. My dad had a drugstore, and he would sponsor a couple of boys. Another boy's dad had a gas station, and he would sponsor a couple of boys, and that is how we got our uniforms. When you got to Northwestern Field in Detroit on a Sunday there were different divisions of sandlot federation teams playing and there were some very big crowds watching sandlot baseball. Amateur baseball was not organized like it is now, when the five- and six-year-olds are playing and they have a nice baseball to play with and a nice bat and uniforms. By the end of the season, we would be taping up the ball with friction tape and by the time we got done with it the ball would look like a football. But that's just the way times were then. It was a wonderful time to grow up. Life was simple and we loved to play baseball. I progressed in these different leagues and went to an amateur All Star game in New York; Detroit's scout wanted me to sign with Detroit.

By age 17, Pierce was turning heads of baseball fans. A left-hander, he possessed a lively arm that delivered an exploding fastball. He attracted the attention of a scout named Lou D'Annunzio. Lou told Detroit's head scout, "Wish" Egan, about his find.

Aloysius Jerome "Wish" Egan was a legend in Michigan baseball circles. As a young southpaw pitcher, Egan fell short of stardom, but as a judge of baseball flesh he was a Hall of Fame scout with numerous major-league stars to his credit. Newhouser, Cullenbine, McCosky, and Houtteman were a few of the players Egan signed for Detroit. A valued member of the Tiger organization, Egan followed Pierce closely during his Federation play.

The Tigers liked Pierce and decided to sign him. They offered him a $15,000 bonus for signing. It was his hometown Detroit Tigers who were giving him the chance to wear that old English D, and in the minds of father and son there wasn't another choice.

Dick Wakefield, a University of Michigan All-American, had the honor of being baseball's first bonus baby. Wakefield received $52,000 to sign with the Tigers in 1941, but he received more promises and incentives that weren't public. Wakefield turned out to be all that the Tigers thought he would be and well worth the price ... for about a year and a half. After the war ended, his lackadaisical attitude, narcissism and gambling habits turned his potential into a big disappointment. His postwar attitude pushed him out of baseball's big show almost as fast as his bonus money passed from his hands into the floating air of good times and bad choices. Bonus babies were scarce after Wakefield's windfall. Pierce became an exception.

Pierce said, "Well, there weren't many bonuses, period. I got what was big money. I got $15,000. I could have got more from Boston or New York, but I wanted to be a hometown boy and play in Detroit. There were not many bonuses given in that time. Wakefield was one of the very few. In those days the fifteen I got was pretty good-size money."

Billy was excited as Egan announced that Detroit not only wanted to sign him but take him to spring training. "I joined Detroit when I was still in high school. I needed one hour of credit with my Lit Two class, so they let me double up on it in January and February. On March 13, I went to Evansville, Indiana."

The signing took place in Zeller's office. Not only did Pierce get a thrill in signing the contract but, as he was about to sign, in walked Charley Gehringer, the great Tiger ballplayer. He was dressed in a full Navy officer's uniform. A star of the 1935 championship team, he was retired as a player and serving Uncle Sam full time. Charley reached his hand to young Bill and welcomed him to the organization.

Life was moving into the fast lane for this 17-year-old. Only a month earlier he had been pitching high-school ball and now was a professional player.

When departure for spring training arrived that 1945 March day, Pierce walked out of his parents' door to join a group of five other players and headed towards his baseball destiny. The wartime camp in Evansville was his first step, but there was little doubt that he was oh, so grassy-green. When he first arrived in camp his voice was still the high-pitched voice of a youth, and some the veterans nicknamed him "Screechy."

He wasn't the only youth going to camp. Art Houtteman, a local American Legion star, was an eighteen-year-old "grassy-green" rookie that Detroit had plans for also.

Pierce remembered his friend: "Art Houtteman and I knew each other well in Detroit. He played for Catholic Central in the Parochial League and I played for Highland Park in the Public League. We got to see each other often. Johnny McHale was a couple of years ahead of us. I didn't know him that well, but when we got to Buffalo I got to know him. My third Detroit buddy, Teddy Gray, was a couple of years ahead and in the Navy. Eddie Mierkowicz was from Wyandotte, a suburban section of Detroit. He was a good hitter and fielder and just a good ballplayer."

Mierkowicz played at Hagerstown of the Interstate League in 1944. There he hit .331 in 139 games, and that gave him marching orders to Evansville.[4]

The 1945 Detroit squad was not a team of youth. Their mainstays were considered graybeards. As the season wore on, sportswriters would label them "the nine old men of baseball." These experienced vets lost a close 1944 pennant race.

Tiger outfielder Jimmy Outlaw said, "We thought we had a good team and thought we would go into the Series in 1945 because we had come so close in 1944. We had the same players back from last year."

Walter O. Briggs, the Tiger owner, had to devote his time during the war to changing domestic manufacturing into war materials. So he trusted his organization to Jack Zeller, an excellent judge of talent.[5]

Zeller made adjustments of his own. During the war years of 1941 through 1944, he began to acquire players to rebuild the 1940 pennant-winning team that had been broken up by the draft. He eased out some older veterans like pitcher Bobo Newsom and outfielder Bruce Campbell and brought up young players, like Virgil Trucks, who had major league potential. The Tigers of 1945 were counting on old veterans, released retreads, and unknown quantities that had some promise.

One respected veteran outfielder Detroit picked up in 1942 was Roger "Doc" Cramer from the Senators. Zeller gave up a good hitter, Bruce Campbell, and an infielder, Frank Croucher, to acquire Cramer. He also sent Newsom, a former 20-game winner, to Washington in 1942, and put Coach Steve O'Neill on a train to Beaumont, Texas, to manage a promising squad, including the bonus baby Dick Wakefield. Zeller sold former star Schoolboy Rowe to Brooklyn in 1942 and brought up Trucks. Trucks broke a number of strikeout records in the minors, and by the 1942–43 seasons he was a winner.

In 1943 Zeller felt Manager Del Baker was no longer effective, and dismissed him. O'Neill succeeded him as the new manager in 1943.

Infielder-outfielder Jimmy Outlaw, a former Reds and Braves journeyman, was still at Buffalo in 1943, and the last month of that season Zeller brought Outlaw to Detroit. Jimmy, a favorite with O'Neill, became a favorite of many Detroit fans. He produced his best playing days for Detroit during the 1944–1945 war years.

One of Zeller's better decisions was to obtain an experienced catcher to replace service-bound George "Birdie" Tebbetts. The oldster, Paul Richards, who had played briefly with the Giants and Athletics, and was a player-manager for Atlanta, was his choice.

Richards was not only old for a major leaguer but had a leg injury that hampered his ability to squat in the normal catching position. That injury forced him to catch with one leg straight out. He was a good judge of pitching talent and well versed in strategy.

Richards was never considered an outstanding hitter, but his understanding of baseball and players was an intricate part of developing a winning team. Richards receives credit for the development of a number of Tiger players, in particular Newhouser, who became the premier pitcher in the majors in 1944.

Zeller realized Richards couldn't physically carry the catching load by himself so he added another catcher, who was in his prime, during this period. He purchased 30-year-old Bob Swift from the Athletics. Like Richards, Swift wasn't a big threat at the plate. Both catchers, however, were top-notch experienced catchers with excellent arms and both were outstanding handlers of pitchers. Richards usually caught Newhouser while Swift was Trout's main receiver. They split the catching chores and were key players during the 1945 season.

Zeller's keen eye continued to roam and spotted the release of infielder Eddie Mayo from the Athletics in 1943. Mayo had big league experience but had been hampered by injuries. Zeller took a chance on him. He proved a most valuable addition at second base, and a big fan favorite in Detroit during this period.

Zeller continued to seek veterans from the major and minor leagues. He picked up a tip from scout Red Phillips in Texas about a semi-pro player from Wichita, Kansas. The scout recommended an outfielder, Chuck Hostetler, who proved to be of value by hitting .298 for Detroit in 1944. When not playing he was a top-notch bench jockey. His boisterous voice could be heard throughout the park rattling the opposition, and even his own club would be amazed at his enthusiasm. Even though he was 39 years old, he was considered the fastest player on the team. He ran exceptionally well for his age and his speed made him a frequent pinch runner.

Phillips also recommended infielder Red Borom, who had been released from the Army on a medical discharge. Red possessed speed. He became one of O'Neill's pinch hitters, runners, and utility players. Red could play several positions, but speed was not the strength of this older squad, and Borom and Hostetler had assets that came in handy. Red spent most of 1944 in Indianapolis. He was recalled to Detroit for a few games in 1944, and in March of 1945 he was ready for spring training and a shot at a full Tiger season. Although he was sent to Buffalo during the year he was soon recalled and finished the year in Detroit.

Red recalls two of his minor league managers:

At Indianapolis Mike Kelly was my manager. He'd been around for years and was strictly what I'd term old school. He wouldn't put up with any lack of effort and despised the use of the "I thought" answer to his question about a particular play. I could relate to his method of communicating.

Bucky Harris managed Buffalo and was the most unusual manager I played for. He had a dry sense of humor, but never offered help as to the way to play hitters, nor did he give any advice about opposing pitchers. I'll say he had a remarkable memory. For instance, his signs for the hitters went like this, if I was the leadoff hitter the signs were cap, belt, leg which meant hit, take, and bunt. The second-place hitter's signs would be belt, leg and cap and so on through the order, but if your position in the order changed, your signs remained the same. How he remembered all that was a mystery to me."

Bob Maier was one of the older rookies at the 1945 Detroit Tiger spring training camp (National Baseball Hall of Fame Library, Cooperstown, New York).

Red and Chuck had their particular roles to play during this 1945 season.

Manpower was scarce, but Zeller believed that he could trim the roster down to 20 players and still play the 154-game schedule. "But we can't keep going with kids under 18 and men over 38," Zeller said. "The big question is whether we'll be permitted to use the 4-F and the 1-C players."[6] Players not in active service that engaged in off-season essential work for the war, but not listed as medically deferred, were classified 1-C. While they worked in defense plants or some type of war work in the off-season, they would be allowed to engage in work necessary to their given occupation. Teachers were an example of such a group. Baseball hoped that its occupation would also qualify for the same status.[7]

There were strong opinions that players should not be granted that privilege. The policy referred to as "work or fight" legislation was before Congress, and its decision might determine the fate of this season. Of men in the 4-F status and the 1-C classifications, Detroit had 21 players, including three catchers and 15 pitchers.

In 1945 the spring roster listed 38 players, a number of whom were not signed. Zeller was secretive about who was out and kept signings a private matter.[8]

Over the war years an assortment of pitching prospects were added to Zeller's list, and several of these contributed rather well, including Frank "Stubby" Overmire, Zeb Eaton, Forrest Orrell, and Walt Wilson.

Two positions that bothered O'Neill and Zeller were third base and left field. The regulars, Mike "Pinky" Higgins and Wakefield, both good hitters, were drafted. Borom, Joe Hoover, Don Ross, and Bobby Maier became strong candidates for the third-base job.

Bob Maier was a rookie brought up from Buffalo in the International League. Hoover, the starting shortstop from the 1944 team, would have competition from Skeeter Webb and Don Ross at short. Ross, a veteran, played 66 games for the 1944 squad.

The left-field position was wide open. O'Neill's first job would be to find some fresh faces to compete for the job as soon as possible.

On March 15, the Navy released veteran player Harvey "Hub" Walker. Hub, a former Tiger and Red outfielder, was the property of the Minneapolis triple-A club. Walker spotted an opportunity to fill the vacant position and called on Jack Zeller. "I'd like another chance to play ball," he said. Zeller arranged for him to travel to Evansville under the condition that he would be given an opportunity to show his skills, and if O'Neill found he could help, Detroit would try to buy his contract from Minneapolis.

Walker knew this would probably be his last season of baseball. He was old for a player and had sustained a knee injury in the Navy. But he felt for this one year he could contribute. Hub would pay dividends with one at-bat. Experience was important for Detroit in a year of player drought.[9]

Detroit had pride in their home-grown talent, and they took satisfaction in a 22-year Detroiter, John Joseph McHale, a southpaw first-baseman. McHale had a cup of coffee with the Tigers in 1943 and again in 1944 for five games in two years. He, like Pierce, was a product of the Detroit sandlots. The Tigers had the power-hitting Rudy York fixed at first base. York was a tremendous hitter, but first base was the only position he could field. This team needed his power. He was crucial to the offense. O'Neill began thinking of converting McHale to the left-field position. Another left-handed bat in the lineup would

Harold "The Prince" Newhouser and Paul "Dizzy" Trout (Corbis Photo).

be a good fit. "I think John will do all right out there. He has a good arm and is fast enough. It's just a matter of adjusting himself," said O'Neill.

McHale had gained his pro experience playing for the Beaumont, Texas, farm club, but the war interrupted his baseball career. Like Walker, he knew his best chance would be left field. He publicly claimed it by saying, "Left field is my job." "He makes the statement with no conceit," said newspaper writer Sam Greene. "He simply has a stubborn confidence in his ability to win a regular assignment."[10]

McHale left Detroit for Evansville with a number of other Tigers around March 13. The group headed for Evansville included Newhouser, Al Benton, Houtteman, Pierce, and Swift. Also on their way were Egan, Berry, trainer Ray Forsyth, clubhouse attendant Alex Okray, and O'Neill. Trout received permission to leave two weeks early. He would visit his former home in Terre Haute, Indiana. He promised to be in Evansville for the first workout. The general order called for pitchers and catchers to report by March 15 and the rest to be there by March 22. McHale became an exception because of the change in his status. It was thought that he be given some early opportunity and instruction concerning outfield play.[11]

At the end of last year, December 12, 1944, Zeller traded infielder Joe Orengo for Chicago's shortstop Jimmy "Skeeter" Webb, who just happened to be O'Neill's son-in-law. Jim wasn't a strong hitter, but he could cover a lot of ground in either direction, and defensively was considered a smooth glove man. Because Skeeter was a weak hitter and a relative of O'Neill, both he and the Tiger manager came under criticism from the Detroit sporting community. O'Neill responded by saying he had no idea of this deal until he woke up one morning and found out that his daughter Olive's husband was added to his Tiger roster for the coming season. Later on, O'Neill said the reason he played Skeeter was that he could cover more ground than any other infielder he had at shortstop and he needed that extra defense.[12]

Webb was a good team player. Defensively sound with a good arm, but weak at the plate, he nevertheless had ability to move runners by bunting or using the hit-and-run play. Besides playing a steady defense he would contribute several clutch hits during the year. He was a type of unassuming but necessary player, who would help mold this club into an effective championship team.

Webb and Mayo made up the keystone center for most of the season.

In January and February of 1945 the Tigers received the good news that two veteran pitchers, Benton and Mueller, had been released and honorably discharged. They became serious contributors to that year's championship.[13]

Zeller did a marvelous job of putting the Tigers together in a war-depleted year, but the stress and intensity left him fatigued. He considered leaving baseball and going home to Texas for fear of total burnout. Mr. Briggs, however, was reluctant to listen to his anxiety. Briggs wanted a championship he could call his own. He had contributed financially to the 1935 championship, but the 1934–1935 squads were considered Navin's teams. Briggs was a man in poor health and confined to a wheelchair. He came close to his dream of a World Series winner in 1940 when Detroit won the American League pennant, but lost the Series in seven to the Reds. He believed that 1945 could be his year if the personnel stayed in place. He engaged in aggressive talks with Zeller, who continued as general manager throughout the 1945 season. The controlling industrialist could be financially appreciative when he wished to be, or when he was forced to be, and Zeller's decision could have involved an elevation in salary.

Zeller's job was difficult. All teams struggled with demands of the military. The government drafted talent for active duty in the armed forces indiscriminately. By now the draft boards were calling for people daily.

One of Zeller's contract negotiations that upset him was a conflict with a promising pitcher from last year. Rufus Gentry was lost to this team because of a salary dispute.[14] In 1944 he posted a 12–14 record for the Tigers and was beginning to look like he could be a big winner, with his fast ball and curve ball coming under control. The Tigers had made a surge at the pennant and Gentry had won five of his last six appearances. Although Detroit lost the 1944 pennant, Gentry looked like an important part of their future. Because he had brought his talent to the front in a pennant race, he thought he deserved a raise, and he told Zeller so. There wasn't much negotiating between management and labor during this time. Management sent the contract. A player received it, signed it, and then sent it back as quick as he could. Otherwise he could be replaced. It was that simple. The reserve clause in the player's contract took away any negotiating power the player might have sought.

Gentry wanted an extra thousand dollars.[15] Zeller couldn't believe the gall of this brazen young pitcher. When he refused to give Gentry the raise, Rufus became a holdout. Zeller then ceased the correspondence. Gentry held out for most of the year but on August 8, when the Tigers looked like they could win it all, he called Zeller and told him he would sign at the original offer and he could be in shape by the September push. Zeller explained to him it would be better to wait until next year and that was that. Gentry lost an opportunity to pocket an extra $6400 as his share of the championship. For the extra thousand he wanted, he instead watched more than six thousand dollars and his career go down the pipes. The year off affected his ability, and then injuries and bad luck followed him. After throwing but three innings for Detroit in 1946, he was done, and by 1949 he was completely out of baseball.

About 260 major league players were classified as 4-F. In an era that had eight teams in the two leagues with approximately 25 players on a team, the 4-F numbers constituted over half of each team's roster. Zeller believed that if a team could retain a part of its 4-F talent, add some experienced players who were deferred because of age, and mix them with a few youngsters while waiting for some of the early draftees to return to their lineups, they might have a shot in the pennant race.

He was performing his job well with the help of the 4-F classifications the Tigers had available. John McHale reflects on Zeller's efforts: "World War II had quite an impact on professional baseball. I often think of the job that Jack Zeller, the general manager, did for the Tigers as a patch-up activity of trying to fill in where the next morning you never knew who your teammate was going to be. The draft board was taking players and people were volunteering for the service. It took a lot of doing to put a roster together for the Detroit Tigers at that time."

Zeller had been mixing his chemistry since 1942, and this year hoped for a quality product. The mixture depended upon the aged ones, and two 4-F arms.

One threw from the left and the other from the right. Newhouser and Trout were the premier one-two pitching punch in baseball that spring. Both were 20-game winners the previous year, and O'Neill depended on them to carry the pitching burden. Detroit's hitting was questionable, but pitching—

that was the Tiger weapon for 1945. The one concern O'Neill had, according to Arch Ward's *Chicago Daily Tribune* column of March 29, was that Trout needed to shed a few pounds. His weight was 20 pounds more than the 215 he carried at the end of last year.

A *Saturday Evening Post* article by Red Smith in March of 1945 explained the history and importance of these two regal wartime pitchers. Smith wrote:

> In 1944 the two had shattered every record set by a two-man pitching staff since 1908. Newhouser, with twenty-nine victories, and Trout with twenty-seven, won fifty-six games, seven more than the pennant-winning Cardinals' Dizzy and Paul Dean in 1934, four more than the total of the Athletics' Lefty Grove and George Earnshaw in 1931, one better than Stan Coveleskie and Jim Bagby, Sr., did for Cleveland in 1920.
>
> They were the league's only twenty-game winners. Newhouser, the only twenty-three-year old to win twenty-nine games since Mathewson polished off thirty in 1903, was the strike-out king, Trout the crown prince. Trout had the league's best earned-run average, made the most starts, worked the most innings, pitched the most shutouts and complete games, with Hal second in all respects. Newhouser was designated "most valuable" player in the league; Trout was runner-up in the voting.[16]

Newhouser's life expectancy was bad. Some called his 4-F deferment a heart murmur, others a leaky heart. The doctor said he was primed for a heart attack and it might happen at a young age. He didn't encourage him to play. "I'm afraid you'll ... put such a strain on the heart that it will cost you years. It might hit you when you're forty-five," he said.[17] He was twenty-three when camp opened.

Paul Trout was assured of a 4-F classification. He had a hearing impairment, flat feet, and poor eyesight, and was the father of a large brood.

For all their infirmities, both had excellent fast balls and were considered top-notch pitchers in the prime of their careers. Wartime baseball and the draft worked to Detroit's benefit. Neither Hal nor Dizzy were going to war, and the Tigers were determined to keep them playing for Detroit.

Webb turned up with a heart murmur that classified him as 4-F. Hoover was rejected due to ulcers. Outlaw had flat feet; York, a knee injury; and rookie Bob Maier suffered a hernia. Mayo's age and his oft-injured back subjected him to home duty. Overmire and Forrest Orrell were also classified as 4-F. Swift was 4-F due to a stomach disorder. Richards's knee injury and age kept him out of the service. Back-up catcher Hack Miller was also 4-F. Outfielders Cramer and Hostetler were safe from the draft due to their age, and Pierce and Houtteman were too young. Most of Zeller's concoction was an elderly group with chronic pains, of various ailments and injuries, mixed with suspect staying power.

The responsibility of engineering this Zeller mix belonged to O'Neill. He was a longtime veteran of the baseball wars as both a player and a manager. A former Cleveland catcher, he had once challenged Ty Cobb as a player. Cobb decided not to mix with him and it was probably a wise choice. O'Neill came from the coal fields of Minooka, Pennsylvania. He was a strong man with the big hands of a catcher and a grip of a miner. Underneath that strength was the heart of a gentle Irishman who was loved by most of the baseball community. Players and sportswriters respected him.

His catching experience served him well during his managerial career and the knowledge of handling pitchers was a plus for him. His credentials were credible, with important stops as a manager with the Indians and a coach for the Tigers, as well as the manager of the farm clubs in Buffalo and Beaumont.

But most of all O'Neill was loved by the veterans. They seemed to understand each other. Although quiet and observant, O'Neill was open to player suggestions, and was patient. But he was more of a manager for the older, experienced player. With all these veteran players this was a tailor-made year for him. When asked what it was like to play for Steve O'Neill, Jimmy Outlaw said, "Couldn't beat him, couldn't beat him. He was one of the best managers I ever played under and I thought a lot of him. He seemed to think a lot of me. In fact I think he was the one that got me back to the big leagues from Buffalo, because I played down there for him. At the end of the 1943 season I went back to Detroit. He was there then, and that was why I came back."

There was not a lot of teaching and instructing done that spring. O'Neill's rapport with younger players and newcomers to the majors could have been better, but he could never quite bring himself to trust rookie players in clutch situations. No matter how talented the newcomer might be, O'Neill would stick with the proven product. He expected results from them sooner or later because they were, or had been at one time or another, major leaguers. Real major leaguers were hard to find during the course of this year.

One sportswriter was moved to comment about the World Series, "Detroit would have been slaughtered without O'Neill; he's the only person who could have kept those old men wired together to go seven games, let alone win the one that counted most." The observation that came closest to being the truth was from the writer who wrote, "It amounts to the fact that Steve, for all of his unswerving optimism, had the good fortune, patience and disposition to realize that he couldn't force any more production out of the 35–40-year-old fellows. So he just geared them and his temperament accordingly, and it paid the richest reward of his 36 years."[18]

This pug-nosed Irishman was the man Zeller depended on to bring Briggs a pennant. Twenty-eight players eventually arrived at Evansville for him to work with.

The Tigers played a lot of intra-squad games. Gas rationing, traveling time, and the weather became difficulties in scheduling games. Between March 24 and April 15, the original spring training playing schedule had included four games with the White Sox, four more with the Indians, and two with the

Pirates. Six games were to be played in Evansville. Circumstances would reduce that schedule until it became so thin that it hardly involved a transportation problem.

There wasn't a lot of complaining. Baseball was happy just to be open for business. Outlaw said, "I didn't call them hardships. We were in a war, and you knew those things were going to happen. We made the best of it ... we just carried on."

Mueller said, "Well, of course it was a time of unrest. You never knew exactly what was going to happen the next day. Before you got into the service, you didn't know if you were going to be drafted, or when you were going to be drafted. You didn't know if you were going to be shipped overseas, so it wasn't a pleasant time. You didn't hear too many people gripe about it. It was a time when people had to come to the front and do things that they might not have wanted to, but at that time they felt they had to do them. I felt that the country did what they had to do to keep the world going."

Patriotism surged through the country with such emotion and enthusiasm that no one would think of not supporting the war effort at this time. Our way of life had never been threatened like this, so life changed and people sacrificed and worked together as a unit on a mission. Tremendous sacrifices were being made in American households. Baseball certainly didn't have much to complain about.

The rainy weather that year from spring training through the regular season would upset O'Neill's pitching plans. During spring training O'Neill was primarily concerned about getting players in shape. They got down to business with what they had.

The Tigers set up headquarters at the McCurdy Hotel. If players were without transportation to Bosse Field, they boarded the Heidelbach bus on 2nd and Main St. near their hotel and asked to be dropped off at the field, which the bus passed on its regular route. Or they could take the taxi and pay $0.50, one way, to the field. A round-trip cab fare at a dollar a day was a lot of money for most newcomers and even some veterans. Players would share cabs to hold down expenses and meet the gas rationing demands of the government. During the regular season sharing cabs became the custom.[19]

The weather was better than the cold and snow from the year before. Mueller looked at the positive aspect of the situation:

I don't remember it being real cold. One thing about it, you had warmer weather in Florida, but it was windy. We got down to business, but I remember O' Neill was laid up with gout [an ongoing problem with O'Neill]. He wasn't able to get to the park. Richards usually took things over when Steve was not there. Art Mills was one of the coaches. It was just the manager and the one coach. It wasn't like it got to be later on when they had as many as three to four coaches on a club.

With few exceptions, pitchers didn't help one another in those days, and sometimes I think some of them were sitting in the dugout hoping you would get your block knocked off. Later they had pitching coaches traveling the minors to work with players; it was pretty difficult then because there just wasn't much teaching going on.

The one thing I remembered ... is that in those years what you did the most was run, which was good. Pitchers sometimes would run an hour at a time, running from right field to left field. You would run some, walk some. Detroit did have a person [to help with conditioning] ... I think the man's name was Neiman ... and he would work with you doing calisthenics for maybe twenty minutes. Outside of that there wasn't too much training. You had your usual batting and infield practice but that was about it."

Pierce said: "Because of the war, baseball was limited. But it was a thrill going to spring training with a major league baseball team even though it wasn't Florida. The veterans were good with the rookies. Houtteman, McHale and I were young rookies and O'Neill, I think, preferred to play his older players. He wasn't a manager for rookies.... [His] record [which was quite successful] speaks for itself."

McHale said: "I went to spring training in 1945 with the Tigers in Evansville. Spring training was a lot different than it is now. You had to get yourself in shape and you really had no instructors to teach you how to pitch or how to hit. The theory was if you couldn't learn it in the minors they weren't going to teach you much in the majors."

Pierce praised the veteran's help for rookies:

I'll tell you they were ... very good. You hear so many stories of hazing and things that happen to rookies. Houtteman, McHale and I were rookies with the club at the time and they were good with us. It was a wartime period. Maybe people were a little more quiet and subdued. Trout and Cramer were great gentlemen, Mayo, Outlaw, Borom, Webb, Swift, and Richards, just all of them, wanted to help you. Newhouser wasn't quite as friendly with young players as some of the others were, but then, some days he was, and he was kind of off and on. Of course Hal was a great pitcher. Nobody had greater years than Newhouser in 1944–45–46, those three years. He was a marvel to watch pitch. Some people say it was wartime, but I'll tell you he had a great curve ball and a great fast ball, and he was a great pitcher.

Coach Art Mills worked on us a little down there. I don't think they were looking for me to do much ... but Art was a good coach because a coach does more than just teach pitching. He will talk to you quite a bit, he will make you do things like running and throwing, and get you in condition to play. Art was good along those lines. Running was the key to the whole thing ... getting your legs strong was number one to getting in shape. That, along with throwing.

That is one of the differences that I see in baseball today: there isn't as much running now as there was then. We were running laps and running sprints. A combination of both because you can run laps all day long, but if you don't sprint once in awhile you can still tear a muscle.... A lot of things we did were in a five-day rotation. Now in those days I wasn't in anybody's rotation but a starting pitcher would pitch one day, rest the next day, throw the third day, rest the fourth day and pitch the fifth day. Or if he were a pitcher pitching on the four-day rotation, which could happen quite often sometimes, he would do a lot of running and throw light on the third day and then pitch on the fourth day. But different pitchers did things different all the time.... Some liked to throw every day. Some didn't throw much at all, but they all ran.

I think in those days pitching control was always a big thing.... It isn't just a matter of how many you walk. If you are behind on the batter, one ball and no strikes, or two balls and one strike, all the time you are going to get hurt, because you got to come in there and they are looking for that pitch. I would say control has always been a major part of pitching. Of course it helps to have a good curve and fast ball.

Pitching location has always been important.... If you were a fast-ball "rising ball" pitcher, that is if the ball would rise, you would try to keep the fast ball up. If you were a sinker pitcher you would try to keep the ball down. Of course nowadays, what I see of the strike zone, you have to throw it down the middle ... from what I see of the strike zone there aren't any high pitches at all. The zone has changed through the years. It has shrunk. Then you would have your catcher move his glove around. You would pitch to him inside, outside, high, low, and you would mix locations up. Some hitters can hit the inside pitch better than the outside pitch and so on.

So the 1945 Tigers started the pre-season work in their northern spring training location, Evansville, Indiana, that year. Due to regulations concerning transportation, and personal schedule conflicts, the players began to trek in slowly. Like a forecast of things to come, the Tigers were delayed for three hours at the start of their workout, March 17, while their diamond dried out following a hard rain. Bosse Field was one of the oldest minor league diamonds in professional baseball, a jewel among smaller professional parks. The Tigers trained in a first-class facility.[20]

Zebulon Eaton, a right-handed rookie pitcher, showed up at camp, becoming the 14th player for the Tigers squad. Pepper games, fungo practice, and limbering-up drills composed most of the workout for the day. The running began, pitchers began to throw carefully, the players worked regularly on fielding, batting practice took place daily, and the manager, coach and players shared game strategies.[21]

On March 18, the baseball travel ban was increased, and the Tigers saw their eight-game exhibition series with major league clubs wiped out by the ban. The Tigers scheduled a four-game Sunday series with an all-star Evansville war-plant nine. O'Neill put his group through a two-hour workout under a bright sun in 70-degree heat, saying the squad would be ready Sunday for the first exhibition game. On March 19, the first infielder Red Borom, 27-year-old second baseman from Wichita, Kansas, checked in for the training season. Seven more infielders and six outfielders were slated for the next day.

Borom reflected back: "I spent most of my time hanging around Richards, Outlaw and Webb. They were very helpful to me and told me about how to play the opposition, and what deliveries pitchers threw, and other things like that. That information came in very handy later on during the season. I don't think O'Neill spoke two words to me during spring training."

Reporters were picking up what news they could find, but many of the clubs were limited to intra-squad contests and light throwing sessions due to rainouts. The exploits of the Browns' one-arm player, Pete Gray, and the Senators' one-legged pitcher, Bert Shepard, were big news.

Gray was the talk of the major leagues. *The Sporting News* for that month reported that the Browns had a special rookie in camp from the Memphis Chicks farm club. The St. Louis writers found him a distinctive curiosity for a baseball player. One such scribe wrote:

> Pete Gray, who only has one arm, is astonishing.... You have to see him field to appreciate him.... The speed with which he catches a ball, gets his glove under his right armpit, slides the ball across his chest, gets it back into the palm of his hand and then snaps the arm back for his throw makes his hand quicker than the eye can see.... His glove has had all the padding taken out.... He wears only about two-thirds of the glove and he keeps his little finger outside.... The palm of the glove is on his remaining long fingers.... He swings a 35-ounce bat and holds it well up on the handle.... His left arm and left wrist are very powerful.... He not only can hit fast balls well, but he is adept at bunting ... and he can run with great quickness and speed.... At Memphis he hit .333, 5 homers and 21 doubles, stole 68 bases and led outfielders in fielding percentage, and was chosen as the MVP in the Southern Association last year. What he does can't be done. Still, I've seen him do it.

While Gray was signed and doing well with the Browns, Shepard had not been offered a contract with the Senators and was relegated to pitching batting practice and doing some sideline coaching. Both were getting a good amount of publicity.[22]

Larry MacPhail of the Yankees saw a publicity opportunity, and decided on the spur of the moment to make a call on the free-agent hero. It didn't matter that Shepard was to pitch in an intra-squad game that day, which he later said he knew nothing about.[23] The one-legged lefty flying ace, who was shot down in Germany, and found himself in a prison camp where his leg was amputated, now found himself back in a plane, winging it to the Yankee training camp in Atlantic City with Col. Larry McPhail. Wearing a fiber artificial leg, and sporting scars from the war on his chin and on his right eyebrow, the determined southpaw worked out with the team by handling bunts and covering first, and then throwing batting practice during a two-hour drill by the Yanks. Afterwards he and McPhail flew back to Washington, where he went to the Walter Reed Hospital for his annual treatment. Everyone had high praise for his playing abilities.

Shepard told a writer 10 minutes before his plane was scheduled to take off that he was going to talk business with McPhail. Shepard said, "I want a job in baseball. So far no one around the Washington club has talked business. If Mr. McPhail wants me, I'll go with the Yankees." He immediately found himself in the middle of a crisis as the owner of the Senators, Clark Griffith, shouted foul long and loud. "When they come right into your camp and snatch them, something's wrong. I consider this brazen piracy by McPhail," spoke the well-known owner. While Griffith was making statements, McPhail and Shepard were at the Pentagon conferring with the War Department representative over what many thought might be Shepard's free agency. It made for a good story for awhile, but in the end Shepard signed with the Senators as a player-coach.[24]

In the meantime, sporadic rain canceled Detroit's first drill in five days. By March 21, O'Neill was looking for twelve unreported players; six of them who did check in were from the Buffalo farm club. The arrival of Bobby Maier and Carl McNabb increased the present team to twenty-three.

On March 22, the *Chicago Daily Tribune* headline read: "Baseball Hails WMC Ruling As Break For Game." The War Manpower Commission loosened the chains from players who were engaged in off-season essential work and granted them the privilege to return to the sport of baseball without danger of penalties. Baseball executives and field managers viewed this as an assurance that the 4-F structure of wartime baseball would remain together and players would not be jeopardized for their status in the draft by quitting jobs for baseball. Baseball owners rejoiced at the announcement.

Zeller reasoned that "the 12 players, out of 35 listed for spring training camp, that have not reported to camp for training were absent for fear that leaving war jobs for baseball would mean induction."[25]

Maier, a rookie from New Jersey, at twenty-nine years old should have been a veteran player of several big-league seasons, but he was another unique part of Zeller's crazy quilt. He had started his career as a player in 1937 with Trenton. He was considered a decent player in either the outfield or infield, and had minor league experience in both positions. In 1944 he became the third baseman for Buffalo, the Tigers' farm team, where he hit .298 and played 154 games. This got him a shot with the Tigers in spring training. His best minor league effort, where he alternated between the outfield and the infield, was at Hagerstown in 1943. He hit an astounding .363 and rapped out 52 doubles to lead the whole country in two-base hits. Maier could hit a baseball. He would turn 30 years old in September of 1945, a suspect age for any rookie.

When spring training rolled around, he said, "The day I left Dunellen, New Jersey, the temperature was 85 to 90 degrees. When I got to Evansville, Indiana, it was snowing." When he opened the door at the McCurdy Hotel, he looked for the manager. Instead, the first two people he met were Trout and Newhouser. "I walked into the hotel lobby and they came up to me, shook my hand, and wished me luck. You could have knocked me over with a pin!"[26]

The man he needed to find was a short, stocky fellow that wore glasses, Clair J. Berry, the Detroit Tigers traveling secretary. The sheet of paper he sent Maier, and the rest of the Tigers, had all the information Bob needed. As he looked at the schedule and additional information, he noticed his meal money amounted to three dollars for lunch and dinner per day. There would be no out-of-pocket cash for the meal. He would "pay" for breakfast by signing the check that the waiter gave to him. When spring training ended and the regular season began, the team would increase lunch and dinner money to eight dollars a day plus the signature on the breakfast check. The major circuit, if you were selected, would be first class.[27]

As old as Maier was, his Buffalo teammate, Walt Wilson, was older. The Tigers brought him up to help share the pitching duties. He was a 31-year-old rookie and a former serviceman. Walt hung on for that one year and gave Detroit some valuable innings during the regular season.

Baseball was still coming under fire for the favorable WMC ruling as well as the favorable treatment given to drafted players in the service. Parents and relatives of boys on the fighting fronts all over the world publicized their bitterness with the partial treatment and the lack of democracy in the service. Organized baseball, led by Larry McPhail of the Yankees, would argue and lobby heavily for the players' rights under Roosevelt's Green Light letter to be classified as work professionals, but not all of the country looked at it that way.[28] McPhail said between 75 and 80 percent of players on baseball's active list at the time of Pearl Harbor were now serving in the armed forces. He defied any other business to match that figure.[29]

Major League Baseball backed the war effort 100% and held many activities to raise funds for the troops and the needs of both the home and war fronts. The business of baseball had already made a $185,093 contribution to the National War Fund that year. The money was a share of the receipts from the 1944 World Series. That was another one of Landis's edicts that the participating teams had little or no say in.

Amid all these events was a strong, but seldom heeded, minority voice telling baseball that it would be easy to solve and survive its problems. Just start using Negro players. Baseball's front office, however, continued to be silent on that topic.[30]

Branch Rickey had been maneuvering towards opening the door for African Americans and was waiting for the right person and the right time. Now he found himself under pressure from minority organizations to open his Dodger camp to two candidates from the Negro Leagues. He gave them a tryout. Rickey wasn't ready and wasn't about to be shoved into making a decision, so he watched, but he was just being polite and biding his time. After the workout he told the reporters that he definitely was not interested in one of the players and had three rookies better than the other. The two players were Terris McDuffie, a pitcher, and Dave Thomas, a first baseman.

On March 23, Zeller contacted the White Sox at their training camp in Terre Haute, in hopes of picking up major competition. It could be done by leaving camp early and, on their way to their opener in St. Louis, staying in Terre Haute to play a series. The Chicago manager, Jimmy Dykes, was agreeable. The games were set for April 7, 8, 9, and 10, but subject to approval by the higher-ups. If they ruled this wouldn't be a violation of side trips involving players the games could be scheduled.[31]

On March 24, the squad was broken into two units. One was called the

"Regulars" coached by Trout and the other the "Yannigans" coached by New-houser. Both player-coaches spent their time in the third-base coaching box for their encounter, cheering their team on. The Yannigans defeated the Regulars, 2–1. Borom tripled late in the game and stole home for the winning run. Overmire and Houttman pitched for the victors while Pierce and Benton did the mound duties for the Regulars. Maier collected a triple and a double in the losing cause. Houtteman was the winning hurler. He gave up two hits in three innings. The losing pitcher was Pierce.[32]

On March 25, the Tigers settled with Rudy York on contract terms. The Big Chief sent word he definitely would leave his farm to return to the club.[33]

In game two the Regulars came back behind the shutout pitching of Trout and Eaton, who shared mound duties for the winners while Newhouser and Mueller pitched for the losers.[34] Maier again tripled and doubled, causing O'Neill to utter a few encouraging words to Coach Mills: "That fellow looks good up there [batting]. He runs well, too, and has a good arm." They believed they might have found a replacement for one of the vacant positions.[35] But Maier knew his abilities and his limitations. He started the season hitting well but he would have trouble with his game towards the end of the schedule. "It's funny," he said, "if you look at my career at the end of every season I used to falter. I don't know why. I guess I ran out of gas, but it was the same result every time."[36]

Maier got off to a fast start in spring training and reporters speculated that he would start in left field as he continued to impress O'Neill. Ross was contributing at third base and if Maier could handle left field the team could improve their weak batting order.

Maier, like Borom, wondered if the manager knew he was in camp. "Steve O'Neill was our manager and a good guy. He had a pug face that made him look like a fighter, but he never did much hollering. He didn't say much to me one way or another. I only knew I made the team when I was still around at the end."[37]

On March 29, the team was washed out again when a downpour chased a few early players back to the hotel and canceled drills. The next day wasn't much better as the diamond stayed saturated. The players could do little but limber up their arms by playing catch in the gravel parking area behind the park.[38]

The team was by now accounted for and needed to reassign players to meet the roster number. On April 2, Zeller shaved the squad to twenty-five. Ralph Ruthstrom, a 23-year-old pitcher, 20-year-old outfielder Mierkowicz, and veteran Bob Gillespie were sent to Buffalo to play for the Bisons. The Tigers got ready to break camp and moved to Terre Haute for the five exhibition games with the Sox. On April 4, they finally played major league competition. Chicago shut out them out 8–0 as pitchers Deitrich, Lopat and Haynes limited the Tigers to four hits.[39]

Houtteman found out the difference between major and recreational hitters as the Sox roughed him up. Mueller and Wilson mopped up the mess. On April 7, the White Sox again tamed Detroit 6–4. The game was soiled by errors as the Tigers submitted meekly to the servings of 37-year-old Thornton Lee, who allowed but two hits in five innings. Overmire was given a robust whipping as the Sox slapped him around for twelve hits. Tony Cuccinello led the Sox with three hits.[40]

On April 8, Dizzy Trout was back in familiar territory near his birthplace. A farmer named Paul James from Centerpoint, Indiana, presented a workman's red bandanna to Trout before he started against the Sox. Dizzy had worked on James's farm as a youngster and promised his former employer that the bandanna would be in his back pocket for that day's game. The red bandanna was Trout's signature throughout his career and projected his image as hard-working laborer. The Tigers rose with a mighty roar and clubbed the Sox into submission, 15–9. An explosive 15-run blast gave Trout an easy win. York and Cramer each posted three hits. York included a homer as part of his three.[41]

Dizzy appeared outside the locker after the game in high spirits and with a foot-long cigar in his mouth. He blew smoke around the entourage of reporters that surrounded him with questions concerning the season. He was never more in his element than when he had an audience to entertain. They asked him about the game, his pitching skills, and the Tigers' chances to snatch the pennant this year. One reporter mentioned Dizzy might finish the cigar by 5:00 if he kept it going that long. Trout was a showman. No matter what he said, one could not help but listen to his entertaining stories. Along with little Jimmy Outlaw, Trout could put a happy face on his teammates' faces. When he walked into the presence of sportswriters their eyes lit up, and their sharpened pencils stood at the ready. Arch Ward, in his "In the Wake of the News" column, described one of Trout's stories with relish: "The voluble Dizzy Trout of the Tigers claims he once made a triple play without pitching a ball to the batter. The bases were filled and there were two strikes on the batter when he resorted to the amazing strategy. He extracted an extra ball that he had hidden in his shirt. With a ball in each hand he wound up with both arms and, being ambidextrous, suddenly threw to third with his left hand and to first with his right. The two unsuspecting runners were called out and the batter was so confused that he swung for the third strike. If you don't believe this, Dizzy has others."[42]

On April 9, O'Neill's unit evened the series by trimming the White Sox, 9–6. Maier filled the outfield position when he cracked a two-run homer off southpaw Lopat and picked up an eighth-inning hit that scored the tying run. Hoover and McNabb had back-to-back hits after Haynes walked the bases full. Detroit exploded for seven more in the eighth. Benton threw seven and Pierce finished the last two, giving up but one run.[43] On April 10, the Tigers turned loose a lean, hungry Newhouser. He scattered eight hits and Detroit ran over the Sox 7–2.[44] Then, led by the fun-loving Trout, Detroit headed for the Chase Hotel in St. Louis where the Browns, the previous year's American League pennant winners, awaited them for the season opener.

5

April

"I hated to pitch batting practice against him ... because he wouldn't swing at a ball unless you threw it right down the middle.... He had a reputation for having a great eye, and he did have. He would not swing at a ball unless it was a strike, you could almost bet on that.... I mean you could throw him five or six pitches and they weren't more than just that far away from the plate ... and he wouldn't swing at it. He would get you aggravated ... but he was a good hitter."

Les Mueller

On Saturday, April 14, I remember looking out my upstairs bedroom window and observing that Maple Avenue was empty. I gazed towards the quiet corner of Maple and Croswell Street; I felt that melancholy, downcast shadow that overwhelmed my small town of Adrian, Michigan, and the whole country. President Franklin Delano Roosevelt, the only chief executive I could remember, had passed away suddenly and unexpectedly on Thursday, after being stricken with a cerebral hemorrhage. The funeral would be held in the afternoon. America was permeated by mourning, and surrounded with a heavy-hearted gloom. The president was listed as a causality of World War II.[1]

Clark Griffith, president of the Washington Senators, and friend of presidents going back to Theodore Roosevelt, spoke for Major League Baseball by saying, "We've lost a warm personal friend and a great champion of baseball."[2]

FDR had established a record for presidents by appearing at seven consecutive Opening Day games at Griffith Stadium, 1934 through 1940. In March of 1945 the president referred to himself as the nation's number-one fan of night baseball. He supported the game in war and in peace. During the winter of 1944, when manpower problems troubled the national pastime, Roosevelt gave it hope by saying the game should continue, but without using healthy young men who could be of greater value to the war effort. Roosevelt had recently commented that, if wartime duties would allow him, he would toss out the first ball at this year's opener between the Yankees and the Senators.

All activities, including baseball's exhibition games, had been canceled out of respect for Roosevelt and his funeral.[3]

I fought through my despondent childish emotions over the death of the president. I continued to stare into the street and couldn't help but wonder, "Who is this guy Harry S Truman?" All of America was asking the same question.

As I pondered further, the radio began to broadcast the funeral procession, which was moving up Pennsylvania Avenue in Washington, D.C. CBS personality Arthur Godfrey was broadcasting his description of the procession and the dirge from a roof on a bank building at Fifteenth and Pennsylvania Avenue. He was watching the movement of Roosevelt's flag-covered casket on a caisson drawn by six white horses. The street was full of combat troops. Men and women of all ages were tearfully sharing the grief of the country's fallen leader. Godfrey's description was a classic historic moment in the history of radio. His broadcast reflected America's agony at this time.[4]

The war, of course, colored everything. As baseball was about to begin its fourth wartime season, it could not ignore the stark reality of Roosevelt's death and the stress the war was inflicting upon the population. After the death of FDR, the picture of an Allied victory and the end to the German and Italian powers in Europe began to take shape. Before the month was finished, the Italian leader Mussolini, his mistress, and a number of followers were captured before they could cross the border into neutral Switzerland. They were shot and hanged in the square of Milan. Hitler, who had married his companion Eva Braun, committed suicide with her the day after the marriage. These deaths and the Russian Army's takeover of Berlin put Germany on the brink of surrendering.

Despite the disturbing news of FDR and the war my thoughts soon turned to the Tigers and baseball's opening day. The world might slow down but it doesn't stop. Life moves on.

Baseball, as *The Sporting News* reported, continued to support the war effort by turning over a $22,837.20 check to the chairman of the Red Cross War Fund. The contribution was raised from the exhibition games of the Yankees and the Dodgers.

War or no war, funeral or no funeral, Newhouser had been itching to get started. The Tigers were still in Terre Haute at the spring training site of the White Sox. Rain had washed out any scheduled activity. But Newhouser believed he needed work. He imposed on Paul Richards to go to the park with him to help him loosen up for the opening game in St. Louis.[5] After an hour of throwing from underneath the stands, he felt he was in sync with his schedule. He said he needed to throw some more the next day, Sunday, and then rest on Monday to have the arm right for Tuesday's opening game against the Browns. At this time in his life Hal Newhouser pretty much ran his own ship. He had his own workout schedule and organized things as he wished.

When he first arrived at the major league level in 1939 he was considered a top prospect, and great things were expected of him. His minor league experience, however, was skimpy. In 1938, 17-year-old Hal was signed and sent to play for Beaumont, the Tigers' double-A farm team. After he worked out for awhile with the Texas squad, Detroit decided he needed more experience, and sent him to Alexandria, Louisiana, which was their class-D club. He posted an 8–4 record and was recalled to the Beaumont squad. But the Exporters were struggling in the basement of the Texas League. Although he pitched well the league was tough, and without much coaching he posted a losing record of 5 and 14. But his fast ball and his curve ball were reported to be good enough for major league pitching. Zeller believed he could play in the majors.

So in 1939 he joined the Tigers. He was as raw and green as any rookie had ever been. A crude, unrefined, spirited pitcher, he had been given little direction in the use of his tools. He gave it all he had, but he soon learned that major league pitching required something beyond just raw talent. The years passed by and at the end of the 1943 season he had a career record of 34 wins and 52 losses. Even though his earned-run average had improved, and he had been selected for the 1942 and 1943 American League All-Star teams, he was far from the polished pitcher that Detroit envisioned.

When Newhouser arrived in Detroit he brought with him a good fast ball, a nasty curve, and a bad temper. Newhouser did not suffer fools, errors, or losses well. He became vocal about it, and his body language would quickly reveal his disposition. His temper clouded his ability and his disposition blocked a congenial relationship with his teammates. The infamous temper gave writers a lot of copy. When he took to the mound he could become an eruptive force if things didn't go according to his script.

A stylish, 6'2", 180-lb., smooth-throwing lefty, Newhouser, under pressure conditions, would become frustrated, erratic, and as wild as a March hare. In 1943 he posted a league-leading 111 walks. His temper and lack of pitching control would aggravate his problems. He was not easy. He had a stare that would reduce the most confident and experienced player to ashes. Any teammate who played behind him and made an error rued the moment he didn't execute the play. Veteran players like Mike "Pinky" Higgins did not appreciate being shown up and felt this attitude had to change.

Even opposing hitters who had success against him would be on the receiving end of that look. The great Red Sox player Ted Williams said, "He was wild when he first came up, and a fiery guy. You would hit one off him, and it was like you had taken his blood. He'd give you that rotten stare. He didn't think anybody was supposed to hit Newhouser. He became a beautiful pitcher, nice effortless style, fine fast ball, pretty to watch. Newhouser had everything. Cronin always said he would have won in any era."[6]

But then if he was taken out of a game, and he had one of those moods, players in the dugout moved. He would fly into the dugout talking to himself, and things could begin to fly. When he headed for the clubhouse, players would know when he completed the journey from the lighted tunnel to the locker area. The sound of popping light bulbs would begin his entrance and a silence would be the clue to the end of his trip. He usually picked up a bat before entering and would knock out the bulbs on his way down. Pop-pop-pop-pop-pop — that clatter, followed by the sound of a thrown bat, would complete his angry walk. His rampage might continue into the locker area. He occasionally would be followed by fellow pitchers Trucks and Hal White, who were interested in watching him complete his tantrum. Trucks related: "He would be having one of those tantrums and White would say to him, 'Go ahead, Hal, I wouldn't take that either.' And sort of egg him on. Then I would chime in with White and he would look at us not knowing what to say. Most of the time he would calm down, because what could he say?"

The Detroit pitching staff was known for its competitiveness and did not always go gentle into that good night. Newhouser was a hard loser, but someone who could top him was Fred Hutchinson. Hutch, who became a regular the following year, was known for tearing up locker rooms, becoming sullen, and even at one time leaving his car at the park and walking home in anger after the game. Evidently it was a very long walk.

Even the easygoing Dizzy Trout could show displeasure and spare no one's feelings with his sarcastic criticism when things went bad. The following year, in 1946, that displeasure resulted in a short but intense brawl with Hank Greenberg. It didn't last long but it took some pretty good-sized teammates and O'Neill to separate them. The Tigers pitchers were a proud group and they believed the idea of the game was to win it.

Dan Daniel, the New York sportswriter, tagged Newhouser as "Hurricane" Hal. Newhouser wasn't fond of that label, but it stuck with him for most of his early career.

After the 1943 season rumors began to fly concerning him. Even if he showed flashes of greatness, his wildness and brat-like attitude had disenchanted the club and the fans. Zeller started to inquire about a trade. But Newhouser was a Detroiter, and he did have extraordinary talent. His biggest supporter was probably owner W.O. Briggs, who took pride in local talent. O'Neill, of course, didn't want to lose a potential winning left-handed pitcher, either. Talented southpaw pitchers were hard to find, and now, during these war years, they were a precious commodity. Briggs might have intervened and squashed any pending deal for trading Newhouser. Whether it was the input and influence of O'Neill, Briggs, or of both men, Zeller decided to drop the idea of trading him, but the rumor mill churned on.

Newhouser heard the rumors and had his own thoughts about pitching in his hometown. In fact he was beginning to wonder if he should continue to pursue a career in baseball. That winter he participated in a bowling tournament in Cleveland, the home of Steve O'Neill. He called him, and O'Neill went to the alley to discuss Hal's future. O'Neill put the trade rumors to rest by telling him there would be no trade. When asked why he couldn't win, Newhouser responded by saying that O'Neill's pitching rotation did not suit him. He requested to pitch every fourth day. O'Neill was agreeable as long as Hal could produce, and then told Newhouser that he would have to set up his own schedule. His habits went beyond just the normal physical activity of most players.[7]

When the war began Hal attempted to enlist in the Army Air Corps and become a pilot. But he flunked the physical. The examiners found that he had a leaking heart. He continued trying to enlist but flunked the physical four different times. The doctor advised him to stop playing ball because of his heart, but he wasn't about to do that. He was under strict orders to get a lot of rest and plenty of sleep, not to eat heavily, and not to get tired. It was a hard if not impossible task for a professional athlete. His activity needed to meet these requirements, as did his diet and daily routine. He ate steaks, received eleven hours of sleep nightly, took iron pills, and made sure he had food in his body before pitching.[8]

People who had no knowledge of these things wondered why he wasn't in the service. This same observation was true of many athletes and entertainers during the war who were in the public eye. People like Frank Sinatra and Newhouser had their critics. Occasionally someone would lash out towards these celebrities. There was a time when he received a one-word letter on yellow paper: "Bastard." These incidents were not uncommon and because of the huge sacrifices being made, people easily resented those who were 4-F but played a sport for a living. Because of all his limitations and the stress of being ineligible to enlist, Newhouser was allowed to work these physical and emotional needs out by himself. O'Neill had been like a Dutch uncle to him throughout most of the 1943 season and had been trying to nurture him along. After his chat with the skipper, Newhouser sensed that he had been given a clear direction and the air had now been cleared between him and management.

During spring training in 1944, Newhouser worked hard. It was here that he developed his relationship with the catcher Paul Richards. Richards was an experienced baseball teacher, and he took the young lefty under his wing. He labored and tutored Newhouser about controlling the release of his pitch so it would be consistent with his chosen location. Hal began to break his pitches inside and then outside of the plate in a manner that would help him stay ahead of the hitter. But the best experience Newhouser received was the control of his changeup pitch. When he left camp in the spring of 1944, Newhouser had developed a change of pace that looked just like the delivery he used for the 90-mph-plus fastball he was gifted with. He also worked on a new pitch called the slider. The slider was gaining popularity among the pitchers of that day. It had a flat, short, late break on it, and looked a lot like a fastball coming up to the breaking point of the pitch. At the last moment the pitch would dart in or away from the hitter. By the time Newhouser had finished the course under Richards, he had control of his blazing fastball, and he possessed a beautiful, breaking curve ball that could make the knees of hitters buckle. But the changeup and his control of pitch locations made his pitches even more effective.

Now the only thing he lacked was a positive attitude and a good rapport with his teammates. Richards had no problem in relating to him the importance of changing his temperament. That Newhouser was disliked by his mates was a fact. Richards, himself, considered Newhouser a spoiled child. Paul was blunt in laying out the need for what today is referred to as anger management. Explaining the dangers a bad temper could produce for a pitcher under pressure, and how teammates would be affected by his temperament, Richards encouraged him to change a negative into a positive. If Hal would support his teammates, as he would have them support him in every situation, the problem could be solved.

Newhouser listened. This was a key factor: he listened and he believed in what the seasoned veteran said, and so he changed. Richards made a believer out of him. He had some moments, but overall his attitude made a drastic turn for the better.

When he would get hot in difficult situations during his mound duties, Richards would use the tactic of holding the ball a little longer than usual before returning it to his hurler, or he would stall around the plate after a pitch and start to adjust his catching equipment for a few extra seconds. He slowed the impetuous young southpaw down, and got him to relax and cool down. The hardest challenge Hal had was to control his temper. There were to be some tense moments, but while Richards controlled the situation they were few and far between.

Newhouser requested Richards to be his main receiver. The bond between pitcher and catcher became a tight one, and Newhouser became not just a good pitcher but a great winning pitcher. A great deal of his success goes to the old veteran catcher from Waxahachie, Texas.

In 1944 Hal won 29 games and just about every award there was including the American League's Most Valuable Player award. His relationship with his fellow players improved dramatically. The press found him much more agreeable and mature. Suddenly, he was—along with the Tigers' other 20-game winner, Dizzy Trout—a mainstay in the Tiger den. After a near miss for the pennant in 1944, he and the Tigers were deadly serious about winning the 1945 flag. His temperament had changed and so had his nickname. He went from being Hurricane Hal to Prince Hal. His disposition became easy and although he might not be as interesting an interview, he became an enjoyable one. Hurricane Hal would on occasion rise to the surface but his appearance would be rare during this period of his career. Prince Hal was front and center most of the time.

The St. Louis Browns were the defending American League champions.

1944 was the first and only time the Browns won a pennant. They had the unfortunate problem of playing second fiddle to the National League St. Louis Cardinals, who played in the same town. The Cards were considered the classiest team in the majors and the Browns were the fellows from the other side of the tracks who played in that other inferior league. Even though they both shared the same stadium and field for home games, it was the Cardinals who drew the larger crowds and whose names were on the lips of most St. Louis fans. In 1944, when the Browns won the American League pennant, ironically, they faced the Cardinals in the World Series. It was the third straight year the Cards had won the pennant, and they defeated the Browns four games to two in the 1944 World Series. Both teams were picked to repeat as champions of their respective leagues.

An interesting side to the Cardinals and their upcoming season this year was a dispute with management and two of their star players. The brothers Mort and Walker Cooper became holdouts even though they signed contracts for the club's ceiling price under the 1943 stabilization act for $12,000. They actually went on strike. The reason was that the Cardinals' shortstop Marty Marion, the previous year's National League MVP, had signed a contract for more money than they were making. They wanted an increase of $15,000. Baseball people were astonished at their rebelling and couldn't recall a time that players refused to play after signing. The unions were nonexistent and players were subjected to the owners' beliefs about salaries. Players had no representation. The public didn't give the brothers much sympathy in a war year when everyone had to tighten up on income.

On April 16, a day before the Tigers started their season, the Boston Red Sox felt compelled to offer a tryout to three African Americans at Fenway Park. Jackie Robinson, Sam Jethroe and Marvin Williams worked out under the watchful eyes of Manager Joe Cronin and Coach Hugh Duffy. They reported they were impressed with the play of Robinson, a former Army lieutenant, but no signings took place. On April 18, just before the start of the Red Sox and Yankees game, the Yankees became the focus of a Negro picket line. There were some twenty people marching around the stadium protesting with signs saying "Jim Crowism in Baseball" and "If We Can Stop Bullets, Why Not Balls?" They were organized by Col. Hubert Fauntleroy Julian, known as the "Black Eagle of Harlem," and the secretary of the League for Equality. He called Yankees president Larry McPhail a czar and said he had conferred with him the day before, pointing out there were no Negro employees at the stadium, either players or service personnel. He declared, "The Negro is entitled to equal rights in sports. If we can fight together, we can play together." It was still a war year and the social issues of the day were coming, but they were still a long way away from being seriously discussed in baseball.

In St. Louis the Browns were favored, but the Tigers were serious contenders.[9]

Big, brawling Sig Jakucki started the opening game against Newhouser at Sportsman's Park in St. Louis. The rowdy Jakucki was many things, a lot of them bad, but on certain occasions pitching wasn't one of his bad traits. He sported a 13–9 won-lost record in 1944, and posted a 3.55 earned run average for the American League champs. When he was right on the mound, he was tough to beat. This day he was right.[10] Newhouser's schedule didn't pay the dividends he had counted on and he got off to a bad start at the very beginning of the game. He gave up two runs on a walk, a single, and a double, followed by an error that sunk him into a deep first-inning hole. Still he kept his composure.

"One-Arm" Pete Gray (AP Photo).

Richards clipped a Jakucki pitch for a round-tripper in the third inning to put the Tigers on the board. But in the sixth the Prince was greeted with an uprising that resulted in his being relieved. A single by shortstop Stephens, and doubles by right-fielder Byrnes and first baseman McQuinn, plus an infield hit by third baseman Schulte, ended Hal's working day. He was replaced by Les Mueller.

Mueller finished up the sixth and pitched the seventh inning, but he gave up two more runs and the game went out of Detroit's reach. Rookie Wilson mopped up the game.

Two significant incidents took place in the game involving Browns outfielder One-Arm Pete Gray. In the seventh Gray got his first major league hit, singling off Les Mueller.

Before that, Newhouser had struck him out with a major league curve ball on a 3–2 count. On his second trip to the plate he ripped a liner to left center that had two bases written all over it, but ageless Doc Cramer made an amazing fielding gem and robbed Gray of a sure double. Cramer's catch was the most sensational fielding play of the day. Pete had already rounded first base when Cramer, on a dead run, crossed his glove hand over his body and grasped the line drive far to his right just a few inches off the ground. The forward lunge for the ball sent the elder center-fielder into a complete somersault motion after the catch. The St. Louis fans groaned, but then gave Cramer his well-deserved applause. The fans recognized a remarkable feat by a soon-to-be forty-year-old major league player. Gray's first hit and Cramer's catch gave people something to talk about at work the next morning besides the war.[11]

Borom remembered Gray's effort to get that first major league hit: "As for Pete Gray, his first time at bat Newhouser struck him out on a 3–2 curve ball. His second at bat he hit a sinking line drive that Cramer made a diving catch on. He was frustrated and as he came by our dugout, Hostetler, our bench jockey, yelled at him, 'You hit the ball good, tough luck, two outs.' Pete replied, 'What a league, they strike you out on 3–2 curve ball pitches and they slide on their bellies like snakes and make catches!'"

Les Mueller said: "Yeah, that's right. I had the honor of giving him his first hit. I don't remember what type of hit it was to tell you the truth, but, yes, he got his first major league hit off of me.... It was unbelievable how he could bat. I think in the Southern Association he had quite a year the year before he came up to the majors. How he could catch a fly ball by getting that glove down after he caught it was tremendous. He was quick afoot, and he had better than average speed."

John McHale commented: "I did see him play and I remember how fast he could run. He was a very fast, quick guy. Interestingly for me, though, was that he hit fastballs very well, but he had kind of a hitch. He had to get the momentum of the bat going. I think it was Newhouser or Trout ... who said, 'When he has to get that momentum going I think if we throw him off-speed pitches that would be the best way to handle him.' It was.... He had a powerful arm. The good arm that he had was developed and very muscular."

Even though Detroit dropped their opener, 7–1, tomorrow would be another day. The season had just started. In baseball there always seems to be a tomorrow or a next year for the faithful.

The next day, April 18, Trout put the Tigers in the win column with a seven-hit, 11–0 shutout performance against the Browns. Detroit unloaded a 21-hit attack on the star pitcher, Jack Kramer, who had accounted for 17 Browns victories the previous year. Webb, Mayo, and Cramer all picked up three hits each while Outlaw led the way with four hits, three singles and a double. Kramer

Roger "Doc" Cramer (National Baseball Hall of Fame Library, Cooperstown, New York).

headed to the showers early and failed to survive the second inning.[12] Red Borom shed some light on Kramer: "Jack Kramer was a good pitcher, but we picked up on his pitches. He was tipping his hand by how he was gripping the ball before the pitch. I don't think he ever figured out why we hit him so well. We knew what pitch was coming during most of the games he pitched against us that year."

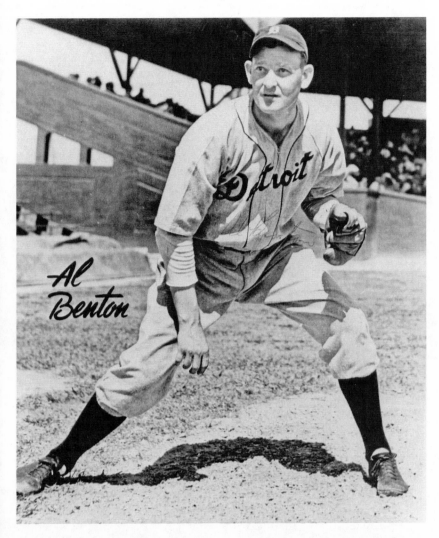

"Big Al" Benton (National Baseball Hall of Fame Library, Cooperstown, New York).

The following day the Browns sent their best pitcher from the previous year to the mound. Nelson Potter had recorded a 19–7 record in 1944. He was known to have good control and an excellent screwball, and he was to give Detroit problems throughout the year. The Tigers countered with their veteran right-hander Al Benton, a native of Noble, Oklahoma.

Benton was a large, powerful man. He stood 6' 4" tall and weighed 225 pounds. Big Al had those huge, flapping ears that made one think of an elephant. His size was intimidating in public and even more so when he was on the mound.

He started his baseball career with the Athletics. Detroit traded for him in 1938. That year he began to experience severe headaches that he believed came from a sinus infection. He lived with headaches daily during his early career, but in spite of his handicap, by 1941 he was considered an important starting pitcher for Detroit. He contributed a 15–6 pitching record to the Tigers' losing season that year. He and "Schoolboy" Rowe (8–6) were the only pitchers with winning records that season. The following year he had a losing record (7–13), but his earned run average was a respectable 2.90. When he enlisted in the Navy he spent almost all of his time at the base at Norman, Oklahoma, where he was involved with the Norman Navy Sky-Jackets baseball team. The headaches landed him in the hospital for about two months in the fall of 1943, and the Navy doctors decided to release him from the service early in 1945.

Although the headaches remained, his arm stayed sound, and he was a welcome sight after a three-year absence for manager O'Neill. Benton felt as if he was set for another big season like 1941. His sinker seemed to be his out pitch. He was inserted into the pitching rotation as the third starter. When the ball was put into the 32-year-old hurler's hand for the third St. Louis game, Detroit expected great things from him.

He did not disappoint them. Big Al scattered four hits and his sinker produced ground balls which in turn set up two double plays. Both pitchers were on top of their game and goose eggs went up repeatedly on the scoreboard, but in the top of the ninth, clutch hits by Mayo and Cramer produced the only run of the game.[13]

Detroit headed home to Briggs Stadium sporting two of the three contests safely tucked away in the Tigers' den. The Detroit baseball season was off and running towards a pennant-winning season.

Detroit faced Cleveland in their home opener on April 20th. A homegrown boy from Hamtramck, Michigan, Steve Gromek, trimmed the Tigers that day 4–1. How Wish Egan missed him was a mystery, and Gromek was to be a thorn in the Tigers' side all year. The Indians finished in the second division in 1945, but Gromek put up nineteen wins against only nine losses along with a 2.55 earned run average, giving him a stellar year with a losing club.

The other pitcher the Indians produced was a young Allie Reynolds. Reynolds would record an eighteen-and-twelve record for the fifth-place Indians and post a 3.20 earned run average. Both pitchers had long careers in the majors. Cleveland was led by player-manager Lou Boudreau, the previous year's American League batting champion, and one of the last successful playing managers in baseball. Sluggers Pat Seerey and Jeff Heath, both outfielders, and catcher Frankie Hayes brought a slugging punch and experience to a wartime-depleted squad. Boudreau was all business when it came to baseball. He couldn't run well due to ankle injuries he suffered playing college basketball at the University of Illinois, and his arm wasn't that strong, but he was a clutch player and one of the best, if not the best, shortstops in the league.

Overmire, the fourth starting pitcher in the Detroit rotation, fell victim to the six-hit pitching of Gromek, losing his first start of the year. Seerey knocked in two of the four runs for Cleveland as the Tribe sprayed ten hits around the field from Overmire's offerings. A pair of back-to-back doubles by Don Ross and Rudy York produced Detroit's only score.[14]

The next day Newhouser pitched and hit the Tigers to a one-run win over the Tribe with a 3–2 victory. It did not come easy. In the eleventh inning Borom, playing shortstop in place of Hoover, led off the inning with a perfect bunt single, stole second, and took third on Richards's sacrifice. With one out, Newhouser stepped up to the plate. Borom relates the incident: "I was on third, with one out, and I kept looking for the squeeze sign, but Richards let Newhouser hit away and Hal hit a single to win the game. Newhouser was a pretty good hitter for a pitcher."

The game was played in icebox weather with a high of 42 degrees that day. It was a typical Michigan spring baseball game at the corner of Michigan and Trumbull. Despite its being a Saturday game, with the ace of the staff on the mound, the attendance was a slim 4,374 due to the cool weather. Newhouser knocked in two of the Tigers' runs and shared the hitting honors with Mayo and third baseman Ross. Both Ross and Newhouser collected two hits, and Mayo's round-tripper accounted for the other run.[15]

The following day, Sunday, the temperature rose, and 23,000-plus fans showed up to see Trout win his second straight game, 6–3.[16] He gave up six hits, but it was a sloppy game for major-league level baseball. The Indians committed four errors behind Allie Reynolds. Trout was in his prime and Reynolds was just beginning to show the stuff that would make him a big winner in the years to come. Borom remarked about Reynolds: "As for Reynolds, yes, he was pretty fast. In fact the double I had off him was a pitch I usually could pull, but this was hit to left center. He was a tough pitcher."

The Tigers won four out of their first six games, but there was a missing person in the dugout. Manager O'Neill watched Detroit lose the opening game to the Browns in St. Louis, and then entered Ford Hospital in Detroit for treatment of gout in his right foot. He was lame and crippled. Since April 19 the skipper had been receiving his baseball news by radio. The news was that he would rejoin the squad during the next month's home stand. A similar attack of gout had laid him up for five weeks the prior year. Steve wasn't worrying about his absence. "They'll do all right; they're in good hands," was his confident comment.[17] Richards, the former acting manager of the Atlanta Crackers in the Southern Association, and Coach Mills, O'Neill's first-base coach, were handling the duties by taking turns in the third-base coaching box where the skipper normally stood. Utility outfielder "Hub" Walker and pitcher "Dizzy" Trout were alternating in the first-base coaching box.

On Tuesday, April 24, 1945, the major league owners had a meeting in Cleveland. The main topic was the selection of a new commissioner. Ford Frick, the National League president, and a number of politicians were on the list.

Roy Cullenbine (National Baseball Hall of Fame Library, Cooperstown, New York).

President of the New York Yankees, Larry MacPhail, added the name of Albert "Happy" Chandler, a senator from Kentucky. After several ballots Chandler was unanimously approved.[18]

A new program called the Malaney Plan was also brought up for a vote. The Malaney Plan would allow for inter-league play. With the 1945 All-Star game being put on hold due to the war, the owners replaced it with war-funding games. Besides the same-city games, Cincinnati would play Cleveland, Brooklyn would play Washington, and Detroit would be playing Pittsburgh. These games would benefit the war-funding effort. Unfortunately the Tigers-Pirates game would be canceled because the Office of Defense Transportation would refuse Detroit permission to detour 62 miles to get to Pittsburgh. The other games were scheduled for July 9 and 10.[19]

The White Sox came into town, but rain and cold weather canceled the games. The Tigers then moved on to Cleveland to play the Indians again. Benton received the call to pitch the opener in Cleveland and spun a beautiful two-hit 5–1 victory.[20] Boudreau and Seerey picked up the Tribe's only hits, with Seerey's double accounting for the Indians' run. Detroit unloaded an eleven-hit attack with Cramer, Outlaw and Ross contributing two hits each to the assault.

But despite the accumulation of hits, which had been lacking in former games, there was an obvious problem with the offense. The Tigers were collecting a lot of singles and a few doubles and once in awhile an occasional home run, but the power charges in their bats were not powerful enough. The only real slugger they had was the home run king Rudy York, and Rudy wasn't producing. Zeller became concerned about it.

The Tribe and the Tigers had a double-header scheduled for the next day. Gromek was his usual brilliant self and shut out the frustrated Detroit squad 4–0, pinning the loss on Newhouser, whose lack of control hurt his game. Although he only surrendered six hits, he gave up eight walks to the Tribe's hitters. Detroit could pick up but five hits from the Cleveland hurler, two of them by Ross, who had been playing a steady third. Rookie Houtteman made his debut by relieving in the seventh, and hurled the last inning without giving up a hit or a run.

Trout took over the duties for the Tigers in the second game of the double-header and shut out the Indians by the same 4–0 score Gromek had recorded for a win in the first game. Trout helped his own cause by clubbing a homer in the sixth inning off losing pitcher Red Embree. That blow produced the first and only run he needed to win the game. Detroit struck for three more runs in the eighth, and Dizzy had control of the game from the first inning, allowing the Tribe only four hits. Borom, Mayo, Outlaw and left fielder Maier all picked up two hits each, with Maier driving in two of the four runs.[21]

In between games Zeller struck a deal with Cleveland. He traded third baseman Ross, and the recent service returnee Dutch Meyer, to the Indians in exchange for their outfielder Roy Cullenbine. Ross and Cullenbine switched uniforms and teams for the second game in Cleveland. Neither, however, played for his new squad in the second game. Ross was not happy with the trade. He talked about leaving the game and retiring. Cullenbine, however, was coming home.[22]

Roy Cullenbine had a history with the Tigers. One of the young hot-shots from the Detroit sandlots and a well-known athlete in Detroit high school circles, Cullenbine, although born in Nashville, Tennessee, grew up in the Motor City and was signed by Wish Egan in the late '30s. In 1939, as an upcoming prospect for the Tigers, Cullenbine became caught in the web of Landis's ruling that released a number of Tigers. Cullenbine was declared a free agent and he was in demand. Brooklyn reportedly gave him a $25,000 bonus for his contract, but when he was slow in responding to National League pitching, they traded him to the St. Louis Browns. There he made a comeback, hitting .317 and knocking in 98 runs in 1941.

Cullenbine always worked pitchers deep into the ball-strike count. As a result of his patience at the plate he picked up a large number of walks and had a high on-base percentage. However, the Browns thought he was being lazy at the plate and just looking for a walk when he should have been swinging away. They sent him to Washington, who in turn sent him to New York, where, as a Yankee, he played in his first World Series. That winter the Yankees unloaded him to Cleveland and he hit .289. In 1944 Roy had a very good year. He batted .284, hit 16 home runs and knocked in 80 runs for the Tribe. By this time he was, at 30 years old, a seasoned veteran and a good switch-hitter.

There were not many hitters who could hit from either side of the plate during this era, so his hitting was an asset. His fielding was average to below average, but his ability to get on base and drive in runs made him a big plus for the powerless Tigers. It was a deal that tipped the scales for Detroit early in the race. Zeller had put another punch into the order and the deal would pay big dividends.

Les Mueller said:

> Roy had a good year, and he did a good job for Detroit. When he came over in that trade ... that was a very favorable trade. He helped the club. He was a likable guy. I hated to pitch batting practice against him ... because he wouldn't swing at a ball unless you threw it right down the middle. He had a reputation for having a great eye, and he did have. He would not swing at a ball unless it was a strike, you could almost bet on that ... and that was the reason he was that way. He concentrated on it in batting practice.... You might throw him five or six pitches and they weren't more than just that far away from the plate ... and he wouldn't swing at it. He would get you aggravated ... because if they all did that we wouldn't finish batting practice, but he was a good hitter that wouldn't swing at bad pitches.... He was just an average fielder. He wasn't the greatest outfielder in the world. But he and Cramer were close and I think Cramer helped him out a lot.

The first month of the pennant race found Detroit in second place, one game behind the White Sox, whom they would entertain at Briggs Stadium on Monday. With Newhouser, Trout and Benton maintaining the front-line pitching duties, the Tigers were on the prowl and looking for a consistent fourth pitcher they could count upon. Their choices were Overmire, Mueller, Eaton, Orrell, and Wilson. O'Neill selected Wilson to pitch the opener against the Sox.

6

May

"The booing wasn't just occasional, it was continuous. When his name was announced, catcalls would be heard throughout the stadium. He couldn't stick his head out of the dugout without being overwhelmed with boos.... O'Neill said, "No matter what ... he had to be distressed by the constant boos. He was afraid to swing at a ball because, if he missed, there would be another salvo.... Frankly, I never saw anything like it."

H.G. Salsinger

The Chicago White Sox occupied first place in the American League by opening the season with a five-game winning streak before the Browns slowed them down with a double-header sweep in Sportsman's Park on the last day of May. As play opened for the month of May, however, the Tigers were nipping at their heels in second place, with but one game separating the pair. The Sox had three fine pitchers in righty Orval Grove and southpaws Thornton Lee and Eddie Lopat. They were paced at the plate by third baseman Tony Cuccinello, who would finish his last year of major league baseball as the runner-up in the American League batting race with a .308 average. He was backed by outfielders Johnny Dickshot and Oris Hockett who hit for .302 and .293 averages. The Chicago team was managed by one of baseball's more colorful characters, Jimmy Dykes.

The Sox, however, had no power at the plate. No regular was able to produce double home-run figures. Dickshot's four round-trippers for the season led the team, and infielder Roy Schalk was their runs-batted-in leader that year with only 65. No one picked them to come close to winning the pennant, and they struggled later in the season, finishing in sixth place behind Cleveland and just above Boston in the standings. All three of those clubs flirted with the .500 number throughout the year, but all fell short of accomplishing the deed. Later in May the Yankees swept Chicago four straight in the Bronx, and after that the Pale Hose declined, but for the better part of the month of May the White Sox held first place in the American League standings. It was to be a two-game

72

stopover for the Sox at Briggs Stadium starting on Tuesday, May 1, as Detroit opened a home stand.

The fans waited patiently for Newhouser to get on the winning side of .500. He had a 1–2 record. Trout and Benton had won their previous starts, neither having lost a game yet. If Newhouser could get himself together, Detroit would have a 1-2-3 pitching punch that could allow them to pull away from the opposition early in the race. But the cool weather wasn't friendly to the lefty. He preferred much warmer weather. The fielding support of his teammates during his outings had been weak, and the team scored only a total of four runs during his starts on the mound. He had knocked in half of those runs himself. Detroiters had faith in their Prince and felt he would eventually lead the way.

During the opening of this home stand, the front office dealt with a problem that could sink the Cullenbine deal. Ross indicated that he was unwilling to report to the Indians. His wife reported her husband told her he was planning to return to their home in Pasadena, California. If Detroit couldn't finalize the deal, Cullenbine would be sent back to the Indians. Zeller was now in conference with Ross at Briggs Stadium concerning his unwillingness to report.[1]

The Tigers decided to grab the opportunity to take over first place without using one of their front-line aces. In O'Neill's absence Richards sent Wilson to the mound to oppose Haynes for the first game. The White Sox were not about to roll over and gift-wrap first place to Detroit. Haynes won only five games against five losses that year for Chicago, but this game was the best game he ever pitched in his life. He shut out Detroit 5–0 on one hit. The right-hander faced only 28 hitters in posting a near-perfect outing. Infielder "Skeeter" Webb sliced a clean hit over second base in the third inning for the only Tiger offense of the day. Manager O'Neill could only sit by his radio and scratch his head in puzzlement over the lack of hitting by his club. The Tigers had no growl at the plate.

A small crowd of 3,000 or so fans attending the game watched in silence as Detroit skidded to third place. Chicago picked up but six hits off Wilson and reliever Mueller, but second baseman Schalk drove in three of their runs with a triple and a single while the Tigers' bats remained quiet.[2]

The next day Benton beat the White Sox 2–1 for his third straight win. The Yanks won again, putting them into a tie with the White Sox for the lead. Detroit moved up to just a half game behind both. The Tigers scored both runs early in the bottom half of the first inning on hits by Mayo, Cullenbine, and York. But errors plagued the Detroit squad. Cullenbine, Webb, Mayo, and York all contributed misplays for this game.[3]

If the defense was suspect, there did not seem to be an immediate concern. Except for third base and left field, the lineup remained set.

After the first month of play the sportswriters inquired about who might be considered the best of the lot. Sportswriter Oscar Fraley interviewed 82-year-old Connie Mack, skipper and owner of the Athletics. Mack's version at this early date was that it would boil down to Detroit, New York and St. Louis, and the race would be similar to the last year's. These three would go down to the wire but the Tigers would finish first.

"Detroit is the one to beat without question," said the A's manager. "Pitching is an important quality, particularly in these times, and Detroit has it. The Tigers were strengthened tremendously by the return of Al Benton. Add him to Newhouser and Trout, and he gives Detroit real all-round pitching strength. They also were helped by the Cullenbine deal. He is a good hitter and will compensate for the loss of Wakefield."

Mack shared 62 years of baseball experience by saying, "The Browns can't be overlooked, for they have key men back. They didn't open with the same rush as last year, but they have to be reckoned with. They found out they could win, and that breeds confidence, a major factor in becoming a champion."

Concerning the Bronx Bombers, he replied, "The ... Yankees' pitchers will hold that team in there. They seem to be having some infield trouble, but Mr. McCarthy [New York's manager] will have them straightened out, and they will be tough to beat." Trying not to belittle the other five teams, including his own, he believed after a careful analysis of each club that none of them would be within shouting distance of the big three. As for the White Sox, Connie just said, "Golly, they certainly started nicely, didn't they?"[4]

Cullenbine and York certainly were capable of giving Detroit a potent one-two power-punch at the plate, and Benton was off to a great start. He might even out-pitch Trout and Newhouser before the end of the season. The Detroit future looked rosy.

The Browns rode into town with their cockiness and rowdy attitude, knowing that they were capable of playing better baseball than their record showed. They had the misfortune of losing five one-run ball games at this early stage. Shortstop slugger Vern Stephens would lead the American League in home runs with 24. The steady play of first baseman George McQuinn contributed a combination of good fielding and hitting, and with outfielder Mark Christman's consistency in the field and at the plate, they were still dangerous. The pitching staff of Potter, Kramer, Jakucki, Hollingsworth, Shirley, and Muncrief was one of the best in the league.

The Tigers welcomed back Steve O'Neill for the first time since opening day.

Kramer ruined O'Neill's return by pitching a four-hit, 5–0 shutout in his first full nine-inning outing of the season. If Detroit had his signs in advance it made no difference on this day. His "stuff" was just too good. Matching goose-eggs with Trout for the first three innings the Browns bunched four extra-base hits for four runs in the fourth inning. Trout gave up seven hits and suffered his first loss. Stephen's third homer of the year started Trout's demise. Mayo's two hits, one a double, led Detroit at the plate.[5]

The next day, May 6, 39,482 fans showed up to back the Tigers in a Sunday home double-header. Swift was behind the plate every day now, including this double-header. Richards was out with a bad ankle sprain from April 29, and would not return to active duty until May 11. The catching load landed on Swift.

He was very capable behind the plate. He did an exquisite job of signal calling and catching for both contests. Newhouser was never better, spinning a one-hit shutout for a 3–0 victory over Jakucki, in what was an outstanding pitching duel. Jakucki gave up only two hits in the first six innings, but the Tigers bunched four hits in the next two frames. Webb, Mayo, and Cramer laced RBI hits in clutch situations to give Newhouser all he needed. Stephens' single in the fourth was the only hit off Hal.

Benton was on the hill for the second contest opposing Shirley. Shirley pitched well, allowing Detroit but four hits. Benton, however, pitched better. He scattered nine hits and shut them out, pitching excep-

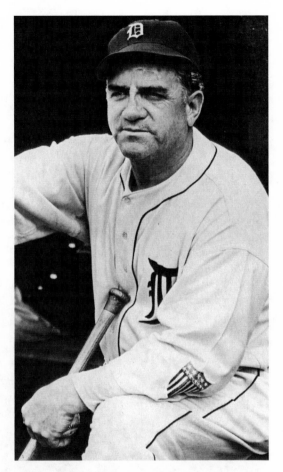

Detroit Tigers manager Steve O'Neill (National Baseball Hall of Fame Library, Cooperstown, New York).

tionally well in clutch situations. His fast ball had picked up speed; he had developed a quick slider, and a wide curve ball, to go with his sinker. The sharp slider was becoming his "Sunday" pitch.

Going into the last half of the ninth, the game was scoreless. Throughout Michigan the voice of Heilmann flowed over the airwaves: "Cullenbine steps in to lead off the ninth. Here is the first pitch to Roy. Cullenbine swings, it's a long high drive to right ... it's trouble, trouble.... It's ... a home run into the upper deck!" Detroiters went home happy that day. The trade was paying off, and it came just at the right time. The crowd watched a rare double shutout victory over the previous year's champions. The team's two shutouts brought the total whitewashing games to five. Four of these were at the expense of the Browns.[6]

Taking off his catching equipment, Swift breathed a sigh of relief. He had gone 0–10 at the plate in the three-game series, but his guiding hand behind the plate was invaluable. Pitching was not the only quality that was needed in making a champion. A durable, intelligent catcher was a must, and Swift was all of that.

Borom, speaking about Swift said, "The first thing that comes to mind is how he didn't take anything off those umpires and you know as long as a catcher keeps his head straight and doesn't turn to say something to them the umpire will be with you. He would needle those umpires, but he was a good handler of pitchers, and he usually caught Trout the whole season and Richards caught Newhouser. So it was a good set-up. When you got two it's not as hard."

The following day, May 7, found the Tigers idle, but Branch Rickey of the Dodgers used the day to announce that he had plans to form a U.S. Negro Baseball League. There was no doubt that Rickey was moving in a direction that would affect African Americans and baseball. Just how this would come about at this time was still a mystery.

The Yanks were en route to Detroit for the next series. Detroit needed their A-game ready to go. The Yanks' "Marse Joe" McCarthy sent Al Gettel out to face Trout in the opener. Dizzy was fit and ready to go. In the 1945 May issue of *Baseball Digest*, Dizzy is quoted as saying, "See that right arm? It's strong from milkin' cows. I milked so many in my day that even now when I meet anybody, I reach for one finger instead of the whole hand." Trout had a hex on the Yankees. His grip was strong enough to have beaten them seven straight times since 1943. His magic worked again as the Yanks fell, 1–0. It was his eighth consecutive victory over the Bombers. York had a perfect day with a pair of doubles, a single, and a walk.[7]

Jimmy Outlaw (National Baseball Hall of Fame Library, Cooperstown, New York).

Snow and cold cut the series to two games instead of the scheduled four. In the final game, Newhouser, trying to even his won-lost record, faced Hank Borowy, who seemed on the threshold of a great year with a 5–0 record. Borowy kept his streak alive by defeating Detroit 7–3, and the Yankees slid ahead of the Tigers in the standings.[8]

With the return of Richards, the catching spots were again normal, but in spite of having his regular backstop, Newhouser's record fell to two and three.

As good as the Tigers had played defensively for Trout, so bad were they for Newhouser. Webb committed three errors, and Mayo, the other keystone player, booted one. Maier replaced Borom at third, and had a mental error, cutting off a throw he shouldn't have, that allowed a run to score. But Detroit stayed in the mix, only a half game from Chicago and New York.

Ross decided to finish the season with Cleveland and was appearing regularly at third in the daily box scores.[9] The Cullenbine deal seemed closed.

The "pepper pot" for Detroit was outfielder Jimmy Outlaw, who said: "Well, when we came to the ballpark ... it seemed we were just one game ahead or one game behind in the race and it depended on who won that day that would determine who would be in first place. I would come into the clubhouse and say, "This is the day! We have to win today!"" The race would be tight throughout the whole season. Jimmy would have a lot to remind his teammates about as the games piled up. The race produced several leaders in the early going, and there was never enough breathing room for Detroit, who was either behind or ahead just a few games in the standings. Jimmy kept reminding them that they had to play hard and focus on winning every day.

Borom remembered Outlaw's drive to win: "Jimmy was the one. He picked on the two biggest men on the club, York and Greenberg, who joined us later in the year, to needle all the time. He kept that clubhouse going between him and Cullenbine.... Jimmy was a very versatile player, a good base runner, and played the infield as well as outfield."

On May 13 the Red Sox journeyed into Briggs Stadium for a Sunday double-header. As hot as Chicago had been at the start of the season, so was Boston cold. They lost the first eight of the year, but then swept their next five, and now were playing at .500. They were energized by a rookie pitcher, Dave "Boo" Ferriss, who won his first two starts with shutouts and had eighteen major-league scoreless innings to his credit. Ferriss was to be one of only three twenty-game winners that year. His feat would be accomplished playing for a seventh-place team. He was the real deal. Ferris could pitch. Trout faced him in the lid-lifter of the twin bill, but Detroit didn't fare much better than the other clubs, losing 8–2, to the phenomenal rookie. The Sox nailed Tiger pitching for fourteen hits, knocking Trout out of the game at the top of the sixth. "Indian Bob" Johnson clubbed a two-run homer to lead the visitors' attack. Ferriss shut the Tigers out for four innings. That set a new rookie shutout innings record of 22. The old record was 19⅔ innings set by "Buck" O'Brien of the Red Sox in 1911.

Rudy York heard the boo-birds of Detroit loud and clear in the first game against Boston when he was called out on strikes four times, all with one or more runners on base. The slugger took every strike pitch thrown without swinging.[10] The fans gave York a hard time during the war years. The booing

Al Benton is carried off by Hub Walker and an unidentified teammate while being examined by a doctor for his broken leg in Philadelphia (AP Photo).

wasn't just occasional; it was continuous. When his name was announced, cat-calls would be heard throughout the stadium. He couldn't stick his head out of the dugout without being booed. York took it in stride, but many believed it affected his play. O'Neill said, "No matter what he says or doesn't say he had to be distressed by the constant boos. He was afraid to swing at a ball because, if he missed, there would be another salvo. He even became jittery on thrown balls. Frankly, I never saw anything like it."[11] York seldom if ever had criticism for anybody. He was happy to have gone as far as he had in baseball and appreciated what the game had done for him. He often said, "Just think what I might have been if I hadn't played baseball." He was an affable person and had many friends inside the game.

In the nightcap, reliable Benton won his fifth straight, defeating the visitors and rookie Jim Wilson with a three, hit 2–0 shutout. York turned the boos into cheers in the second contest by scoring the first run on Outlaw's single, and then knocked in Maier with the insurance run in the seventh. Benton labored hard. The Tigers could only manage five hits against Wilson, another Red Sox rookie pitcher, but Big Al was stingy, and tough in the clutch.[12]

On May 17, Trout had a bothersome mole cut off his chin at Ford Hospital. He blamed the mole for his Red Sox battering. He thought Hollywood might call at anytime for a screen test and the mole just wouldn't do.[13]

This seventh-place Boston team was one of two clubs that would record a winning record against the Tigers. Wilson and Ferriss pestered Detroit all year long.

Borom found out later, during a game at Fenway Park, that he knew Ferris. Red said:

> Rudy York had a lot of trouble hitting Ferriss, but Boo Ferriss and I go back a long ways. When I was in my second year of pro ball I was in Cleveland, Mississippi, in the old Cotton States League. Ferriss was our batboy. I didn't know until nine years later that I would be hitting against him in the majors. We played a game in Boston in 1945 and to get to your clubhouse you would have to go through their dugout. When we came out for the game someone called out, "Hey Red." He was warming up to pitch. I went over to him and he said, "You don't remember me, do you?" I said, "Well, I know one thing, you are having a great year." He said, "I was your batboy back in Mississippi." He lived in a town called Shaw and would ride his bicycle on those pea-gravel roads that they had in Mississippi five miles to Boyle, another town about three miles outside of Cleveland where we played. I've kept in touch through the years. He became the baseball coach at Delta State College in Cleveland. He is a fine fellow. It really amazed me when I found out that it was our former batboy [who] was pitching against us.

Rain, rain and more rain fell as the Tigers and the Athletics both had seven straight games postponed due to the bad weather. In the entire American League every game between May 14 and 17 was rained out.

On May 19, Detroit finally got an opportunity to swing back into action. Their opposition was the other club that compiled a winning season against them in 1945. The Senators checked into the Book-Cadillac Hotel to begin a two-day, four-game series.

Trout once more took the lead game of Saturday's twin bill. He hadn't felt up to par lately, but seemed up to the task as he shut out the Senators for five innings. In the sixth inning, however, Trout labored. He made one of the three Detroit errors that day and now he was struggling to keep control of a game that was on the verge of slipping away. He gave up run-scoring hits to first baseman Kuhel and outfielder George "Bingo" Binks. Bearing down, he injured himself by straining a side muscle and young Houtteman rushed in to relieve him. Houtteman became a victim of infielder Torres' eighth-inning 3-run triple and the Senators won 6–2. More serious was the injury to Trout. He was sidelined for four days. His return was questionable.

Later in the year Trout addressed the injury and attributed it to overswinging. "I hurt my back early in the season trying to hit a knuckle ball, which Roger Wolff of Washington fed me. It was one of those crazy things and I swung at it vertically. Right straight up and something snapped, and it took me weeks to get back in shape."[14]

O'Neill's worst nightmare was lack of efficient pitching, with an increasing number of games in a short time, and Trout's recovery rate didn't help his bad dreams.

The winner for Washington was Wolff, one of the four Senator knuckleball pitchers. The Senators had been picked to finish in the basement of the junior circuit. Owner Griffith didn't believe his club had a shot at the pennant, and had arranged to finish his team's playing schedule earlier than normal, so he could rent the field to the Redskins football team. That decision came back to haunt him.

This unique pitching staff of knuckleballers gave the Senators a legitimate crack at the pennant. Wolff posted a 20-victory season. Fellow knucklers Dutch Leonard, Mickey Haefner, and Johnny Niggeling had win numbers of 17, 16, and 7. The only non-knuckler, Marino Pieretti, chipped in with fourteen victories for the year.

The "knuckle" pitch, easy on the wear and tear of pitching arms, was used to advance the older veterans' time at the major-league level. Detroit, later in the year, would pick up two knuckleball throwers, George Caster from the Browns, and Jim Tobin from the National League Boston Braves, to help save their tired staff. Ted Lyons of the White Sox had used the pitch to extend his career. Most pitchers depended upon the normal fast balls and a curve for their "bread and butter." This Washington staff, however, had been basic knuckleball pitchers for some time and that pitch was their "bread and butter." When a team faced them they had to adjust their hitting habits and their mindset. It was tough to switch gears after seeing high, hard ones thrown at them.

At this time no one took the Nats seriously. They were only .500, and fifth in the standings. The Tigers dug in to get a split. Newhouser was their man, and he opposed knuckler Haefner, the Senators' only lefty. The two hurlers worked well for the first three innings. Neither allowed a run. Newhouser shut out the visitors for four innings. In the bottom of the fourth Cullenbine homered. When Cramer and Webb walked, the Prince singled both home. His six-hit, 3–0 shutout gave Detroit a split.[15]

It was the seventh shutout recorded by Detroit in this young season. Outlaw and third baseman Maier accounted for five of seven hits. The hitting, with the exception of Cullenbine's clutch homers, was timely, but not strong.

By May 20, the American League opened with a record of 43 postponed games. Contrast that with the 68 average of postponements in a season and it looked like the rain and the double-headers would set a new record. The league postponement record was believed to be 97. The rain meant one thing to O'Neill: there would be a burden of double-headers that would wear down his pitching staff. Somewhere in mid-season Detroit would have to play off three games at Chicago and seven at Briggs Stadium. Four of Detroit's home games would be with Philadelphia and one each with the White Sox, Yankees and Red Sox. O'Neill said, "It looks like quite a load. To get over this hump, we'll have to get some wins from Wilson, Mueller and Overmire."

Benton, Trout, Newhouser and Overmire had accounted for thirteen victories in twenty-two games. "We can't expect these men to keep on carrying the club," O'Neill said. "They need help to meet the demands of all those double-headers. Last year I thought we made a race for the pennant and we should've won it because of good weather. We had one game postponed at home and two on the road. If we'd had to double up in August and September, it would have been bad. We didn't have the depth. Newhouser and Trout were overworked, as it was."

This year O'Neill believed Benton would take up the slack that was missing the previous year. He said, "Al is a workhorse. He will do his share and more. Even so, I can see trouble ahead unless we get a lift from the pitchers who have been unable to get started. I am not criticizing or complaining. They just haven't had a chance. I think they will deliver when the weather settles down and the race gets straightened away."

Turning to the relatively weak hitting attack displayed by the Tigers, the skipper said, "Nobody can perfect his timing under the conditions we've had this spring. When I look at our team batting average and some of the averages, I have to admit they're pretty low, but I understand why. What we need is sunshine. The consolation is that the other clubs also have been hit hard. We're no worse off than the other contenders."[16]

Sunday, May 20, Overmire, making his first start in over a month, beat Washington 4–1 on a seven-hitter. Maier and Cullenbine had a pair of hits, Cullenbine and Mayo drove in the runs, and Overmire held the Nats at bay for his second win.

Benton sought his sixth straight win of the year in the second contest and the Nats sent out a rookie, non-knuckler Pieretti, who simply outpitched Benton by allowing but three hits and whitewashing the weak-hitting Tigers 1–0. Benton lost his shutout streak of 32 innings when Binks doubled in the ninth for the only score.[17]

The big news of this baseball Sunday was not in Detroit. It was in St. Louis. The Yankees took on the Browns in a twin bill, and the Browns swept both games, 10–1 and 5–2. The sensational "One-Arm" Pete Gray was the center of the buzz. Before about 20,000 fans, Gray played what were the best games of his major-league career. He picked up three hits in the first game and drove in two runs while scoring one. He made three putouts in the field, one of them a long running catch of a Frank Crosetti hit. In game two he executed a hit and run that tied the game, and he handled six putouts flawlessly. His last catch was a knee-high grab of a fly ball hit by Bud Metheny.[18] The sweep saw the Yanks slip into third while St. Louis and Detroit shared second, two games behind Chicago, which had taken a Sunday pair from the Red Sox.

Detroit ended their home stand and prepared for a sixteen-game road trip. The teams traveled almost exclusively by train, which seemed romantic and adventurous to fans. But being on the road was difficult for players in a pennant race.

Outlaw reminisced about the train rides: "Oh, we talked hitting some, you know, and what other players were doing, just killing time mostly. I didn't mind riding the train, but one trip I didn't like was the Boston to St. Louis ride. Most of us got close with each other because of the trips. We got to play cards all the way down to the next stop. We would pull those seats back and start to play gin rummy or something. Most of the time, we had a private dining car. The Tiger car was a Pullman. If we were traveling all night we had it to ourselves."

The train rides were close to ending and with them an era in baseball was about to disappear. It wouldn't be long before plane travel would be common. But at that time the train was in vogue. Some enjoyed the ride and others didn't. Borom was one who enjoyed it: "Oh yes, all the travel was done by train. Nothing was beyond St. Louis and the trips weren't too long. I enjoyed the train. You were with the guys and associated with them. You could walk around the train, not like the plane flying one, two, three hours and sitting most of the time. We had two Pullman cars. Of course the road secretary had to handle all the arrangements, but it was a joy to get on a train after you had been riding those school buses in the minors like we had in the Cotton States League."

Pierce had a little different take on the trains. He was old enough to remember the train rides and young enough to fly in planes and make comparisons. Pierce said:

The trains, well, the first time I got a lower berth they told Houtteman and me, "You guys can have the lower berth if you sleep together." The two of us would have to sleep in a lousy lower berth. Most of the time, we would get the upper berths, because we were rookies, which is logical. It was nice you had your own little private room where the bed came down. They called it a roomette. But before that it was upper and lower berths.

I would rather go by plane. You would get there much quicker, and get your sleep. I remember all the stops and goes on a train. One time I was on a train and it was going so slow, I looked out the window, and I saw a group of pigs going by and the pigs were moving faster than we were traveling. I don't know how long it takes from Boston to Chicago, but it's a long ride and the plane is just so much better.

But train rides weren't terrible. We had some decent ones, but let's say you play a ballgame, you get there in a couple of hours and get your sleep that night. Now they have a rule which says if you have a night game you never play a day game following a night game because on a plane you might not get in until one or two in the morning.

The camaraderie on a train was a little closer. On the train we played cards, we played a lot of cards. We played pinochle because you could set the things up so you could play four in a group. If it wasn't pinochle it was hearts. Those were the two main games. We definitely talked baseball. That is one thing that is missing today. I don't think players get the chance to talk that much baseball, not just on planes, but also the rooms in the hotels. We always roomed with roommates. I think today it is in contracts that some players room by themselves. That takes a lot of the camaraderie away.

Detroit boarded the Tiger Pullman Special and headed for Philadelphia, where the Athletics would host a four-game series. The camaraderie was strong and the Tigers were looking forward to playing the A's, who had lost fourteen of their last eighteen games.

Baseball announced on May 23 that the Cardinals accommodated Mort Cooper by trading him to the Braves for $60,000. This ended the salary dispute with the three-time twenty-game-winning pitcher. Management didn't believe one player was indispensable.

On that same day, Jess Flores opposed Newhouser in the opener of a three-game series. Flores held the Detroiters to one run until the eighth, when Tiger bats exploded for six tallies. Newhouser pitched intensely. He struck out eleven and scattered seven hits, and had a shutout until Bobby Estalella hit a homer in the ninth. Everyone had at least one hit in the 7–1 win. Cullenbine, Webb, and Richards picked up two each.[19]

The victory moved Detroit into second place, one game out of first, because the Yanks dumped the White Sox and the Red Sox sank the Browns.[20]

Then the next day O'Neill's worst nightmare came true.

Benton was the cornerstone of Detroit's staff. He had been dominating during this young season and he was the difference O'Neill hoped for, but now Trout's injury left Benton and Newhouser to pick up a heavier load. "Big Al" faced the A's Thursday, May 24, at Shibe Park. Detroit was nursing a close 2–1 lead on a homer by Cullenbine, a triple by Maier, and a Mayo single. In the bottom of the fourth, O'Neill grimaced when Bobby Estalella hit a wicked line shot from a Benton offering right back through the middle of the mound. The ball struck Benton on the right ankle and knocked him down. Benton picked himself up and when he put weight on his leg he felt the pounding pain from the blow. Muller remembered the incident: "Yes, yes, I did see it. It was very scary. You could tell he was injured very badly. He was one of our better pitchers and it was a loss to our club."

If Big Al was nothing else, he was a "gamer." The leg was broken, but he wasn't ready to believe it and wasn't ready to give in to the pain. He was going to throw to the next hitter, which he did. A ground ball forced him to cover first base, and on his way to the coverage his leg collapsed underneath him. His teammates carried him off the field. Hub Walker and several other Tigers helped him into the locker room. It was a tough break, but O'Neill, ever the optimist, said, "I believe Al could be available after three or four weeks." Given the type of injury it appeared to be, most felt it might be more like two or three months.

This injury took away Detroit's chances to waltz through the American League race. Shirley Povich, the reporter from the *Washington Post*, said, "If the Tigers don't win they'll know why by being able to trace their failure to the drive off of the A's Estalella's bat that resulted in Benton's fractured leg." Povich lauded Benton, saying he was overshadowing Newhouser and Trout with his pitching, and that was a considerable feat inasmuch as those two were the prior year's top pitchers in the circuit.

That day Detroit faced a tough right-handed side-arm pitcher named Russ Christopher. He shut the Tigers down for the rest of the game while Mueller and Houtteman finished for Detroit. The A's battered Houtteman, as the Tigers not only lost a starting pitcher, but also a ball game 7–2.[21]

O'Neill called on lefty Overmire to pick up the pitching slack. Overmire, more of a control pitcher than a power one, was amongst the shorter players in the league that year at 5'7", and he was also one of the grittiest. Matching opposing pitcher and former Tiger ace Louis "Bobo" Newsom pitch for pitch, Overmire finally gave up a run in the bottom of the seventh, but Newsom couldn't hold. York's double in the eighth scored Mayo and tied the game. Richards slammed his second double of the day in the top of the ninth, scoring Outlaw with the winning run. The A's slapped "Stub" around for ten hits and three walks, but he gave up just one run.

The 2–1 victory before 19,240 fans shot the Bengals back into a tie with the White Sox for second place, both now a game and a half behind the Yankees.[22]

The next day, May 26, O'Neill chose Wilson to help plug the pitching gap. The New England farmer threw a complete game. While the A's slugged out eleven hits, the Tigers broke loose at the plate for a 12-hit attack. The result was a 5–4 win.

They did it the hard way, by blowing a 4–0 lead and allowing the A's to tie the game in the fifth. Wilson pitched hard and threw four consecutive shutout innings. He took the win when Cullenbine, in the seventh, singled in Mayo for the fifth run.

The victory put Detroit into second place alone. The Yankees dropped the Sox, 13–0, at home. It was Chicago's fourth straight loss.[23]

Detroit had twelve more games on the road, five of them before the end of the month. The two double-headers, one with Washington on Sunday, and another with New York on Wednesday, plus a single game with the Yanks on Thursday, would complete their work for May. In the first week of June the Detroiters would have to swing back through Boston and Cleveland before heading back home.

Newhouser was called upon to beat the Senators and he did just that, posting a 3–1 win over knuckleballer Niggeling in the opener. Newhouser sweated the win. He threw shutout baseball for the last six innings. York clubbed a round-tripper, and O'Neill thought if he could keep it up the Tigers' attack would improve one hundred percent.

With no front-line pitchers available for the second game, O'Neill dipped into his second-line staff and put the ball in Joe Orrell's hand. Orrell pitched well and nursed a 1–0 lead for seven innings. But Detroit couldn't hit the left-handed knuckler Haefner. Outlaw and Cullenbine picked up two hits, and Outlaw's double drove Cramer in with the lead run in the second, but that was all Haefner gave up.

In the eighth Orrell finally bent and allowed doubles by Case and Kuhel to tie the game.[24] In the ninth, Torres singled in Binks with the winning run.

After the split, Detroit journeyed to the "House that Ruth Built." This encounter in the Bronx had become important. Detroit's staff was starting the game feeling overworked.

New York, a major market for baseball, had 67,816 fans show up to see what the second-place Detroiters were made of. The attendance was the largest number of paying customers this year. The teams split the twin bill with identical 3–2 scores. The Tigers sent their lefties to the mound. Overmire won the first, but Newhouser, pitching with only two days' rest, lost the second.[25] Overmire scattered eight hits and once more pitched himself out of scoring threats throughout the game.

In their losing effort the Tigers were unable to score after getting men on first and third with no outs, but their ace, Newhouser, found difficulty being off schedule, and his control suffered as he issued eight free passes.

For the third game of the Yankee series, O'Neill called on the bespectacled Les Mueller to fill the void. This was his first major league start of his career before about 7,000 New York fans. It was a twilight game. Mueller remembers the assignment: "Yes, you don't forget those kinds of games. I was experiencing quite a thrill to be pitching at Yankee Stadium against the Yankees. I pitched a good ball game. The one thing I remember was that Richards caught that game. Believe it or not I don't think I threw more than, maybe, a half a dozen curve balls. I threw practically all fast balls. They had a lot of left-handed hitters. Richards had me pitching kind of up and in all day and I had very good luck. The thing I remembered most about that game was that I threw practically nothing but fast balls. Richards handled pitchers quite well."

As the twilight began to fade into evening Mueller completely handcuffed the Yanks, tossing the Tigers to a 2–0, 2-hit victory while facing only twenty-eight batters. It looked like Detroit had unveiled a new pitching star. The 26-year-old, 6'3" right-hander was being compared to Boston's rookie, Dave Ferriss.

Mueller, from Belleville, Illinois, was honorably discharged from the Army the previous October because of migraine headaches, but on this night he gave the Yanks the headache by showing a better than average pitch. What small number of breaking pitches he threw set up his fast ball, and the Yankee hitters were off balance all evening. Both hitters that singled in the first and fourth innings were erased on double plays. His pitches moved sharply and were difficult to hit solidly. He threw like a veteran that evening and showed remarkable poise for his first major-league start. He disposed of his foe in only ninety-four minutes.[26]

Detroit scored twice in the fourth. York, Cramer and Outlaw put together hits. A Yankee error sent them home. The play of the night belonged to Cullenbine, who electrified the crowd with a running catch of Johnny Lindell's liner to right in the seventh.

The Detroiters had taken the series from the Yankees in the Bronx, and although still in second behind New York, they had left New York just a game out of first place.

As the game was in progress, O'Neill sent his pitching staff to Boston for the next games to get them some early needed rest. Newhouser, Wilson, Overmire, and Trout were en route by train to Boston before Mueller retired his last hitter.

Trout rejoined the staff after a long rest period due to his side and back injury. He was eager to start the month of June in his regular rotation. O'Neill was smiling and thinking that even with the heavy away schedule and two pitching injuries, he had dodged a bullet on this long road trip. But the trip wasn't quite finished yet.

Still very conscious of the sacrifice that war had inflicted on the nation, the *New York Times* columnist Arthur Daley wrote that it would be a very nice gesture on the part of Major League Baseball to honor all recipients of the Medal of Honor with lifetime passes. "It's little enough to do for those who have done so much," he wrote. In Detroit the groundskeeper at Briggs Stadium, Jim Conway, exhibited the Purple Heart and Bronze Star medals won by his son, 1st Lieutenant James Conway, in Italy. Young Conway single-handedly cleaned out a group of German snipers and in his effort suffered a bullet wound to the knee.

7

June

"The Tigers knew when he was throwing a fastball and when he was throwing a curve. You can imagine what a handicap that would be to the pitcher.... But those are the little things that help you win games.... When you win the pennant by one game every game was big."

Les Mueller

Detroit finished the first month and half of play a half game behind the Yankees. They posted a 13–9 win-loss record for the month despite injuries to Richards, Trout, and Benton. The White Sox dropped to third, four games out, and the Browns sat in fourth, four and a half games behind.

Detroit opened with a road trip in June, playing a four-game series with the Red Sox. Wilson faced Emmett O'Neill June 1 at Fenway Park. In the bottom of the fifth O'Neill was forced to make a pitching change.

Looking into his thin bullpen, the Detroit manager decided to give young Pierce his major-league baptism.[1] Pierce looks back on the day:

I think I threw three and a third. The first batter I faced was "Boo" Ferriss [the paper recorded the first hitter as Metkovich]. I went in with the bases loaded. I came in from that right-field bullpen. That was a long walk in those days for an 18-year-old.... Cullenbine was talking to me while I was coming in, 'Take it easy, don't worry about it,' he said. Cramer came over, Mayo; they were all talking to me on the way in. I got the count to 3 and 2 and I walked Ferris [Metkovich].... Then I got them out for the next three innings. We were behind ... and ended up losing 4–3 [the score was 6–4]. That was my first appearance in baseball.

I always looked at Boston and tried to push that wall back with my hand. It looked like it was right on my back. If you had control you could pitch away from the hitter and have good luck. I pitched three and a third innings. I shut them out, so it was a pretty good outing. Steve O'Neill, the manager, came up to me after the game and said, 'Bill, son, I am so proud of you.' But you know I never got into another ball game after that until I was sent to Buffalo, June the 26th. I was figuring, boy, if he wasn't proud I would have been long gone. He was so nice, but I never got into another game until I got to Buffalo. [Note: Pierce did relieve against Chicago for two innings on June 10, giving up two runs and four hits.]

O'Neill decided Joe Orrell could help the Tigers draw even with Boston. Orrell turned to the Detroit traveling secretary, Clair Berry, and said, "I'm going downtown and buy a new suit of clothes ... I always have a good day after I buy a new suit."[2] But when the swift-throwing Joe returned from his shopping spree there was no suit, just a pair of new shoes, the next day the Red Sox hurler, Clem Hausmann, defeated the Tigers and Orrell, 5–1. The only run the Tigers could produce arrived gift-wrapped on a throwing error by shortstop Eddie Lake. Rookie Houtteman took over in relief and Sox outfielder Johnny Lazor buried one of his pitches into the right field stands to cap the ballgame.[3] Joe should have bought a suit.

After losing the first two, and dropping two games out of first place, O'Neill put his one-two pitching punch of Trout and Newhouser on the hill for the next day's double-header.[4]

Trout, making his first appearance since his layoff, took the ball for the first game to oppose Jim Wilson. Both pitched well, but Trout was rusty due to his long recovery, and lost a close game 4–3. Newhouser now was the last chance to salvage the series.[5] He rode to Detroit's rescue in the second game and won his sixth victory by the same score Trout lost the opener, 4–3.[6] The nightcap had a three-run fifth that was highlighted by batterymate Paul Richard's leadoff homer over the "Monster," and then hits by Webb, Mayo, and Cullenbine put the game away.[7] The Tigers left Boston with tails dragging, but still just two games away from the Yankees.

The skipper couldn't complain. He had dipped into his bullpen and received excellent pitching from Mueller, Orrell, Wilson, Pierce, and Overmire during the road trip.

The real problem was the lack of hitting. York, the only power hitter, wasn't hitting. O'Neill dropped Maier to seventh in the batting order. He had been the more consistent hitter and O'Neill said, "I believe he needed to have his hits count for something."[8]

The next series against Cleveland started June 5. Detroit's hitting problems became obvious when they were shut out in the first game. Mueller received his second start of the year and it was a rough one. Red Embree opposed Mueller.[9] Embree was to be inducted into the armed forces on Monday. This was his last start, and he wanted it to be a good one. It was. He tossed a six-hit, 9–0 win at Mueller's expense.

On June 6, Stubby Overmire defeated Cleveland, 8–1, and earned his fourth win in a row.[10] The large run production and the clutch pitching of Overmire put a smile on O'Neill's face. Never overpowering, Stubby was guided by Richards, and used his control and change of speeds to hit his mark.

Doc Cramer led the way, hitting a triple with the bases loaded in the sixth.[11] The New Jersey carpenter had four RBIs to go along with four hits. That was a batting punch O'Neill was looking for. Al Smith took the loss for Cleveland.

Newhouser took on Reynolds the next day and rang up his seventh

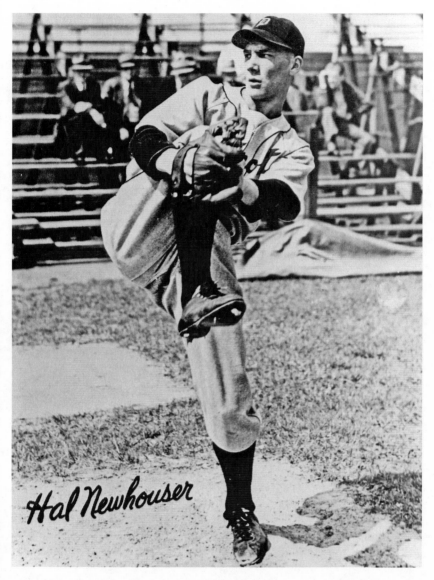

Hal Newhouser (National Baseball Hall of Fame Library, Cooperstown, New York).

victory with a five-hit, 3–2 gem over the hard-luck Reynolds.[12] Detroit was starting to hit. They had a total of eleven hits for that contest. Webb, Mayo and Maier each had a pair. Cramer, after a fast start, had slumped. Working on ways to break his hitting slump, he discovered that he had fallen into a bad habit with his batting stance. He corrected the stance and the balls started to drop in for hits.[13] Late in the game Cramer made a throw to home plate which saved the win for Newhouser. This prompted O'Neill to comment that Cramer in his book had an arm that stacked him the best of all time. O'Neill reminisced about the best throwing arms he had witnessed in his long player and managerial career. He commented on the following players: Ruth, a fine arm that was accurate and strong; Cobb didn't have a strong arm; Speaker, accurate but not strong; Musial, a very good arm; Joe and Dom DiMaggio, very good arms; Henrich, a strong arm; Ted Williams, just a fair arm; and down the line he went, rating them as he had seen them. But Cramer he believed was as good as any and maybe the best. This was high praise for the Tiger outfielder.

Newhouser was now pitching well. He had won five out of his last six games, three of them by one run, and even though the hitters hadn't been tearing the cover off the ball, there was a bump in the batting order. Outlaw, Cullenbine, Cramer, Mayo and Maier were all making the team growl a little louder at the plate.

The hitting problem still centered on the Big Chief. Rudy York's lack of run production had the Detroit executives wringing their hands. He had only hit two homers in forty games. His excuse was that the spring rains shut down batting practice, and while the pitchers continued to throw under the stands to keep themselves polished and poised, the hitters are restricted from batting practice due to the rainfall.

The Tigers, happy to be home again, started June 8 with a four-game series vs. Chicago. They took three out of four, using aces Trout and Newhouser in relief to save the second and third games.

Joe Orrell must have picked up a new set of clothes from his favorite Detroit haberdasher, because in a twilight game at home, the big 6'4" hurler choked off the Sox, giving up only four hits, and won a 2–1 victory.[14] The win put the Tigers into first place. Detroit scored both runs against Lee in the fourth. Hits by Cramer, Outlaw, Maier and Swift lit up the scoreboard for two runs. When Orrell weakened in the ninth with runners on second and third, O'Neill rushed in Trout from the pen. Trout was ailing again, but he shut the door on the Sox.

Saturday, June 9, Mueller received the starting assignment.[15] Chicago's starting pitcher, Haynes, was throwing a no-hitter, and nursing a one-run lead going into Detroit's fifth. Cuccinello scored in the second on infielder Michaels's base hit. Detroit rebounded when Outlaw started the Tigers off by hitting a line shot safely into right field. He advanced to second on an error by the fielder, and came home on Swift's single. Mueller then hammered a Haynes pitch into the lower left-field bleachers, putting the Tigers on top 3–1. It was Mueller's only major-league career home run. In the sixth, however, shortstop Webb fumbled a grounder and Mueller allowed a hit and a walk, and committed a balk, which put Chicago back into a 4–3 lead. By the end of the seventh the Sox had secured a 6–4 lead, gratis of another error by Mayo that led to two more runs. Reliever "Zeb" Eaton, making his first pitching appearance of the year, shut the Sox out for the rest of the game. Maier and Swift led off the last inning with base hits and Eaton drove a double into center field, scoring both runners. Webb was safe on an error and Mayo made up for his miscue with a long triple to left-center, bringing in the tying and winning runs. The Tigers, with four straight victories, stayed in first place.

That same Saturday, Major League Baseball picked up a black eye. The manager of the National League Brooklyn Dodgers, Leo Durocher, was arraigned on a charge of feloniously assaulting a fan at Ebbets Field.[16] Durocher and a "special policeman," Joseph Moore, were arrested on charges of assault at a game between the Dodgers and the Phillies.[17] The Dodgers were about to go on a seven-game winning streak which would put them into the National League's first-place slot for a time. The evidence was too thin to convict Durocher, but a civil suit forced him to pay a settlement to the victim.

O'Neill sent Trout back to the hill. He shut Chicago out for eight innings, and picked up a 3–2 victory over Humphries in the opener of a twin bill. Cullenbine hammered his fourth homer in the first and scored all three Tiger runs. In the ninth Trout faltered and was relieved by Newhouser, who closed out the inning to save the win.

There would be no sixth straight victory. Overmire, in the nightcap, didn't last past the fifth inning.[18] The Sox swamped him with eight hits in 4⅔ innings. Richards's grand slam wasn't enough as the Tigers took a 9–4 loss. They fell into second place with the split and the Yanks slipped back into first with a win over the Red Sox.

Tuesday, June 12, at Detroit, before 19,000-plus fans, the Tigers hosted the Browns for the first of three games. St. Louis was still in third, four games away from the Yankees, and but two and half behind Detroit. Detroit won the opener 2–1 in eleven innings.[19] The aces of both clubs, Kramer and Newhouser, pitched the entire game. Mayo and Cullenbine tied the game 1–1 in the third by slamming a double and a single. That score held up until the bottom of the eleventh, when Maier singled in Cramer with the winning run. St. Louis left thirteen runners on bases. This was Hal's eighth win. He gave up nine hits, but only one tally. The Browns suffered their fourth one-run loss in the last five games.

The win was significant for the Tigers because they jumped back into first place when the Yankees dropped a 5–3 game to Washington. Detroit never again relinquished first place. They did, however, have to glance over their shoulder for the rest of the year.

Now Detroit's bats boomed. York found his groove in the second contest and drove in four runs.[20] The Tigers nipped St. Louis, 6–4, behind his homer and two singles. Hoover contributed a round-tripper while filling in for Webb. Orrell was the winning pitcher with relief help from Eaton and Mueller. York had the distinction of hitting his first homer of the season in Detroit and hit what probably was the longest single of the year.[21] He drove a 400-footer to dead

Paul "Dizzy" Trout (Brace Photo).

center field in the first, but settled for a single when he tripped over first and fell flat on the ground, rolling over twice, before rising.

The big news out of New Jersey was that Greenberg could be out of the Army by Friday.[22] Greenberg, at 34 years old, had been out of baseball for four years. His nine seasons with Detroit had been outstanding ones. His lifetime batting average stood at .325, he had hit 249 home runs, and one year hit 58, a mark topped only by Ruth and equaled only by Foxx. Famous for his runs batted in, he had come within one of tying Gehrig's American League record in 1937. He was the American League's MVP in 1935 and again in 1940. He would be the first real superstar to return to the majors.

Trout pitched the closer against St. Louis on the 14th. He pitched brilliantly, allowing only five hits, but lost 3–2, despite the fact that Detroit gathered nine hits against their nemesis, Jakucki, who picked up his fourth victory of the year. Two of the hits off Trout were home runs by Vern Stephens.[23] He accounted for all three runs batted in. Trout would have been better served by pitching around him, but then "Diz" enjoyed challenging the best. Gray, the one-armed outfielder, retired from the game with a shoulder injury when he fell making a catch in the fifth inning.[24] The loss left Detroit but a half game ahead of the idle second-place Yankees.

That same day word arrived that Greenberg had been discharged.[25] Under a league ruling he would be entitled to his old salary for at least 60 days. At the time of his enlistment he had the highest salary in baseball at $55,000 a year.[26] He indicated he would need several weeks of practice before entering the lineup.

Questions in baseball circles were raised about the veterans that would be returning from war in mid-season. Critics thought their ability would prove too rusty to play against major-league competition. It was debatable whether a player could be separated from baseball for several years and return with all his previous skills.

Jack Zeller, however, believed Greenberg would return and compete well. Zeller had a good point when he said, "He is younger than many of the players who are holding regular jobs in the major leagues this season." Rudy York had no doubt Greenberg would return. "He'll be at the ball park at 6 in the morning, batting and fielding. I wouldn't be surprised if he was in playing form in four or five days," said Rudy. O'Neill concurred. "Hank is a hard worker and one of the most aggressive and conscientious players I've ever seen. With Hank back we'll take a lot of pressure off of York."[27]

Detroit now journeyed to Chicago for a five-game series with the White Sox.

O'Neill picked up a two-headed win-win coin against Chicago as Trout and Newhouser grabbed back-to-back victories. Dizzy opened the series by relieving Overmire to win the first game, 7–5, and then in the final contest Newhouser tossed a six-hitter, allowing but one run, to complete the sweep, 6–1.[28]

Richards had punched out a grand slam against Chicago recently, but O'Neill played a hunch that it wouldn't happen again and went to his bench.[29] He was making some strange decisions, but they were working out. Pinch hitter Hostetler batted for Richards, and singled home two runs in the top of the ninth. Trout picked up credit for the 7–5 victory. In the game Detroit's ancient center fielder, Roger Cramer, became but the thirteenth player in modern major league history to reach the 2,000 mark total in singles. He achieved the distinction against Ed Lopat of the Sox. Cullenbine and York also contributed to the win with home runs.

The Tigers then lost three games in a row. Thirty-seven-year-old Lee tamed the Tigers on June 17 in the opener of another twin bill, 6–1. Pitchers Orrell and Wilson were ineffective.

The next contest went to the Sox as well when Haynes outpitched Mueller and reliever Eaton, thereby receiving credit for Chicago's 7–5 victory.[30] It was the last game Haynes would play that year. He injured himself when he jammed his right leg sliding into third base. The result was a compound fracture and a dislocation of the right ankle.

The fifth game, on June 18, matched Trout against Bill Dietrich. The hookup became a pitcher's duel. Both hurlers pitched shut-out ball until the bottom of the ninth, when Mike Tresh squeezed home the winning tally with an excellent bunt. The 1–0 defeat evened Trout's record at 6–6.[31]

The Tigers returned home nursing a slim one-game lead over New York. O'Neill was aware of the Tigers' precarious situation. Even though he had received good pitching from his second-line hurlers, the whole staff had started to struggle. He dismissed talk of a pennant and kept everyone on task for the game of the day by saying, "We're just trying to win one game after another. We hope we win enough of them. None of the boys are talking pennant. They're just out there playing one game at a time. We will need another pitcher or two to help Trout and Newhouser carry the load."[32]

That evening, at the Del Prado Hotel in Chicago, O'Neill spoke with Red Borom and asked him if he wouldn't mind going to Buffalo to help out the minor league team. He said the manager, Bucky Harris, had asked for some help to bolster the club and one of his needs was an experienced infielder. Red was disappointed and asked O'Neill how long he would be there. The skipper said two weeks. O'Neill was getting ready to put a strong burden on his veterans. On June 20, Red arrived in Buffalo, but he wasn't alone. O'Neill also optioned McHale and Houtteman with him to help Buffalo out. The three showed up a couple of hours before game time. Later, on June 26, O'Neill sent Billy Pierce to join the group in Buffalo.

When he arrived in Buffalo, Houtteman lost a strange game to Jersey City, 2–0. He had held the Jersey team hitless and faced only twenty-two hitters for seven innings, but two scratch hits in the eighth combined with two errors to put him in the loss column. After two weeks had passed, Borom made sure the skipper hadn't forgotten him by placing a phone call to O'Neill reminding him of his promise. True to his word, O'Neill brought Borom back to Detroit. Houtteman also returned later to give the bullpen some needed relief. McHale and Mierkowicz enjoyed a good year playing for the Bisons and both, along with Pierce, would be recalled later to be eligible for the World Series.

The season was a third gone, but even after losing the Chicago series there were many who believed Detroit had the pennant in their hip pocket because Greenberg would rejoin the club in Detroit.[33] Too, Newhouser had been unbeatable in June. Detroit ace Al Benton was expected to return from his leg injury in a few weeks. He should strengthen the shaky pitching staff. But O'Neill stayed realistic despite the boastful Tiger fans talking of a sure pennant. He said, "We just don't have the mound strength, and the hitters are called on for too much. But we all hope we'll be there in October if we can win a game at a time and keep our heads above water from now until then."

The water would get pretty high before the Tigers could be assured of safe ground. The Yankees would win the next seven of eight games. The Runt's voice would be heard in the dugout and the clubhouse daily: "This is the day ... the day we have to win."

Les Mueller remembers Outlaw: "Jimmy Outlaw was the type of player that was always hustling. The type of guy that would get his uniform dirty and he did a good job. This was especially true when Greenberg joined us, and they moved him from the outfield to third base. Maier didn't play as much anymore and Outlaw played third most of the time with Greenberg in left field. He was a pepper pot. He was the type of guy who was always kidding around ... in the clubhouse or the dugout, and kept the guys loose."

The Tigers, back in Detroit, faced the Indians and their nemesis Gromek. They finally managed to find a way to defeat him, 4–3, in the first contest. O'Neill gave the Indians a different look and sent young Zeb Eaton out to face Gromek. Eaton struggled, but confounded the Indians long enough to benefit from a third-inning three-run rally, and by the fifth inning led in the game 4–1. York's two-run triple and RBIs by Swift and Cramer produced four runs for the young hurler to work with. Eaton was as wild as a March hare, allowing seven passes along with four hits. The Tribe left nine runners on base as they ducked away from Eaton's pitches. Finally O'Neill removed him after the Tribe touched him for a pair of runs in the sixth.

Mueller and Overmire saved the win for him by closing the Indians down with only two more hits. O'Neill was still pushing the right buttons.[34]

Baseball received another blow in the public eye the next day, Wednesday, June 20. The St. Louis Browns turned a game with Chicago into a fistic brawl. Sigmund Jackucki, Ellis Clary and George Caster led an assault upon a batting practice pitcher named Karl Scheel, who was a very vocal bench jockey for the White Sox. The razzing between the two clubs had turned ugly. Scheel, according to the Browns, became so verbally abusive in the eighth inning that he crossed the rhetorical line of cordiality with pitcher George Caster. His loquacious crudeness caused Caster to whip around and throw the baseball violently, and with bad intentions, at Scheel in the Sox dugout. That brought out Sox manager Dykes, who loudly protested to Umpire Passarella. Almost immediately the Browns' dugout, led by Jackucki, poured out onto the field, headed into the Sox' dugout, and physically attacked Scheel. Manager Dykes rushed to his player's rescue and suffered bruises and minor spike wounds during the resulting free-for-all. St. Louis wasn't the only club that Scheel had verbally assaulted during the season. Cleveland and Detroit felt his barbs as well, and many thought Dykes encouraged Scheel's behavior to unnerve the opposition. Scheel never played a game, but he was always on the bench, using his sharp tongue to annoy and insult. This time it took the help of the police to restore order and Scheel was removed from the dugout to the trainer's room, where he received much-needed first aid. St. Louis's manager Sewell had his hands full with this rowdy, brawling, drinking bunch of players and suffered with them when American League President Harridge fined him $250 for his failure as a manager to control his ball club. Each of the three members of that group that led the fight was fined $100.[35]

That same day Newhouser shut out Cleveland, 5–0, and he recorded his fifth consecutive June victory and his 10th of the season. Cullenbine clubbed his sixth homer and Outlaw collected three hits in three appearances for a perfect day. Detroit reached lefty Al Smith for six hits in seven innings and handed him his sixth defeat of the year.[36]

Greenberg had arrived in Detroit, according to Zeller, and prepared to go through a ten-day practice schedule designed to put him into the lineup by June 30. O'Neill remarked, "I don't know yet where he'll play but we have a little time to figure that one out."[37]

Before the third game with Cleveland on June 21, Greenberg engaged in his first practice session, working both in the outfield and at first base. Youngsters jammed the left-field stands to cheer Hank in the preliminary to the Cleveland game. Detroit sportswriter Sam Greene watched the first batting practice curve ball to Greenberg since his departure from the Tigers. It was a beanball. Zeb Eaton released the pitch with great enthusiasm, but it failed to break and headed straight for Hank's head, forcing him to duck. He smiled and asked Eaton to throw another. The next one hit the dirt in front of the slugger, forcing him to do a quick dance. Holding up his hand, Greenberg requested just fast balls after that. He even said please after his request. He drove the next pitch deep into left field and, according to Greene, "Baseball in Detroit again returned to normal."[38]

Detroit finished off the Tribe, 5–1, for a three-game sweep. Overmire spaced out seven hits and handcuffed the Tribe while the hitters tapped Jim Bagby for nine hits in six innings. Outlaw continued to bat well and had two hits, one a triple, to pace the Tigers.[39]

The team headed for St. Louis the next day, but Greenberg stayed in Detroit to work out four hours a day and focus on his batting. O'Neill assigned Pierce and Houtteman to pitch batting practice to Greenberg during the team's absence. Pierce recalls: "Remember, he was actually in the war. He wasn't playing ball. A lot of the players in the service got to play ball while they were in the service. He was actually in the combat. Hank ... wanted to get practice. Art Houtteman and I stayed back when the team took a road trip to throw batting practice to him. He could hit that ball, and he was a first-class gentleman, a nice man. He treated us well. I remember he took Artie and me out to lunch, and everyday he wanted to, but as young teenagers we had some things to do too."

Red Borom said: "He took batting practice about a week or more and I think he took so much batting practice he had blisters all over his hands."

Trout got off to a bad start even before the game. After leaving the train and his Pullman compartment, he discovered his wallet missing. Also missing was $50, no small loss in 1945. Against the Browns, Detroit handed Trout a two-run lead in their opener at St. Louis. But by the fifth inning he was struggling. He walked three hitters, forcing in a run, committed an error from the mound, and gave up three hits in that fateful inning. It led to an 8–4 loss. York's three hits went for naught. Trout's collapse sent him to the showers and the Browns picked up three more off Wilson, Orrell and Eaton.[40]

On June 23 the skipper put Mueller back in the rotation because Benton still wasn't ready for service. Mueller grew up in Belleville, Illinois, which was a short toss across the state line into Missouri and the city of St. Louis. It was like a homecoming for the Belleville native and he wanted to pitch well. He did. He picked up his second victory in five starts, 5–1. Detroit staked Mueller to a three-run lead in the fourth and added two more insurance runs for him in the ninth inning. His catcher, Swift, cracked out three hits and drove in two of the Detroiter's five runs. The Browns couldn't touch the 6'3" side-arming Mueller. He evened the series for Detroit.[41] Kramer absorbed the loss.

Mueller spoke about Kramer, repeating Borom's words earlier, and added this:

> I don't remember much about that game, but I remember something about Kramer. He was one of the Browns' better pitchers and he had a pretty good record, but Detroit wore him out. The Tigers knew when he was throwing a fast ball and when he was throwing a curve. You can imagine what a handicap that would be to the pitcher when you know what pitches were coming. There was something he did in his windup that someone on the Tiger bench picked up and of course they relayed it to all of the players. I think he was turning his glove one way on the fast ball and another way on the curve ball. It was something that was very obvious to the batter. The hitters didn't have to get it from the coach. The batter watched and as a result Detroit won [the pennant] by one game. So, maybe, if the Browns had knocked us off a few times it could have been a different story, but those are the little things that help you win games. Of course when you win the pennant by one game every game was big.

In the first game of the next day's double-header, Newhouser picked up his eleventh victory, 5–1. He had pitched twenty-three scoreless innings until the Browns broke the streak in the ninth with a solo drive by Christman. Cramer paced the Tigers with three hits and two runs batted in. It was the ace lefty's sixth straight win in June. In the second contest Trout picked up a win in relief of Wilson. Cramer again starred at the plate with three hits, including a rare home run. Shirley and Potter suffered the defeats.[42]

Despite the Tigers' fine record, the Yanks kept pace, and were only a game and a half behind them. The scribes began to see a favorable pattern developing for Detroit. Arthur Daley of the *New York Times* wrote, "Newhouser and Trout finally hit their stride. Once Benton recovers the Bengals might be out of reach. Greenberg also is due to bring his big bat and can make a tremendous difference if he finds his old groove."[43]

O'Neill received the official news that the Office of Defense Transportation had notified the Pittsburgh club that the benefit game against the Tigers for July 10 at Forbes Field would be canceled due to the extra sixty-six miles Detroit would have to travel to play. Detroit and Pittsburg were the only teams canceled. The other benefit games would be played. There were still doubts about playing the World Series that year.[44]

The Tigers' next series was at home on June 27, against Washington. The Nats now stood at the .500 level and resided in fourth place, six games behind the Tigers. Washington took two of the three games with Newhouser getting credit for the only win.

Emil "Dutch" Leonard overcame Trout 9–1, despite Trout's circuit blow. Trout was always a crowd pleaser who swung from his heels and this time he connected, but of course that wasn't what he being was paid for. On the mound he failed to earn his salary. The Nationals walloped him with thirteen hits.[45]

The next day the lean, grave, sober form of Newhouser appeared on the Tiger hill. A serious man doing serious business, he outpitched Roger Wolff and won the second game of the contest 5–2. Scattering but six hits, Newhouser achieved his seventh straight pitching victory. Although Newhouser achieved a win, the Senators gave notice they were more than a decent squad. In the fifth, Harlond Clift hit one of the longest round-trippers ever in Briggs Stadium. It landed some 20 seats deep on the wrong side of the fence in deep center field. O'Neill demanded the umpires examine Clift's bat the next time he came up to hit. They did and they found nothing wrong with it. His homer tied the game at one-all. Then the Senators clipped off three more hits in a row for another score off Prince Hal. But Newhouser settled down. In this game Cullenbine fielded a base hit by George "Bingo" Binks, and when Binks took a wide turn at first, Cullenbine threw a rocket strike to York at first and Binks was a sure out. Binks would be involved in a few strange plays during the year. The last one would be very costly to the Senators. The Tigers struck back with Cramer, York, Richards and Webb getting key hits to support their ace. Detroit won the game, 5–2, despite the shaky fifth inning.[46]

The Senators bounced back to take the final match 8–3. Overmire's attempt at winning the series for Detroit fell short. The Senators treated him as harshly as they had treated Trout. The 5' 7" Pieretti had a big day.[47] He cuffed the Tigers with six hits and breezed through the game for the win.[48]

The Tigers licked their wounds, happy to see the Senators leave town, and welcomed Connie Mack and his basement-dwelling Athletics.

Mr. Mack opened the series with Newsom for the first game of the series.

The A's and Bobo fell, 4–1, before the Tigers. Newsom gave up but two runs in seven innings but his replacement, "Jittery" Joe Berry, didn't fare quite as well. He was ripped for four hits and two runs in the eighth. Mueller pitched a fine game for Detroit, giving up three hits and one run, although he needed help from Newhouser, who came out of the bullpen in relief once again to save the game. Mayo knocked in three of the Tiger runs with a pair of doubles.[49]

The Tigers posted an eighteen-and-twelve record for the month of June. Much of the credit goes to Newhouser, who raised his record to twelve-and-four and was *The Sporting News* player of the month.[50] With a slim game-and-a-half grip on first place, Newhouser in top form, and the return of Greenberg, Detroit fans looked optimistically towards the second half of the season.

The Tigers' nine old men turned a little grayer during this festive month of June as Dizzy Trout celebrated his 30th birthday on Friday, June 29.

8
July

"I remember him.... He was at Buffalo with us.... The pitchers would take batting practice and we made him hit left-handed.... He hit too many homers, and we would lose all the baseballs.... He had tremendous whip-like power.... He could hit a ball a mile. Boy, he was strong!
                                                                    Bill Pierce

It had been seventeen days since Greenberg had been mustered out of the Army. The last ten of those days he had practiced hard in an attempt to regain his former skills. Greenberg was not an ordinary player. He was a player that had been instrumental in winning three Tiger pennants and a World Series. Fans rooted for him because he put his duty to the country ahead of his own personal gain. They rooted for him because he had overcome racial and religious bias to achieve his goals. They rooted for him because he had challenged Ruth's home-run record, and tied Foxx's major league home-run record for right-handers in 1938 with 58 homers. His 183 runs batted in for one season in 1937 put him third in the books behind Gehrig and Wilson. He was awarded the American League's Most Valuable Player Award in 1935 and again in 1940. He was the first player to win the award for playing two different positions. For all that, fans rooted for him.

But Americans most of all rooted for him because of his work ethic. He was not a natural. He had worked hard at the game all of his life. Before games, he would be found working at his skills long before regular practice would begin. He was a genuine Tiger star from the prewar glory days of the past. Greenberg was independent, hard-working and successful, the son of a Romanian Jewish immigrant, and Americans throughout the country had no choice but to admire his values and work habits. He was a shinning example of what a person, an American, could do or become in a free democratic society.

On July 1 in Detroit, Greenberg jogged out to left field in the first of two games against Philadelphia. One might have excused him for some special posturing after four years in the service. But as he remarked in his book, *Hank*

Greenberg: The Story of My Life: "I came out in front of 55,000 people, the largest crowd of the year in Briggs Stadium. Everybody was cheering like mad. After four years in the service, the greeting was nice, but it didn't matter all that much to me. I was just glad to be back alive. I just went out there to do my job."

The Tigers' fans went home happy as Detroit beat the A's 9–5 and 5–3. A combination of Trout, Benton and Overmire got the pitching job done.

In the first game Greenberg went hitless his first two trips to the plate. York, however, clubbed a three-run homer to start a six-run attack.

In the eighth, Greenberg stepped to the plate for his last opportunity. Reliever Charlie Gassaway, a 26-year-old, left-handed wartime player, put a pitch right down the middle of home plate and Hank crushed it. It landed 375 feet away in the lower left field bleachers. The explosive roar of the crowd could be heard for miles down Michigan Avenue. Greenberg sat out the second game.[1] His homer seemed to answer any question about his return. Fans believed he was back. The Tiger bench was shaking his hand and slapping him on the back as if it had been Lefty Grove or Bob Feller instead of Gassaway who delivered the gopher pitch. Jimmy Outlaw immediately labeled Hank "Big Stick," and the friendly giant did indeed deliver the big stick to the Detroit lineup.

York punched in four runs in the first game and batted two more across in the second. Trout won his eighth game, but needed help for the last two innings. His reliever, Benton, making his first appearance since he broke his leg on May 24, was welcomed back by the crowd with cheers that matched Greenberg's ovation.[2] He had been out of action for 40 days. With the hitting greatly improved, the pitching staff beefed up, Newhouser in a solid winning routine, and "Hammering" Hank back again, pennant fever overwhelmed the city of Detroit.

For the first time in four years a box score of the first game the next day registered the names of Greenberg and York in the HR category. Before the war, 1937 through 1940, they were an explosive home-run duo at Detroit. What they had in common was a love for baseball; otherwise they were contrasting opposites.

York was a rural small-town product of the Deep South. Born in Ragsdale, Alabama, and a longtime resident of Cartersville, Georgia, he typified the southern "good old country boy." Greenberg was a northern urbanite from the largest city in America. Rudy was of Cherokee Indian, German and Irish descent. Hank's background was a historical European, Jewish, Romanian culture.

York was overwhelmed with the hustle and bustle of the city life and partook of things he never knew existed. "Man, I saw the sights, I'll never forget the first time I saw Yankee Stadium. I said to Gehringer, 'They don't play baseball here, do they? It's too big.' You can imagine what it was like the first time I saw a subway. I thought they'd run right out from under the ground."

Rudy York and Hank Greenberg (Brace Photo).

Greenberg, a tall, well-dressed gentleman in the latest fashion of the day, even had his own personal tailor. He could be found, and welcomed, in many of the upscale restaurants and social events in the city.

Greenberg knew the value of a dollar. When Detroit asked Hank to move to left field to give Rudy the opportunity to play first base in 1940, Hank demanded his salary of $40,000, plus a bonus of $10,000, for the move. He got his wish, and with business investments he did quite well financially.

York, however, lived for the moment and ended up with very little at the end of his career. Rudy partook of the fast life. When he first broke into the major leagues an irresponsible use of women, drink, tobacco and the dollar was an ever-present scene in his social life. He reflected later on his choices. "I made something like $250,000 in the majors, but when I was through, I had nothing to show for it except a brick bungalow in Cartersville, Georgia. I spent it as fast as I made it. One year [1941] with the Tigers I earned $40,000. Maybe it was because I wanted all the things I didn't have as a kid. We were so poor when I was a youngster I quit school at 13 to go to work."[3]

There was another problem. Gehringer said, "Quite often Rudy would fall asleep and drop his burning cigarette. I don't know how many mattresses he burned up.[4] We always said he led the league in burned mattresses."

York responded about the fires by saying, "You would have thought I led the majors in arson. By the time the stories made the rounds, I was supposed to have set fire to every hotel in the country." As far as his drinking was concerned he asserted, "I had a reputation for boozing, but it was all out of proportion. I had some drinks just like the other fellows, but it was nothing like some people said. I'm an Indian and all an Indian has to do is being seen drinking a beer and he's drunk. Any time an Indian puts on a baseball uniform he becomes something of a character."[5]

Trucks had this to say about York: "Oh, man, he was a strong man and a good guy. But he led the league in hotel fires. No one wanted to room with him, but it would have been better rooming with him than it would have been rooming above him, because all the smoke would go there. He would fall asleep with a cigar or a cigarette. He did that and that is where the rule came in by the government, that there is no smoking in bed at the hotel. That rule went into effect. They put signs up on the door where you couldn't smoke. Rudy had a lot to do with that."

Both men were slow afoot. Rudy led the league in errors three times in his career. New York writer Tom Meany wrote, "Rudy York, part-Indian and part-first baseman." That phrase, and the one word "Chief," followed York everywhere.

Mueller, however, thought York was a decent fielder despite the league-leading errors: "Rudy was a good hitter, a lot of power, and he wasn't the worst fielder in the world either. He didn't look like a nimble fellow. Like I said, he was a big, heavy-set guy. He had shoulders, big broad shoulders, but he had a good pair of hands. He didn't make that many errors."

York also thought he wasn't all that bad of a fielder. He defends his fielding ability to his son in a letter:[6]

A lot of these big-league sports writers would try to make you believe I wasn't much of a fielder. Well I can read you another line that said I was the best first baseman the Red Sox had during the Tom Yawkey regime, and there was a guy by the name of Jimmy Foxx there before me. The fielding averages show that your old man was a pretty good first baseman. I never was under .980 in the majors, and in 1947 I led the American League with .995.

Because of the pivot he's got to make it's difficult for a right handed first baseman to make the double play at second. Still, in 1943 I set a league record for assists by a first baseman, and the next year I set a major-league record for double plays by a first baseman.

Greenberg led the American League first basemen in fielding percentage in 1939, but when he was rotated to left field in 1940 to make room for Rudy at first, he led the league left fielders in errors. He was dependent on his center fielder to run down those long drives in left center that his lack of speed restricted him from reaching, but he did have a decent throwing arm.

Both were well liked by their teammates. Mayo, speaking of Rudy, said in Richard Bak's book *Cobb Would Have Caught It*, "Rudy was the smartest base runner I ever saw. You know how intricate the signs can be, the take-offs and everything. They change according to the inning or the situation. Rudy would get on second base and it was fabulous how he could steal their signs. You could count on it. He'd be on base and rub his shirt: I've got 'em. He'd tip off the signs and you could go to the bank with it."

Hank, on the other hand, would show his appreciation by sitting down and talking to people one-on-one, especially a rookie or a new player from another team. That attention meant a lot to players, that Greenberg would treat anyone like a regular guy. Greenberg would pick up the tab at restaurants and even have his tailor make a suit for someone had gone out of his way to help him. Mueller said this:

> Greenberg was a hard worker a very astute man about baseball. I remember well one year, I went to spring training with him ... I was warming up to go into a game and after I had pitched, Greenberg came up to me and said, "Les, I was watching you when you were warming up and did you know you hardly ever threw a strike?" That amazed me, you know. Here is Greenberg, a superstar, and he is watching me, just a rookie kid, warming up and he comes and tells me that. He was a very nice fellow.
>
> How nice he was, as short of a time I was with Detroit, twice when he was the general manager with Cleveland and then with the White Sox, when they got into the World Series I'd drop him a note saying I'd like World Series tickets and he sent me World Series tickets to those games both times."

Red Borom tells of York's sweet side: "Rudy would give you the shirt off of his back. When I went to spring training I went up there in a hurry and I didn't have but one pair of spikes and it was kind of muddy and snowing up there in Evansville. Rudy called everybody kid, and my locker was next to him. He saw me with those old spikes and said, 'Kid, what is the shoe size you wear?' I told him and he said, 'I wear the same,' and he threw them over and said, 'Kid, keep these.' He would give you anything he had."

Greenberg's return was just what the Tigers' offense needed. Detroit now had both of its great sluggers swinging back to back, and opposing pitchers not only had to be concerned with Cramer, Cullenbine and Mayo, but also had to face two of the most powerful hitters in the history of the American League. One way or the other the Tigers were going to score runs with Greenberg in the lineup.

As the season moved along O'Neill looked for ways to rest his older players.

Boston arrived in Detroit for four games and the teams split evenly. The lowly Sox shocked the Tigers in the opener. Wilson outpitched Newhouser and beat the Tigers, 4–0.[7] On Wednesday, July 4, Ferriss beat Detroit in the first contest of a double-header by edging Trout in a close 4–3 Sox victory. The Tigers salvaged a split in the next contest as Benton resumed his winning ways and beat Boston 5–2, with relief from Overmire.[8] Mayo and Greenberg struck home runs for the Tigers, who delivered a twelve-hit attack, three of them courtesy of Maier. Hausmann acquired the loss.

The Tigers won the last game Thursday when Greenberg smacked a two-out pinch-hit single in the ninth that drove in the winning run for a 9–8 victory.[9] Mueller, the starting pitcher, was bombarded, giving up seven hits and a pair of walks in four innings, but Eaton finished well for the win. Detroit needed to rest Richards and Swift, so bullpen receiver Jim "Hack" Miller caught the whole game.

Zeb Eaton (National Baseball Hall of Fame Library, Cooperstown, New York).

Mueller remembered the harsh Red Sox treatment:

I remember Shellenback, the pitching coach in Boston in 1945, came to Detroit, and one of the first things he told me was, "Les, they were calling your pitches in Boston. They knew what you were throwing." The game I pitched against the Red Sox in Detroit was one of the worst games I've ever pitched. I really got hammered. I don't remember what the score was, but I felt so sorry because we had a catcher on the club, Hack Miller, a third-string catcher and mainly a bullpen catcher. He started that game and I think it is the only game he got in all year. After the game, when we went into the clubhouse, Zeller, the general manager, came in. He just blasted Hack Miller. He more or less seemed to blame him because I had pitched poorly. To this day I don't know why he thought that. I guess he thought he didn't call the pitches good or he should have come out, and talked to me, and try to settle me down. Anyway, I never heard him talk like that to anybody, because Jack was a very nice person. I felt sorry for him when I found out later I had been tipping off my pitches.

The Yanks, on July 6, replaced the Red Sox. A crowd of 31,288 fans went home unhappy as New York, led by third baseman Grime's three hits and Stirnweiss's triple, gave Overmire a 5–4 defeat. In the eighth O'Neill rushed Trout in to put out the fire, which he did, but his arm was ailing and Dizzy was vocal about the pain.[10]

Newhouser, the next day, was ready and the Tigers evened the series with a tenth-inning 3–2 victory. Cramer's bat was too much for the Yanks. He had four hits in five attempts. He opened up with a double and ended with a triple. The triple, followed by York's hit in the bottom of the tenth, was the game-winner. Newhouser won his thirteenth and Bill Zuber absorbed the loss for New York.[11] Cramer was his usual brilliant self on defense, but during the game he injured his hand with a one-handed running grab of Hershel Martin's hard-hit fly ball.

Les Mueller (courtesy Les Mueller).

Detroit split a double-header with New York on the 8th. A total of 56,164 fans jammed Briggs Stadium to watch Trout get knocked out of the box with a seven-run beating before the fifth inning concluded. Trout had finally lost to the Yankees. He had dominated the Yanks since August 25, 1943, with eight straight victories. But this was the day the string ended. Detroit rallied, but fell short and lost 8–6.

Detroit won the next game as Benton pitched a gem. Greenberg and Cullenbine drove in the runs and Benton, hobbling around with a cast, beat New York, 3–2.[12]

The traditional All-Star Game had been canceled due to war restrictions but the leagues selected a dream team for each league anyway. The Tigers had five selections to lead the American League, while the Cardinals dominated the National League with eight candidates. Cramer, Cullenbine, Benton, Newhouser and Mayo represented the Tigers for a dream game that didn't get played.[13]

Greenberg, looking for his "baseball legs," had to retire from the second game with the Yankees in the fifth inning. Outlaw would caddy for Hank until his legs strengthened enough to endure double-headers.

Since his return, Greenberg had played in seven games, clubbed three homers and a double, and drove in six runs. His .286 batting average for the team was second only to Mayo's .287. A few months earlier critics had wondered if Hank would be worth his $55,000 salary. He had made up for that and more. Huge crowds began to hike into Briggs Stadium to watch the old Tiger perform.[14]

Detroit finished the Yankee stand, but a new face settled into second place. The Senators, riding a six-game win streak, replaced the Yanks. Detroit hit the road for a sixteen-game jaunt that started in Boston.

They boarded the train minus Trout. He had been shelved due to a back injury. He entered Ford Hospital for a complete physical. His record at this juncture was 8–10. The previous year's twenty-seven wins was but a memory. Trout had been complaining of back problems and other injuries for about two weeks, but he continued to take his regular turn and also relieved at O'Neill's request.

Beside Dizzy, the Tigers left hurlers Orrell and Jerry Burke, a new rookie, at home. Orrell had developed serious dental problems and needed teeth to be pulled, and Burke slipped and fell, seriously injuring his pitching arm.[15] Burke never pitched a major league game and lost his potential to be a major leaguer.

Too, Greenberg spent Monday and Tuesday in New York taking massages to ease his leg pains. Bothered by sore leg muscles since he'd started workouts,[16] Greenberg believed he overdid his workouts.

Cramer's bruised, swollen left thumb also forced him out of the lineup.[17] This was a big loss. Cramer was "old school," and would have played through the injury if possible. His equipment was "old school" as well.

McHale comments on Cramer and his gear:

Roger Cramer, our center fielder, was as good as a center fielder that ever played. The Hall of Fame Veterans Committee talks about "Doc" Cramer a lot. He is the best player nobody knows. He had almost 3,000 hits [2,705], he was a great outfielder, had a great arm, and he had the worst glove I ever saw a major league player use. It looked something like a motorman's glove that train engineers would wear. It was very flat (not much lining), but he had very powerful hands and arms; he didn't have to use a glove. He was the first guy I ever saw make the sliding catch, where you put your leg under, slide and catch the ball. I never saw that catch before I saw him make it.

Detroit's fortune, in Boston, took a bad turn. Wilson trimmed Detroit 2–1 by outdueling Newhouser, and Richards sprained his bad ankle trying to steal second base. He was carried off with torn tendons in his right ankle. The next day, using crutches to leave the hotel, he returned to Detroit. He stayed there until the road trip ended. Webb also broke down with a twisted ankle. Hoover would replace him. Detroit hoped to return, after this swing, without too much of a deficit to a more stable lineup.[18] The injury list, however, started to get serious. Zeller recalled Houtteman from Buffalo to help fill a pitching void in the bullpen.

The Sporting News' front page had a Willard Mullin cartoon that reflected Greenberg's return and it posed an important question. The larger of two Greenberg figures was stretched across a large gorge as a bridge between two signs, named May 1941 on one side, and July 1945 on the other. The bridged figure was titled "The Greenberg That Was." Crossing on the back of that figure was a smaller Greenberg figure who was balancing his way across the back of the bridged figure. This second figure was named "Greenberg Today." He was sweating as if the crossing was difficult. The gorge was titled "4 Years in the Army." Mullin's headline read, "Starts Bridging Big Gap With Bat." Hank's conditioning and endurance were being questioned.[19]

On July 13 Ferriss proceeded to contribute to the Tigers' bruises by pinning a 5–1 defeat on them. Overmire hit the showers in the third due to a four-run surge. Eaton relieved, and pitched shutout ball the rest of the way.[20]

Adding insult to injury, the lowly Red Sox made it three straight the next day. Mueller lost, 7–1, and Sox pitcher Emmett O'Neill held the Tigers to three hits. Detroit snuck out of Boston after being embarrassed and headed to New York.[21]

The Senators now moved within two games of the Tigers.

Unable to shake off the Boston blues, Detroit extended its losing streak to four games by dropping a 5–4 decision to the Yanks. The game was played at Yankee Stadium in rain and mud. *The Sporting News* reported that the mucky ground tried the patience of pitchers; the runners' feet sank into the soggy baselines up to the shoe tops; and outfield puddles checked the speed of hard-hit drives. Hank Borowy, the Yanks' pitcher, had a 2–0 lead, but struggled on the rainy, muddy field. Benton wasn't having much luck either, so O'Neill decided to pinch hit "Zeb" Eaton in the fourth inning. The Tigers had the bases jammed. Cramer, York and Swift packed the muddy sacks. Eaton stepped into the box and ran the count to two and two. Then he began to foul off a half dozen offerings of varying speeds. Finally Borowy ran out of patience and grooved a fast ball. With a quick swing of Zeb's bat the ball left the neighborhood. He didn't just hit the ball out of the playing field. The ball caromed off the facade of the top tier in left field, 450 feet away from home plate. It was an awesome explosion and it put Detroit on top, 4–2.[22]

Pierce described Eaton:

> I remember him. He could throw hard. He threw a ball as hard as anybody. He was at Buffalo with us. The pitchers would take batting practice and we made him hit left-handed, because he hit too many homers and we would lose all the baseballs. Then he would hit lefty and lose all of *those* baseballs. He had tremendous whip-

like power. I remember his strength of hitting the ball in batting practice. He could hit the ball a mile. Boy, he was strong! For a pitcher he had a good fast ball too. But he didn't get a chance to pitch a lot. I know we got tired of him in Buffalo, because they would only give you so many balls for batting practice and he would lose them all.

Bob Swift (AP Photo).

The Yankee president and part owner, Larry MacPhail, was in the stands that day. He felt his pulse quicken with the Eaton blast and became disillusioned with his star hurler. An impetuous baseball genius, McPhail did things on the spur of the moment. He was not happy with that home run. Borowy was on his way to a twenty-game winning season, but McPhail decided to get rid of him even though the Yanks won that game, 5–4. The trade would become a factor in the Cubs' quest for the National League pennant.

Overmire stopped the bleeding by winning 9–4 the next day. He was backed by a booming twelve-hit attack that featured doubles by Greenberg and Cramer, and Cullenbine's eighth homer. Swift, catching regularly now, added three hits as the Tigers mauled the Yanks. Zuber suffered the loss.[23]

Detroit then traveled to D.C. to open a four-game set with the Nationals. Detroit was still on top by three games. Trout had been cleared for duty and joined the squad on the road, and O'Neill was delighted to see him.

Newhouser and Benton's performances helped Detroit to sweep the twin bill and to increase their lead to five games. Newhouser struggled, but won 6–4 over Haefner. He gained his fourteenth win against six defeats. Benton then shut out the Nats and Pieretti, 5–0. York paced the team with four hits and batted in four runs.[24]

The Senators turned the tables on Detroit the next day and took a pair, 4–3 and 3–1. Overmire and Eaton absorbed the losses. Leonard and Wolff "knuckle-balled" the Nats back into contention.[25]

In the second game the Tigers pulled off one of the rarest of plays. The seventh found Case on second and Myatt on first, when Torres ripped a liner towards right field off reliever Wilson. Second baseman Mayo, playing a deep second base, made a leaping catch of the blow for the first out, then threw to Webb, doubling off Case at second for out number two. Webb's fast peg to York at first base forced Myatt and completed a triple play.[26]

Eaton was relieved in the fifth inning. Zeb was wild again. He had struck out four hitters, walked five, and had one wild pitch while giving up six hits. O'Neill decided to take him out of the game. Eaton at times could be a popinjay. He wanted to stay in the game, and he left under protest. Mueller remembered the incident:

> He [Eaton] had a pretty good fastball, but he was a cocky kid. I remember back in Washington.... O'Neill came to take him out of the game and he didn't like it. I think he kind of talked back to O'Neill and he didn't want to come out of the game. It just so happened that the next day I happened to get into a cab with O'Neill and he was talking to me. He said, "If that cocky S.O.B. tries to show me up again out there I will beat the hell out of him." He was upset. I was surprised and I didn't comment.
>
> Oh, [O'Neill] was a strong man and he was a big guy. He was a very, very likable fellow. He was a ballplayer's manager. I know when I went to Beaumont he invited me out and we went out and ate chicken together. You felt as good with him as you would with a player. Everybody liked O'Neill.... When Eaton was at Beaumont and some of those other places he let his temperament affect his pitching. Yeah, he would get mad, you know. That temperament got the best of him and he would lose control.... Yeah, he was very belligerent. I never heard of him getting into any fights or getting into any trouble with any of the players. It's a good thing he didn't because he was that way. They would just let him go and fuss at himself.

On July 21, in Philadelphia, Mueller made history. The Tigers and Athletics played to a 24-inning, 1–1 tie, and tied a thirty-nine-year old league record. They struggled for about five hours like two great wrestlers caught in each other's grip without one or the other gaining an advantage. Mueller pitched nineteen and two-thirds innings. Then, after walking two men with two outs in the twentieth inning, O'Neill relieved him.

Les gave up five walks, struck out six men, and allowed thirteen hits in his outing. It was an amazing display of pitching endurance. The A's' Christopher hurled thirteen innings and then gave way to Joe Berry. Umpire Summers called the game because of darkness. He said he couldn't see, and they couldn't turn on the lights because rules prohibited turning on lights to complete daytime games. The two squads played for four hours and forty-eight minutes.

The A's scored in the fourth when Dick Siebert was safe on York's error, then Estalella doubled and Buddy Rosar singled, scoring Siebert. In the seventh Cullenbine walked, York singled, and Cramer's fielder's choice scored Cullenbine to knot the score.

Outlaw saved the game in the tenth with a great throw to Swift at home plate that nipped the A's' runner, Peck. Detroit filled the bases once in the twenty-second inning and again in the twenty-fourth, but both times Maier failed to hit safely. The A's left eighteen men on base and Detroit fifteen. There were three seven-inning stretches during the game. The 4,325 fans stayed until the end.[27]

George Kell played third base that day for the A's and he commented on the game:

Russ Christopher was a tall, 6'3", string bean who pitched from down under. Not really side arm, but down under. He was really tough on right-handed hitters. I remembered we played Detroit a 24-inning game and Christopher pitched 13 innings of that game. He came in at the end of the 13th inning and said, "I've had it. That's as far as I can go." Mr. Mack said, "Wait, the game is not over!" He said, "That's as far as I can go—13 innings!" He swung off to the locker and Mr. Mack said, "Oh my, my, my!" That's about as strong as he could say it. Mueller pitched side arm, threw hard, and had good "stuff." He was a pretty good pitcher.

Swift had been catching one game after another since Richards reinjured his ankle. This was his eleventh straight ball game behind the plate. That included the two double-headers Detroit played in Washington the last two days. Now he was catching a marathon game. Kell said of Swift: "Swift was a good catcher, an outstanding catcher. He was almost a manager on the field, Bobby, was.... Yes, he was that type of guy, and he wasn't that bad of a hitter."

Outlaw spoke of Mueller: "Yeah, he didn't want to come out. When O'Neill came out to the mound he said he didn't want to leave, he wanted to pitch. Steve said, 'You have had enough.' So he took him out. It was a good thing. When we played the make-up game to play off that tie we played another 16 innings."

Borom said of that game: "Well, of course it was a day ball game and finally they called the game, but the game went twenty-four innings. At one point O'Neill came out there after nineteen and two-thirds innings and Mueller questioned him, saying, 'What's the matter, are they calling it on account of darkness?' O'Neill came out to change pitchers, which he did. When they called it we were tied one and one."

Mueller called that game "the long game:"

That game is a record for me in the sense that nobody has pitched that long in a major league game since. I think it is the longest tied game that has ever been played in the league. As far as modern day games there hasn't been anything like that. I remember I met Kell when the players came back for the last game at Tiger Stadium. We talked about the game and he said, "A lot of these guys gripe now when they go 0–4 or 0–5." I kind of kidded him and said, "Yeah, I tell a lot of people that a Hall of Fame guy went 0–10 against me," and he got a kick out of that. I had good stuff that day. There were a lot, a lot of balls, hit to the infield. There were a tremendous amount of assists that day.

Detroit was responsible for thirty-eight assists, seventy-two putouts and three errors in this long game. The errors were committed by Webb, Mayo and York. Mayo led the players in the field from both teams with twelve assists.

Mueller continued to comment about the highlight of his major league career:

It never occurred to me to come out of that game, I felt OK. And I don't think that long game bothered my arm. I was up in Detroit years ago and talking with New-houser and he said, "You know, before that ballgame Steve talked to me and said I don't know who I am going to pitch tomorrow, but whoever starts is going to have to go all the way." He said that because the night before we played and lost a dou-ble-header in Washington and used a lot of pitchers in that series. Our staff was beat up at that time. Newhouser told me I was still throwing as hard in the twentieth inning as I had in the whole game.

Swift caught me in the long game. I often think of that game and to me it was amazing that Swift caught the whole twenty-four innings. It was a pretty warm day in Philadelphia, and I think it would have been as hard as or harder on him than it was on me. To be back there catching, huh, that was a long, long day and Swift caught the whole ball game.

Connie Mack was quite a manager. He owned the club and managed it. He had his office above the ballpark and would leave the game and retire to his office until the game was close to ending and then come down again. They had an elevator that always got him and brought him down again. During the long game about the eighth or ninth inning the elevator man went up to get him and bring him down. I don't know if he stayed in the elevator or not, but because the game went until it got too dark to play I believe he made several trips up and down in that elevator.

Mueller was named Player of the Week by *The Sporting News*.

At Philadelphia 7-21-1945

Detroit	AB	R	H	PO	A	E
Webb-6	10	0	2	8	10	1
Mayo-4	9	0	0	6	12	1
Cullenbine-9	7	1	2	8	0	0
York-3	9	0	3	28	6	1
Cramer-8	10	0	1	2	0	0
Outlaw-7	8	0	1	2	1	0
a. Greenberg	0, Hit for Outlaw (22)	0	0	0	0	0
Hostetler-7	0	0	0	0	0	0
Maier-5	10	0	1	3	5	0
Swift-2	9	0	0	12	0	0
Mueller-1	7	0	1	2	3	0
Trout-1	2	0	0	1	1	0
TOTALS	81	1	11	72	38	3

Philadelphia	AB	R	H	PO	A	E
Hall-4	11	0	2	6	8	0
Peck-9	8	0	2	1	0	0
Siebert-3	9	1	1	31	2	0
Estalella-8	10	0	5	5	0	0
Rosar-2	9	0	2	13	2	0
McGhee-7	8	0	2	9	0	0
Kell-5	10	0	0	2	7	0
Busch-6	10	0	1	3	11	1
Christopher-1	5	0	0	1	2	0
Berry-1	3	0	0	1	2	0
b. Burns	0, Hit for Berry (22)	0	0	0	0	0
c. Metro	1, Hit for Burns (24)	0	1	0	0	0
TOTALS	84	1	16	72	34	1

a. PH-22nd
b. PH-24th
c. PH-24th

RBI: Rosar, Cramer. 2BH: Estalella, Cullenbine. SACRFICES: Siebert, Rosar. DOUBLE PLAYS: Det — 5–3, 5–4–3, 3–6–3, 6–4–3; Phil — 6–4–3. LEFT ON BASE: Det —15, Phil —18. WALKS: Muller — 5, Christopher — 2, Berry — 5. STRUCK OUT BY: Christopher — 8, Mueller — 6, Berry — 2, and Trout — 2. HITS OFF OF: Mueller —13 (19⅔), Trout — 3 (4⅓), Christopher — 5 (13), Berry — 6 (11). UMPIRES: Summers, Rue and Boyer. TIME OF GAME: 4:48. ATTENDANCE: 4,526.

After playing twenty-four innings the day before, the Tigers and A's went out the next day, July 22, and split a twin bill. Swift continued behind the plate for both games. Newhouser outpitched Steve Gerkin, 9–1, and picked up his fifteenth win of the year. Detroit blasted out thirteen hits. Newhouser helped his own cause by knocking in three runs with two hits. Mayo played, despite a sore back, and picked up three hits.

Game two was a pitching duel and it was a heartbreaker for Benton, who gave up but three hits and no earned runs, but still got tagged with a 2–1 defeat. York's hit scored Cullenbine, giving Detroit a 1–0 lead, but Maier's error cost the Tigers two runs and the ball game. The game was called at the end of the sixth due to rain.[28]

Doc Cramer added a few more gray hairs to the starting lineup when he had a birthday that turned him into a 40-year-old. After the game, when reporters congratulated him on his birthday, the cantankerous Cramer insisted that the baseball records were wrong: he was only 39 and his birthday should be listed as July 22, 1906, instead of 1905. But of course the record book still stated he was born in 1905, and along with Chuck Hostetler, Cramer became the second 40-year-old Tiger in the den.

In the last game of the Philadelphia series Overmire got the short end as Newsom beat his old mates, 1–0.[29]

On the 27th, the Tigers finally returned to Detroit with its friendly fans. One could hear the sounds of batting practice coming from Briggs Stadium. The chatter of the players, the crack of the bat colliding with the ball, the snap of leather as the ball jarred the gloves, the ballpark odors of hot dogs, mustard, and beer, the haze of tobacco smoke, and the din of the crowd all added up to a lazy July baseball day in Detroit. Above that noise was a player's voice singing as he took batting practice. Rudy York was swinging easy in the cage and moving those big shoulders ever so timely as he swatted lightning-fast grounders through the infield and drove long liners towards the outfield fences. They might boo him, but he loved being here in this cozy hitter's park with its dark green background. He was no Johnny Mercer or Bing Crosby, but what did he care? He and his Tigers were in first place, and Detroit was the best baseball park in the world.

Red Borom remembered Rudy: "The 1945 Tigers didn't have any musicians or singers on the club that I remember. Oh, we went down to Swift's one night in the basement of his home there in Detroit. I do remember there were about six of us and Hostetler played the guitar, but that was about all that I ever saw. I remember Rudy. He used to sing ['Mairzy Doats'] when he was taking batting practice.... I remember that. Rudy sang that song all the time."

York had good reason to enjoy this stadium. *The Sporting News* reported why Briggs Stadium was such a players' gem:

> Briggs Stadium in Detroit is considered a ball players' ballpark and that includes the clubhouse accommodations. The visitors' clubhouse is as nifty as the host clubhouse. The Tigers' room is more elaborate. There are two rubbing tables, and all kinds of apparatus, including what players call the "whirly-pool," in which hot water at any desired degree is swirled around bruised and aching muscles. Visitors' quarters have 28 lockers, cross ventilation, four showers, an automatic heater, two rest-rooms with a separate room for trainers, equipped with washstand, rubbing table and electric light sockets that permits use of various appliances carried by trainers. Separate tunnels to the dugouts prevent heckling of visiting players.

In 1945 Briggs Stadium was a state-of-the-art facility.

Detroit opened up a home stand by sweeping a three-game series from the White Sox and in doing so the Tigers maintained their three-game lead over upstart Washington.

Mayo and Newhouser were the heroes of the first game. Newhouser threw a shutout and won his sixteenth, 1–0, when Mayo hit a ninth-inning homer. Chicago had runners on base in every inning, but Swift threw out four of them on attempted steals. Detroit had but two hits until Mayo broke up the game with his round-tripper. Johnny Humphries, who gave up only three hits, took the loss.[30]

On July 27, the same day Newhouser and Mayo starred as heroes, the Yanks shocked the world of baseball when MacPhail carried through on his impulse and sent Borowy, who was 10–5, through waivers to the National League. New York said the deal was done to solve a roster problem. He was passed over by fifteen teams before the Cubs picked him up for $97,000. The deal was a mystery to everyone. Why would a team get rid of a potential twenty-game winner? The writers couldn't figure that one out, and no one could figure out MacPhail. The deal took the Yankees out of contention and sent Manager McCarthy into a depression. MacPhail became a hard pill for McCarthy to swallow.

Detroit broke out the hitting sticks for Trout the next day as the Tigers were on the prowl once more. The illustrious Dizzy won his ninth of the year, 8–3. Detroit backed Trout with seventeen hits and blew through three Chicago hurlers. Maier and Bobby Swift, who by now must have been playing on memory and instinct, collected three hits each. Grove took the loss for the Sox.[31]

The big news that day, July 28, had nothing to do with baseball, but it put a scare into the people of New York and the nation as a whole. That morning at 9:49 A.M. a ten-ton B-25 bomber smashed into the 79th floor on the north side of the Empire State Building. Lt. Colonel William Smith was piloting a U.S. Army bomber on a foggy day with very little visibility. He didn't see the building until the last moment and tried to climb and twist away. He didn't make it. The blast created a hole in the building eighteen feet wide and twenty feet high. When the high-octane fuel exploded, flames shot down the side of the building and through hallways and stairwells. An engine and landing gear flew across the floor, through walls and out a window, falling on top of a twelve-story building across the street. The other engine flew into an elevator shaft and landed on an elevator car where it plummeted downward in a slower, safer manner due to safety devices. The casualty list was fourteen dead, twenty-six injured, and the damage worth one million dollars.[32]

Ed Mierkowicz and Billy Pierce were playing at that time for the Buffalo club and were with the team in New York waiting to travel to a game in New Jersey. Mierkowicz said:

Yes, we were staying at the McKelpin, a hotel in midtown Manhattan a block from Grand Central Station. When you look out the window it looks like it was just next door, but the buildings are so high, they look a lot closer. I looked out that day and there was a lot of commotion. There was a big black mark on the building and the tail of the plane was sticking out. That was about the only thing I can remember, but there was a lot of commotion there. The streets were closed off.

People were saying why didn't it burn like 9–11? Well, when they filled the gas tanks up for the 9–11 planes they were filled up much more, and these wouldn't burn as much. The Empire State Building stayed up. The structure wasn't damaged much at all.

Pierce said:

I remember that vividly. I was with Buffalo at that time. I was there the day after it hit the building. In the street I saw pieces of the plane that fell down from the 79th floor. I never will forget the newspaper articles about the two sailors who ran up one-hundred flights or something like that, taking medication for the injured upstairs. They were talking about what this one person had said as the plane hit, and a ball of fire, which was the engine, came through and went right down the elevator shaft. I remember we happened to be there with the Buffalo team staying in a hotel a couple of blocks away. It was a terrible thing. People don't know. They say, "Nothing ever hit the Empire State Building or anything like that." Oh, yes it did!

The next day, July 29, Benton racked up his ninth win despite giving up thirteen hits. Chicago fell 4–2. The Tiger attack featured six hits that produced four runs. Mayo contributed several outstanding fielding gems during the contest, while Cramer and Cullenbine provided the firepower, with each knocking in two runs with a single in the first and a double in the sixth.[33]

On Tuesday, July 31, the Browns found a red-hot Detroit team ready to play. Detroit picked up their fourth straight win at St. Louis's expense. Richards had recovered enough from his ankle injury to catch Newhouser that day. Newhouser, who probably could have used a rest himself, twirled twelve long innings to give the Browns yet another one-run defeat, 5–4. He scattered nine hits, fanned seven, and won his seventeenth triumph. This started a Detroit six-game winning streak, which was their longest win streak of the year. Outlaw's hit with the bases loaded, and one out in the bottom half of the twelfth, brought in the winning tally. The extra-inning win was Detroit's fourth of the year, and the Prince had pitched in all four. Maier and Greenberg produced triples while Mayo accounted for two of the five runs batted in. Jakucki picked up the loss.[34]

At the end of July, Detroit had increased its lead to five games over the parvenu Senators, who continued to hold onto second place. Despite the lead, Detroit had barely played over .500 baseball for the month, posting a 14–12 record. The pitching staff was again feeling the strain, but the hitters were producing. The Tigers put up 107 runs on the "big board" to the opposition's 91. O'Neill had concerns about the wear and tear on his veterans. The make-up twin bills were coming up. The skipper had to look hard at the health of his front-line staff.

9

August

"The first time at bat, I had heard about his fast ball, I thought I had better take a pitch or two; he got two strikes on me in a hurry with that fast ball, but what they didn't tell me was that real snake he had, about like this, that dropped right off the table, and he struck me out on three pitches. He beat us that night 4–2."

Red Borom

Detroit's late three-game surge at the end of July kept them in first place. The 14–12 record gave them some space on the Yanks and the Senators, who were five games back.

The *Detroit News* sports editor, H.G. Salsinger, the dean of baseball sportswriters, interviewed Hal Newhouser. Unfortunately the subject of the New York Yankees became the topic of his conversation. Newhouser spoke harshly of the Yankee club. "I hope the Tigers finish first, but if they don't I hope the Yankees won't win the pennant. Nobody likes them because they are lucky. They play half their games in the softest park in the league, where a bloop fly to right field is likely to fall into the stands for a homer. They walk with a swagger as if they were special. Actually they've got only one real player, Snuffy Stirnweiss."

Mr. Salsinger, in his column, then pointed out to Detroit's ace that the Yankees built their own luck and it is so much parsley that luck has anything to do with their past success. No team wins eleven flags in eighteen years on luck.[1]

Newhouser was asserting the long-felt impression of a large legion who through the years had expressed a dislike for the Yanks, but he let his personal feelings be publicly known. It was not a good public relations moment for the club. After losing eight of twelve on their last swing, Detroit needed to take care of their own business and not bother with things like the luck of the past Yankee clubs.

O'Neill had two major concerns now: avoid injuries and rest the veterans. The Tigers started August at home by sweeping the Browns with a 9–8 win on August 1, and a 6–0 victory on the 2nd. Detroit now had a six-game winning streak. Although Trout was driven out of the box in the fifth of the 9–8 win, Mayo, York and Greenberg homered, and then Cullenbine's bases-loaded double gave Eaton credit for the win.[2]

The next day Mayo hit a pair of homers to support Benton and beat Kramer. It was Big Al's fifth shutout of the year. His ERA became a minuscule 0.89.[3]

Every winning club has more than just a few stars or a natural talent to become a champion. The ingredient needed is the strength to continue to play hard despite setbacks, injuries or management problems. Every club needs a spark plug, a self-starter, one that can provide leadership. Eddie Mayo became the clutch spark plug for these 1945 Tigers.[4] It doesn't matter if they are winning or losing, the competitive spirit to win that Mayo displayed is the stuff that wins games. His efficiency in the field, his clutch hitting and take-charge leadership, were the assets the Tigers needed.

Because of travel restrictions and rained-out games, a six-game series was not unusual. Chicago crushed the Tigers at Comiskey with five wins in such a series.

Their bats fell silent on August 3, as 40-year-old Earl Caldwell shut them out 5–0, subduing Overmire and Orrell.[5]

The following day, Chicago made it two in a row by defeating the club's anchor Newhouser, 3–2. A perfect ninth-inning squeeze bunt by Tresh did Detroit in. Grove received credit for the victory.[6]

On that same day, August 4, the Senators, who had a red-hot month of July and were breathing down Detroit's neck, were playing their fourth double-header in four days and looking at another twin bill on the morrow. The Nats' manager, Ossie Bluege, had the common problem of providing enough effective pitching for the demanding schedule. The Senators beat the Red Sox in their first game, 4–0, but in the nightcap their starter Sandy Ulrich came apart in the 4th inning, and was relieved by Joe Cleary, a rookie who only got one out and then failed to retire another hitter. If he didn't walk them, they hit him, and quickly the score ballooned to 14–2. Cleary, who never pitched in the majors again, owns one distinction. He sports the major league highest ERA record of .189.

Manager Bluege, after a huge argument with the rookie about his pitching ability, replaced Cleary with Bert Shepherd. Shepherd, a World War II amputee, had lost a leg when, as a pilot, he was shot down flying over Germany. He originally signed as coach and batting practice pitcher. Bluege activated him after an exhibition game with the Dodgers in which he pitched well. The one-legged twirler was a good pitcher — a great one considering he had but one leg. In desperation Bluege brought him in to finish a losing cause and rest his pitching staff. This became his only major league appearance and he turned in a stellar performance. He pitched five and one-third innings, giving up one run on three hits. It was the stuff movies are made of. But it was the only time he pitched in the major leagues.[7] The pennant race was just too close for Bluege to experiment with an amputee.

Meanwhile, Chicago hit Detroit hard on August 5, sweeping a pair, 12–8 and 3–2. Trout left in the top of the seventh of the first game as Detroit wasted 12 hits, including Greenberg's fifth homer. In the nightcap Mueller dropped a heartbreaker. He had Chicago shut out with one out in the ninth. A combination of three hits and an error scored three ninth-inning runs for the Sox. York's homer was of no avail.[8]

On August 6 the teams split. Detroit took game one, 6–2, behind Benton's eleventh win and the timely hitting of York, Outlaw, Maier and Swift.

Chicago's Humphries beat Eaton in the second game 7–0, and meanwhile the Senators took two from Boston and were but a fractional few points away from the Tigers.[9]

The split of the double-header was buried on the sports page and paled in comparison with the news of the dropping of the atomic bomb on Hiroshima. The world now would remember Harry S Truman, and he would be much more than just the man who replaced Roosevelt after FDR's death. He would be the man who ended the war and saved American lives. The bomb's destruction was enormous. Over 70,000 people lost their lives, and about 60,000 buildings were destroyed.[10]

The Tigers returned to Briggs Stadium to face the Red Sox in a double-header. They won the first, 5–2, with Overmire on the mound, but dropped the second, 7–4.

Detroit finally beat Dave Ferris in the first contest and they did it with an eleven-hit attack. Greenberg slammed out three hits and started a long 15-game hitting streak.

An injury marred the second game, which went twelve innings. Greenberg's screaming line drive knocked Red Sox pitcher Jim Wilson to the ground unconscious in the tenth inning. The hit struck him behind the left ear, and he suffered a fractured skull. *The Sporting News* reported, "Wilson is all finished for this year, although it is believed he will be able to pitch again. Greenberg's liner was hit so hard, it lifted the Red Sox pitcher off the ground, spun him around, and dropped him flat on his face."[11]

Mueller recalled the scene: "Well, you knew the fellow was very seriously hurt. Greenberg hit a vicious line drive. He fell just like a tree. He just went down. You worried for his life at that point."

Maier reported Greenberg's concern for Wilson: "One ball he hit, I never saw anything like it in my life. We were playing a twilight game and it was getting dark. He hit the ball so hard that you heard the crack of the bat and then you saw the pitcher fall. He'd hit the pitcher in the head. The guy was on the operating table for quite a few hours, and who was at the hospital the whole time? Hank Greenberg wouldn't leave the hospital until he knew that Wilson came out of the operating room alive. Nobody can say anything bad about Greenberg as far as I'm concerned."[12] Wilson never became the pitcher Boston hoped he would become after being hit by the Greenberg drive. After a long rehabilitation he ended up playing for several teams and flirted with a few .500 seasons. His career ended in 1958.

Newhouser was losing 3–1 in the ninth of the nightcap when O'Neill pinch-hit Eaton for him with two down and one on base.[13] "Mighty Zeb" tied the game with a two-run homer, but reliever Walt Wilson couldn't hold, allowing four runs in the 12th.

The Tigers were but half a game ahead of Washington. Zeller came to the rescue of the overworked pitching staff by completing two deals in August for veteran pitchers,

Joe Hoover (National Baseball Hall of Fame Library, Cooperstown, New York).

George Caster of the Browns and Jim Tobin of the Braves, who were both knuckle ball "flippers." They would benefit the staff and contribute to winning the pennant.[14]

The same day, August 9, that Truman announced the dropping of the second atomic bomb on Nagasaki, Detroit shelled Boston with fifteen hits and routed them 11–5.[15] Trout finally went the distance, but Mayo's arm and back injuries necessitated a rest period. O'Neill inserted Borom at second. He, Greenberg, and York each had three hits. Rudy hit two homers and knocked in four runs. The addition of Greenberg helped York and Cullenbine to see more hittable pitches and took some pressure off both sluggers. Detroit developed into a group of power hitters that could explode suddenly and score at will. Borom, in his utility role for Mayo, played efficiently and became a table setter.

On August 10, Detroit's bats were stilled. Benton lost a 9–0 game to young Randy Heflin. But they managed to stay ahead of the Nats, who lost to Chicago, 6–3.[16]

The next day, Detroit clipped the Red Sox, 5–4. They put up a four-spot in the second. Caster did a great job for four and one-third innings in relief of Mueller. It was Caster's first win since his trade from the Browns to Detroit. George Woods took the loss. O'Neill rested Webb and replaced him with Hoover. Joe had two hits, one a double, scored two runs and knocked one in. Borom chipped in with a hit, scored a run, and knocked in two.[17] O'Neill's replacements were contributing well.

Hosting New York on Sunday, August 12, before 53,189 screaming fans, Detroit started a successful series by sweeping a double-header from the Yankees. The other newly arrived reliever, Jim Tobin, Detroit's fourth pitcher, crushed a three-run homer in the eleventh, and gained credit for the 9–6 win. Newhouser in the nightcap picked up his eighteenth win, 8–2, with ease.[18] Greenberg continued to swing a big stick. His .290 average included five homers and eighteen RBIs. Cullenbine's hits, one a circuit shot, drove

Jim Tobin (National Baseball Hall of Fame Library, Cooperstown, New York).

in three runs and helped spark the 8–2 win for Newhouser. Tobin's performance so impressed *The Sporting News* that they named him their Player of the Week.

Greenberg commented about his physical condition after the games: "I thought I was in good shape when I came out of the Army. But I guess I was in good condition as a man, not as an athlete." His advice to the other returning players from the armed forces was: "Keep in shape: condition determines the success of any sports comeback."[19]

Hustling Jimmy Outlaw alternated in the outfield, giving Greenberg and Cramer necessary time off.

With the success of Castor and Tobin the Tigers' staff began to feel some relief, much to the annoyance of their competitors. Shirley Povich's article in the *Washington Post* opened a door against the way the waiver rule was being used. He believed the waiver rule should be probed because of the transactions that had raised some questions about the acquisition of Tobin by the Tigers and the Cubs' new pitching star Borowy from the Yankees. Castor, of course, came from the Browns, who are in the same league as Detroit, but Tobin from the Braves, and Borowy from the Yankees, were inter-league transactions that required permission from the rest of the clubs in the prospective players' leagues. Povich said, "When the waiver list cleared the desks someone had their eyes closed. Perhaps it is time for the new commissioner to do some deep digging into the wavier rule."

On Monday, 41,956 fans watched Detroit beat the Yanks twice. Borom drilled six hits off the Yank's pitching in ten trips to the plate. Five were in the first game, as Detroit overpowered them 15–4. Trout went nine again to win his eleventh. Detroit misused the Yankees' hurlers consistently, gathering twenty hits for the day. Maier hit a pair of doubles, Richards tripled, and York homered. *The Sporting News* said that Rudy York commented amount the lack of home runs that year. He said that two out of eight balls used in the American League were dead and handicapped power sluggers. *The Sporting News* also mentioned that the huge number of double-headers being played made sunglasses a priority for many players, due to the sun's being high in the sky in the early part of the game. Whoever could survive the double-header schedule might just win the flag.

In the nightcap Caster won his second game in relief of Benton, and Detroit completed another sweep. York's eleventh homer helped sink New York 11–9. The Yanks' ineptness on the field caused one New York writer to say, "Any resemblance to an orderly game was unintentional and purely co-incidental."[20]

On August 14, all of America rejoiced. Japan surrendered and President Truman declared it V-J Day. Celebrations took place throughout our nation's cities and towns.

Bill Pierce realized the impact of the times:

> I think wartime, when you lose friends, we all think about it. I had thought about it too, because I knew at my age I was due to be going into the service. Then the war ended and that stopped that. V-J Day, I remember the bombs' ending the war and it is just a happiness that was a real happiness. It's nice to win the World Series, but when the war ends that is a very big thing, because we lost so many men.
>
> Boys, some that I knew, in fact the day the war ended in Germany, a boy I knew in high school was shot by a sniper, probably within hours of the war ending there. We also lost a boy in our neighborhood on one of the naval ships. So as soon as the war ends it's a solemn but a very happy thing to see it come to an end. I thought that the atomic bomb was the thing that brought the war to an end. I think it probably saved more lives than it took. It was sad for the Japanese, because they lost a lot of innocent people. But I don't know how many people, Americans, Australians, etc., and Japanese would have lost their lives if we would have kept going island to island and into Japan. I think we would have lost a lot more lives. The two atomic bombs ended the war quickly with a devastating end, but it did end it. As a truly American I was glad we had the bomb and they didn't.

Del Baker Jr., whose father Del Baker, a former Detroit manager, was presently coaching in Boston for the Red Sox, said, "Oh yeah, oh yeah, you know, I think he thought it was a wonderful thing. If my father were sitting here right now he probably would say we should have dropped a few more. He was very strong about his beliefs concerning our country and that no other country should give us any sort of a problem. He was just a proud American. That was probably the sentiment of most Americans at that time in history."

For baseball the end of the war could change the 1945 pennant picture as veteran players returned from the service. Names like Joe and Dom DiMaggio, Trucks, Feller, Cecil Travis, and Ted Williams flashed into the minds of American League fans. The World Series was no longer in doubt; it would be played. The writers believed this year would be the last of mediocre play. The returnees could affect this year's race. Detroit was especially interested in the release of Trucks from the Navy. The rumors gave Tiger fans hope for boosting a tired pitching staff.

George Caster (National Baseball Hall of Fame Library, Cooperstown, New York).

Detroit's five-game win streak was halted by the Senators. They shut the Tigers and Tobin out, 8–0, in their series opener in Detroit on August 15.[21]

Leonard held the host team to four hits. Tobin had a nothing ball that had nothing on it but the stitches and the cover. The Nats pounded Detroit's pitchers for eleven hits. Four errors, two by Maier and two by Hoover, aided the Senators.

The Tigers' ace, Hal Newhouser, before 31,681 home fans, brought his intense competitiveness into the pennant race the next day, beating the Senators 9–2 for his nineteenth win. York, Cullenbine, Cramer, Maier, and Richards all hit well that day.[22] The Senators, however, took the next two games, and won the series 3–1.

Haefner outpitched Overmire 3–1 on Friday, in a duel of left-handers. An error by Maier set up the winning run.[23]

The Nats beat Benton on Saturday, with help from the Detroit infield. The sportswriters' concerns about mediocre play proved true as the Tigers fell, 11–5, despite an upper-deck blast by Roy Cullenbine, and three hits each from Cramer and Greenberg. On the field, however, Webb, Borom, York and Hoover all displayed interesting ways of mishandling a baseball.[24]

The Senators were now but a game and a half behind Detroit. The Nats left, and the A's arrived for an eight-game series. Detroit took advantage of the lowly A's for six victories out of the eight scheduled contests.

In the first of two games, 37,767 fans rejoiced as Greenberg and Cullenbine belted back-to-back homers. Both sluggers, along with York, were swinging big sticks during the stretch run. Mayo then celebrated his return to the lineup with three hits to help spark Trout, and the Tigers, to a 6–1 victory. It was Trout's twelfth victory.

The nightcap turned into an extra-inning game that Detroit lost 8–3. The A's scored five in the eleventh and Christopher survived for the win while Tobin had the loss.[25]

On August 20, Detroit ripped the "Mack-Men," 4–0 and 4–1, in a twin-bill sweep. The first contest featured Newhouser's whitewash. He became the first 20-game winner and was backed by circuit clouts from the bats of Cramer and Cullenbine.

Mueller coasted to a four-hit, 4–1 victory in the second game. Triples by Mayo and York and a double by Hoover scored runs. Charlie Bowles and Flores absorbed the two losses. Greenberg went hitless in both games and that ended a 15-game hitting streak.[26]

The next day, August 21, the papers advertised Philadelphia's obnoxious, flamboyant, rubber arm "Bobo" Newsom as being the starting pitcher for both contests. A throng of 21,303 fans turned out to watch "Old Bobo," a former Tiger hero, and the Tigers do battle. The A's split the twin bill.[27] Newsom left in the seventh inning of the first game leading 6–3, but reliever "Jittery" Joe Berry gave it up when York's homer tied the game. Berry, however, achieved his victory in the eleventh inning. Hits by Irv Hall and Mayo Smith, a .212 hitter in his only major league season, off reliever Houtteman gave Berry and the A's a win.

Newsom took an early lead in the nightcap, but Cullenbine's thirteenth round-tripper in the seventh cut Bobo's lead to 6–5. After a rain delay Detroit overcame Newsom when Greenberg doubled to the tie the score and York singled him home for the game-winner. Caster, in relief of Overmire, picked up the victory.

On Wednesday, August 22, Trout registered his fourth straight victory as the A's fell, 4–1. Greenberg bashed his seventh homer into the upper deck in left, and Lou Kneer, who was the pitcher with the most American League losses (16) for 1945, was awarded the loss.[28]

The next day the Tigers feasted again on Philadelphia, 4–3, as Tobin had enough on his "nothing ball" to keep the A's at bay and go the distance. Don Black was the loser. Webb's squeeze bunt-hit in the sixth provided the winning run.[29]

The Tigers ended the twenty-one-game home stand with 14 victories, but the Senators continued to breathe down their necks, climbing to just a half a game away from them. Detroit left home for a short road trip to Cleveland and St. Louis, looking over their shoulders as Washington continued their hunt for the Tiger.

Bob Feller was the next big baseball star to return to the majors from the service. On August 22, Chief Specialist Robert W. Feller, U.S. Navy, became "Rapid" Robert Feller, pitcher phenomenal, property of the Cleveland Indians. Here truly was the All-American Boy. As much as Greenberg was respected and admired in Detroit, so much and more was Feller loved in Cleveland. He last pitched major league competition in 1941, when he won 25 games for the Tribe. A three-time twenty-game winner and a four-time strikeout king, he possessed one of the greatest fast balls in the game. The 26-year-old Feller had opportunity to play baseball in the armed forces, but he also had an active combat record, serving 29 months of his four-year hitch as chief of an antiaircraft gun crew on the battleship *Alabama*, which was involved in heavy combat. With the war over and citizens looking for entertainment, Feller stepped front and center as baseball's new number one ticket.[30]

Cleveland wasted no time in using him. On August 24, 46,477 roaring fans jammed Cleveland Stadium to see Feller pitch against Newhouser. In his first start back in an Indian uniform Feller fanned twelve and beat Newhouser, 4–2.

Feller sizzled the ball by everyone except Richards, who was the only hitter who managed to avoid the unwanted K.[31]

Cleveland scored twice in the third on Heath's two-run homer. The voice of the Indian announcer, Jack Graney, called the shot with his usual enthusiastic voice: "It's going, going, gone, a case of Wheaties for Barbara Ann!" The General Mills Co. gave Wheaties to any Indian who homered for Cleveland. Barbara Ann was Heath's daughter.

In the third, Richards doubled, Outlaw walked, and Borom singled home Richards. Cramer followed up with a hit that drove in Outlaw. But after that, Feller shut the door, and the Indians went on to score runs in the third and fifth innings. Outlaw had the honor of ending the game the same way he began it, with Feller blazing a third strike past him.

Red Borom, playing second base, vividly remembered facing Feller for the first time:

> He came back from the service and the fans gave him a big night in Cleveland. The club gave him a jeep and all kinds of presents. His wife received a fur coat. The park was full, and by the way, Tris Speaker [the old Cleveland player/manager, and a Hall of Fame member] attended that game. Feller and Newhouser got caught up

"Rapid" Robert Feller and "Prince" Hal Newhouser (Corbis Photo).

in a duel. It was a night ball game and I was playing second base. The first time at bat, I had heard about his fast ball, I thought I had better take a pitch or two; he got two strikes on me in a hurry with that fast ball, but what they didn't tell me was that real snake [curve ball] he had, about like this, that dropped right off the table, and he struck me out on three pitches. He beat us that night, 4–2.

That was the start of a great rivalry between Newhouser and Feller that continued throughout the forties and into the early fifties. David Jordan, the

Some of the World War II veterans that contributed to Detroit's 1945 championship season. *Left to right:* Al Benton, Red Borom, Les Mueller, Hank Greenberg, Tom Bridges, Walt Wilson. Absent from picture: Virgil "Fire" Trucks, who returned just before the end of the season (courtesy E.J. Borom).

author of Newhouser's biography, reported that Feller said, "Newhouser was far from being at top form, and I felt a strong sense of personal rivalry as I faced him that night." The great pitching match-ups featuring the two drew large crowds for years to come.

The next day Fort Meade officials boosted Detroit's pennant hopes by discharging Tommy Bridges, a former Tiger pitching star of the thirties and early forties. Bridges, known for his great curve ball, would join the Tigers immediately, so Detroit had another veteran to help them pursue the American League pennant.

Red Borom shared memories of Bridges:

Tommy came back out of service, and we were lucky to get him back. That was the first time I met him. I had number 10 when I started the season, but that was his number and I had to give it back. I wore 30 the rest of the year.

He was known for his curve ball but every once in awhile he would load one up [spit ball]. One day he was warming up to pitch batting practice in front of the dugout. Richards was catching and standing close to me. He threw his mitt to me and said, "Here, you catch him." He threw a couple of fast balls and then he motioned for a curve. He didn't throw a curve ball with a regular motion; he threw it like this. The ball just dropped out of it. It was just like a straight drop. The first pitch hit me on the belt buckle and he motioned again. That one hit me on my knee. I threw Richards the mitt back and Paul said, "You had enough?" I said, "You catch him."

Bridges, like I said, would load one up now and then, and in one game he pitched in relief and struck this guy out. It was the third out, and as he passed the umpire on the way to the dugout the ump said, "What in hell kind of pitch was that?" Bridges replied, "I don't know, but wasn't it a beaut?" We were fortunate to get Bridges, Trucks and Greenberg back when we did.

What fans didn't understand, however, was that Bridges was "ballplayer-old" when he went into the service. The 38-year-old Bridges' great pitching days were behind him, and he would give Detroit relief, but he couldn't be counted on to be a starter anymore.[32]

As the season wore on, Washington had one series left with Cleveland, while the Tigers faced the Indians three times. With the race so close, Feller would face Detroit three times, and Washington but once. The games he pitched might make a difference that would favor the Senators. The Nats would close out a week ahead of other contenders. They would have to idly wait and hope for help from the other clubs.

On Sunday, August 26, the Indians staggered Detroit with a sweep of a double-header in Cleveland. Reynolds and Gromek pitched the Indians to 3–1 and 5–4 wins over Trout and Benton. Reynolds posted his fourteenth win in the first game.

In the second contest the Tigers scored in the first on Outlaw's RBI and nursed it into the fourth inning before Cleveland took the lead 2–1. The Indians added one more in the fifth and another in the sixth to retire Benton. Tobin, in relief, got out of trouble and going into the ninth Detroit was down 4–1 when York, still swinging the big stick, tied the game with his fourteenth round-tripper, a three-run bludgeon that stunned Gromek. In the ninth Gromek singled, moved to second on a sacrifice, and scored on infielder Mickey Rocco's hit. Gromek won his sixteenth and opened the door for the Nats. But the Yanks swept the Nats 3–2 and 7–1 in New York, keeping Detroit up by a game and a half.[33]

After losing three to the Indians, Detroit staggered into St. Louis for a two-game series with the dangerous Browns. The Detroiters managed to split the series. Newhouser won his 21st, 10–1, on August 28, and stopped the Tiger bleeding by riding the heavy artillery bats of his sluggers. Detroit unloaded on Kramer in the first inning with Cullenbine's three-run clout in the first, Greenberg's two-run four-bagger in the eighth, and Maier's two-run whack in the third. Newhouser mowed the Browns down, with Maier's three hits leading all Tigers hitters.[34]

A super relief pitching job by Bob Muncrief and a clutch hit by Gene Moore in the eighth inning sent the Browns past the Tigers, 5–4, in Wednesday's game.[35] Mueller started the game, but was forced to retire in the third after giving up four walks.

Mueller felt bad about his performance. "I remember that very well because that was Les Mueller Day at the ballpark. They honored me before the ball game. I think they gave me a war bond of some kind and a big basket of flowers. I guess that was for my wife, but it should have been for me on that particular day. But as often happens when a player is given a day ... I had pitched a good game against the Browns earlier, but that game was no good. I felt bad about it."

The Tigers limped back to Detroit after losing four out of the five road games. Cleveland was waiting for them and continued the abuse by slamming Trout for eleven hits, beating him 7–2. Center fielder Felix Mackiewicz slugged a three-run four-bagger and Reynolds picked up his fifteenth victory.[36]

Detroit finished August with a disappointing 18–17 record, but amazingly, the Yankees dumped the Senators six times in three double-headers, keeping the Tigers a game and a half in front of the Nats. The Browns were just four games off the pace, and the Yankees five and a half. Detroit, with a shaky pitching staff, faced a thirty-three-game September schedule. Twenty-five of the games were on the road. The race, rushing to its September end, found Detroit's pitchers grossly overworked, but with a strong hitting attack and some help from Zeller's trades, they continued to maintain high pennant hopes.

10

September

"Jimmy went to a novelty store and got a combination ashtray with about an 8 ft. rubber hose on it where you could prop the cigarette at an angle on the ash tray and smoke out of the hose if he was lying in bed. He also put a note with the gift and told him, 'Try this, as we are trying to win a pennant here and need no more distractions.'"

Red Borom

The St. Louis Browns had a situation blow up in their face that very likely destroyed any opportunity they had for repeating as champions of the American League.

The inability of the team's management to control ace pitcher Sig Jakucki reached the point of no return when manager Sewell suspended him indefinitely for being out of shape, for insubordination, and for the general good of the team. *The Sporting News* reported Sewell said, "I actually believe the club will be stronger without him."

Jakucki had a twelve-and-ten win-loss record, and was second in wins only to Nelson Potter's thirteen, but his drunkenness, his abuse of Pete Gray, and his pugilistic nature on and off the field caused Sewell and the Browns to part ways with him. Jakucki's animosity towards anyone, but particularly towards Pete Gray, led to dissension of the highest kind. The hostility started early enough in the season. Gray couldn't tie his shoes and needed help. One day he made the mistake of asking Jakucki to help him. Jakucki's reply was quick and curt: "Tie your own G.D. shoes, you one-armed S.O.B." It was all downhill from that time on.

When he reported intoxicated to board the train to Chicago with the team on August 31, the skipper told him to leave and go home. Jakucki refused, threatened Sewell, and then boarded later anyway. When the manager learned he was aboard he asked the road secretary, Charley DeWitt, to stop the train at the Delmar Station in West St. Louis and had the police remove him. In spite of the removal he somehow showed up at the Del Prado Hotel in Chicago later that evening, but was denied a room. Sewell said, "I suspended Jakucki; that suspension still stands, and I'll go further and say he'll never pitch again for the Browns."[1] After all that, any chance the Browns had for the flag ended, and Detroit had one more leg up the ladder towards the pennant.

Meanwhile, in Detroit, while the Browns were descending the ladder, Newhouser and Feller faced each other for the second time on September 1, but neither was around at the finish. Borom, who was playing second for the injured Mayo, had quite a day as the Tigers squeaked out a 5–4 win. Red recalls the game. "Feller and Newhouser tie up again in Detroit. So this time I am going up there swinging. I hit the first pitch a couple of times up and got base hits. I got four base hits in a row off of him [Feller]. The last time at bat of the first game I had a hit off of him, so I actually had five straight hits off of him. In that game I was the leadoff man in the ninth. I believe Ed Klieman, a right-handed pitcher, was pitching by then. I caught the second baseman playing back, so I drugged [bunted] him. I went five for five in that ball game and scored the winning run. That was the only times I faced Feller."

In the seventh inning of that game with one out and the Indians up 4–2, Newhouser reached back for a little extra on a pitch and immediately knew he had injured himself. When he left the field he had trouble raising his arm. From then on Newhouser would struggle with serious pain in his arm and back. Caster relieved him and squirmed out of the inning without damage. In the bottom of the seventh Feller ran out of gas, and the Tigers put together three straight hits to shave the Tribe's edge to 4–3, sending Feller to the showers. Klieman did relieve for Cleveland, and when Cullenbine's single filled the bases again, York came up with a walk that forced in the tying run.

Borom's perfect bunt led off the Tigers' ninth. A walk to Cramer and Greenberg's single loaded the sacks. Then York's smash to center scored Red with the game-winning run.[2] Tobin picked up the victory in relief. It was only the second victory in the last seven games for the Tigers, but the Tribe punished Detroit the next day as Bagby beat Mueller, 3–2.[3] A great catch by center fielder Mackiewicz off Cullenbine's liner saved Bagby's victory. The rumor mill churned out a report that Newhouser's back and shoulder injury might prevent him from making the next road trip because he was planning to check into Henry Ford Hospital on the morrow.

Detroit entertained Chicago on September 3 and the old veteran Tommy Bridges was called upon to make his first start since his discharge from the service. A holiday turnout of 53,953 fans jammed Briggs Stadium for the Labor Day double-header with the White Sox. The Tigers did not disappoint and took a pair from the Sox with two 6–5 scores. Bridges lasted into the seventh and received credit for the win. He needed relief help, however, from George Caster. York's homer and Mayo's clutch hit helped bring home the victory.

Bob Maier commented, "Do you know what it is like to get booed by 50,000 people? Well, I found out. It happened in Detroit. It was late in the season, and we had Bridges pitching for us. Tommy was a saint in Detroit and if you made an error when he was pitching, boy, they let you know it. It was the sixth or seventh inning, and I made a boot. And then it came: 'BOOOO!' Lucky for me we won the game, by one run!"[4]

In the nightcap Chicago chased Benton from the box in the first inning after he gave up four runs, but Tobin's superb relief pitching choked off the White Sox hitting attack. The Tigers tied the game in the second, and then in the eighth Tobin's second American League homer drove in two runs to clinch the win.

The large crowd boosted Tiger attendance to a record 1,160,677 for seventy-two games. The city of Detroit had a strong case of pennant fever.[5]

Now Detroit faced a 23-game road trip which included seven doubleheaders. This eastern trip might well determine the American League pennant.

Injuries and age were taking their toll. Benton, unable to finish games, had not been the same pitcher since he returned from his broken leg. Greenberg hit well despite a bad ankle, but needed more rest from the field, so Outlaw, Mierkowicz and Hostetler caddied for him as needed, but the Tigers desperately missed his bat when he wasn't playing. Borom and Hostetler were pinch-running for him whenever the opportunity arose. As for pitching, Overmire and Mueller were struggling on the mound, and Trout had returned from his previous injury strong enough, but he was always overloaded by O'Neill with starting assignments and relief work. Newhouser's back was questionable, and Cramer had strained his back, and his bruised thumb still hadn't healed. The biggest loss, however, had been Mayo. His clutch hitting, steady fielding, and optimistic attitude those past months were the soul of

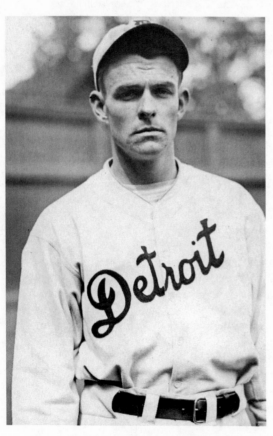

Tommy Bridges (National Baseball Hall of Fame Library, Cooperstown, New York).

the club. Those that filled in for him did a fine job, but the leadership Mayo provided was a missing ingredient that only he could provide. His arm and back injuries restricted his playing time. Webb's bad ankle had limited his fielding range and his playing time had been shortened. Richards was playing consistently, in spite of his bad ankle.

These were baseball's old men facing the demands of a long, strenuous and stressful baseball season. The acquisition of Caster and Tobin had helped at the right time, but both were well over 30, an age considered old in mid–20th century baseball, and either one or both could physically break down in the middle of this pennant race at any time.

Hoover and Borom were playing well in substitute roles, but Detroit missed its take-charge guys. The heavy load of playing daily fell upon York and Cullenbine, both of whom hadn't missed any playing time.

O'Neill recalled McHale, Mierkowicz, Pierce and Houtteman from Buffalo, to give some relief to players, and to give them some experience. Yet O'Neill wasn't about to give these inexperienced rookies too much time in the lineup with a flag at stake. He used them late in the game when the game was out of sight or to rest one of the veterans. Because he anticipated a close race at the end of the season, he used players carefully so the veterans could be healthy enough to bring the flag home. Every game was important. As Outlaw continued to say, "Today is the day!" The measure of a champion is the determination one has going down the stretch, and the killer road trip now challenged the will of Detroit.

The Tigers boarded the train for New York City where the Yankees, only four and half games behind Detroit, winners of eleven of their last fourteen games, awaited them. Newhouser did not make the trip, but Trout now, hopefully, could be counted on. Both aces had been burdened with heavy use. Steve O'Neill was feeling fortunate that Trout was with them even though Newhouser wasn't. Trout was a fellow who could bring a smile to a person's face and was a fun guy. He was also a giving individual. Joe Falls, the old Detroit writer, covered the Tigers a few years later and said this of Dizzy: "Just before the Detroiter's final dispatch whistle from the Michigan Central Station, Dizzy Trout would board the train at the last minute. He would have several bags of corned beef sandwiches from Boesky's Deli on Dexter, corralled in his arms. Trout's generosity was over-flowing as he would hand out the travel snacks."[6] It wasn't reported that he was handing out sandwiches to reporters and players on this trip, but his disposition and smile could give a big positive lift to the ball club.

The suspicion in NYC was that the Tigers were faltering under the stress of the pennant race. The stretch journey had begun. Detroit, like a boxer after receiving multiple blows, was staggering from six of eight losses to the Indians and Browns before they recouped enough to slip by Chicago with two close one-run wins. Arthur Daley's *Sports of the Times* column in the *New York Times* made an accurate observation by saying, "Oddly enough though, every time

Detroit appears to be hanging groggily on the ropes, awaiting the coup de grace, they've managed to let go with a haymaker from the floor and knock down the nearest tormentor." With the other contenders, St. Louis and Washington colliding with each other at the same time the Tigers and Yanks were, this race could get mixed up in a hurry.

At Yankee Stadium, Steve O'Neill handed the baseball to Dizzy Trout and told him to "go and get them!" That he did. Detroit writer Joe Falls, years later, explained the famous Trout routine he was known for, and what the Yanks must have experienced on that day: "He went into his big rocking, back and forth motion, and heaved that high, hard, fast one towards the plate, challenging the hitter to do something with it. When the strike was called and he had snapped back the return throw from the catcher with his glove he would turn his back to the plate, step off the mound, gaze out to center-field, and then that workman's red bandana came out of the back pocket. He would clean his glasses; and wipe the back of his neck. Then he would pivot back towards the rubber, and return for the next challenge." That was pure vintage Dizzy Trout. "Old Diz" challenged the Bombers on this day and he mowed the Yankees down, shutting them out 10–0. The veterans became flag-inspired warriors, drawing first blood with a first-class pitching job and a fourteen-hit attack to back it up in the series opener.

The old Tiger, Doc Cramer, cranked out his fifth home run of the season and Greenberg still, swinging the big stick, chipped in with his ninth. Eddie Mayo punched out three hits and took charge of the infield. Jimmy Outlaw had three hits and Cullenbine picked up two.[7] Detroit looked nothing like a faltering bunch of old men trying to keep their balance, as the writers would make them out to be. The ferocity of the attack gave notice that the Tiger, although lame, still had a big bite and was a very dangerous creature.

New York manager Joe McCarthy had trouble swallowing this painful beating, one of the worst the Yanks had absorbed that season. Running out of pitchers, he tapped his longtime batting practice pitcher for relief. Paul Schreiber hadn't pitched major league baseball since 1923. Ironically, Schreiber held Detroit hitless for three and one third innings.[8] McCarthy, however, had to watch in dismay as the Yankees slipped five and half games back into fourth place behind the Browns. Late in the game, with the lead seemingly safely tucked away, O'Neill sent rookie Eddie Mierkowicz into the game to give Greenberg a rest. Hank's legs were giving him painful problems. The gossip over baseball's back fence had Greenberg getting married after the season and then looking for a job beyond playing ball. He said, "Baseball, before I joined the Army, used to be fun, and now it's work. How those legs ache. I have to force myself all the time."[9]

In Washington the writers were still looking for the miracle that would hold that Tiger. "All of a sudden," one scribe wrote, "...it's a four-team scramble for the American League pennant instead of the well-defined two-club race between Detroit and Washington."[10]

Hank Greenberg (National Baseball Hall of Fame Library, Cooperstown, New York).

The Tigers, Senators and Browns were now tightly packed into a close race. Detroit's earlier losing streak had been offset by the Yankees' wins over the Senators, and the Nats' losses had allowed the Tigers time to recover.

Skeptics, however, continued to believe that there wasn't a solid club in the division, and the Tigers, with only a two-and-a-half-game lead over the Senators, could still blow the race. Critics said Newhouser, Greenberg, and Mayo were all injured and these were three indispensable men for the Bengals. Almost everyone believed that Newhouser, the pitching key for the Tigers, had to be healthy for Detroit to win the flag.

The Browns were only four games out and had a younger and healthier infield. The emergence of Muncrief as a solid front line pitcher for the missing Jakucki might just be the answer to their pitching problems. They were still the former champions who must be reckoned with. Luke Sewell, the St. Louis manager, summed up the flag scramble by saying, "There isn't a club of the eight which can't be beaten four straight by any other club regardless of their respective standings at the time."[11]

The Yankees, in spite of the beating they had taken the day before, had been playing their best baseball up to that point of the year. Charlie "King-Kong" Keller's return from the service, combined with the steady play of George "Snuffy" Stirnweiss, gave the Yankee lineup a good possibility to increase their run production. Red Ruffing's recent reappearance from the Army was expected to improve their pitching prospects. They had an opportunity to amend the pennant picture, because they still had six games at home with Detroit. If those two squads split or if the Yanks took four of the games, the Nats, Browns, and the Yanks would all have a good chance of displacing the first-place Tigers.

The playing ability of the players that year might not have been up to critical par, but the race was exciting enough and most of the stadiums had been drawing large crowds.

On Wednesday, September 5, 51,511 New Yorkers streamed into the house that Ruth built and witnessed a split between two pennant contenders. Cullenbine poked his fifteenth homer into the lower right field stands in the first inning and three Tiger paws slid across the plate. But the Yanks came back with two in the bottom of the first and one in the third to tie the score. The score went back and forth until the ninth inning. New York had a 7–5 lead when the roof caved in on them. With two mates aboard, Mayo launched a round-tripper into the right field stands, and then Greenberg left the neighborhood with a 425-foot drive. Cullenbine and York added a double and a triple. Final score: Tigers 10, Yanks 7, with Caster the winner in relief of Overmire.[12]

In the second game, Benton again was battered and left the game in less than three innings after giving up six hits and a walk. Stirnweiss's homer and Nick Etten's triple were the key blows for the Yankees' 5–1 victory. Joe Page shut down the big Tiger hitting machine on three hits and three walks.[13]

On Thursday, September 6, the squads continued to battle each other in yet another twin bill. The Yanks took the first game with a vengeance, evening the series at two each and swatting the old Tigers 14–5. Jim Tobin's "flutter ball" wasn't fluttering, and the Yanks drove him out of the box in the third inning. He gave up six hits and three walks during his short stint. Four home runs highlighted the New York attack. Catcher Aaron Robinson, a recent returnee from the service, jacked out two of them, while Keller and Metheny accounted for the others. Wilson and Caster mopped up the mess for the Tigers. Rookie Pierce pitched to two batters, and McHale pinch-hit for Tobin as O'Neill continued to use his rookies in spots. Cullenbine's homer in this game was the only bright hitting spot for the Tigers.[14]

The nightcap became crucial since the Yanks had squared the series and Detroit's pitchers were struggling. Tiger hurlers in that first game gave up 15 walks and 13 hits. It was a shocking misrepresentation of a major league staff. The winner of this game would take the edge in the series.

Mueller started the second game and remembered its importance:

Oh, yeah ... the second game of a double-header in New York. Well, I tell you, that was a big ball game for Detroit. I don't recall who started that first game, but it was one of the fellows who started quite often, you know. We got beat very bad, it was a big score, and the Yankees hammered us. I was scheduled to pitch the second game of the double-header. That was the one time I was shocked. I think they were getting concerned, because there was a game or two differences in the standings at that point.

Tommy Bridges came up to me and says, "Les, you can beat these guys!" I thought that was unusual that Tommy would come up and say that. It made me feel good. I pitched a 3-hitter against them. I pitched real well. I remember Richards caught that game. There was, in that game, a very tough situation with the game being in the balance. Crosetti was batting and I got a 3–2 count on him. Richards kept calling the curve ball, the curve ball, and the curve ball, on the 3–2 count. Boy, I thought, this is tough, but I got them over and finally got him out with the curve ball.

We won that game, and Sunday when we went to Boston I was walking into the park with Dizzy Trout, and Joe Cronin, the Red Sox manager, who didn't know me from Adam, spoke to Trout and said, "Hi, Diz, that was a big game that kid won for you the other day in New York." I felt good that Cronin felt that way about it.

Detroit won the game behind the solid pitching of Mueller, 5–1. Cullenbine stroked his second homer of the day and seventeenth of the year with one on in the seventh, wiping out the two-run edge that Etten's home run had given the Yanks in the second. In the eighth, Detroit loaded the bases with a pair of hits and a walk. Greenberg's hard-hit grounder to Grimes at third resulted in an error that allowed Detroit to pour three runs across the plate and close on the frustrated New Yorkers. Just as everyone thought the Tigers had run out of pitching, Mueller became a stopper. Hoover subbed for Webb in the second game and had a pair of hits for the hungry Tiger. This was becoming a real team effort with the bullpen and the bench contributing needed help in this pennant race.[15]

Detroit still had two important contests with New York. The Senators won a double-header from the Browns and picked up a half game, putting them only a game and a half back. O'Neill felt he had to go with Trout for the last game in the series, but he needed a starter for the game of the 7th. That starter should have been Newhouser.

A few days earlier, Zeller had phoned Newhouser and asked him to come to New York. Hal quietly flew in and checked into the New Yorker on the 6th. He was still ailing and his effectiveness was in doubt. This assignment was to be a test of his arm. O'Neill told him that relief as early as the first inning would be ready, if needed. Before the game he took a shot of Novocain from the Tiger trainer, an osteopath, Dr. Forsyth, to dull his pain. The novocaine procedure was kept as quiet as it could be in that time. When it was later revealed that Forsyth had injected Newhouser it became a scandal in some circles. He pitched and remembered the contest as a strange encounter:

> It was the most peculiar game I ever pitched. In the first inning I needed a strike on Keller, so I peeled off a curve. It was a good one, but a terrific pain shot up my back and I knew I couldn't throw any more like it. I called in my catcher, Richards, and told him what had happened. "Might as well forget about a curve," I said, "I just can't throw one." From then on it was first a fast ball and then a change-up. The Yanks kept looking for that hook again, but by the time they finally figured that I couldn't throw it any more it was too late. I beat them 5–0 on a four-hitter. Believe me, you don't beat the Yankees very often on just one curve ball![16]

James "Skeeter" Webb (National Baseball Hall of Fame Library, Cooperstown, New York).

Two double plays helped pull Newhouser out of early-inning jams. Mayo, back in action, had four hits and York crushed a homer to ignite the offense. The Prince didn't issue a pass and pitched to only twenty-nine men in notching his twenty-second victory of the year. It was his sixth shutout and his twenty-sixth complete game. O'Neill said of Hal's performance, "I thought he was just as good as ever. If he's got a pulled muscle, I hope every pitcher on the club gets a pulled muscle quick."[17]

Trout faced Joe Page, who had handled the Tigers easily in the earlier series encounter. By the third inning Detroit had sent

Page to the showers by hanging a four-spot on the scoreboard. Trout picked up his fifteenth victory, 11–4, though he wasn't around at the finish. The Yanks shelled him in the seventh and Overmire was rushed in for needed relief. A drive by Metheny, which had been put on course for the stands, was speared by Cullenbine, and that helped Overmire to work his way out of the seventh. Stubby finished the game giving up but two singles in his relief role. Greenberg and Hoover both had three hits each, and led a sixteen-hit attack against the weak Yankee staff. Hoover added a pair of doubles and then Greenberg, in the eighth, launched his eleventh homer of the year. It landed deep in the right-field pavilion. The Tigers' win crumbled the Yanks' hopes. The weary Tiger pitchers were grateful for the rise in the team's offense. Extra-base hits from their bats played a major part in disassembling the Yankee hopes.[18]

At Boston on September 9, Detroit defeated the Red Sox 6–3 in the first game of a twin bill in Fenway Park, but had to hold on to an eleven-inning 3–3 tied contest in the second game, which finally was called due to darkness. Benton retired early again, and gave way to Caster in the sixth inning of the first game. The eight and nine hitters, Outlaw and Richards, each had three of ten Detroit hits, but Richards practically won the opener single-handedly by accounting for five of the runs-batted-in and scoring the sixth himself. O'Neill went to the pen and waved in Trout to protect the 6–3 lead. He did his job, but his frequent starting and relief use was a concern. O'Neill, however, was holding nothing back on this eastern swing.

In the second game York tied the score in the eighth by hitting his sixteenth homer of the year over the left-field wall. Then in the 11th with two outs, and Pinky Woods at third, York made a great stop on infielder Jim Bucher's hard hit and threw him out to snuff a game-winning rally. O'Neill used Tobin, Eaton, Caster and Henry Oana, just up from Buffalo, in relief during the tied game; and Borom, McHale, and Mierkowicz were substituted in both games as injuries kept Greenberg and Mayo out of the lineup for several days.[19]

In Philadelphia the Browns lost a double-header to the A's, which dealt St. Louis another severe blow to their pennant hopes. The second game added insult to injury when Dick Fowler of the A's, recently discharged from the Canadian Army, no-hit the Browns for the first no-hitter of the season. The 6' 4" right-hander's achievement set tongues flapping about veterans who were returning from the service to play winning ball for their old teams. Fowler's no-hitter gave him *The Sporting News* player of the week award.[20]

Dave Ferriss defeated the Tigers again on Monday, September 10, 9–2 in the opener. Les Mueller couldn't duplicate his pitching feat in New York, and was out of the box by the fifth after giving up ten hits, still not aware that Boston knew his pitches. Wilson and Pierce relieved, while Maier played third as Outlaw replaced Greenberg in left field. Jimmy picked up two hits, one a triple, and scored a run in the losing cause. O'Neill was wheeling and dealing his players in an attempt to keep his patches on the quilt in order.

The second game was a duel between Overmire and Emmett O'Neill. The rookie Mierkowicz, subbing for the injured Greenberg, pulverized a ninth-inning pitch for a double off the left field wall that drove York home with the winning run. Oana relieved Overmire and shut the door on the Red Sox, giving Stubby a well-earned victory. The Nats split a pair with Chicago and stayed a game and a half back of the Tigers.[21]

Detroit sent Trout to the mound on Tuesday, September 11, when Newhouser's injury didn't allow him to take his regular turn on the mound. Being the warrior he was, Trout pitched a two-hit shutout, and won 5–0. His win gave him his seventeenth victory of the season. Detroit's big hit came in the seventh when Cramer hit a three-run homer.[22]

While Dizzy and his fellows were taking care of business in Boston, the Senators lost again to Chicago and were now two and a half games behind the Detroiters.

The long road trip clearly had an auspicious start, with Detroit shattering the Yankee pennant hopes by taking the first series, five games to two, and two of three from the Red Sox. Any thought of clogging up the pennant race was squelched in those two series.

"The race is again a two-team battle," wrote the scribes. Washington and Detroit had the inside track. Although neither club had been playing well, both rose to the occasion and narrowed the options. The Yanks and Browns had been hot clubs and it had looked like it was going to be a wide-open race, but after that week the clock was running out for them.

"Detroit had figured to be the pitching class of the league, but now it's depending upon hitters for victories. Benton had been knocked out of the box in his last six starts and O'Neill is weakening Trout with overuse. The Tigers, however, were unleashing a murderous hitting attack involving Greenberg, York, Cullenbine, Cramer and Mayo."[23]

The series against Washington would be the big test between winning and losing the pennant. But before that, the Tigers had to play the Athletics a four-game series in Philadelphia.

Detroit departed the Kenmore in Boston and checked into Philadelphia's Benjamin Franklin Hotel. They opened the series at Shibe Park with a double-header on the 12th. The second game was the makeup game for the 24-inning tied game played earlier in the year.

In the first game Bobo Newsom pitched with only two days' rest. He had been piling up as many innings as was possible. He was tired; the fast ball didn't have the zip and the curve ball didn't break much anymore, but the arm was rubber. He performed by spot pitching. It kept him in the game, but he didn't have a chance to win on this day.

Newhouser was to start the first game and he began to loosen up to pitch for Detroit when after a short warm-up period he walked back to the dugout. Then, just before the start of the game, Benton appeared. Newhouser complained of a bad back and the lump under his shoulder blade confirmed that his problem was a bad one.

Big Al chalked up a victory, but once more he didn't have the stamina to last nine. Caster came to the rescue. Detroit raked Newsom for 12 hits before he left in the eighth. York's seventeenth homer and Cullenbine's three hits paced the attack.

O'Neill struggled with his pitching alignment. Because Newhouser had to be rested, and double-headers were eating up the arms of his pitching staff, there seemed to be no relief in sight. The skipper decided to start Prince Oana for the 24-inning makeup game.

Oana had been pitching in Buffalo for most of the year, but the big Hawaiian was no rookie. He had been kicking around the majors off and on for more than a decade. Desperate for experienced throwing talent, O'Neill gave him a try. He nearly pulled it off. His fast ball whistled coming to the plate and the curve was sharp. He held the A's to a single for eight and two-thirds innings. But Detroit had trouble with Lefty Gassaway. In the seventh, Cullenbine singled and stole second, then Outlaw's single scored him. In the ninth Oana found himself with one runner on base and two outs, and he was just one strike away from a victory. He worked the count on Estalella to three and two. The compact 5'8" Cuban shot a rocket off the left-field wall on the next pitch for a double and the tying run scored.

In the eleventh, York singled and Outlaw tripled to take the lead again, but the A's countered. Again Oana had two outs when he gave up a single to Bill McGhee. O'Neill brought in Caster to relieve. He intentionally walked the dangerous Estalella, but gave up a run-scoring single to Dick Siebert and the game was tied again. Don Black took over for the A's in the thirteenth and made the Tigers harmless kittens the rest of the way. In the bottom of the sixteenth, O'Neill reached into the bullpen and pulled Trout out for relief to salvage a tie as darkness approached. The twenty-four-inning makeup game had become a forty-inning monster! Mayo Smith immediately singled off Trout, and then he scored the winning run when the next hitter, that man, Estalella, in the dimness of the sixteenth inning, laced his second double into left field. In the Tiger dugout, Eddie Mayo, with a sore shoulder that resulted from a crash with York when both went to field a ball, and Greenberg's use of a cane to move around on his bad ankle, along with Newhouser's bad back and its lump, painted a sad picture of a crippled Tiger. Detroit's injuries and the series with Washington were now the main focus of the baseball world.[24]

The next day, September 13, Detroit blew another ball game to the lowly Athletics 3–2, while Washington shut out the Indians 4–0. Washington was now breathing hard down Detroit's neck, just a half game away from the shaky, wounded Tigers. Tobin had been getting people out all day long with his flutter ball but he fell apart in the ninth inning. After getting the first out in the ninth he gave up a long triple, a sharp single, and a double. Those three blazing hits brought O'Neill out of the dugout to make a pitching change, but Tobin's pleas convinced him to let him stay in the box. Tobin then intentionally walked Kell and then sent Buddy Rosar down swinging for out number two. The bases, however, remained loaded. Ed Busch worked Tobin to a full count, and the next pitch was called ball four, which allowed the winning run to score. O'Neill shook his head in disgust for second-guessing himself and listening to Tobin's pleas. Tobin's protest that the last pitch was a strike changed nothing. The Tigers still had another loss to deal with.[25] Detroit continued to play without the services of Greenberg and Mayo for another day. They, however, stole the fourth game of the series from Philadelphia on September 14, 1–0. Bobby Maier was the center of attention:

> Going into September we were in first place, but the Senators were just a couple of games behind us. The day before we went into Washington for a big five-game series, we beat the Athletics, 1–0, on a play where I stole home. I got to third base in the fifth inning and Steve put the squeeze play on. The Athletics called for a pitch-out and their catcher, Buddy Rosar, thought he had me dead. He ran out to tag me, but I slid around him and scrambled to the plate. When the umpire, Art Passarella, called me safe, Buddy went haywire. Passarella eventually threw him out of the game.
>
> Buddy knew darn well he didn't touch me. He was arguing that I went out of the baseline, which I don't think I did. My foot marks were in the base paths, my body was there. He just missed the tag because he was looking at the guy going from second to third. The next inning it started to pour and we couldn't continue the game. It rained so hard the dugouts were filled right up to the top with water.[26]

The game was called and Detroit had a 1–0 steal. Mueller was the winner and Fowler absorbed a tough loss.

Sitting on the visitors' bench in Shibe Park, Red Borom watched an object drop into the dugout next to him from the stands above. It was a .22 caliber bullet. Red decided to keep it as a good luck piece for the pennant stretch run.[27] With an even break in that series, Detroit left for Washington assured of the leader's role to start the tangle with the Senators the following day.

Both Greenberg and Mayo, two key Tigers, looked like cripples, but declared that they intended to play in the opening double-header against Washington. The Tigers' ace pitcher Newhouser said just as positively he would work the first game. Newhouser, who for two days had complained of that painful lump under his shoulder blade, threw hard that day and said he felt fine. Greenberg's left ankle was still badly swollen and it caused him to limp slightly, but the club's doctor gave him a pain-killing injection and told Hank he could play. Mayo's shoulder hurt him every time he swung a bat or stooped for a grounder, but he said, "I'll be in there. I don't know how much good I'll do, but I'm going to give it all I got."[28]

Shirley Povich of the *Washington Post* reported in his September 14 column, "Mayo may not be in the lineup at all after hurting his shoulder in a collision with Rudy York at Yankee Stadium. Incidentally, Mayo couldn't have picked a worse guy to collide with. York collides with gusto." At 6'1", 210 lbs., Rudy was a tough bump.

Rumors surrounded York about his status as a Tiger for next year. The reporters were saying he would be offered for sale this winter. McCosky and Wakefield would return from the service along with some fine rookie outfielders, and Greenberg would have to move to his old position at first leaving York out of the lineup.[29]

York had again started a fire in his hotel room by falling asleep with a cigarette in his hand. He was becoming a dangerous menace, but Jimmy Outlaw had an idea. Red Borom recalled Outlaw's solution: "It's a fact that Rudy burned up a couple of mattresses going to sleep with a cigarette in his hand, but I think Jimmy Outlaw might have cured that. It was in Philadelphia when it last happened that he burned a

Eddie Mayo (Brace Photo).

mattress, so Jimmy went to a novelty store and got a combination ashtray with about an 8ft. rubber hose on it where you could prop the cigarette at an angle on the ash tray and smoke out of the hose if he was lying in bed. He also put a note with the gift and told him, 'Try this as we are trying to win a pennant here and need no more distractions.'" Outlaw was all about winning and he didn't want anything to take away the focus of winning the pennant.

The Shoreham Hotel in D.C. was busy. Red, sitting in the lobby, watched the traffic go by. He spied an old friend from the entourage of General Wainwright. Colonel Holmon, Red's former Ft. Reilly commander, was on Wainwright's staff. Red had played for Fort Reilly when he was in the service. Renewing his acquaintance, he offered him precious, hard-to-get player tickets to the game. Wainwright and Holmon were among the many privileged fans with tickets at Griffith Stadium. The series sold out early. The Senators were causing a stir in the capital city by winning nine of their last eleven games. The city of Washington had pennant fever and the stadium was packed to the brim.[30]

The pennant race had tightened up in the past week and O'Neill, complaining, said, "I wish Washington would get off our necks." Now his team could do something about it. This team had always had the ability to come through when the pressure was the tightest and this should be a rip-roaring series.[31] If either team could sweep, the advantage would be theirs, but a 2–3 split would leave both squads hanging and the race still in doubt.

Newhouser and Overmire faced the Senators' Haefner and Leonard in the twin bill. Just as Trout had a long string of wins over the Yankees, so Newhouser had a similar string of victories over the Senators. They had not defeated him since 1943. Overmire, however, had been a soft touch for them all year.[32] Making matters worse for Detroit was Bridges' bruised finger on his pitching hand. It wasn't responding to treatment.

Major General Claire Chennault of Flying Tigers fame threw out the first ball and the big confrontation began. The series had drawn baseball writers from all over the country. They overflowed the old press box. No extra seats were to be found.

The best-laid pitching plans often go astray. After one scoreless inning the rain came. In a few moments the field turned to mud. When the game resumed the score was zero-zero and Rudy York was at bat with the count of one and one in the top of the second inning. The rain delay had affected Leonard. When play resumed York worked Leonard for a walk, Cullenbine had an infield hit, and after Outlaw forced York at third, Maier singled to right, drawing first blood for the Tigers. Leonard developed an arm problem and headed for the dugout, and Detroit had a two-spot on the board at the start of the bottom of the second inning. Instead of Newhouser, O'Neill brought in Overmire to continue the pitching duties. The advice came from Richards. Newhouser was standing around idly, waiting to warm up again when the game would resume. Richards convinced O'Neill that the smart thing to do would be to save their ace. Richards said, "Some pitchers can't warm up twice in one day and keep their stuff, and Newhouser is one of them. The series is too important. We could save him for tomorrow." O'Neill liked the idea and agreed to hold Hal back.

Even without the services of Newhouser and Greenberg, who had found out his ankle wasn't up to the task, the hitters took over and slammed the Washington relief corps for eleven hits and seven runs. Although the Senators knocked out Overmire in the sixth, forcing Caster to relieve, it was too little too late for the Nats. Detroit growled again in the top of the seventh on hits by Castor and Mayo, which were followed by Cramer's triple and Cullenbine's double. Castor then sailed through the Washington batting order and pitched Detroit to a 7–4 victory.

O'Neill rested Mayo for the second game. He replaced him with Webb, and inserted Hoover at short. With both announced starters used up, the always-willing Trout was sent out to the hill a day earlier than normally scheduled for the second game. He gave up two runs in the first and then settled down, allowing only one more in the sixth. The hot bats of his mates clubbed the Senators' pitching for a 7–3 win and a sweep.

Outlaw went five for nine, four in the nightcap, in which he scored 3 runs and knocked in a run. He also made the fielding play of the day by catching a liner off the bat of Travis in the third and making a peg to York that doubled Kuhel off first.

In the sixth, York smacked his eighteenth and last home run of his career as a Tiger. It was an awesome blow into the deepest section of the park, 421 feet away. Only seven hitters hit home runs at Washington's spacious Griffith Stadium during the 1945 season and two were inside-the-park home runs. York hit two of those seven in 1945, one earlier in the season over the left-field wall, and this one over the center-field wall. The whole Washington team hit but one homer at home in 1945 and that was an insider by Kuhel. Trout won his eighteenth, and Detroit's lead bulged to two and a half games.[33]

The enthusiasm from the Motor City was evident in the locker room when ten thousand "go get 'em" letters from Detroit fans were dumped in the Tigers' dressing room before the games. Lyall Smith, the sportswriter from the *Detroit Free Press*, conducted a campaign for encouragement. The Detroiters responded and put forth their best effort.[34] Series fever rose to a high-pitch level in Detroit.

Trout took a little tour around Washington with sportswriter Joe Williams of the *New York World-Telegram*. "An old catcher named Gabby Street once caught a ball thrown from the top of this Washington Monument," the writer related. "Did, eh?" said Mr. Trout. "And you guys call me Dizzy."[35]

The following day, September 16, Wolff outpitched Newhouser with a five-hit, 3–2 win for the second-place Senators. With their backs against the wall, the Nats beat their old nemesis, ending Newhouser's streak at 10 straight vs. Washington.

The second game saw Detroit come back to beat the Nationals 5–4 in another close game. Detroit jumped starter Johnny Niggeling with hits in the third by Cullenbine, Outlaw, Swift and Benton which, combined with a Washington error, sent Detroit into a 3–0 lead. The Tigers added two more in the later innings.

Benton received credit for the win, but again he couldn't finish the game, leaving in the seventh. It was the eleventh straight time Benton failed to go the route. The ailing Bridges relieved him for less than two innings. The Senators attacked Bridges with hits by Lewis and Kuhel and when Cullenbine committed an error the runners scored. Caster relieved Bridges. An error by Hoover allowed Washington another run, ending Caster's appearance, and O'Neill waved Trout in to put out the fire with the tying run on third, and the winning run on first. He saved it with the help of a great fielding gem by Webb which preserved the Tigers' two-and-a-half-game lead.[36]

Sitting around the lobby of the Shoreham the next day, Tiger players watched the downpour fall while receiving news of the postponement of Monday's contest. Despite the fact that Detroit had to play three games more than the Senators and were sitting on a two-and-a-half-game lead, there was no boasting from the players that they had sewed up the pennant. They might be confident, but no one was making noises about going to the Series. The next day was an off-day and the game was rescheduled for the 18th at 2:00 to give Detroit time to depart for their 8:30 train to Cleveland. O'Neill was ready to start Oana against Washington's Walt Masterson, who was pitching well after being released from the Navy the last week, but with the extra day of rest the skipper asked Trout if he would like to work that game and the big righty jumped at the chance. Trout had eighteen wins and wanted a shot at another twenty-win season, but this would be his eighth mound appearance in fourteen days, during which he had won five, lost one and saved one. He had been a tower of strength for the pitching staff on this road trip.[37]

O'Neill received some good news. Fire Trucks, who won 16 games in 1943, would receive his discharge from the Navy and would be eligible for the World Series.

Trout didn't have it as the heavy work load finally caught up to him. He was pounded and five other bullpen relievers gave up sixteen hits in a 12–5 loss that cut Detroit's lead to a game and a half. Clipped for six hits and four runs in the first inning, Dizzy was forced to make an early exit. A parade of pitchers progressed across the stage. The Senators treated them all the same — badly. Overmire, Caster, Newhouser, Oana, and Eaton all took their lumps. The Nats were alive. Leonard had the win and Caster the loss.[38]

Reliever Caster had been of great value since he came to Detroit. Even though he was tagged with the loss, he had appeared in 18 games and put up five straight victories before this losing effort. The Tigers could have hardly hoped to stay in the race without him. He took up a large amount of slack in relief, especially with the injuries that on occasion prevented Newhouser, Trout and Benton to do their best. He seemed to enjoy pitching in tight situations, and his consistency was a windfall for the Detroiters.

The Tigers scored all of their runs in the sixth and Borom remembered an incident that took place with his good-luck piece. Red said:

> As I watched from the dugout I had been playing around with my good-luck charm, the .22 caliber bullet that dropped into my lap in Philadelphia, and I built a mud casing around it while I was sitting on the bench. We got a rally going and Greenberg pinch-hit a double. O'Neill called for me to pinch-run for him. I wasn't thinking and I stuffed the muddy bullet in my back pocket and trotted out there to replace him. When I got there I thought, what if I have to slide? That bullet would be a hindrance. So I called Hank back, and I said, "Put this on the bench shelf for me, will you?" He looked at the muddy bullet in the strangest way and left with it cupped carefully in his hands. When I returned it was right there where I wanted it to be. I sure didn't want to lose my lucky piece.

A tired and crippled bunch of Tigers left Washington. It had been an interesting series with Detroit holding its lead in the AL race by a game and a half.

The Tiger rock that their road opponents couldn't move was Dizzy Trout. Forced to take up the pitching slack caused by Newhouser's injury, Trout was amazing on this road tour. He took the ball six times in twelve days, three times as a starter and three in relief. He was credited with four victories and one defeat in the outings. Players and fans believed last year he was overworked late in the failing September drive for the flag. He had paid a physical price for it. Now, once more, he held the Tigers and their pennant drive together in a late September push. *The Sporting News* believed he was more than the player of the week — that he was the player of the month each September. Trout was the Tigers' "hoss," and although he definitely needed a rest he was a most willing workman.[39]

It was late when the team pulled into the Statler Hotel in Cleveland, tired and bruised, but still in the lead. Somewhere in the midst of all their weary thoughts the name of Bobby Feller must have appeared. They knew he would pitch one of the games against them. Who would start in opposition to Feller? Would they be able to hit well against him, or would he dominate as he was known to do on occasion?

Les Mueller relates his thoughts concerning the series first game:

> Yeah, well, I can tell you the story on that game, because I remember that game quite well. That was one of those games where I came into the ballpark that day and Steve O'Neill came up to me and said, "Les, I don't know but you may have to pitch today."
>
> They had intended to start Bridges. Tommy's arm had been bothering him a little bit. So if he can't go, they said, you will be pitching. I said fine.
>
> When it got time for the pitchers to warm up, Bobby Feller was warming up for the Indians. It wasn't two minutes later when Steve came up to me and said, "Tommy's arm is bothering him." Now you know darn well and good that Tommy, being an old veteran pitcher, thought, "To hell with that, let Mueller pitch. I'll pitch against some other team." I pitched and I pitched quite well, but Feller pitched a one-hitter. I think that was the time I hit a big foul ball off of him. Yeah, Jeff Heath hit a home run off of me. That is how they got their two runs off of me."

The Indians, playing at League Park, only had three hits off Mueller. It just happened that one of them was Heath's fifteenth homer of the year, with first baseman Rocco, who had walked, aboard. Don Ross had singled in the first inning, and in the second inning Pat Seerey blasted a long double. Mueller survived both of those hits. But Heath's two-run blow occurred in the third inning and put two on the big board. That blow was all Feller needed. The only hit Feller gave up was a blooper into right field that outfielder Fleming hesitated about trying to catch it and then played it safe by letting it drop. Feller dominated and if Fleming had caught the ball he would easily have had a no-hitter. Outlaw had looped out that single in the fifth, and Richards walked right behind him. O'Neill then put Borom in to pinch-hit for Mueller. Red had five straight hits off Feller, but this time he hit into a fielder's choice, and Feller then forced

Webb to ground out for the third out of the inning, ending any threat. Caster threw three hitless and scoreless innings. Bridges must have had a sudden rejuvenation because he threw the last inning without giving up a hit or a run. Mueller graciously took the loss.[40]

Both Greenberg and Mayo returned to the lineup, but against Feller they could only contribute a walk between them. Washington picked up a half a game without playing.

The game of September 20 against the Tribe turned into a Detroit nightmare. Benton pitched beautifully for seven innings and nursed a 1–0 lead into the eighth; O'Neill was beginning to believe that he had regained his early season form.

The Tigers run came via a Cramer walk, a Cullenbine single, and Outlaw's fielder's choice in the fourth. But in the eighth the Tigers were overwhelmed by three avalanches in one inning. Hits, errors, and a soaker from the heavens overturned Detroit's smooth ride. Dutch Meyer singled, Cullenbine's error advanced him, and then Cullenbine mishandled Rocco's hit, and Meyer went to third. Heath grounded to York, who threw late to home, allowing the run to score. O'Neill once again called on Trout for a bail-out, but this time, Dizzy poured gasoline on the fire. He walked Fleming and gave up a single to Ross. Seerey then grounded to Mayo, who made a poor throw to second that allowed another score. Hayes singled, and Ross scored. Maier erred on the throw and the runners advanced. It was a Tiger avalanche of misfortune and misplays. Caster relieved Trout. Reynolds singled, scoring Hayes, after Seerey was put out at home on Al Cihocki's attempted squeeze play. The rains then blew in and the game went on hold for 42 minutes. When play resumed, Meyer singled Cihocki across the plate. Rocco finally ended the fracas by grounding out. Was that a typical wartime contest or just a bad day at the office?

There were, however, some good plays in that game. Cramer made a great one-handed catch of infielder Elmer Winegartner's drive. A beautiful stop and toss by Mayo on Rocco's grounder was an above-average play, but the only good news for Detroit was that the Yankees beat Washington and the Tigers lost no ground to them in the race.[41]

The Tigers finally returned to friendly Briggs Stadium. Instead of resting his troops on an off-day, the skipper invited them out to look at their home park, which they hadn't seen since sweeping the Sox on Labor Day. While they were there, he insisted that they might as well gorge themselves on some batting and fielding practice.[42]

O'Neill had a couple of problems to solve. One was, what about Newhouser? Was he recovered from his shoulder ailment? O'Neill decided to start him the next day against the Browns, who were playing for third place. The other question was, what about Greenberg? Should he be rushed back into the lineup? He had showed in Cleveland he was still off his game in the hitting department, and handicapped in his fielding because of the ankle injury. Outlaw, who had been subbing, had been doing the job in a big way. The good news arrived in Detroit when they were told the Yankees beat the Senators 5–3. The Tigers were up a game and a half.

On Saturday, Newhouser went to the pitcher's box, and Greenberg started in left field. Mayo picked up his glove and trotted out to second base. Detroit battered the Browns with a great display of power and pitching skill, 9–0. Newhouser threw a four-hit shutout and hurled one of his finest games of the year as he notched his twenty-third victory. He also swung a potent bat. He tripled in a run in the second, and doubled in a pair of runs in the third. The Tigers knocked Muncrief off the hill and into the showers as they scored seven times in that 3rd inning. Newhouser, Richards, Cullenbine and Greenberg all had a pair of hits. Greenberg's ankle appeared improved and he played the entire game.[43] The Senators kept pace, however, beating the A's. Wolff defeated Christopher 2–0.

Mueller was sitting in the bullpen next to George Caster when Pete Gray trotted past them. Caster said to Mueller, "I hope he breaks his neck." Gray was unpopular with the St. Louis players. Mueller explained the problem:

> He was very unpopular with the other players. One of the reasons was that Mike Kreevich was an established player and played pretty well for the Browns. A lot of the players thought that Kreevich should have been playing instead of Gray because Kreevich didn't play as much when Gray joined the club and the Browns then traded him to the Senators late in the year. Chances are if Kreevich would have played every day he probably would have helped them, but that is something you don't know for sure. Caster was there in St. Louis part of the year and then he came over to Detroit. He said what he did because that was just the way he felt about it. It was just one of those things, I guess.

On the 23rd, Potter turned the tables around on Detroit and shut them out 5–0. The Tigers curled up like kittens before Potter, who allowed but two hits. The whitewash was his eighth straight victory. Greenberg's single in the fourth and Cullenbine's double in the seventh were all Detroit could muster. Dizzy Trout gave up three hits and three runs in the first inning. He had nothing left but a willing disposition for punishment, and the skipper finally retired him in the second. The parade of pitchers began as Mueller, Overmire, Caster and Tobin all took their turn in the box.[44]

Dizzy was trying to get by with effort but he didn't have any gas in his arm to work with and he was fussing with his catcher. Outlaw relates the story: "I'll tell you a little tale about Trout and Swift. They were having trouble with signs and Trout was shaking him off. Swift ran out of signs and he finally walked out halfway to the mound and he said, 'Trout, if you don't start throwing what I am calling for, I am going to come out here and bite your head off.' I was standing right there at third base and I heard him. Trout said back to him, 'If you do, you will have more brains in your stomach than you do in your head.' That settled it and they went back and played ball."

Although the Browns earned their runs cleanly in the first inning, there was a glaring weakness in the Tiger defense. A limping Greenberg was slow fielding hits that went for extra bases, and that allowed runners to advance easily. He also wasn't able to get himself into a good throwing position for a toss to the plate on a fly ball in the sixth inning, and that allowed a run to score. The defeat, however, didn't cost the Tigers any of their lead over the Senators.[45]

In a strange turn of events the Senators lost their first game of a double-header to the A's, 4–3. Washington had a chance to close to within a fraction of Detroit until the sun suddenly came out from behind a dark overcast sky. It was there just long enough to block the Senators' opportunity. In the bottom of the twelfth inning the game was knotted at 3–3 when the A's Ernie Kish hit a high fly to center. It appeared that the Senator's "Bingo" Binks would make a routine catch. As the ball came down, Binks began to wander about like a blind man in the opposite direction from the falling baseball. When the ball plopped to the ground, Kish was standing on second and Binks was rubbing his eyes. A cloudy day had suddenly become sunny and Binks had neglected to take his dark glasses to the outfield. Now the dangerous George Kell stepped up and promptly lined a single into right field that scored the winning run for the A's. The Nats returned the favor by the same 4–3 score in the nightcap, but they could not undo the damage of the first game. There were no more games to play. The Senators had ended their season early, and their only chance was to pray the Tigers would lose. Detroit had to win but two of four games to lock up the flag.

The Senators' locker room was filled with sorrow and little forgiveness. Their anger towards Bingo Binks showed. A victory for the Nats would have cut Detroit's lead to a half game. The Senators looked to be, as Mr. Povich, Washington's main sportswriter, liked to say, "A gone gang."[46]

Detroit, however, still had to find a way to win two games to take the pennant outright. Trout had bogged down dismally, and Benton hadn't finished a game in a long time. The sluggers had stopped slugging, but Detroit had Newhouser back. O'Neill was holding the ace. How he played him was important.

On September 26, 41,000-plus fans crammed into Briggs Stadium to witness a double-header between the Indians and the Tigers. O'Neill played his card boldly. In the first game he sent the ace into action looking for a win and at least a tie for the pennant. The slender southpaw pitched an outstanding game and whitewashed the Indians 11–0. It was his eighth shutout and his twenty-fourth victory. He also ran his strikeout total to 206 for the season. Three quick double plays by Mayo, Outlaw, Hoover and York pulled him out of the few jams he was in.

In the first inning, Detroit gave the hometown boy all he needed by clipping eighteen-game winner Reynolds for four hits, including Cullenbine's eighteenth and last homer of the year. Greenberg slugged his twelfth with two aboard and the Tigers scored four in the seventh. Newhouser banged out three hits himself to help his own cause.

In the second game Steve Gromek, the Indians' ace hurler, disappointed the huge crowd by freezing the Tiger bats and nipped Detroit's flag chances with a 3–2 win. Throwing a snappy fast ball and a wide sweeping curve, Gromek made the Detroiters look helpless. Tempers ran high when Outlaw scored in the fifth on a squeeze play, and the Tribe's catcher Hayes, according to Outlaw, tagged him more heavily than was necessary. The Runt jumped up roaring mad, and it took all four umpires to halt the milling around and get the contest underway again.

Benton pitched well for five innings, allowing but one hit. In the sixth, however, two hits and an error by York allowed all three of the Tribe's runs to score. Caster relieved Benton and Bridges relieved Castor, but Gromek prevailed. The Tigers headed for St. Louis for two games still one win away from the flag.[47]

Writer Joe Williams wrote about the problems in securing the pennant: "What has hurt the Tigers down the stretch is the failure of Benton to regain a winning form following the broken leg. In the matter of stuff on the ball he ranks next to Newhouser. For five, six or seven innings he can make the ball do tricks. But he lacks leg stamina, and weakens in the late innings. The Indians got him out of there in the sixth yesterday. It was his twelfth successive failure to complete a game."

O'Neill had to make a serious pitching decision. Should he use Newhouser in St. Louis or save him in case Detroit and Washington ended the season tied and there was a playoff? The ace had been brilliant in his last 2 starts and if he beat the Browns, the Tigers would clinch the flag. Much was at stake, including O'Neill's pocketbook, because Mr. Brigg's generosity allowed Tiger managers to receive a $10,000 bonus for leading their team into a World Series.[48]

Shirley Povich explained the philosophy of the Detroit owner in his morning column by writing:

A few years ago Mr. Walter O. Briggs Sr. stated his baseball ambitions very simply by telling his general manager, Jack Zeller, "I want the best baseball team, the best stadium and the best playing field in the major leagues. The rest is up to you." The difficult item among those three demands would be getting the best baseball team. Briggs' money hasn't been able to swing that, yet. Ball games are one of the few things that money won't quite buy. If it could, the Tigers would be out in front by 20 games at this point instead of a mere game ahead of the comparatively impoverished Washington Senators of Clark Griffith, with the pennant still undecided.[49]

Detroit players took exception to those words. If nothing else could motivate Detroit to clinch the pennant in St. Louis it would seem that Mr. Povich's *This Morning* column in the *Washington Post* would do more than even Mr. Briggs' money could. Perhaps one should let sleeping dogs (and Tigers) lie undisturbed!

Virgil Trucks joined the Tigers just in time. He accompanied Tom Bridges and Paul Richards to St. Louis to scout the game on the 28th between the Indians and the Browns. The Browns beat the Indians 2–1 in a game called in the last of the sixth inning by rain. The win assured the Browns of at least a tie for third place. The threesome compared notes for the important game on the 30th between the Tigers and the Browns.[50] The rains had poured in the Midwest for ten days, and the field was soggy. The groundskeepers did everything possible to allow the game to be played. If it hadn't been such an important contest it most certainly would have been postponed.

On September 30, 1945, the Browns and Tigers finally attempted to play the double-header at Sportsman's Park. Early darkness was dropping over the field and a small mist fell throughout the game. It rained off and on throughout the contest and the field was so muddy that the players had difficulty wading around.

Trucks held up well but ran into trouble in the sixth. O'Neill played his ace again. Newhouser entered the game and got out of the trouble, but he gave up the lead in the eighth. Detroit was down 3–2 going into the ninth.

Never was a title to be won in a more dramatic fashion than this one. The rain which had delayed the game for nearly an hour threatened to come down in sheets and the game could be called at any time. All of baseball wanted this title to be won on the field and the umpires strived to keep the game going so the pennant could be won or lost on the field.

Nelson Potter threw well for the Browns, but in the ninth, he got himself into trouble by giving up a pinch-hit to reserve Hub Walker. Webb bunted Walker to second and occupied first when the throw to second missed its target. Borom ran for Walker and then Mayo sacrificed both runners. When Cramer stepped in to hit, the Browns decided to walk him and pitch to Greenberg, hoping he would hit into a game-ending double play.

The Browns had made a fatal mistake. On Potter's second pitch Greenberg brought the curtain down on the 1945 American League season with a grand-slam home run that brought Mr. Briggs's championship back to Detroit. Al Benton finished up the ninth inning and Detroit beat the Browns 6–3 in one of the craziest game situations ever played. The attempt to play the nightcap failed when the storm unleashed its fury. The Prince had registered his twenty-fifth win, and he and Greenberg were being toasted in Michigan homes, taverns, and workplaces as Detroit's game heroes.[51]

After the game Greenberg embraced his teammates and posed for pictures. He tried to put into words the emotions of clubbing the game's winning drive that gave Detroit the American League pennant. "I've had thrills, but never..." Struggling to finish the sentence, he stopped to gather himself for a second or two, and then said, "That was the sweetest home run I ever hit."[52]

Across the room was the happiest Irishman in the nation. Steve O'Neill, a big league manager and a coach for sixteen years, finally had his opportunity to manage in the World Series. He was cheerfully beaming in the splendor of his managerial pennant and held court amongst a bevy of reporters who hung on his every word.

A weary Paul Richards and a tired Newhouser congratulated each other and breathed a sigh of relief. The game could have turned out differently for those combatants.

Greenberg almost became the dupe instead of the hero. In the inning when the score was tied at 2–2, he was trapped off third base and run down with only one out. He seemed to have had a notion he could sneak home on York's infield out, but Gutteridge's toss across the diamond put him out and left big Hank looking like a chump.

O'Neill could have worn the robe of the fool too, for he had used up his pitching ace, Newhouser, in what was beginning to look like a squandered relief job when St. Louis tied the game and then took the lead. There was some indecision in the sixth when Trucks tired and allowed a double and a walk to lead off the inning with no one out. Richards went out to talk to Trucks, and it was his choice to keep him in the game. O'Neill stepped in and called for Newhouser from the pen, but at the finish the responsibility shifted from Detroit's personnel to the Browns' manager Luke Sewell. Never should one pass anybody to get to Greenberg. That was an American League truism.

The Tigers tied one on, and celebrated to the fullest on the train going back to Detroit. Greenberg, still in the glow of his pennant-winning heroics, spoke with confidence by saying, "Newhouser will win two and Trucks will win two, and that will finish the Cubs. I don't see how we can win the series inside of four games, though."[53]

O'Neill heaped special praise on Roy Cullenbine by saying that he was the most underrated player on the Tigers and thought he was Detroit's most valuable player. "He did everything for us from hitting home runs to playing the best right field in the league. When he wasn't winning games for us he was saving them."[54]

When asked about Hank's winning homer in the misty gloaming he took a deep breath, stood up, spread his gnarled hands approximately one foot apart and said, "That ball missed being foul by about this much."[55]

The happy band of players also managed to give a few jabs to the second-place Senators. The morning before Detroit won the pennant, a newspaper quoted the Nats' owner, Clark Griffith, who said, "The Senators will win. I feel it in my bones." In the midst of all the Tiger pennant merriment, Eddie Mayo flippantly replied, "It must just have been Griff's rheumatism after all." The Tigers were an exhilarated group of athletes looking happily towards the biggest show in any town — the World Series.[56]

The bottom line was that Briggs's Tigers were going to the World Series to play the Chicago Cubs and Griffith's Senators were going home to listen to the radio. The first Series game was scheduled for Wednesday. The Tigers were a 10–13 favorite to win the Series. As a young fan I rejoiced and eagerly anticipated the start of the Series.

9-30-1945

Detroit	AB	R	H	PO	A	E
Webb-6	3	1	1	3	3	0
Mayo-4	4	0	1	3	3	0
Cramer-8	5	1	1	2	0	0
Greenberg-7	5	1	2	1	1	0
Cullenbine-9	4	1	1	0	0	0
York-3	5	0	0	6	1	0
Outlaw-5	2	0	1	1	1	0
Richards-2	4	0	1	10	1	0
Trucks-1	2	1	0	1	1	0
Newhouser-1 (L)	0	0	0	0	0	0
a. Walker	1	0	1	0	0	0
b. Borom	0	1	0	0	0	0
Benton-1	0	0	0	0	0	0
TOTALS	35	6	9	27	11	0

St. Louis	AB	R	H	PO	A	E
Gutteridge-4	3	1	1	6	3	1
Finney-7	2	0	2	1	0	0
Byrnes-8	2	0	0	2	0	0
c. Christman-PH	1	0	0	0	0	0
Gray-8	1	1	0	2	0	0
McQunn-3	4	0	1	5	2	0
Moore-9	4	1	1	0	0	0
Stephens-6	4	0	2	2	2	0
Mancuso-2	4	0	0	5	0	0
Schulte-5	4	0	0	3	4	0
Potter-1 (L)	3	0	1	1	0	0
TOTALS	32	3	8	27	11	1

a. Hit for Newhouser (9)
b. Ran for Walker (9)
c. Hit for Byrnes (6)

Detroit	0	0	0	0	1	1	0	0–4-(6)
St. Louis	1	0	0	0	0	0	1	1–0-(3)

2BH: Gutteridge, Potter, McQuinn, Moore. HOME RUN: Greenberg. SAC. HITS: Webb, Mayo. DOUBLE PLAYS: Detroit, 2–4, 5–4–3. LEFT ON BASES: St. Louis 5, Detroit 9. BASE ON BALLS: — Off Trucks 2, Potter 5, and Newhouser 1. STRUCK OUT: — By Trucks 3, Potter 4, and Newhouser 5. HITS-OFF: Trucks 3 (5⅓), Newhouser 4 (2⅔), Benton 1 (1), Potter 9 (9). WINNER: Newhouser, LOSER: Potter. TIME OF GAME: 2:23. ATTENDANCE: 5,582. UMPIRES: Pipgras, Berry, Rue and Hubbard.

11

How Detroit Succeeded in Winning the Pennant

"Trout, a hulking man with a booming voice, who ... did an iron man stint in leading the Tigers to the 1945 American League Pennant ... would recall, 'You didn't worry about sore arms or three days rest. You just kept burning them in, hoping the plate umpire had 20–20 vision.'"
Chicago sportswriter

Detroit had no hitter reach the magic .300 mark for the year, with the exception of Hank Greenberg, who posted a .311 average for 78 games. Nor did they have a hitter with 20 home runs, or a player who recorded 100 runs batted in for the year. Their pitching staff depending on two pitchers for 559.6 innings, well over a third of the number of innings played; while three more starters labored for 488.7 innings, leaving the remainder of innings to be spread out by eleven other hurlers, some who threw as little as 1, 5 or 11 innings for the campaign. Detroit's age made them susceptible to physical breakdowns and a gradual loss of their athletic reflexes was noticeable. The injuries during the course of the year hampered their star pitchers, their sluggers and their spark plug. When those key combatants came back for competition they still had nagging physical damage to deal with during the course of play. So how did everything fall in place for Detroit?

One factor was the experience that all these old veterans had. Greenberg and Bridges had successfully completed three previous pennant campaigns that resulted in three league championships and one World Series victory. Greenberg, Bridges, Richards, Cullenbine, Benton, York, Cramer, Newhouser, Trout, Mayo, and Caster all had been part of pennant-winning teams in the past. They understood the effort that was needed to win the flag.

All of them were covetous of the pennant, especially considering that they had come so close the year before and lost out at the last moment to the Browns. Eddie Mayo summed up their feelings about losing the 1944 pennant by say-

155

ing, "I remember 1944 vividly. We had a one-game lead over St. Louis with four games to go. Washington came to town and the Yankees went into St. Louis. We won two out of four and the Browns won four straight. That was a crusher, a real crusher. That spoiled the whole winter for me."[1] No Tiger wanted to repeat that scenario. Detroit was a savvy, hungry team in 1945.

The second factor was Detroit's administrative staff. Jack Zeller was a very competent GM and he filled the needs of the team. He swung an off-season deal for Webb that improved the defensive part of the infield; kept or added Borom, Hostetler and Maier; and stocked the young talents Houtteman, Pierce, Mierkowicz and McHale. He swung a deal for Cullenbine early in the season which gave Detroit an extra hitting punch, and Cullenbine experienced a career year. Tobin and Caster were valuable pickups by Zeller late in the year when the pitching staff was physically breaking down. Caster in relief was dependable and endured well in the stretch run. Without his steady relief work Detroit would have been hard pressed to win the flag. Tobin chipped in with starting and relief jobs and some very timely hitting. Steve O'Neill knew how to handle a veteran team. He knew when to rest and when to elbow them. His disposition was to give older players professional space. He inquired about their concerns and took their advice under consideration. His managerial decisions during the season were successful. An impressive fact about O'Neill's career as a manager was that he never had a losing season. Eddie Mayo's opinion of O'Neill was common of most of the veterans: "I played for Steve O'Neill. In my opinion, he was the greatest humanist and manager of ball players that I've ever known. He was a great strategist and a very understanding man. He was the kind of manager who said, 'You're a major-leaguer, you know how to play ball,' and left you alone."[2]

Paul Richards was an

Rudy York (National Baseball Hall of Fame Library, Cooperstown, New York).

integral intermediary between players and management. His authoritarian approach towards fundamentals and cohesive team play was respected and his influence with Newhouser was a winning proposition. Uncle Sam helped by returning key players throughout the year. Mueller and Benton were onboard early. Mueller contributed to the pitching staff in spot starts and in relief. His role helped to bolster the staff. He defeated the Yankees in several crucial games. The return of Greenberg gave Detroit an explosive "pop" in their bat chemistry that was significant for the pennant drive. Bat power is in most cases a God-given gift and in 1945 Detroit had been blessed with three of them in Hank, Rudy and Roy. York, Cullenbine, Mayo and Cramer all protected Greenberg in the lineup, making it difficult to pitch around him. Hank responded well, hitting a team-leading .311 average, contributing 13 home runs and 60 runs batted in for Detroit during the second half of the season. The drama of his pennant-winning blow became a legend for the ages. Benton posted a 13–8 record despite serious injury, and was second in the league earned-run department with a very impressive 2.02 average. The return of Bridges wasn't anywhere near as important as the contributions of Mueller, Benton and Greenberg, but he did win one game and helped in relief. Considering Detroit won the pennant by one and a half games his return proved helpful. Virgil Trucks's release from the navy at the end of the season, even if it was just for that one pitching stint of 5 and a third innings, gave Detroit a fresh arm at just the right time. Stubby Overmire gave the Tigers another lefty and a change-of-speed pitcher who contributed a 9–9 record and could be counted on as the fourth starter in the rotation and a willing reliever for the pitching staff.

Bob Maier's early start and his hitting ability amounted to a bonus. Jimmy Outlaw's hustle, enthusiasm, and diversified talents of switching between the infield and outfield spots made him an asset that gave O'Neill confidence in playing him as both a starter and as a needed reserve. Outlaw's cooperative optimism helped make this a career season for him. Mayo had his best year and spark-plugged the team with 10 homers and 24 doubles. His glove was invaluable in the field. His leadership was the glue that held the team together.

The utility players, Borom, Walker and Hoover, filled in well for injured starters. Red added extra speed, and made fielding, bunting and hitting contributions. Hoover had an extra punch in his bat for an infielder, and delivered 10 doubles, 5 triples and a homer in his limited play. Walker's pinch-hit started the game rally that won the pennant. Over all of the factors given were Newhouser and Trout. Trout carried the load late in the year despite an overused pitching arm, always ready to pitch even when his arm and back disagreed. His clutch pitching gave O'Neill confidence in using him for starting or relief roles, and O'Neill felt he was his stopper. A Chicago writer summed Trout up after his death by saying, "Trout, a hulking man with a booming voice who did an iron man stint in leading the Tigers to the 1945 American League Pennant ... would recall, 'You didn't worry about sore arms or three days rest. You just

Hank Greenberg (National Baseball Hall of Fame Library, Cooperstown, New York).

kept burning them in, hoping the plate umpire had 20–20 vision."[3] Even more so was Newhouser. He stopped the bleeding; he was the go-to guy and the headliner of the squad. Newhouser was the king of pitchers in the mid-forties. No other pitcher has ever won back-to-back MVP awards in the history of baseball, but he did in 1944 and 1945. In 1945 he won the historical pitching triple-crown, finishing first in ERA average, wins, and strikeouts. His 313 pitched innings topped the league. O'Neill used him as frequently as it was possible to do so. Newhouser carried a heavy load.

The Browns' inability to beat Detroit was a factor. Kramer never knew Detroit had knowledge of his pitches and it cost the Browns dearly. The dismissal of St. Louis's pitcher Sig Jakucki helped to neutralize one of Detroit's main rivals during the stretch run. The failure of New York to beat Detroit became a factor, and just as important was New York's success against Washington that happened just at the right time and played to the Tigers' advantage. The Yankee infield remained unstable and when they sold Borowy, a 20-game winner, they lost any opportunity for the flag. MacPhail never admitted he made a mistake. Griffith's decision in shortening his schedule for an extra football game in the fall became an unknown factor. His team really pulled a great upset after finishing last the previous year and contended for the flag right down to the wire. Griffith misjudged its talents. Binks's misplayed fly ball at the end of the year against the A's kept the Senators from sweeping the last-place A's team, putting less pressure on Detroit. A peek-a-boo sun became their undoing.

Another factor would be the final statistics of the year. The Tigers topped the league in wins, winning percentage, and doubles; finished second in runs scored, home runs, and the least number of errors committed, third in stolen bases and team fielding percentage. The team pitching statistics were boosted by Newhouser's outstanding year. The pitchers led all teams in strikeouts, shutouts, and saves, and were second in the earned run department.

Then there was the spirit of Detroit manifested in word and deed by Jimmy Outlaw and Mayo. Nothing fancy, just all-out 100% hustle, and encouragement every day of every game. Even though Washington led the league with road victories (46–31), Detroit's home win record was tops in the league (50–26). Detroit's 38 victories on the road was second best, while the Nats 46 home wins was only the fourth best in the American League. The chemistry of these known components helped acquire the 1945 pennant for Detroit.

12

1945 Statistics

American League[1]

Team	W-L	%	GB	Runs	2B	3B	HR	BA	SB	FA	E
Detroit	88–65	.575	0	633	227	47	77	.256	60	.975	158
Washington	87–67	.565	1½	622	197	63	27	.258	110	.970	183
St. Louis	81–70	.536	6	597	215	37	63	.249	25	.976	143
New York	81–71	.533	6½	676	189	61	93	.259	64	.971	175
Cleveland	73–72	.503	11	557	216	48	65	.255	19	.977	126
Chicago	71–78	.477	15	596	204	55	22	.262	78	.970	180
Boston	71–83	.461	17½	599	225	44	50	.260	72	.973	169
Philadelphia	52–98	.347	34½	494	201	37	33	.245	25	.973	168
League	88–65	.575	0	676	227	63	93	.262	110	.977	126
Leader	Det	Det	Det	NY	Det	Was	NY	Chi	Was	Clev	Clev

Team Pitching	CG	BB	SO	SHO	SV	ERA
Detroit	78	538	588	19	16	2.99
Washington	82	440	550	19	11	2.92
St. Louis	91	506	570	10	8	3.14
New York	78	485	474	9	14	3,45
Cleveland	76	501	497	14	12	3.31
Chicago	84	448	486	13	13	3.69
Boston	71	656	490	15	13	3.81
Philadelphia	65	571	531	11	8	3.62
League	91	440	588	19	16	2.92
Leader	St. L	Was	Det	Det & Was	Det	Was

1945 Detroit Tigers Team Batting[2]

Pos.	Player	Age	G	AB	R	H	2B	3B	HR	RBI	BB	SO	BA	OBP
C	Swift B.	30	95	279	19	65	5	0	0	24	26	22	.233	.298
1B	York R.	31	155	595	71	157	25	5	18	87	60	85	.264	.331
2B	Mayo E.-LH	35	134	501	71	143	24	3	10	54	47	29	.285	.347
3B	Maier B.	29	132	486	58	128	25	7	1	34	38	32	.263	.317
SS	Webb J.	35	118	407	43	81	12	2	0	21	30	35	.199	.254
OF	Cullenbine R.-SwH	31	146	523	80	145	27	5	18	93	102	36	.277	.398
OF	Cramer R.-LH	39	141	541	62	149	22	8	6	58	36	21	.275	.324
OF	Outlaw J.	32	132	446	56	121	16	5	0	34	45	33	.271	.338
OF	Greenberg H.	34	78	270	47	84	20	2	13	60	42	40	.311	.404
C	Richards P.	36	83	234	26	60	12	1	3	32	19	31	.256	.315
INF	Hoover J.	30	74	222	33	57	10	5	1	17	21	35	.257	.324
INF	Borom E.J.-LH	28	55	130	19	35	4	0	0	9	7	8	.269	.307
OF	Hostetler C.-LH	41	42	44	3	7	3	0	0	2	7	8	.159	.275
INF	Ross D.	30	8	29	3	11	4	0	0	4	5	1	.379	.471
OF	Walker H.-LH	38	28	23	4	3	0	0	0	1	9	4	.130	.375
OF	Mierkowicz E.	21	10	15	0	2	2	0	0	2	1	3	.133	.187
1B/OF	McHale J.-LH	23	19	14	0	2	0	0	0	1	1	4	.143	.250
C	Miller H.	32	2	4	0	3	0	0	0	1	0	0	.750	.750
C	Welch M.	20	1	2	0	0	0	0	0	0	0	1	.000	.000
P H	Kerns R.-LH	24	1	1	0	0	0	0	0	0	0	0	.000	.000
P H	McNabb C.	28	1	1	0	0	0	0	0	0	0	1	.000	.000
P	Newhouser H.-LH	24	40	109	9	28	5	1	0	17	7	10	.257	.302
P	Trout P.	30	42	102	11	25	3	2	2	11	2	23	.245	.260
P	Benton A.	34	31	63	2	4	2	0	0	3	2	21	.063	.092
P	Overmire F.	26	31	53	5	10	2	1	0	3	4	6	.189	.246
P	Mueller L.	26	26	44	5	8	3	0	1	4	2	10	.182	.217
P	Eaton Z.	25	26	32	2	8	1	0	2	10	0	7	.250	.250
P	Tobin J.	32	17	25	2	3	0	0	2	5	1	5	.120	.154
P	Wilson W.-LH	31	25	19	1	1	0	0	0	0	0	9	.053	.053
P	Orrell J.	28	12	15	0	2	0	0	0	0	0	6	.133	.133
P	Caster G.	37	22	11	0	2	0	0	0	1	2	3	.182	.308
P	Houtteman A.	17	13	5	0	0	0	0	0	0	0	2	.000	.000
P	Oana P.	37	4	5	0	1	0	0	0	0	0	0	.200	.200
P	Bridges T.	38	4	3	0	0	0	0	0	0	0	0	.000	.000
P	Pierce W.-LH	18	5	2	0	0	0	0	0	0	0	1	.000	.000
P	Trucks V.	28	1	2	1	0	0	0	0	0	1	1	.000	.000
Total	Team (team age)	32	155	5257	633	1345	227	47	77	588	517	533	.256	.322
Rank	Among 8 AL teams	NA		4	2	3	1	5	2	NA	4	5	5	6

Code: LH — Bats Left Handed; SwH — Switch Hitter; NA — Not Available[2]

1945 Detroit Tiger Team Pitching

POS	Player	Age	G	ERA	Won	Lost	SV	GS	GC	ShO	IP	H	R	ER	HR	BB	SO
SP	Newhouser H.	24	40	1.81	25	9	2	36	29	8	313.3	239	73	63	5	110	212
SP	Trout P.	30	41	3.14	18	15	2	31	18	4	246.3	252	108	86	8	79	97
SP	Benton A.	34	31	2.02	13	8	3	27	12	5	191.7	175	68	43	7	63	76
SP	Overmire F.	26	31	3.88	9	9	4	22	9	0	162.3	189	81	70	6	42	36

POS	Player	Age	G	ERA	Won	Lost	SV	GS	GC	ShO	IP	H	R	ER	HR	BB	SO
SP	Mueller L.	26	26	3.68	6	8	1	18	6	2	134.7	117	63	55	8	58	42
RP	Caster G.	25	22	3.86	5	1	2	0	0	0	51.3	47	25	22	3	27	23
RP	Wilson W.	32	25	4.61	1	3	0	4	1	0	70.3	76	40	36	4	35	28
RP	Eaton Z.	31	17	4.05	4	2	0	3	0	0	53.3	48	28	24	0	40	15
RP	Houtteman A.	28	13	5.33	0	2	0	0	0	0	24.3	27	17	15	1	11	9
SP/RP	Tobin J.	37	14	3.55	4	5	1	6	2	0	58.3	61	31	23	2	28	14
SP/RP	Orrell J.	17	12	3	2	3	0	5	1	0	48	46	18	16	1	24	14
SP/RP	Oana P.	37	3	1.59	0	0	1	1	0	0	11.3	3	2	2	0	7	3
SP/RP	Bridges T.	38	4	3.27	1	0	0	1	0	0	11	14	6	4	2	2	6
RP	Pierce W.	18	5	1.8	0	0	0	0	0	0	10	6	2	2	1	10	10
SP	Trucks V.	28	1	1.69	0	0	0	1	0	0	5.3	3	1	1	0	2	3
RP	McLaughlin P.	34	1	9.01	0	0	0	0	0	0	1	2	2	1	0	0	0
TOTAL	Team Age	28	155	2.99	86	67	16	155	78	19	1392.4	1305	565	463	48	538	588

1945 Detroit Tiger Fielding

Catchers	G	PO	A	E	DP	FP	PB
Swift Bob	94	358	60	5	12	.988	7
Richards Paul	83	361	44	2	7	.995	4
Miller Hack	2	4	1	0	0	.1000	0
Welch Milt	1	3	1	0	1	.1000	0
TOTAL	155	726	106	7	20	.992	11

Shortstop	G	PO	A	E	DP	FP
Webb Jim	104	215	343	25	71	.957
Hoover Joe	68	126	163	17	35	.944
Borom E.J.	2	3	4	0	1	.1000
TOTAL	155	344	510	42	107	.953

First Base	G	PO	A	E	DP	FP
York Rudy	155	1464	113	19	142	.988
McHale John	3	5	1	0	0	.1000
TOTAL	155	1469	114	19	142	.992

Second Base	G	PO	A	E	DP	FP
Mayo Eddie	124	326	393	15	91	.980
Borom E.J.	28	62	82	5	15	.966
Webb Jim	11	30	25	0	8	.1000
TOTAL	155	418	500	20	114	.979

Third Base	G	PO	A	E	DP	FP
Maier Bob	124	142	226	25	19	.936
Outlaw Jim	21	18	42	4	5	.937
Ross Don	8	6	18	1	0	.960
Borom E.J.	4	1	7	1	0	.889
TOTAL	155	167	293	31	24	.937[3]

Outfield	G	PO	A	E	DP	FP	LF	CF	RF
Cullenbine Roy	146	321	23	7	3	.980	2	0	145

Outfield	G	PO	A	E	DP	FP	LF	CF	RF
Cramer Roger	140	314	7	3	4	.991	0	140	0
Outlaw Jim	105	192	13	7	6	.967	82	17	8
Greenberg Hank	72	129	3	0	0	.1000	72	0	0
Hostetler Chuck	8	8	0	1	0	.889	6	1	1
Walker Hub	7	5	0	0	0	.1000	5	0	2
Mierkowicz Ed	6	8	0	0	0	.1000	6	0	0
Maier Bob	5	2	0	0	0	.1000	5	0	0
TOTAL	155	979	46	18	13	.983	155	155	155

Pitching	G	PO	A	E	DP	FP
Newhouser Hal	40	16	66	0	5	.1000
Trout Paul	41	13	65	9	9	.897
Benton Al	31	11	44	2	4	.965
Overmire Frank	31	11	33	2	2	.957
Mueller Les	26	6	20	3	2	.897
Wilson Walt	25	3	20	0	1	.1000
Tobin Jim	14	3	16	1	0	.950
Eaton Zeb	17	4	11	2	0	.1000
Caster George	22	3	9	0	0	.923
Orrell Joe	12	4	8	1	1	.1000
Houtteman Art	13	2	8	0	0	.1000
Oana Prince	3	0	1	0	0	.1000
Bridges Tommy	4	2	4	0	0	.1000
Pierce William	5	0	2	0	0	.1000
Trucks Virgil	1	1	1	0	0	.1000
McLaughlin Pat	1	0	0	1	0	.000
TOTAL	155	79	308	21	24	0.949[4]

1945 Detroit Tigers Team Leaders

Batting

Batting Average — Eddie Mayo .285
On-Base % — Roy Cullenbine .398
Slugging % — Roy Cullenbine .451
Games — Rudy York 155
At Bats — Rudy York 595
Runs — Roy Cullenbine 80
Hits — Rudy York 157
Total Bases — Rudy York 246
Doubles — Roy Cullenbine 27
Triples — Roger Cramer 8
Home Runs — York and Cullenbine 18
RBI — Roy Cullenbine 93
Bases on Balls — Roy Cullenbine 102
Strikeouts — Rudy York 85
Stolen Bases — Jim Webb 8
Singles — Roger Cramer 113
Extra Base Hits — Roy Cullenbine 50
Times on Base — Roy Cullenbine 250
Hit by Pitch — Cramer and Cullenbine 3

Pitching

ERA — Newhouser 1.81
Wins — Newhouser 25
Won-Lost % — Newhouser .735
Hits Allowed 9 IP — Newhouser 6.86
Base on Balls — Overmire 9 IP 2.33
Strikeouts 9 IP — Newhouser 6.09
Games — Trout 41
Saves — Overmire 4
Innings Pitched — Newhouser 313.3
Strikeouts Total — Newhouser 212
Games Started — Newhouser 36
Games Completed — Newhouser 29
Shutouts — Newhouser 8
Home Runs Allowed — Mueller & Trout 8
Base on Balls Allowed — Newhouser 110
Hits Allowed — Trout 252
Losses — Trout 15
Earned Runs Allowed — Trout 86
Wild Pitches — Newhouser 10

Sacrifice Hits— Roger Cramer 15
Grounded into Double Plays— Rudy York 23
Caught Stealing— Bob Maier 11
At Bat per Strikeout— Roger Cramer 25.8
At Bats per Home Run— Roy Cullenbine 29.1
Outs— Rudy York 467
American League MVP: Newhouser
The Sporting News: Player MVP Mayo, Pitcher MVP Newhouser[5]

Hit Batsmen— Tobin 4
Relief Games Finished— Castor 10

1945 American League Hitting Leaders

Batting Average
Stirnweiss— NYY .309
Cuccinello— CHW .308
Dickshot— CHW .302

Total Bases
Stirnweiss— NYY 301
Stephens— SLB 270
Etten— NYY 247
York— DET 246

Strikeouts
Seerey— CLE 97
York— DET 85
Byrnes— SLB 84

Slugging %
Strinweiss— NYY .476
Stephens— STB .473
Cullenbine— DET .451

Doubles
Moses— CHW 35
Binks— WASH 32
Stirnweiss— NYY 32

Stolen Bases
Stirnweiss— NYY 33
Case— WASH 30
Myatt— WASH 30

Games Played
York— DET 155
Cullenbine— DET 154
Etten— NYY 152
Stirnweiss— NYY 152

Triples
Stirnweiss— NYY 22
Moses— CHW 15
Kuhel— WASH 13

Extra Base Hits
Stirnweiss— NYY 64
Stephens— STLB 54
Moses— CHW 52

At Bats
Stirnweiss— NYY 632
Hall— PHA 616
York— DET 595

Home Runs
Stephens— STLB 24
Cullenbine— DET 18
Etten— NYY 18
York— DET 18

Hit By Pitch
Crosetti— NYY 10
Grimes— NYY 6
Hall— PHA 6
Meitkovich— BOS 6

Runs Scored
Stirnweiss— NYY 107
Stephens— STB 90
Cullenbine— DET 83

RBI
Etten— NYY 111
Cullenbine— DET 93
Stephens— STB 89

Hits
Stirnweiss— NYY 195
Moses— CHW 168
Stephens— SLB 165[6]

Base on Balls
Cullenbine— DET 113
Lake— BOS 106
Grimes— NYY 97

1945 American League Pitching Leaders

ERA
Newhouser— DET 1.81
Benton— DET 2.02
Wolff— WASH 2.12

Hits Allowed/9 IN
Newhouser— DET 6.86
Wolff— WASH 7.20
Potter— STB 7.47

Total Hits Allowed
Ferris— BOS 263
Newsom— PHA 255
Trout— DET 252

Wins

Newhouser — DET 25
Ferris — BOS 21
Gromek — CLE 19

Strikeouts

Newhouser — DET 212
Potter — SLB 129
Newsom — PHA 127

Saves

Turner — NYY 10
Berry — PHA 5
Caldwell — CHW 4
Johnson — CHW 4
Klieman — CLE 4
Overmire — DET 4
Reynolds — CLE 4

Innings

Newhouser — DET 313.3
Ferris — BOS 264.7
Newsom — PHA 257.3

Base on Balls Allowed/ 9 IN

Bonham — NYY 1.10
Leonard — WASH 1.46
Wolff — WASH 1.91

Complete Games

Newhouser — DET 29
Ferris — BOS 26
Gromek — CLE 21

Shutouts

Newhouser — DET 8
Benton — DET 5
Ferriss — BOS 5

Home Runs Allowed

Kramer — STB 13
Bevens — NYY 12
Grove — CHW 12
Newsome — PHA 12

Base on Balls Allowed

Reynolds — CLEV 130
O'Neill — BOS 117
Newhouser — DET 110[7]

Losses

Newsom — PHA 20
Kramer — SLB 15
Trout — DET 15

13

The Fall Classic

Nine "Cubbies" and their wives were sent to the boats.... After inspecting the small rooms the Cub players decided to get off that "tub" and demanded either they get rooms in the Book-Cadillac like the rest ... or the series could be played without them. The leader ... was captain Phil Cavarretta.

Peter Golenbock, *Wrigleyville*

The Tigers' pennant-winning victory in St. Louis added more bubbles to an already large, fired-up caldron in Detroit, Michigan. The city was bursting with excitement, with the end of the war bringing big new changes to an urban center that had to unload its industrial arsenal and retool its factories and stores to more domestic needs. The ever-increasing population of returning veterans and the imported labor forces that fueled the plants during the war had left Detroit overpopulated. The popular saying of the day was, "The joint is jumping!" That was certainly applicable at this time to the city of Detroit.

The World Series came along, and on the eve of the series a person couldn't buy or beg a place to sleep because of all the congestion. Every hotel was filled. Hotel managers doubled up guests by agreement with each other to meet the demand. The Book-Cadillac Hotel placed cots in a sample room vacated by a furniture convention. Every conceivable bit of space was being used to meet the large influx of baseball fans. The Detroit Convention and Tourist Bureau had arranged with the downtown hotels to handle as many of the visitors as possible in private homes, apartments and smaller hotels, and even solicited for spare rooms in hope of making the plan work. The place was not only jumping; it was shaking.[1]

Two Great Lakes passenger steamers were pressed into service during the emergency and moored at the foot of downtown Woodward Avenue in the Detroit River to take on the overflow. One hotel said it had turned down 10,000 applications for reservations within the last two weeks. Restaurants and bars set themselves for a crushing demand. The World Series was another facet to an already busy post–World War II society.[2] Thousands of people swarmed into Detroit daily. Celebrities came from everywhere. Heavyweight champ Joe Louis, just discharged, would attend all of the games in Detroit and Chicago.[3] Film and radio stars, the top political figures of the day, and of course the brass from major league baseball and other sports figures, had their own tickets.

Ten war veterans, four of them totally blind, the other six only partially blind, headed into Detroit for the series from Menlo Park, California. The Army flew them in and the *San Francisco Examiner* was handling the expenses of the party. Accompanying them were three "orientors" trained to work with blind patients. Their enthusiastic attendance at local games in California, despite their handicaps, caused them to be selected from the blind rehabilitation program at Dibble Hospital in California.[4]

Baseball notables arrived, including Will Harridge, the American League president, who came in from Chicago with his wife. Lew Fonseca, a retired 12-year major league veteran and former 1929 American League batting champion for the Indians, came in the capacity of a filmmaker to supervise movies that were being made of the series. The Book-Cadillac Hotel would house them, and the Statler Hotel would host Commissioner A.B. Chandler, along with National League president Ford Frick.[5] The Wabash and Michigan Central Railroads arranged for special trains to Chicago for local rooters.[6]

Everything else was on hold. The city ignored strikes and threats of strikes. The oil workers' strike had upset the city transportation systems. Buses and streetcars carried heavier loads because the service stations were shut down. Calls for cabs were heavier than ever and even they had to worry about fuel supplies.[7]

The Cubs were affected by the hotel schedules when they arrived in Detroit. They had dallied in making arrangements and were short on accommodations. Nine "Cubbies" and their wives were sent to the boats on the river. After inspecting the small rooms the Cub players decided to get off that "tub" and demanded either they get rooms in the Book-Cadillac like the rest of the Chicago gathering or the series could be played without them. The leader of the group was Cub captain Phil Cavarretta. Manager Charley Grimm had a problem of finding suitable quarters, and was busy with Secretary Bob Lewis until the early hours before he got the club housed in five different hotels.[8]

The Cubs were formidable opponents. They edged out the Cardinals for the National League Championship. Their American League pickup from the Yankees, Hank Borowy, had a record with the Cubs of 11–2. He had a league best ERA at 2.13, but most important he beat the Cardinals 4 times. His full season record was 21 and 7.

Besides Borowy, Chicago had a 20-game winner in Hank Wyse, and two veterans, Claude Passeau and Paul Derringer, who recorded 17 and 16 victories for the year. Their starting lefty, Ray "Pop" Prim, posted a 13–8 mark. It was an excellent pitching staff.

Captain Phil Cavarretta leads the Chicago Cubs into Detroit for game one (courtesy Dr. Paul Rogers).

Detroit lacked a .300 hitter, but Chicago had three of them: third baseman Stan Hack, .322; second baseman Don Johnson, .302; and Cavarretta, whose .353 topped the league.

Detroit, however, might have had a slight edge in the home-run department. Chicago's Bill "Swish" Nicholson had an off year but punched out 13 homers, and a young flashy outfielder, Andy Pafko, belted 12 of them, but no other Cub reached double figures. Cullenbine, York, Greenberg and Mayo, with 18, 18, 13, and 10 clouts, gave the Tigers a slight home-run edge.[9]

Pafko also drove in 110 runs, whereas Detroit had no 100 RBI man. Cavarretta, Nicholson and Lowrey contributed 97, 88 and 89 RBIs for Chicago, while Cullenbine's 93 and York's 87 RBIs were tops for Detroit.

Grimm was one of the most successful managers in the Cubs' history. This was his third National League pennant; the others had come in 1932 and 1935. A favorite of owner P.K. Wrigley, Charley was a character. He was nicknamed "Jolly Cholly" for his optimistic attitude, which made him popular with his players. His teams were known for their solid defenses, and were tops in fielding percentage and fewest errors. He depended on pitching and excellent fielding for a winning year.

The Cubs set a major-league record by winning 20 double-headers in 1945. Eighteen wins out of their first 19 double-headers also set a record.[10] Grimm's managerial move, much like Detroit's O'Neill, worked well during the year. While Detroit set a record for winning the pennant with the lowest number of wins (88), Grimm's Cubs posted an admirable 98–56 victory season. Harry Hollingsworth's famous or infamous chart, depending on one's bias, "How All 200 Pennant Winners Since 1901 Rank," lists this Cub team as number 36 out of the first 200 flag winners. The chart stops at the 2000 season. Even today this Cub team is highly rated. In comparison, this 1945 Tiger team ranked 179 out of 200 on Hollingsworth's list. It is simply amazing that the talent could be so far spread between the two teams.

So why was Detroit a 10–13 favorite? Hal Newhouser, the American League's MVP, gave them the edge. His fierce competitive spirit and talent made him almost unbeatable. Even though Hal, Benton and Trout were going into the series arm-weary and injured, Detroit had been given a pitching boost with the return of a healthy and well-conditioned Virgil "Fire" Trucks. And then there was Detroit's ability to have big-run innings. Their firepower could explode at any time for multiple scores.

O'Neill thought out his pitching schedule and said Newhouser would pitch the opener in Detroit; if he won, Overmire would pitch game two, and Trucks game three. If Newhouser lost, Trucks would start game two and Overmire game three in Detroit. Trout would open the fourth game in Chicago. O'Neill respected the Cubs; he said Detroit would win, but it would take six games to do that.

Trucks's return gave O'Neill confidence. He felt that Seaman Trucks would win any game he pitched: "I think he is faster than Feller and has the best curve ball I've seen all year. He can't miss."[11] Trucks was clocked at 105 mph with an Army radar gun earlier in the year. Much like power hitters, power pitchers have God-given arms and their fast ball is a gift. When he signed his contract, Trucks was so confident he'd make good that he ran off to a tattoo artist and had him pen a tiger on his right arm. When he pitched for Cochrane at the Great Lakes Naval Base, Mickey said he was the best pitcher he had.

Grimm had a healthy respect for Detroit, but believed it would be the Cubs who would win in six.[12] His 20-game winners would start the first two games.

Borowy would open in Detroit, then Wyse and Passeau would close the series there.

When asked what he thought about pitching the opening game, Borowy poured fuel on the writers' fiery pens by saying, "Naturally, I like the assignment of pitching against the Tigers in the opener. I always like to face clubs I can beat, and I think you'll find I've beaten this club pretty often." In fact, Borowy had beaten Detroit eleven times in his career, two of them that year as a Yankee, and Newhouser was one of his victims.[13]

Due to gas restrictions it would be a 3–4 series. Detroit would host the first three and Chicago the last four games if needed, so there would be no extra back and forth traveling and waste of energy. Briggs Stadium had been painted and maintenance crews were shining up the big park. Concession crews packed in huge supplies of hot dogs, beer and soda-pop for the vendors. Both infield and outfield were in excellent shape for playing.[14] The managers listed probable line-ups and batting orders for the first game of the series:[15]

Chicago (N)		Detroit (A)	
Hack, 3B	.322	Webb, SS	.199
Johnson, 2B	.302	Mayo, 2B	.285
Lowrey, LF	.282	Cramer, CF	.275
Cavarretta, 1B	.355	Greenberg, LF	.311
Pafko, CF	.297	Cullenbine, RF	.272
Nicholson, RF	.267	York, 1B	.264
Livingston, C	.254	Outlaw, 3B	.271
Hughes, SS	.248	Richards, C	.256
Borowy, P	11–2	Newhouser, P	25–9

The police force was ready for extra-hour duties, and the city had rearranged its bus and trolley schedules in anticipation of any urgent needs over the next three days. The WOP placed a ceiling on parking lot charges, which would run from 25 to 75 cents.

Meanwhile Red Borom had a problem he needed to take care of. As Borom explained:

Each player was allowed twenty tickets at six dollars each for the games in Detroit. This was a total of $360. I had requests for all twenty of them. But only six came, including my brother and his friend, plus my friend Fred Barnes, who was in the army on leave. He was in uniform and just when I thought I was stuck for 14 sets of tickets, Fred asked me for the tickets and said he'd get rid of them. I had to be at the ballpark at 10 A.M. to sign several dozen balls. Fred made the lobbies of three hotels jammed with ticket seekers. He gave a spiel about having to return to duty and would sell his tickets for what he paid for them. Well, he met me at the clubhouse and had a roll of bills in each pocket. The total was over $800, so I split it with him.

On October 2, both teams took a pre-game practice to check the field and acquaint themselves with conditions. It was cold at the stadium. Chilling, penetrating winds blew across the field. Players and spectators shivered in the frosty atmosphere. Trucks, Overmire and Trout all tuned up on the sideline. The Tigers, sporting turtle-necked jerseys, methodically went to work.

Grimm was a witness to some lusty hitting. In particular, Cullenbine, the switch-hitting outfielder, went in for some long-distance clouting. Greenberg, Mayo and York followed with some fence busting of their own. Tiger right-handers Caster, Bridges, Houtteman and Wilson pitched batting practice in anticipation of the Cubs' right-handed ace. Newhouser maintained his schedule by running about the field after the rains departed. Later big Hank Greenberg toed the pitching slab and pitched for 15 minutes. "Cobb ruined his arm doing that," warned an old-timer. Paul Richards was another who took a turn pitching. Richards came to the majors with the Dodgers as an 18-year-old short-stop and ambidextrous pitcher, but catching and teaching became his forte.

When Cullenbine banged out another one Grimm said, "He must have hit a thousand in there." Roy then parked one more into the upper deck, causing Grimm to yell out "Cut that out, Cullenbine. That is your 9,000th homer today. I hope Nicholson belts one his first time up. If he does he won't stop all through the workout. They never do." After more than an hour, rain fell and halted the Tigers' business. Two hours later the Cubs took the field and put in a session of forty-five minutes, allowing Nicholson, Pafko and Cavarretta the opportunity to deposit baseballs in the upper right and left-field decks as well. When the "Big Nick" finally got his turn he drove one upstairs and then concentrated on liners into the lower stands. Cavarretta managed to put two out before the session ended.[16] York observed the hitting and commented, "They're dangerous."[17] All the Cub hitters seemed to enjoy the better hitting background. More rain fell and the tarpaulins were spread out, the Cubs fled for cover, and practice ended. The stage was set to pull up the opening curtain for the next day's performance.

The new commissioner, Happy Chandler, made his debut, conducting the pre-series rules session with the managers, umpires and scorers. The umps for the series were Art Passarella, American; Lou Jorda, National; Charlie Berry, American alternate; Jocko Conlan, National; Bill Summers, American; and Lee Ballanfant, National alternate. Reporters wondered who explained the rules to whom.[18] The happiness of this occasion was enhanced for one Tiger player. Les Mueller's wife gave birth to a baby boy the day before the opener of the 1945 Series.[19]

These two teams had a history. The Cubs and Tigers had not distinguished themselves well in previous series play. The Cubs hadn't won a series since 1908 and it was over Detroit. The Tigers had won but one series and that was over the Cubs in 1935. There were five players, two from the Tigers and three from the Cubs, that had played in the 1935 World Series: Greenberg and Bridges from Detroit, and Lon Warneke, Hack and Cavarretta from the Cubs. Much was made of who would finally win their second World Series.

14

Game One

"[This] was the first time I had been to a World Series and the bunting is all over the field and the excitement is there.... It's a feeling of accomplishment. It's a feeling of excitement for your city.... Let's face it, you are playing the game as well as you can to win it for yourself and your team, but you are thrilled for your city to have a champion. Detroit fans were the greatest fans in the world.... Detroit had the greatest fans I had ever seen at that time."

Bill Pierce

As this series was a rematch between two old opponents, it was natural that players and fans would revisit memories of their last encounter with each other, the 1935 series, because baseball memories die hard. Warren Brown reported that "Smiling" Stan Hack was looking the field over in Detroit six years after the Cubs lost to the Tigers just before he dressed out for the annual mid-season All-Star Game in 1941. When Brown asked him what was going on, Hack replied, "I just wanted to see if I was still standing there on third base." Stan probably still had that same thought when he first looked at third base in Briggs Stadium for this 1945 series. In 1935 Tommy Bridges had given up a lead-off triple to Hack in the ninth inning of game six with the score tied at 3 each. Bridges left him there by retiring the next three hitters. Detroit then scored the winning run in the bottom of ninth, ending the series and giving the Tigers their first world championship.

From his box seat in Briggs Stadium, Happy Chandler basked in the limelight as photographers took numerous pictures of the new commissioner. Known as the Kodak manufacturers' best friend, he posed for every 2-A Brownie in Detroit, throwing out "first balls." Over 54,000 fans, who had braved bitter cold and shivering winds, waited patiently for the ceremonies to conclude and the first pitch of the World Series.[1]

It was more like football weather than baseball. Baseball should be played in the Indian summer of a fall season, but the temperature registered slightly above a wintry 36-degree mark that morning. It was so cold that Hank Borowy

Hank Borowy's strong shutout pitching in game one gave the Cubs a jump-start for the series (Brace Photo).

used hot bricks under his jacket between innings to keep limber. He used one as a foot warmer and another on his arm.[2] Like most pitchers, he hated working in cold weather. He said, "My big toe was frozen until 'Doc' Lotshow brought some warm bricks to warm my feet between innings." Hal Newhouser tried to warm his hands in the dugout on an electric heater.[3] Prince Hal received a pain-killer shot that was injected into his left shoulder before the game. After that, aspirin was the only medication he needed.[4] The growth in the shoulder area was "an enlarged muscle, like what Walter Johnson had," said O'Neill. The writers referred to that analysis in the managerial guild as psychology. The scribe Red Smith explained, "Newhouser wore a high collar dickey of black jersey beneath his shirt. The collar was not for warmth but so when they fill the bases nobody can see the lump come up."[5]

Despite the weather, the excitement of the first game spread throughout the city. The war had ended and people clapped for something else beside a victory in the trenches or on the high seas. It was a time to relax, a time to rejoice instead of stressing through another day's news of battles. The 1945 World Series was a good reflection of our nation's emotions at that time. The series set attendance records. The press, radio and film media carried it to markets throughout the country and the world.

A couple of rookies, Pierce and Houtteman, took in the scene with all the enthusiasm of their youthful years and watched the famous and the important in a setting of such pre-game celebration that it produced a feeling of pride in the home-bred Detroiters. They would be hard pressed not to be proud of being part of this setting and their city.

Pierce remembered:

> The World Series itself, I mean, to me it was the first time I had been to a World Series and the bunting is all over the field and the excitement is there. The people in politics are there and those are people you never had to meet before. It's a feeling of accomplishment. It's a feeling of excitement for your city. When you win it, you win it for yourself, let's face it, you are playing the game as well as you can to win it for yourself and your team, but you are thrilled for your city to have a champion. Detroit fans were the greatest fans in the world. I don't care if it was football, baseball, hockey, or basketball, Detroit had the greatest fans I had ever seen at that time.

Even before the first pitch had been thrown, the New York, Washington and Chicago writers had a field day denigrating both clubs. New York writer Dan Daniel, in his article of September 27, 1945, ranked both teams among "the all-time stumblebums." He reasoned Chicago had been defeated in seven of their last nine Series opportunities and Detroit had lost five out of six appearances in the Fall Classic. At the start of the festivities, Chicago's Warren Brown, a writer for the *Chicago Sun* and the *Chicago American*, the H.L. Mencken of sportswriters in 1945, and a Baseball Hall of Fame writer, was asked who he thought would win the World Series. He replied with his historical line, "I don't think either one of them can win it." Frank Graham, another New Yorker, later wrote in his gentle poetic style of the two combatants, "It's the fat men versus the tall men at the office picnic." The *Washington Post*'s reporter Shirley Povich spared no one in his reporting. Many of the writers were scathing, sarcastic, and insulting in their observations of this World Series. Brown wrote a chapter about the 1945 series in his book, *The Chicago Cubs*, and named it "World's Worst Series."

The reporters did the teams an injustice. It was far from the worst of the World Series contests and, even though the scribes attempted to throw a negative slant upon it, the general public enjoyed it greatly. It wasn't a smooth and elegant series, but it was an interesting and exciting series that went the full seven games and had both good and bad play within it. Baseball has always been that way no matter what teams are playing; stuff happens. The players played as well as some and not as well as some other players in previous World Series games. The bottom line was that they played in a difficult time and for that alone they should have some credit.

Mueller had some thoughts about the negative writers and said:

> Yeah, well, I thought that was ridiculous. That actually made me angry because I thought it was very unfair, not so much for myself, but what are they thinking of these guys like Stan Hack and Cavarretta, Greenberg, Cramer, Trout, Rudy York and Cullenbine? These guys had played for years in the big leagues. It was typical; something to write that would cause comment. It was the big leagues and there was no question that there were a few players on each team that weren't big league ball players. I always felt myself that I was a big league ball player. I didn't feel out of place. Most of the clubs thought it was overrated and they talked too much about it, because all the ball clubs had players that either had been in the big leagues for several years, or a number of them that played a lot more years after the war in the big leagues."

The stuff that happened to Newhouser in game one, however, was bad. To the utter amazement, dismay, and confusion of 54,637 frostbitten fans, Detroit could not field, pitch, hit or run the bases with any aptitude, expertise, proficiency or elegance befitting a champion. Losing a game is one thing if you play well, but to lose with the sloppiness that the Tigers displayed for that game was something fans in any city would not tolerate. Before the finish, fans that had come to cheer left booing their heroes.[6]

Newhouser, a twenty-five-game winner and the pride of Detroit, was jarred. He was the victim of a poorly played inning by some of his mates, and an inning of his own making when the Cubs' hitting attack led to his quick dismissal from the mound.

The *Washington Post*'s Povich jotted some short notes from the crowded press box as the innings went by and used them in his "This Morning" column to run the next day. He began by addressing the weather, which was bad. The cold air and the wind made everyone uncomfortable and it was not a suitable day for the grand old game of baseball. He said, rightly so, that the weatherman was giving the series a cold stare and was keeping the sun under wraps.[7] The new commissioner threw out the first pitch of the series to Detroit's catcher Richards, and the Washington reporter can't help but mention that it looked like a knuckler floating up there. He might have been lamentably thinking that it should have been the Senators and their knuckle-ball staff facing the Cubs.[8]

The first hitter Newhouser faced was Smiling Stan, the Cubs' third baseman. He induced him to ground out to his counterpart at third, the Tigers' Jimmy Outlaw. The next hitter, Don Johnson, the Cubs' second baseman, bounced a single over second base, a hit that barely squeaked through the infield. Without hesitation and respect for Richards's strong throwing arm, Johnson stole second. He aggressively went into the base, cutting second base-

Richards applies tag with Newhouser backing up the play, during a regular season game. In the first game of the 1945 Series, however, the reliable Richards was guilty of two passed balls, and allowed base runners two stolen bases out of four attempts (Paul Richards' collection, Waxahachie Museum, Waxahachie, Texas).

man Mayo's fingers. The Cubs came to play hard.[9] The two second basemen became a cooperative pair, sharing the same pair of sunglasses, exchanging them at every half inning. Johnson's aggressive slide didn't seem to ruin the relationship, as Mayo knew it was all part of the game.[10] The Cubs had speed and they were trying it out in the Tigers' lair.

Lowrey then hit a fly to Cramer in center. Now with two outs it seemed like Newhouser could work his way out of the inning. But Cavarretta hit a slow dribble to Mayo, who was playing in his usual deep position. Umpire Lou Jorda called Cavarretta safe, and that opened the floodgates. Cavarretta's speed barely beat the throw by Mayo and Johnson moved over to third. The fans thought he was out, but of course he wasn't.

When Richards allowed a passed ball, Johnson scored the first run of the series. Povich showed his disgust for both Newhouser and Richards by saying Chicago played as though they had little respect for either. "Johnson singled as if he never heard of Hal Newhouser and then stole second as if he never heard of Paul Richards." After Richards allowed a passed ball that gave the Cubs the first run of the series, the reporter penned, "Thus far, Richards is distinguishing himself in a positively negative sort of way."[11]

Cavarretta moved to second on the passed ball. Then Detroit intentionally passed the dangerous hitter, Pafko, to set up a force play at each base. Swish Nicholson, a former NL home-run champion, hit a long, high, fly ball to right field. Cullenbine moved backwards below the upper deck overhang, with his arms up, and lost sight of the ball. When he couldn't see the ball he thought it had found its way into the upper deck for a homer. Much to his surprise it dropped just short of the upper deck, fell through his extended arms, and caromed away from the startled fielder. By the time the ball was retrieved, both runners had crossed the plate and Nicholson was standing on third. O'Neill came out for a chat, but decided to continue with Newhouser.

The Cubs' catcher, Livingston, rifled a bullet to right field for the only really legitimate hit of the inning. Nicholson trotted across the plate for the 4th run of the inning. The crowd was silent and then a few boos could be heard throughout the stadium. When Livingston tried to steal second, Richards awoke and rose up from his sleep, and gunned him down with a perfect peg. Povich accurately summed up the situation by saying, "It's 4–0 Cubs, at the end of the first inning and for a team that has to step on the gas to catch up the Tigers are in the wrong town. What with both Borowy and Detroit's oil workers throwing strikes, it does not look good for the Tigers."[12]

Detroit looked like they might still make a game of it. Webb and Mayo led off the bottom of the first with back-to-back hits, but Cramer crushed those hopes by hitting into a double play. Detroit had opportunities because Borowy had trouble locating the plate, but the Tigers couldn't take advantage of it. Greenberg and Cullenbine both walked, and then York popped out for the last out. Newhouser, however, hadn't given up by any means. He proceeded to make sure the ball would not be put into play in the second inning by striking out the next three batters in 1-2-3 order. Borowy continued to feed off of double plays with the Cubs' slick-fielding infield. Outlaw popped up, Richards walked, and both were erased when Newhouser hit into a double play.

In the third the Cubs caught up with Newhouser, and all of their hits were streamers, not a cheap one in the lot. Johnson doubled over Cramer's head in center. Cramer caught the ball after lunging for it, but then dropped it. Now the cloud that shadowed Newhouser's face showed he wasn't pleased with the behavior of either the Cubs or his mates.[13] Lowrey's sacrifice put Johnson on third and he scored on Cavarretta's clean, crisp single. Pafko powered a double to left center, knocking in Cavarretta. When Livingston drove a hard single into the outfield for his second hit the score went to 7–0.

Newhouser was forced to take that long walk to the dugout and Benton made his appearance from the bullpen. On the way down the dugout steps, amidst the noise of boos, Newhouser's disposition changed from "Prince" to "Hurricane Hal." He grabbed the knob of a bat and quickly departed into the corridor that led to the clubroom. Players listened to the light bulbs popping as he moved through the tunnel into the clubhouse and wondered what damage would be done to the facilities.

Referring to the Detroit player's skills, Povich scribbled, "That performance will never be surpassed in World Series history.[14] Not without an investigation, at least."

In the bottom of the third, Webb grounded out, and Mayo struck out. Then Borowy had another wild streak. He walked Cramer and hit Greenberg with a pitch, but Detroit again failed in the clutch when Cullenbine popped up to second.

The Cubs pitched Greenberg tough. Borowy didn't give him any good pitches. A fast ball clipped his hat and removed it from his head. An inch lower and he wouldn't have been a problem to the Cubs for the rest of the series.[15]

Benton settled in and put the Cubs down with little difficulty. Hughes flied to Cramer and Borowy whiffed for out number two. Hack beat out an infield hit when Benton, York and Mayo could not reach the ball, which was hit a little to the right of the mound. But Benton's sinker ball retired Johnson on a grounder to Outlaw ending the inning.

Detroit did nothing in their half of the inning and Tobin took over the pitching chores for the fifth. He flipped his flutter ball past the Cubs and shut them out.

Detroit opened their fifth with a base hit by Mayo.

Andy Pafko (courtesy Dr. Paul Rogers).

After Cramer fouled out, Greenberg lined a hard single to center field. Mayo then challenged the throwing arm of center fielder Pafko, and Andy's throw landed in Hack's glove at third like the sound of a rifle shot. Mayo slid head-first into the base, more than just a trifle late. Umpire Jocko Conlan, resplendently dressed with his usual bow tie, called him out without hesitation. Povich's comment was, "The darnedest thing just happened. Eddie Mayo, the smartest guy on the Tigers, tried to go from first to third on Greenberg's single at a time when the Tigers were seven runs behind and was thrown out. The Cubs will be glad to learn that Mayo represents the Tigers' best baseball brains.... [T]hey will assume they have nothing more to fear from the Tigers."[16]

The next inning Tobin again whitewashed the Cubs with little trouble. The Tigers' sixth was another frustrating inning. York led with a single, Outlaw was safe on an infield hit to Hack, and the runners were on first and second, but Richards and Tobin flied out and Webb grounded out. Detroit had watched another opportunity slide away.

The weather demanded Povich's attention again: "This is the same kind of a raw afternoon that prompted the late Joe Jacobs' immortal crack of the 1935 Cubs-Detroit series after he was inveigled into attending a game despite his protests of fresh-air poisoning. Shivering in the cold that day, Fight Manager Jacobs gave tongue to the famous 'I shoulda stood in bed' line that will live forever in American literature."[17] Indeed, it was a cold, cold day for a baseball game.

Another reporter cracked, "York's long single in the sixth was one any hitter could of [*sic*] had a double on and if that was all they could show the Cubs the Tigers ought to throw the towel in and spare us the rest of the games."

Tobin retired the first two hitters he faced in the seventh and then broke down, allowing two runs. With two outs, National League batting champion Cavarretta pounded a Tobin floater into the upper deck in right field for the first home run of the series. As Captain Phil trotted around the bases the heavy envelope of silence fell upon the faithful few. The depression muffled the crowd as they sat in disillusionment. Pafko followed with a single. He stole second on Tobin, and went to third on another Richards passed ball. Then Nicholson's single scored the final run.

Mueller threw the last two innings for Detroit without allowing any runs or hits. This was the last time Mueller would toe the rubber for the Tigers during the regular season.

Borowy was cruising and he had no problem retiring Detroit in the last two innings. He recorded a 6-hit 9–0 shutout, and put the Cubs up 1–0 in the Series. Povich's comment summed it up: "The score is 9–0; Cubs at the finish, the same score by which forfeited games go into the record. It's obvious that the Tigers could have achieved the same result by not showing up today."[18]

Borowy pitched a fine game in shutting out the Tigers, but in the first six innings, Detroit left ten men on base and two others were wiped out on double plays. Tiger fans couldn't believe that this was the same Newhouser who had humbled the American League sluggers for the past two years. His performance and the play of his mates ended in a humiliating defeat. They seemed to be outclassed in every phase by the Cubs.

The betting odds switched almost immediately after the game and the Cubs became favored. The Bruins mauled a docile Tiger club that muffed scoring chances and baseballs in the field. The box score showed an amazing statistic by relating no errors for either team.

Red Borom thought: "Well, he [Newhouser] just had a bad day that day, and they got to him early. But he did come back and we wouldn't have won the World Series without him." Mueller commented: "It was expected that Newhouser, win or lose, would pitch a tough game, but it was just one of those things. On a given day a bad team can beat the very best team, and the same with the players. A pitcher or hitter can have an off day. Evidently that is what happened to Newhouser, because he didn't have many days like that."

New York reporter James P. Dawson summed up the Detroit mood when he wrote, "The quiet of the Tigers' clubhouse was understandable. They had no cause for celebration or demonstration. They acted as they were expected to act, with an air of the completely suppressed, moody, irritable, and unresponsive to sympathetic, encouraging talk of the morrow. From Manager O'Neill down the line to the bat boy, they were sobered. Their wings had been clipped. Their hopes had suffered a setback."[19]

Moving to the Cubs' locker area, Dawson wrote: "Grimm held his forecast of a Cub victory in six games and said, 'The break for us came when Cavarretta beat out that hit to Mayo, after Johnson's steal. After that it was easy. Newhouser was in the hole several times and we just hit every time he got the ball over. Nevertheless, he's a great pitcher, don't forget that.'"[20] "O'Neill offered no excuses," said Dawson, and quoted the manager, "'There is nothing you can say about a 9-to-0 beating; they just clubbed us plenty. They deserved to win. They had class today. But, tomorrow's another day.'"[21]

The whipping was the worst first Series game shutout score since Dizzy Dean beat the Tigers and Elden Auker in 1934, 11–0. The only other 9–0 shutout first Series game was back in 1905, when the Giants' Chris Mathewson beat the Athletics 9–0.[22]

Newhouser had calmed down by now and offered his thoughts about the pounding. "I feel terrible. I had plenty of stuff and my control was all right. If only I could have gotten past that first inning things would have been different. But Johnson stealing second was one of the things that started them off."[23]

Of Newhouser's catcher, Dawson reported his opinion of the game this way: "Richards was critical of himself, not particularly because of two passed balls, because one was a knuckler and the other he was too quick with his motion when he thought he had the ball in his glove. But he resented strongly Johnson's theft of second right after the first hit of the game. 'He never should have got away with that. Shucks, he had no start on me. I should have caught him had I made a good throw. There were three times we could have gotten off the hook in that first inning and it would have been a different ball game. That stolen base, the scratch hit to Mayo and Nicholson's triple.'"[24]

Cullenbine was quoted as saying, "I should have caught Nicholson's triple which slipped off my fingertips when I got under the ball near the stands. I would have grabbed it if I made a one-handed stab for it on the run."[25]

Cramer said the ground was slippery and wet after the recent rains and that's why he fumbled around in center field like he did.[26]

Detroit must not have believed what the gossip said about the machine-gun arm of Pafko when Mayo was easily thrown out. "Handy Andy" chopped him down with authority on both attempts. Mayo said little except that the spiked index finger of his right hand wouldn't bother his return for the next day's game.[27]

Writer Joe Williams reported, "The Tigers not only looked like a bad ball club in the opener, but, to confirm it, played bad baseball." Williams went on to list the sins of the day and then made a telling comment by saying, "To one who has seen them only at scattered times it was astonishing to note the group lack of speed. Few of the Tigers can run, and Greenberg and York, their long hitters, must hit the ball for deep distances, to get extra bases and be of help in rallies."[28]

The Tigers didn't feel the series was lost by any means. Doc Cramer sounded the keynote for the Tigers' dressing room. "They're still a long way from home," he said.[29]

Cullenbine followed that with, "Sure, I'd rather lose that way than 1 to 0, they just beat our brains out."[30]

Richards added, "We didn't guarantee to beat 'em four straight."[31] Perhaps he hadn't heard Mayo's quote on the train ride home after Detroit clinched the pennant.

Columnist Arthur Daley of the *New York Times* described the atmosphere in Michigan when he wrote, "It was a very glum crowd which filed out of Briggs Stadium after the game. With the incomparable Newhouser beaten, Detroit hopes were lower than the mercury in the thermometer. And brother, that was pretty low."[32] In Adrian I was a sad and confused eleven-year-old trying to hold back tears. It was difficult to understand how my Tigers lost so badly. I thought maybe the Tigers are not as good as I thought they were. I hoped the Tigers wouldn't embarrass themselves in tomorrow's game. Povich's words in his game summary went through my heart like a dagger: "The Tigers were a hapless bush-league outfit today."[33]

Game One, 10-03-1945, at Briggs Stadium in Detroit

Chicago	Pos	AB	R	H	RBI	PO	A	E
Hack	5	5	0	1	0	3	0	0
Johnson	4	5	2	2	0	3	4	0
Lowrey	7	4	0	0	0	1	0	0
Cavarretta	3	4	3	3	2	8	1	0
Pafko	8	4	3	3	1	4	1	0
Nicholson	9	4	1	2	3	0	0	0
Livingston	2	4	0	2	2	5	0	0
Hughes	6	3	0	0	0	2	4	0
Borowy	1	3	0	0	0	1	1	0
TOTALS		36	9	13	8	27	11	0

Pitching	IP	H	R	ER	BB	SO		
Borowy (W)	9	6	0	0	5	4		
CHI (Line Score)	4	0	3	0	0	0	2	0
DET (Line Score)	0	0	0	0	0	0	0	0

DET	Pos	AB	R	H	RBI	PO	A	E
Webb	6	4	0	1	0	1	2	0
d. McHale	PH	1	0	0	0	0	0	0
Mayo	4	4	0	2	0	4	1	0
Cramer	8	3	0	0	0	6	0	0
Greenberg	7	2	0	1	0	0	0	0
Cullenbine	9	3	0	0	0	0	0	0
York	3	3	0	1	0	8	0	0
Outlaw	5	4	0	1	0	1	4	0
Richards	2	2	0	0	0	7	2	0
b. Hostetler	PH	1	0	0	0	0	0	0
Newhouser	1	1	0	0	0	0	1	0
Benton	1	0	0	0	0	0	0	0
a. Eaton	PH	1	0	0	0	0	0	0
Tobin	1	1	0	0	0	0	1	0
Mueller	1	0	0	0	0	0	0	0
c. Borom	PH	1	0	0	0	0	0	0
TOTALS		31	0	6	0	27	11	0

a. Struck out for Benton in 4th
b. Grounded out for Richards in 9th
c. Grounded out for Mueller in 9th
d. Flied out for Webb in 9th.

Pitching	IP	H	R	ER	BB	SO
Newhouser	2, ⅔	8	7	7	11	3
Benton	1, ⅓	1	0	0	0	1
Tobin	3	4	2	2	1	0
Mueller	2	0	0	0	1	1

DOUBLES: Johnson, Pafko. SB: Johnson, Pafko. TRIPLES: Nicholson. DP: Cubs 6–4–3, 4–6–3. HOME RUN: Cavarretta. PB: Richards, 2. HPB: Greenberg by Borowy. LOB: Chi 5 — Det 10. ATTENDANCE: 54,637. TIME: 2:10. UMPIRES: Summers, Jorda, Passarella, Conlon.

15

Game Two

"I'll tell you something about Al Benton. When the shares were cut up ... they gave me a half of share.... I didn't argue about that and I thought it was great. Benton ... said, 'Well, I think you should have ... a full share.... I don't think we would have won without you.' He wrote me out a check for $100. He said that is what it would cost each player to give me a full share. I said, 'Al, I don't want that.... I'm happy to get what I got.... He said, 'You take it or I'll stuff it up your nose.' He was ... 6'5" and weighed about 240 lbs. I wasn't going to argue with him so I took it.... He insisted so I had to take it, because I didn't want to get beat up on."

Virgil Trucks

It was a very moody, sullen and chilled crowd that filed out of Briggs Stadium after the first game of the 1945 Series. The peerless Newhouser had lost and Detroit's hopes were lower than an anchor that held the boats in the middle of Lake Erie.

The Yankee castoff, Borowy, had received perfect support, while the Tigers, by contrast, seemed to have the willies in the field although the box score showed no errors. The slowness of Detroit in fielding, their bad decisions on the bases, and poor clutch hitting gave the sportswriters much fuel for a rip-roaring fire.

The victorious Cubs manager, Charley Grimm, looked up his friend Warren Brown, who had predicted that neither team was capable of winning, and asked him, "How come?" "Because I've seen both teams play," replied the seer of baseball writers.[1] Something had to happen to change such a depressing media outlook.

The Cubs were deciding how to pitch the dangerous Greenberg. Borowy, in the first game, had walked him, hit him with a pitch, allowed him to line a single, and then fanned him in his last at bat. He had kept the big slugger at bay.

When Detroiters woke up the temperature had jumped 10 degrees higher than the previous day.[2] A very welcome 60-degree reading by game time allowed favorable weather conditions for the second spectacle. It was a new day and a new opportunity.

Spirits went up with the change in the weather, and a young, confident Alabama right-hander rose to the challenge. Virgil "Fire" Trucks knew he could beat the Cubs because he had pitched against them as a member of the Great Lakes team a year earlier. The Irish-Indian-American from Leeds, Alabama, was sure of himself, and he was cocked, loaded, and ready with that God-given fast ball to bring Detroit back into this series.

In spite of the dark clouds spread by the scribes, three thousand half-frozen fans were in line at the bleacher gates early that morning. It would be another sellout. Four boys from Brewton, Alabama, about 50 miles from Trucks's home town, had made their way to the front part of the line to see their old buddy pitch.[3] The procession of fans was led by two women who took their positions at 7:30 P.M. the night before and came equipped with blankets,

heavy coats, jugs of coffee and sandwiches. They spent the night curled up in the blankets. The series seemed to have enthusiastic fan support.[4]

The Cubs' players were having difficulties with the overflow of people that crowded their comfort zones. First it was the lack of hotel space that had led nine of them to be shipped out to boats on the river. That was settled by splitting the team up into a number of hotels. Now the Cubs' wives were seated in the outfield and out of the sight of the players, who were concerned about their seat location and their safety so far away.

The sailor Trucks and the soldier Green-

Virgil "Fire" Trucks (Brace Photo).

berg contributed to a much-needed win. With the war so recently ended, people were still in a patriotic mood, and in October of 1945 that mood superseded all other feelings. The band played its share of marching music, and filled the atmosphere with proud feelings for the red, white and blue. When Detroit won on the strong arms and heavy bats of former servicemen, the writers, almost to a man, jumped on the flag-waving bandwagon with such lines as the one Chicago's Arch Ward wrote in his *In the Wake of the News* column: "The Cubs are not the first strong team to learn you can't whip Uncle Sam's Army and Navy or the men who have made them the greatest fighting forces the world has known."[5] The second game of this Series went down in baseball history as the "Army-Navy" victory. When referring to Detroit's two heroes they called them Bluejacket Trucks and Captain Greenberg.

The photographers pleaded for the two starting pitchers to stand together and have pictures taken before the contest started. The confident Trucks had no problem with that, but the Cubs' superstitious starter, Hank Wyse, had to be coaxed out for the pictures. Later Wyse said, "I remember when we got to warming up; they wanted pictures of Trucks and me shaking hands. I shook hands and wished him good luck and walked off and he beat me; and I told myself: Damn, you all will never get me to do that again."[6]

In the first inning Trucks was wobbly as Hack beat out a hit to short. Hack took second when Johnson sacrificed to York. This was Hack's first of a three-for-three day, all of which were of the infield variety. Lowrey lined an honest hit to left and Smiling Stan headed for the plate. Greenberg, the left-fielder, snatched the ball off the first hop and rifled a perfect peg to Richards, who was blocking home plate. Hack had no chance and Umpire Lou Jorda called him out with authority.[7] The gem of a throw surprised Hack and the Cubs. They had been running at will up to now, believing the Tiger outfield would do them no harm. Lowrey had taken second on the play and was in scoring position, but now there were two outs. The old ball player turned commentator, Al Simmons, observed in a prophetic voice, "They're trying to be 'Fancy Dans' [on the bases and in the field]. That'll cost 'em."[8] He was right. Cavarretta rolled out to York, and the threat was over. No runs scored. Greenberg's assist changed the flow of events.

Wyse, the Chicago ace, threw only eight pitches to retire the Tigers in the first inning. Two simple fly balls and an easy high-fly-out quickly ended the inning.

Trucks whipped through the Cubs' lineup one-two-three in the second. Two infield pop-ups and a harmless fly to center made short work of the visitors.

In the Tigers' second inning, Rudy York was called out on strikes without taking a cut, and the fans made sure he heard them growl loud and clear.

Trucks had settled in, although Hack, with two outs in the third, picked up his second hit when York fielded his grounder and waved Trucks off the bag.

Rudy tried to race Hack to first. Hack outran York for his second hit. Trucks said, "York had a bad habit of waving off the pitcher covering first base. I was covering and he waved me off. He done [sic] that in my second game and it cost me."

Virgil focused on the hitter, Johnson, and struck him out to end the inning. The Tigers went gentle, one-two-three in the bottom of the third.

In the Cubs' fourth, with one out and no score, Cavarretta hit a routine fly to right center. Neither Cramer nor Cullenbine seemed to have a jump on it and the ball found safe landing. When Cramer was slow in retrieving it, Cavarretta took advantage of the nonchalant attitude, and challenged one of the best arms in baseball. He sprinted safely into second, stretching the hit into a double.[9] Pafko grounded out, but Nicholson singled sharply to right center, scoring Cavarretta. The Cubs again went up 1–0, but Trucks bore down, forcing the catcher Paul Gillespie to fly out and ending the threat.

Detroit threatened in their half of the fourth to no avail. Cramer led off with a hit to center and advanced to second when Greenberg grounded out to Hack. Cullenbine walked, bringing up York. The hard-hitting first baseman connected and lined a drive to center, but the ball found refuge in the glove of Pafko. Outlaw ended the inning by grounding out to Johnson.

Trucks continued to hold the Cubs in the top of the fifth. Hughes and Wyse both rolled out harmlessly. Hack lined a hit to center and took an extra base on Cramer for a double, but Johnson's simple grounder to Mayo ended the inning.[10]

Wyse was getting Detroit out rather well. He gave up but two singles to Outlaw and Cramer and a pair of walks to Cullenbine. As he approached Detroit's fifth inning, he had not allowed a run. Detroit's mighty run-producing lineup had played 13 innings without scoring a run. The Cubs' pitching had stymied the Tigers. When Richards flied to deep left and Trucks grounded out it looked like more of the same.

The old baseball adage said, "The best of things can happen with two outs." And it was to come true for Detroit in this fifth inning.

The Tigers' light-hitting shortstop, Webb, singled to left, and Mayo walked, putting runners on first and second, with two down. Cramer drove a single over third, and Webb touched the plate, ending the Tigers' scoreless drought. The game was tied 1–1. Mayo was standing on third and Cramer took his lead off of first.

The towering figure of Greenberg stepped into the batter's box. Wyse was in trouble. Greenberg hadn't done any damage so far. The decision to pitch to him was Grimm's. Charley decided, even with an open base and two outs, to pitch to him. Wyse went one and one and then threw a deciding pitch. It went out a lot faster than it came in. The former Army Air Force captain dropped a 3-run bomb into the bleachers. Detroit's first round-tripper of the series was a high caliber line shot that easily cleared the lower deck screen, 375 feet from

"Hammering Hank" Greenberg (National Baseball Hall of Fame Library, Cooperstown, New York).

the plate, and about 25 feet to the left of the center field flagpole. The crowd cut loose and emitted such a terrific clamor that the tumult rocked the stadium and echoed deep down Michigan Avenue. Big Hank's mates grabbed, hugged and mauled their slugger on his return. Even the reserved, sober president of the American League, Mr. Harridge, nearly fell out of his seat slapping Hank on the back.[11] When this sailor, Trucks, had his stuff, a 3-run lead was money in the bank. The Cubs managed but one more hit off the flamethrower. Detroit's four-spot held up for the rest of the day.

Just as quickly as Detroit erupted in the fifth, so quickly did the Tiger bats fall into a deep silence again. The mighty York gave the Cubs a scare in the sixth when he connected and drove a long drive to center that threatened to leave the playing field until the glove of Andy Pafko appeared. Pafko shocked the hometown fans by climbing up the fence and spearing the drive with finesse and grace. The hit actually went farther than Hank's homer but, when you look in the book, it was just the first out of the sixth.[12]

Secory pinch-hit for Wyse in the seventh and flied out. Erickson, in relief, threw two innings of shutout ball. The Tigers did threaten in the seventh. Webb, with one away, scratched out an infield hit. Lowrey then made a fine grab of Mayo's troublesome short-popper into left, but Cramer singled again, and Greenberg walked to load the bases. Cullenbine lined a hard shot into right, but Nicholson made an excellent catch to end the inning. The Cubs' outstanding defense had prevented a blowout inning.

Becker had the privilege of ending the game when he hit for Erickson with two outs in the ninth. Trucks finished strong, putting him away as his fourth strikeout of the day, and the last out of the game. The series was now even and the roar of the Tiger could be heard throughout the state. Detroit had that victory spirit as they entered the clubhouse, but their emotions were in check. There was no special horse play. They showed a professional appearance of just doing their job knowing that they would have to go out and perform again tomorrow. They still had to win three more contests.

The only noise came from the locker of Greenberg. The 6'4" giant, along with Trucks, was the center of the reporters' attention. Tobin, the former National Leaguer, strolled over to Hank's locker and Greenberg thanked him for coaching him on how to hit Wyse. He then revealed to the inquirers that Tobin knew Wyse and been sharing that information.[13] Greenberg always listened. A good tip for him went a long way.

Trucks responded to the writers as well. "I was relying on control, and I was trying to get the ball exactly where Richards gave the target," the 24-year-old hurler said. "Hank's home run helped everything. It seemed that I got some slick, smooth balls as the game wore on; ones that had not been thoroughly roughened up, and I lost my control midway in the game, but I never felt tired, and after Greenberg hit that homer I had no worries. I felt stronger at the finish than at the start. In fact I'm ready to go out there at them again right now."

Trucks was elated. "I felt great out there," he said, paused a moment, and flashed a grin before adding, "I feel better now." He also gave credit to the Navy Great Lakes manager, Mickey Cochrane: "Mickey taught me a lot about pitching and helped me improve my curve ball. If I am better now, he should get credit for it."[14]

The photographers called for pictures, but as usual Hank was modest about his achievement and wouldn't pose unless Virgil posed with him. One of the photographers asked Hank to plant a kiss on Virgil's cheek, to which the big guy replied, "What the hell, here we're supposed to be hard, rough, tough men and you want me to give the guy a kiss?" He refused to do that, but he did hug Trucks with a big bear squeeze and said to him, "You certainly pitched a beautiful game." Trucks merely grinned.[15] When asked what type of pitch it was, Greenberg replied, "I hit a curve, high and inside, and if I said I got a thrill out of it, it would be an understatement. We'll get started now, I'm sure."[16]

Richards was lavish in his praise for Trucks. "He's the one I liked to see out there with the assignment he handled today. He's been out of baseball for two years and doesn't even know the names of some of his teammates, because he hasn't been back long enough to get acquainted. Another fellow in his spot would hesitate about such an important job. But he just said, 'Give me the ball.' He seemed to tire about the fifth or sixth, but came on again, and at the finish he was stronger than ever."[17]

A vanquished Newhouser was smiling in a quiet corner. When asked what he thought, he said he was ready for another shot at the Cubs whenever O'Neill gave him the nod.[18] Cramer's bat found its groove and his three hits encouraged O'Neill in his concern about the lack of hitting. Cullenbine's slump, however, continued and he shook his head and moaned about the robbery Nicholson pulled on him when he picked off his hard hit with the bases loaded in the seventh.[19]

In the Cubs' dressing room the downhearted Wyse was still replaying Greenberg's homer. "He hit a curve that hung high inside as I was trying to get the outside corner of the plate. It wasn't even a strike. I didn't intend to put it there. I wanted it low and outside where I had been pitching him. I expected him to let it go past. York hit a better pitch, a low, outside sinker. But it didn't go into the stands."[20] Years later he said, "I heard Tobin, who used to be with the Braves, was calling pitches from the catcher. He was in the scoreboard calling pitches. I don't know for sure but I wouldn't doubt it."[21]

Manager Grimm was jovial in spite of the loss and praised Trucks for pitching a magnificent game. "Tomorrow's another day," he told his players:

Just like yesterday, today is only today. But I am going to start respecting Greenberg's arm. He threw a strike nipping Hack at the plate, and you knew as soon as you heard the crack of his bat that that drive of his was going some place in the fifth. Trucks pitched a fine game. Pretty good pitching: fast, very fast, and a good curve, don't overlook that. I haven't seen anyone in the National League as fast as him.[22] Wyse had good stuff. It was just one of those things. We have those Detroit outfielders on the run, turning first base, and we'll have them on the run tomorrow, too. I'll pitch Passeau and Livingston will catch."[23]

Back in the Tigers' lair Manager O'Neill, sitting at his desk in his fenced-in cubbyhole, said he was taking every game in stride, he then countered with, "I figure to throw left-hand pitching at the Cubs tomorrow and Overmire is the pitching choice, so we can take care of Nicholson and Cavarretta. Those are the guys we've got to stop." He waved the reporters to the dressing quarters and said, "Go out and talk to those fellows. They're the ones who won the ball game."[24]

The trivia question of the year was, "What American League pitcher won more games in one World Series than he had during the entire major league campaign?" The answer, of course, would be Virgil Trucks, who had one Series win and no season wins.[25]

Trucks and Greenberg were the difference in game two. The *New York Times* said, "Virgil's fast-ball was alive and his curve had sharper bends than a pretzel." A rumor spread that after the reporters left O'Neill, someone heard him whistling that tune "The Army and Navy Forever, Three Cheers for the Red, White and Blue!"[26]

When interviewed by the author, Trucks said, "Well, being defeated as we were in the first game 9–0, you would have thought the worst and beating your leading pitcher who had won 25 ball games that year, you would think we were in trouble. I don't know why they decided to pitch me in the second game, but they did. I was very fortunate to go all the way and win again through the hands of Hank Greenberg. If he doesn't hit that three-run homer for me I may not win."

Trucks related what that win meant for at least one of his teammates.

I'll tell you something about Al Benton. When the shares were cut up after the World Series they gave me a half of share, which I thought was very good. Benton came up to me and said, "Well, I think you should have gotten a full share. You pitched good in the last game of the year and you won a World Series game. I don't think we would have won without you." He wrote me out a check for $100. He said that is what it would cost each player to give me a full share. I said, "Al, I don't want that. I'm just happy to be here." He said, "You take it or I'll stuff it up your nose." He was about 6'5" and weighed about 240 lbs., I wasn't going to argue with him, and so I took it.

He was mad because they hadn't given me a full share. He was a great guy. I don't think he should give me his part and the other players not give me a share too. But that didn't bother me. I thought the players were very kind to give me a half of share for one game. I told him, but he insisted, so I had to take it.

Concerning the comments of the media about the shoddy plays in the Series, Trucks said: "I think the players all played their positions very well. That's what you have to do to win. They covered the ground they were supposed to cover and they executed the plays the way they were suppose to be executed and that's why we won. I frankly say and believe that. I was there and I saw it they all worked hard as well as the Cubs did. The Cubs worked hard and they did the best they could do. The Cubs' players shouldn't be ashamed of the job they had done."

The box score showed no errors for the second straight game. Povich gave the Tigers no quarter and wrote in the morning paper:

> The series standing is tied.... But darned if the Cubs don't look like the best ball club on the basis of what's happened.... Greenberg is the only reason why the Tigers are not two down in this series. Aside from that and Trucks' seven-hit pitching there has been little to delight the Detroit fans. Both yesterday and today, the dashing Cubs made the Tigers look like impossible dolts. That the Cubs have all the speed in this series is obvious. Hack made Cramer look like a chump again on a ball hit past Mayo, Hack ended up on second when Cramer failed to come up with it cleanly. Mayo was playing so deep because he no longer can get a jump on the ball and couldn't make the play when it came up. Cavarretta at first and Johnson at second make lumbering York and Mayo look like stationary guards. The most obvious superiority of the Cubs is in the outfield. Pafko, Lowrey and Nicholson are making the Tiger outfielders look like rank bushers. Tomorrow should be the hitters' ball game and the club that wins that will be the hefty favorite to take the series.[27]

After reading that, one might wonder why the Tigers didn't put their gloves away and just forfeit. But baseball is a strange and unpredictable game.

The headline of the day was "Run Over By Trucks."[28] Benton was right. "Fire" Trucks was worth a full share. For a season total of 18.2 innings, 5.1 of those on the last day of the season, and 13.1 in the World Series, Trucks earned a half share, which amounted to $3,221. 66.[29] He was worth every penny of that share and maybe more.

Game Two, 10-04-1945, at Briggs Stadium in Detroit

Chicago	POS	AB	R	H	RBI	PO	A	E
Hack	5	3	0	3	0	0	2	0
Johnson	4	3	0	0	0	2	4	0
Lowrey	7	4	0	2	0	3	0	0
Caverretta	3	4	1	1	0	8	0	0
Pafko	8	4	0	0	0	4	0	0
Nicholson	9	3	0	1	1	2	0	0
Gillespie	2	4	0	0	0	3	2	0
Hughes	6	3	0	0	0	2	0	0
Wyse	1	2	0	0	0	0	0	0
a. Secory	PH	1	0	0	0	0	0	0
Erickson	1	0	0	0	0	0	0	0
b. Becker	PH	1	0	0	0	0	0	0
TOTALS		32	1	7	1	24	8	0

a. flied out for Wyse in the 7th
b. struck out for Erickson in the 9th

Detroit	POS	AB	R	H	RBI	PO	A	E
Webb	6	4	1	2	0	0	4	0
Mayo	4	3	1	0	0	3	3	0
Cramer	8	4	1	3	1	2	0	0
Greenberg	7	3	1	1	3	2	1	0
Cullenbine	9	2	0	0	0	2	0	0
York	3	4	0	0	0	11	1	0
Outlaw	5	4	0	1	0	1	0	0
Richards	2	4	0	0	0	5	0	0
Trucks	1	3	0	0	0	1	1	0
TOTALS		31	4	7	4	27	10	0

Pitching		IP	H	R	ER	BB	SO
Chicago	Wyse (L)	6	5	4	4	3	1
	Erickson	2	2	0	0	1	1
Detroit	Trucks (W)	9	7	1	1	2	4

LINE SCORE   Chicago
(1.) 0   (2.) 0   (3.) 0   (4.) 1   (5.) 0   (6.) 0   (7.) 0   (8.)   (9.) 0

LINE SCORE   Detroit
(1.) 0   (2.) 0   (3.) 0   (4.) 0   (5.) 4   (6.) 0   (7.) 0   (8.) 0   (9.) X

DOUBLES: Cavarretta, Hack. HOME RUN: Greenberg. SACRIFICE:: Johnson. LEFT ON BASE:: Detroit, 7, Chicago, 8. ATTENDANCE: 53,636. UMPIRES: Jorda, Passarella, Conland, Summers.

16
Game Three

"When in hell are we ever going to get going?"   Tiger fan

"I remember his stuff was awfully good and he kept it low."
John J. McHale

"He's saying its cold, he's got arthritic fingers, but he must've had sandpaper in there because he shut us out on one hit."
Eddie Mayo

"He was throwing sliders ... but they were real good sliders."
Paul Richards

"His slider broke like a hummingbird."   Eddie Mayo

"My 'stuff' was our outfield."   Claude Passeau

"Good Old 'Mr. Chips,' what a sweetheart."   Charley Grimm

I bundled up for the cool weather outside, bolted from the breakfast table, and ran out the door for school. Sprinting to Toledo and Elm Streets, I joined the rest of the gang from the hill: Tony, Big Bill, Jimmy T., and Bobby C., on their way to school. It was Friday, the end of the school week, and there was one more game in Detroit before the series moved to Chicago. Everyone was excited about yesterday's Tiger win over the Cubs. I eagerly joined in the conversation and started talking about Greenberg and his home run. When our group passed through Monument Park, all of us waited a moment for the traffic to slow down before crossing a busy Church Street. Just as we were about to dash across the street to the school, Tony said, "Smitty, you know Greenberg is a Jew, don't you?" The question caught me by surprise and I replied, "What does that have to do with him playing ball?" "Nothing," he said, "I just wondered if you knew he was Jewish." Before I answered back, we had sprinted across the busy street, up the steps to St. John's Lutheran School, through the open door, and into the warmth of the hallway. The question went unanswered.

The truth was I didn't know he was Jewish, and for some reason that bothered me. I had never thought about it before. I wondered what the implication of being Jewish meant for a ball player, and came to the realization it didn't have any bearing at all on baseball. So I dismissed the importance of the conversation, but it produced a strange feeling within me.

Hank Greenberg struggled with discrimination when he entered organized baseball. As a minor league player in the agricultural South and a major league player in the northern industrial Midwest, the New York City native found himself in a very different culture and environment from the Bronx he grew up in. He heard vicious taunts, and found players taking cheap shots at him both at the plate and on first base. He had fights with teammates and challenged opposing players because of his religious heritage. As polite a gentleman as he was, young Hank could be a very tough guy who would react when pushed, insulted and challenged. The last time the Tigers and Grimm's Cubs met in the World Series in 1935, Greenberg was greeted with a barrage of insults from the Chicago bench. It was so bad that Umpire George Moriarty had to issue a strong warning that he would clear the bench if the Cubs didn't tone it down.[1] But that type of hate talk, or, as the players of the day would say, bench jockeying, had simmered down considerably after the war started, and in 1945, although it most certainly hadn't disappeared, one didn't hear as much of that type of raucous disrespect on the playing field. This World Series chatter was different from that of the mid-thirties. The rough and tumble dugout enmity and malice seemed to have become more restrained for the time being.

In fact Dan Daniel, writing for *The Sporting News* after the series ended, said, "I was impressed with the utter civility of the contesting players with each other. What a tremendous difference compared with the Tigers against the St. Louis Gas House Gang in 1934. Base runners did not try to cut infielders down around second. York and Cavarretta carried on considerable palaver with opposition whenever they reached first base. No enmity, no riding from the benches, just fine sportsmanship while playing."

It seems that war helps to keep sports in a proper perspective. The end of the war had tempered some of the racial and religious hatred in society as well, and if a person was a service veteran he was first of all an American through and through. A new generation had put a lot of the old bias behind it because of the international conflict that had caused so much death and sorrow. After the war a new culture began to appear in the United States that tried to avoid ethnic, racial and religious confrontations. Toleration was a part of a transition that was taking its first baby steps to find a place in American society.

It was reported, "David Greenberg, a retired business man from New York City, and father of Detroit's slugger Hank Greenberg, was perhaps the proudest father in attendance at this game. Hank proved he is a star in any uniform whether it is the uniform of a major-league athlete or Uncle Sam's military service." David Greenberg would have no problems in Detroit as his son was not only known but much loved and respected.[2]

Jimmy Outlaw commented about the question of Greenberg's Jewishness: "When I was around Greenberg that was all over I think, most of it. I got a book here that's got a lot of stuff in it that tells about when he first starting playing. You see, I didn't know him then, but my dealings with Greenberg were A-OK. He never even brought up religion. He never said anything about it, never said anything about my religion, and you wouldn't even know that he was Jewish.... He had already had his real good years at that time and his reputation was made."

Shirley Povich predicted a hitting contest for game three, but he was wrong: there was no resemblance to a hitting contest in this game. It would be dominated by pitching.

The World Series had its beginnings in the early years of the twentieth century, and the Tigers had won but one series in six attempts. That championship happened in 1935 over the Cubs. The Cubs won the pennant ten times, but only two World Series, both at the expense of Detroit, in 1907 and 1908.

Their first Series appearance in the 20th century was in 1906, when they lost to their southside cousins, the White Sox, 4 games to 2. In that series a Cub pitcher, Ed Reulbach, pitched a one-hitter that beat the Sox 7–1. Reulbach was a creditable hurler who won 181 games over 13 years. Three times he led the league in winning percentage. On October 10, 1906, he had a no-hitter going until the seventh, when first baseman John "Jiggs" Donahue slapped out the only hit of the game for the Sox, a single to center field. Reulbach, a nineteen-game winner that year, walked six men in the contest. When shortstop Tinker booted a grounder in the fifth, one of those walks accounted for the unearned run.[3] This game was considered the standard for the best-pitched World Series game in the history of baseball. That was about to change.

The Tigers put Frank "Stubby" Overmire on the hill for game three, and the Cubs sent Claude Passeau to the mound. They were a contrast in appearance and pitching style. Overmire, the shortest member of either club at 5'7", 170 lbs. threw lefty and hailed from Moline, Michigan. He broke even in 1945 with a 9–9 record. Stubby was not an overpowering pitcher. He changed speeds and pitched to locations. When he was on his game, he could frustrate hitters. He had a slider that kept batters off balance. After a few innings, however, batters could adjust and, if his control was off, they hit him sharply.

Overmire had that baby-faced look and that youthful apple-cheek appearance which could mislead someone into thinking he was a teenager. The huge Rudy York was standing arm in arm with him before the game when Cubs coach Richard "Red" Smith began to laugh at the contrasting sight and shouted out to York, "Who's that with you, Rudy, your little son?" Signed by Wish Egan, who found him on the campus of Western Michigan College where he played his college baseball, Stubby was a bargain at a $400 signing bonus for the Tigers.

He was a pitcher, however, who needed a fast outfield, a solid infield, and good batting support.[4] The short southpaw was expected to control the left-handed power hitting of Cavarretta and Nicholson.

Passeau, on the other hand, was a 6' 3", 198 lb., eleven-year veteran from Lucedale, Mississippi, and Grimm's most experienced pitcher. He had seen service with the Pittsburg Pirates and the Philadelphia Phillies before going to Chicago in 1937, where he became a consistent winner. In 1940 and 1942 he won 20 and 19 for the Cubs. He was a tough, competitive righty. He believed the inside of the plate belonged to the pitcher, and he pitched there with regular success. In 1945 he won 17 games for the pennant champions.[5] He became a victim of elbow calcium deposits during the 1944 season. Grimm's nickname for him, "Mr. Chips," probably was due to the elbow problem. He seemed to have overcome the elbow problem and bounced back into winning form for this year's Cubs pitching rotation.

Passeau had a special ballplayer's superstition. His uniform number was 13, as was his auto tag, the serial number on his rifle, and the last two numbers on his life insurance policy. His address was 113 London Street, he spent 13 years in the majors, and his name is 13 letters long.[6] When it came to pitching, however, the number 13 had nothing to do with it. He knew how to pitch. He did have a reputation for "doctoring" the baseball. He could treat a ball harshly by roughing it up and helping it to move in unnatural ways.

A tarpaulin covered the infield at Briggs Stadium through the night. It was removed thirty minutes before game time. Crews of 33 workers were needed to take away the overlay.[7] Detroit, once again, sold out the park. Even though the weather had not been very cooperative, the attendance was beyond belief. The largest of the three-day attendances for the games took place this day. A horde of 55,500 hungry baseball fans jammed the stadium eager to watch the Tigers devour the Cubs.[8]

The weather slowed the fans' movement to the park and it drizzled through out the morning. The weather, however, warmed up more

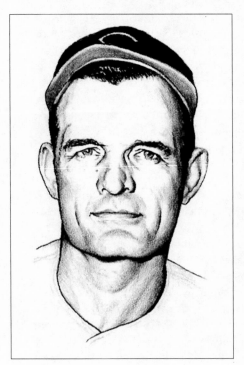

Claude Passeau (artwork ©1997 John Phillips, Perry, Georgia).

so than it had during the first two contests. About noon the sun tried to sneak out and showed itself, but it never quite made a permanent appearance. The rains began to let up, and under the gray skies and drizzle, the players prepared to play on a damp field.[9] There was a discussion of postponement of play and the new commissioner made the decision by stepping on the turf with one highly polished shoe. That action was followed by the words, "The game goes on." It was the first decision Chandler had to make in his new position.[10]

One item of interest that took place off the field happened to the commissioner, who was unable to reach his box between first and home at the prescribed time. It seems that he had lunch with Spike Briggs, the owner's son, and afterwards the two of them headed for the park in one of Detroit's super deluxe autos that the owner helped to furnish, and the limousine, halfway to the park, ran out of gas. Fortunately, Jr. knew to park the car and find a corner for the first trolley stop, which took them to the stadium.[11]

The spectacle of this pageant took place in the grandstand when 300 battle-maimed veterans from Percy Jones Hospital in Battle Creek, Michigan, were wheeled and carried to seats donated by fans. The hospital had been overlooked in the dispensing of passes, and after an appeal was made, more than 500 fans gave up their tickets for the vets.[12]

Sitting in the press box above home plate was the legendary H.G. Salsinger. He was one of the official scorers for this series. "Sal" first covered a World Series for Detroit in 1909 when Hughie Jennings' AL champs, led by a young Ty Cobb, lost to the Pirates in seven games. It is doubtful that there was anyone else who could claim they saw those 1907–09 Tigers play in those first Detroit World Series games from the press box. This would be the last time Detroit played a series Sal would report on.[13]

Passeau, this day, was an image of an artistic master of pitching on the mound at Briggs Stadium. Completely in control, and using all the cunning and trickery at his disposal, he turned the Tigers into kittens with intimidating sinking fast balls and wide breaking curves. After the game, Mayo said of Passeau, "His slider broke like a hummingbird."[14] He set the Detroit squad down in a mercurial sequence and faced but 28 hitters. With the exception of one walk and one single, the Tigers couldn't get to first base against him. His poise, control and sequence of pitches completely overwhelmed Detroit. The Tigers were shut out 3–0. The Cub hurler turned in the finest World Series pitching performance since 1906 and set a new standard for a pitched World Series game. It was a beautiful piece of professional pitching for the right-hander.

His teammates backed him up with outstanding performances in the field. Passeau had but one strikeout. Greenberg went down swinging in the second and everything else the Cubs fielded with the speed and energy that had won them the National League flag.

Rudy York, Passeau's old minor league roommate, knocked out the only hit, a long single in the second inning that rolled to the left-field wall, and might have been a double for another runner. Catcher Bob Swift picked up a walk to lead off the sixth inning, but a double play eliminated him. That was the sum total of the Detroit offense for the day.

It was the third time this year Detroit had barely avoided having a no-hitter thrown against them. Outlaw had dumped a catchable fly ball to the opposite field against Feller in Cleveland in Feller's 2–0 win on September 19, and Webb sliced a clean single over second base against the White Sox' pitcher Haynes on May 1, 1945, for the only hit in a 5–0 defeat. The silence of the Tiger bats was too much for one fan who leaped to his feet and loudly shouted, "When in the hell are we ever going to get going?"

Overmire gave it all he had and pitched very well. He kept Detroit in the game, giving up only four hits in six innings before leaving for a pinch hitter. The game was scoreless until the fourth. Then Lowrey banged a double against the wall in left. Greenberg didn't seem fast enough to catch up with it and it cleared his head. Cavaretta sacrificed Lowrey to third. Overmire walked Pafko to set up the double play possibility. The infield shifted for the pull-hitter, but Nicholson popped a lazy fly to short left. Shortstop Webb ran into short left field and reached out as far as he could for the ball. He came close to making a great play, but it was a dying quail, and what would have been a routine catch if he had been in his normal position dropped just short of his reach. Lowrey scored. This was Nicholson's third straight game in which he had knocked in a run.[15] He led all hitters in the series with five runs batted in, and the Cubs for the third time drew first blood. Stubby retired Livingston on a short fly to Cramer for the second out. It wasn't Stub's day. Hughes dumped a lazy fly into right for a single, and when Cullenbine failed to throw to the plate, Pafko scored from second. Povich's observations about Detroit's age, slowness and skills looked to be absolutely true.

Frank "Stubby" Overmire.

The Cubs picked up their last run in the 6th against reliever Benton. Livingston doubled off the wall in right and the Cubs again used a sacrifice, this time by Hughes, to advance the runner to third. Passeau helped his cause with a long fly to Cramer in center field to score Hughes for an added security run.

It was a cool, bleak afternoon for the home fans. The Cubs flashed a lot of leather at Detroit in that game. Hack robbed Mayo of a sure hit when he fielded a hot shot in the first inning and threw him out. Cavarretta dove to the ground to stab Mayo's second slammer in the fourth and tossed to Passeau for the out. Lowrey followed that up with a fine catch of Cramer's liner to left center. In the fifth, Hughes picked off a line shot by Outlaw to end the inning. In the sixth, after Swift had walked, Borom ran for him, and then the speedy Johnson made a fine grab of pinch hitter Walker's slow roller, picked it up, tagged Borom on the base lines and threw almost in the same motion to Cavaretta for a smooth, quick double play. Borom, of course, disagreed with the call: "Johnson missed the tag and the umpire missed the call. Johnson knew it and the ump knew it, but in the book I am still out."

After that, Passeau became so dominant that the Tigers offered only weak grounders, pop-ups and routine fly balls, which the Cubs handled with little effort. Pinch hitter McHale ended the torture when he popped out to catcher Livingston for the last out in the ninth. The Cubs swarmed Passeau, and the first to embrace him was Captain Cavarretta. Passeau headed for his catcher and gave him a big hug in appreciation of a job well done, and the rest of his mates congratulated him all the way to the locker room.

Detroit committed the first recorded errors of the series. Fortunately neither error led to any Cub runs. Mayo muffed a grounder by Hughes in the seventh, which put runners on first and third with two outs, but then Lowrey made the third out with a grounder back to the pitcher. In the ninth, with two outs, Hack singled and attempted to pull off a steal, but Richards, in for Swift, shot a bullet to shortstop Webb that would have made the third out, but Webb dropped the ball. The next hitter struck out so neither error caused damage.

In the clubhouse Passeau was informed of his historic performance, news that brought a smile to his face. He said, "The best things I had today were those outfielders making plays behind me. I had good control and took my time. I just got 'em out, one at a time." When asked again, "What was your best stuff, a curve or fast one?" he said, "My best stuff was our outfield."[16]

Manager Grimm blurted out, "What a ball game Mr. Chips pitched! Old number 13. Every time Passeau rattles his right elbow it sounds like china in a wash boiler. And our good friends over there — Mr. Hughes and Mr. Nicholson, it was those two hits those guys got that won for us! Those hits were just a couple of cuties. Both of them put together wouldn't have hit the screen. Good old Mr. Chips, what a sweetheart!" Grimm then cut loose with a piercing two-finger whistle that echoed throughout the room.[17]

The Tigers didn't have much to say in their dressing room. The reporters watched them file silently into the clubhouse to their lockers as if in a funeral procession. One of the reporters said, "O'Neill will be here in a minute and he'll say, 'You can't win if you don't hit.'" A few minutes later, O'Neill strode in and blurted out: "Well, you can't win if you don't hit."[18] O'Neill then spoke soberly while he peeled off his uniform, "Passeau was too much. He was just too tough." He then praised Overmire. "Frank pitched good ball, today. Neither one of the balls that drove in Chicago's runs off Overmire were hit soundly. Nicholson's single that scored Lowrey wasn't hit well; Hughes' hit to right that scored Pafko wasn't either. It's a tough one for Frankie to lose."[19]

Richards said, "He was making that perfect pitch, time after time, especially when he'd get behind a hitter. He was throwing sliders, but they were real good ones."

Cullenbine, who still hadn't had a hit, shook his head, remarking, "I just couldn't hit it."[20]

John J. McHale reflected back about the game. "I do remember his 'stuff' was awfully good and he kept it low. He had a lot of pitches that were tough to hit. He just baffled us completely."

Mayo, as reported in Bak's book *Cobb Would Have Caught It*, said, "What I remembered about that series is that it was cold, very cold. I remember Passeau pitched one game in Detroit. He was a great pitcher, but I think he pulled a snow job on the umpires and us. He had rheumatic hands, and had to twist the ball in his glove to get a grip on it. We were all so naïve. He's saying its cold, he's got arthritic fingers, but he must've had sandpaper in there because he shut us out on one hit."[21]

Les Mueller: "It's possible, I don't know, but I think he had a reputation for doctoring the ball even before that game ever started. He was a pitcher that would do that, you know. I think there was a tendency to do that in those days; especially your older pitchers ... some of them were still throwing spitballs, which were illegal."

Red Borom: "As to Passeau's one-hitter there was not much comment that I heard except from the older players

Harry "Peanuts" Lowrey (artwork ©1997 John Phillips, Perry, Georgia).

such as Bridges and Cramer, who said to give him credit as he'd been around a long time and pitched a good game."

Reporters pressed down on O'Neill and asked about future pitching plans. O'Neill replied, "We'll give 'em Trout, Newhouser and Trucks in the next three games and that ought to win the series for us."[22] It was the stuff the press was looking for. Trout, Newhouser and Trucks, the T.N.T. guys from the industrial arsenal of the world. That was the connection that would keep the patriotic line going.

O'Neill's words were not pie-in-the-sky kindling wood. The manager not only had faith and believed what he said, but he turned out to be a prophet.

The dashing Cubs had a two-one advantage and were in a position to end the Series. All they had to do was split a four-game series at home and they would be champions of the world for the first time since 1908.

Red Borom said: "As far as being down 2–1 in the Series all of us were thankful that Trucks won the second game, and I think he and Greenberg were the keys to the Series."

The representatives who promised to have everyone in Chicago for the game on the special World Series trains lived up to their word. The Tigers took the 4:30 P.M. train out of Detroit with reservations at the Hotel Stevens along Lakeshore Drive in downtown Chicago. Several American League executives, including league president Harridge, joined them. The Cubs left 15 minutes later on the next special. The last train, a newspapermen's train, finished the expedition, and departed at 5:30.[23]

The Cubs seemed to be such a peppier team and to have so much more life and fire than the Tigers. Perhaps it was the energy and warmth of manager Grimm.[24] He and his coach, Red Smith, brought a contagious attitude that projected enthusiasm. The teams had played 26 and a half innings, and Detroit had scored in only one of those innings. They had a lot to ponder on the way to the "Windy City."

Game Three, 10-05-1945, at Briggs Stadium in Detroit

Chicago	0	0	0	2	0	0	1	0	0
Detroit	0	0	0	0	0	0	0	0	0

Chicago	*POS*	*AB*	*R*	*H*	*RBI*	*PO*	*A*	*E*
Hack	Third Base (5)	5	0	2	0	1	1	0
Johnson	Second Base (4)	5	0	0	0	1	1	0
Lowrey	Left Field (7)	4	1	2	0	4	0	0
Cavaretta	First Base (3)	2	0	1	0	10	1	0
Pafko	Center Field (8)	2	1	0	0	3	0	0
Nicholson	Right Field (9)	4	0	1	1	3	0	0
Livingston	Catcher (2)	4	1	1	0	3	0	0
Hughes	Shortstop (6)	3	0	1	1	1	4	0
Passeau	Pitcher (1)	4	0	0	1	1	2	0
TOTALS		33	3	8	3	27	9	0

Detroit	POS	AB	R	H	RBI	PO	A	E
Webb	Shrotstop (6)	3	0	0	0	2	3	1
d. McHale	Pinch Hitter	1	0	0	0	0	0	0
Mayo	Second Base (4)	3	0	0	0	2	1	1
Cramer	Center Field (8)	3	0	0	0	4	0	0
Greenberg	Left Field (7)	3	0	0	0	1	0	0
Cullenbine	Right Field (9)	3	0	0	0	1	0	0
York	First Base (3)	3	0	1	0	12	0	0
Outlaw	Third Base (5)	3	0	0	0	0	3	0
Swift	Catcher (2)	1	0	0	0	2	0	0
a. Borom	Pinch Runner	0	0	0	0	0	0	0
Richards	Catcher (2)	1	0	0	0	3	1	0
Overmire	Pitcher (1)	1	0	0	0	0	1	0
b. Walker	Pinch Hitter	1	0	0	0	0	0	0
Benton	Pitcher (1)	0	0	0	0	0	3	0
c. Hostetler	Pinch Hitter	1	0	0	0	0	0	0
TOTALS		27	0	1	0	27	12	2

a. ran for Swift
b. grounded into DP for Overmire (6th)
c. grounded out for Benton
d. fouled out for Webb (9th)

Chicago	IP	H	R	ER	BB	SO
Passeau (W)	9	1	0	0	1	1

Detroit	IP	H	R	ER	BB	SO
Overmire(L)	6	4	2	2	2	2
Benton	3	4	1	1	0	3

DOUBLES: Hack, Livingston, Lowrey. SAC. CAV.: Hug, Paf. DP: Chi, 4–3. UMPIRES: Conlan, Jorda, Passarella, Summers. ATTENDANCE: 55,500. TIME: 1:55.

17

Game Four

"I've got a ticket! The goat has a ticket! Why not?"

Billy Sianis

"Dizzy did good.... He was really throwing that ball. He was all business ... and he won us a ball game...."

Jimmy Outlaw

"I was throwing my atom ball.... I stood up there and threw it at 'em and they swung and missed it."

Dizzy Trout

Chicago fans were cocksure their beloved Cubs would close out the Series in the next two home games. The happy fans stuffed Union Station for several hours before the squad arrived from Detroit. When the special pulled in at 10:15 P.M., a noisy demonstration greeted the heroes who made their way out of the station, through an aisle-constricted cheering crowd. "This time we are going to win; they can't stop us," said Grimm. The Cubs were in the highest of spirits and eager to finish off the Tigers.[1]

As the Tigers' special sped towards the "Windy City," Joe Williams, the sportswriter, was having a conversation with Detroit's manager. Williams had bet on the Tigers and was trying to convince O'Neill he had the wrong pitcher for game four. If Detroit was going to make a series of it they absolutely needed to win this fourth game. The sportswriter believed the Tigers were in the desperate stage of the series and it called for desperate measures. Ignoring the fact that the Cubs had mishandled Hal Newhouser in game one, Williams said to O'Neill, "Newhouser was still the best pitcher in the American League and that first game was just one of those things that wouldn't likely happen again." O'Neill quietly replied, "Just the same, I'm starting Trout." Williams countered by saying, "Newhouser is still the ace and the rules of the game say you must lead with your high card." O'Neill shook his head and said, "No." Williams tried again and replied, "Please, Steve, he's your ace, and besides, I have a few bucks riding on the Tigers." Now the Detroit manager began to become irritated and raised his voice to the scribe, "I'm not interested in your bucks. I'm interested in the Tigers and the World Series. Trout is my man!" Now it was Williams's turn to shake his head. Frustrated, the writer replied with the age-old Socratic question of, "Why?" The discussion heated up when O'Neill said, "He's my man!" The manager continued, "All year long he wins tough games and this is the real tough one. He is my man!" Like a pouting child, Williams replied, "Trout can't carry Newhouser's glove!" Now O'Neill was upset and firmly replied, "I don't want him to carry anybody's glove. I just want him to win this game for me and I am sure he will!" Just then Mrs. O'Neill interrupted the conversation. "How about those nylons you were going to get for me?" That was more than the Tiger manager wanted to handle and he put his head in his hands and said, "Will both of you get out of here? Nylons! I'm trying to win a World Series and here is Williams trying to switch my pitchers. Leave me alone, please!" Both writer and spouse made a hasty exit. Williams spoke to Mrs. O'Neill as they departed and said, "He's worried? How about keeping in mind that I have a few bucks riding on the Tigers to win the Series and why doesn't that stupid husband of yours pitch Newhouser?" That raised the ire of the wife and she closed the conversation with, "Mind your own business. Steve is managing the Tigers and he doesn't need help from you. Besides, we were talking about nylons." With that, she turned her nose up and moved to another section of the train. Mr. Williams was left to bluster and complain to himself and hope that this manager knew what he was doing.[2]

This preference for Trout was a decision that would help determine the World Series.

If Briggs Stadium was spruced up for the Series, it was matched in neatness and price by the Cubs' owner, Philip Knight Wrigley. The Wrigley Gum Company CEO didn't have the love for baseball that his father had. He was no Briggs, who worshiped the Tigers from their early days and continued to be a rabid fan as well as an owner.

Peter Golenbock's book *Wrigleyville* gives an insight into the life of the man known as P.K. He had shown little interest in the game until his father passed away and he inherited the team, but when the team was his he believed he had been given a great responsibility to protect and promote this team and the stadium for the people of Chicago. It was out of duty to his father and the city that he assumed control of the club. Winning and losing, he believed, were not as important as having a good, clean time with family and friends at the ballpark.

The park was a place for Chicagoans to bring the family for an outing and to enjoy themselves. He believed the park should be tidy and sparkle like a diamond. His pocketbook was bottomless when it came to improving the field. The theme of fan and family became his slogan for the park.

In the late 1930s, after many failures in his attempt to provide greenery to the park, he ended up with the ivy upon a bleacher wall in center field. The field was known for the yacht flags and the boat theme bordering the scoreboard. The friendly efficiency of the workers in the park and their supervisors, as well as the closeness of the seats to the field and players, made the park the place he envisioned to bring friends and family for a few hours of food, drink and fun. During World War II, Wrigley overwhelmed the public with advertising that promoted his gum. His gum was even in every serviceman's overseas gift bag. The gum was a big success, and as the money flowed into the coffers, he made the park a great place for the city of Chicago.

But he was a shy man who was interested more in ideas and things than people. Things like business methods, motors, planes, boats and technology captivated him. He was not a social creature at all. He had few if any friends and didn't care for publicity. He avoided reporters and didn't care to have his picture taken. He had not attended the Detroit series but had been busy organizing ticket sales for the games in Chicago and preparing the stadium.[3]

Wrigley decided to maintain the red-carpet hospitality that Briggs had rolled out in Detroit. The one group that would be the main recipients of these efforts would be the reporters. Povich's morning article in the *Post* after game three reflected his appreciation of the hospitality that he would find in Chicago: "If anyone can outshine Briggs it is Wrigley. His care of the park made Chicago's North Side the show place of the National League, and beside that the meal fare is more chi-chi than Detroit."

Wrigley's ushers labored in the security squad of supervisor Andy Frain. They were good advertising examples for excellent service and disciplined hospitality. Povich referred to Chicago and its park as a first-cabin facility, and wrapped up his praise with these words: "In Detroit, Mr. Briggs is very proud of his ball park, manicured lawn, gleaming green paint, elevator service, cocktail lounge and dining room. But the fact is that the only man who can contest him for the favor of the press is Mr. Wrigley."[4]

Billy Pierce thought of Chicago's field from the viewpoint of a pitcher. "I'll tell you, strictly speaking as a pitcher, that looked like an awful small ballpark. That left field and center field, unless it's down the line, is what we call the power alleys, are short, and if the wind happens to be blowing out, those fly balls are dangerous, they are trouble. But it was a thrill to go to another ballpark, a major-league park in the National League, especially for a World Series with all the excitement going on. The green vines in Wrigley weren't there because it was the fall season, so they had turned brown by that time. It was very exciting; I remember they had a big band out there. I think Art Houtteman and I had the job, after we pitched batting practice, to go out and catch fly balls to protect the band."

Just as in Detroit, Chicago hosted capacity crowds. It was a dark and cloudy morning, and rain threatened the fourth game. Batting practice was eliminated for the second straight time due to rain. The gloomy start to the day motivated the ground crew to keep the tarpaulin over the infield.[5] Manager Grimm thought he saw a patch of light just about noon and joyously cried out "Roll 'er up!" So they rolled it up, but instantly rain began to fall, and the manager popped out of the dugout in a flash and screamed, "Roll 'er down!" The canvas remained snug until game time.[6]

All of a sudden the curvaceous movie star from 20th Century–Fox's latest, soon-to-be-released movie *The Dolly Sisters*, June Haver, rushed onto the field during warmup practice and planted a juicy kiss on Jolly Cholly's cheek. That caused a large number of cameras to start clicking. She then headed for the most bashful Cub on the field, Hank Borowy. Borowy was still blushing from the kiss when the first pitch of the game was tossed.[7] The movie star became like a slab of butter on a roll, so why stop now with those cameras following her wherever she went? The next stop was the Tigers' den. Right on her heels were a number of photographers. Red Borom remembers the incident well: "She came right for Richards, but he was married and didn't want his wife to see any such pictures, so he pushed her over to me, and I got kissed. The pictures were taken, but I never received one. Usually the photographers and newsmen would leave them in your locker as a gift, but not this time. Then Phil Silvers, the comedian, slinked into the dugout, and said, 'Come on, guys, lets get it going. I've got a few shekels bet on you fellows.' It started to get a little crowded around there for awhile."

Also this was the genesis of the goat and its curse. Virgil Trucks remembers the goat: "At the series in Chicago I saw a goat outside of the entrance to the stands. I didn't know why until later. This guy owned a tavern near Wrigley Field and he took the goat to the game. But they wouldn't let him in with the goat. He even bought a ticket for the goat. He still couldn't get in. So that's when he put a curse on the Cubs that they would never play or win a World Series again. And until this day they haven't."

One version of this saga is that the owner of the goat, Billy Sianis, a Greek immigrant from Paleopyrogos, Greece, and a Chicago tavern owner, adopted the goat as a pet. The goat wandered into his bar, limping after falling out of a truck.[8] He nursed the goat to health and named him Murphy, or as some recalled, Sinovia.

He had two $7.20 box-seat tickets to game four, and one was for Murphy. Before the game, both paraded about on the playing field by the American League box seats. Murphy wore a blanket that read, "We Got Detroit's Goat."[9]

Andy Frain took great pride in his job. He had 525 employed in usher squads for this series and they were equipped with walkie-talkie radio sets so communications could be instantaneous in case a serious problem arose.[10] Andy also had access to over 300 city policemen, as well as 43 Navy Shore Patrolmen and 25 Army MPs, all of whom patrolled about the stadium.[11] When the parading was over, Sianis and Murphy went to their box seats. Shortly thereafter the ushers showed up investigating complaints about a smelly goat, and they

WORLD FAMOUS
BILLY GOAT
TAVERN & GRILL

LOWER LEVEL

Established in 1934 the Billy Goat Tavern, was located across from the original Chicago Stadium, it was from there William 'Goat' Sianis, put the Curse on the Chicago Cubs.

In 1964 the Billy Goat Tavern moved to Michigan Avenue. It was the inspiration for a Saturday Night Live skit, is frequented by reporters and has become an Historic Chicago Tourist Landmark with its famous 'cheezeborgers'.

How long will this curse last? (courtesy Alicemaude Hernandez)

informed Mr. Sianis the ticket wasn't meant for goat admission. Sianis believed a ticket is a ticket, and it had nothing to do with being human or animal; besides, hadn't he brought Murphy to games during the season? An argument ensued. Frain confronted Sianis, but Billy had tickets and he proudly said, "I've got a ticket! The goat has a ticket.... Why not?"[12] Mr. Frain was annoyed, and waved the goat's ticket in the air saying, "If he eats the ticket that would solve everything." The goat did not eat the ticket.[13] Then Mr. Frain replied, "We can't have animals in the ballpark." Mr. Sianis decided to appeal to a higher authority and said, "Call Mr. Wrigley!" This was done. When the official reply was conveyed it said, "No goat allowed. The goat smells and we don't want a smelly goat in the park." Mr. Frain carried out his duty and both goat and man were removed. When an outraged Mr. Sianis asked why, he was told, "The goat smells."[14] Billy Sianis's nephew, Sam Sianis, said that Billy went back to his tavern at 1855 West Madison, where he allegedly put a curse on the Cubs by saying, "The Cubs are going to suffer because of what they did to my goat!" People interpreted that to be a curse. The Cubs' fortunes went south as the years went by and so the legend grew.[15] The tavern, however, did well. As interesting as the hullabaloo was, Detroit had just the pitcher to match the kissing movie star and the smelly goat. Dizzy Trout took a back seat to no one.

O'Neill had held Trout back to get him well. He had a tired arm and a sore back, and had been ill with a cold and a sore throat.[16] His back injury from the regular season added to his misery. But now he had enjoyed five days of sufficient rest, and this, O'Neill believed, would be the perfect time for the big guy to pitch. The manager asked him how he felt the morning of the game, and Dizzy replied, "I'm fit, boss; I'm ready to pitch the game of my life." "And you're just the boy who can do it," replied O'Neill.[17]

In spite of second guessers like Williams, O'Neill planted Trout on the mound. Detroit's second package of explosive T.N.T. pitching was scheduled to go off in Chicago, and according to O'Neill, this once again would even up the Series.

Charley Grimm started Ray "Pop" Prim as Trout's opposition. The lefty was two months away from his 39th birthday. A 6'0", 178-lb. native of Salitpa, Alabama, who now lived in California, he had recorded a 13–8 season for the Cubs. This was his best year in the major leagues. He had been effective for the Cubs. He reached his peak in July of 1945 when he won five straight games and contributed 27 scoreless innings for the Cubs' pennant drive.

Prim's schooling took place in Jackson, Alabama, and he wasn't the only native from the area playing in this series. Jimmy Outlaw was born in Orem, Tennessee, but grew up in Jackson. The Tiger third baseman had a lot in common with Ray Prim. They both lived in Jackson; their homes were about four blocks from each other. Both finished high school in Jackson, Prim in 1928, and Outlaw in 1930. Both played on the high school baseball team and were coached by Eddie J. Pace. They both played on the hired summertime semi-pro club of Jackson in the Tri-County League and both had the same manager in that league. Both played at Auburn University, Prim in 1929 and Outlaw in 1932. Both chose professional baseball over a college degree. Outlaw stayed in Jackson for the rest of his life while Prim moved to Whittier, California, where he had a successful automobile business. Prim spent most of his career playing in the Pacific Coast League and is in the PCL Baseball Hall of Fame. Outlaw is a member of the Alabama Sports Hall of Fame. It was ironic that a small town like Jackson would have two native sons playing against each other in a World Series.[18]

This was the first time Chicago had hosted a series since October 6, 1938. That year the Yankees won the championship with a four-game sweep over the Cubs.[19] If the Cubs could win this series it would be the city of Chicago's first crown since the 1917 White Sox beat the Giants.

Suddenly there was a split in the clouds, the drizzle faded, and the band played "It Ain't Gonna Rain No More." The commissioner pointed to the field with one hand, kept his fingers of the other hand crossed, and pitched out the first ball of game four.[20]

The Cubs made short work of Detroit in the first inning. Hack threw out Webb. Then Pafko stole a hit from Mayo with a running catch of a sinking liner. Cramer bounced out, pitcher to first and a scoreless inning went up on the board. Detroit was but a tame kitten in the hands of the Cubs' pitching staff.

Trout had made one request before he toed the rubber: "Give me four runs and I'll win in a breeze."[21] Cavarretta said after the series, "Trout did the job. They had Newhouser, but Diz was the best pitcher in the whole series."

As the Tigers took the field in the bottom of the first they probably weren't aware of the fact that they had set a series record for senior citizens. Nine old men went to their positions. Their ages at this time were: Trout, 30; Richards, 36; York, 32; Mayo, 32; Webb, 33; Outlaw, 32; Cullenbine, 30; Cramer, 40; and Greenberg. 34.[22] During this era most players slowed down drastically at age 30. On this day baseball had fielded the oldest group ever to play in a World Series game.

These old men cut the Cubs down in order. Webb threw Hack out at first as York made a beautiful scoop of a low throw with a long stretch to post the out. York then snatched a drive from Johnson by moving far to his right and beating Johnson to the bag in a foot race. Lowrey ended the inning by slamming a liner straight into Cullenbine's glove in right field.

Good pitching and good defense dominated this game for both teams during the first three innings. The sluggers Greenberg, Cavarretta and Nicholson all struck out in the second. York made another play when he handled a smash from Pafko and threw to Trout. The playing in the field was looking first-class. Pafko returned the favor for the second time when he made another super play, hauling in a long drive by Richards in the third. Both teams were hitless after two and a half innings.

The first hit of the game came from the Cubs' catcher, Livingston, who singled in the third. Diz then started to set a tone that became his signature for this game. He took time and walked from the mound to the brick wall in front of the box seats to kick mud off his shoes and make everyone wait impatiently until he was ready to pitch again.[23] He returned to the mound, only to pull out the bandana and clean his glasses. Umpires, players, and fans gawked and jeered, but Trout was in no rush. When he was ready again he fielded Hughes's bunt and forced Livingston at second. Prim then sacrificed Hughes successfully to second, but Hack bounced to Outlaw and Dizzy had his reprieve. At the end of the third, Trout and Prim were locked in a scoreless duel.

In the top of the fourth, Detroit changed the tempo. Hack made a dazzling stop to retire Webb, but then Prim made a mistake by walking Mayo. Prim began to falter working out of the stretch and the Tigers took advantage. Bang-bang-bang went the next three bats. Almost as quick as one could blink an eye, two Tigers had put their paw prints on the plate and two more were in position to score. Cramer singled Mayo to second, Greenberg hit a hot shot past Hack, scoring Mayo, and Cullenbine broke his three-game slump by pounding a hard drive down the left field line, scoring Cramer. Greenberg was perched on third and Cullenbine on second. Prim had some big trouble and the pen heated up. In came "Oom" Paul Derringer, the old Cincinnati ace, who had won 16 games this season. But Derringer wasn't the ace he had been.

Trout frustrates Cubs with stalling tactics. Here he converses with his catcher Richards. Manager Grimm of the Cubs wanders on the field in protest. Cubs runner Johnson, umpire Passarella, and Tiger infielder Jimmy Outlaw patiently wait (Paul Richards' Collection, Waxahachie Museum, Waxahachie, Texas).

Towards the end of the year he had experienced difficulty. He was using his experience to get by.

He walked York deliberately to set up the twin killing. Outlaw hit a grounder to Johnson at second for what should have been the inning-ending double play the Cubs needed. The execution was too slow. Johnson's throw forced York, but Hughes's throw to first couldn't catch the speedy Outlaw, one of the faster of the old men. Greenberg scored on the miscue. Richards, like Cullenbine, had struggled with the bat, but he ended his slump by drilling a pitch to center that brought Cullenbine home with the fourth run. Trout ended the flurry with a ground ball to Johnson. Dizzy had his big 4 on the board.

The Cubs flew into the dugout to retaliate and, when Johnson singled to center, followed by Lowrey's hit to right field, it looked like the Cubs were off to a good start and would return the favor of sending the visiting starting pitcher to the showers. Caster rose from the bullpen bench and started to loosen up.

Then Bridges rose from the bench and started to break off a few of those famous curve balls. But Trout took his time on the mound and the racket in the stadium grew louder. He was the center of attention. What more could he ask for? He lived for the moment.

The Cubs' favorite, Phil Cavarretta, received enormous encouragement from the crowd to drive in the runners and Dizzy off the mound. Diz set him up with breaking pitches and off-speed pitches. Then, with the count 3–2, he blazed a fast ball into the heart of the plate, and Cavarretta went down swinging. Then it was Pafko's turn. He was forced to wait in the box while Trout pulled out the big handkerchief and swiped his glasses for a quick view of the signals. He proceeded to jam Pafko with a high-inside, hard pitch that Andy rolled to Mayo for the second out. One more out and the big fish would be out of the jam. "Swisher" Bill Nicholson strolled into the batter's box. As the slugger got himself set at the plate the Tiger pen went into action and was now warmed up and intently listening, watching, and waiting for a call should it come. Wrigley Field was alive with fans shouting for Trout's head. When Nicholson straightened up into the ready position, Trout stepped off the mound. The shoelaces needed to be tied. When he stepped back onto the mound he fired two quick strikes past the slugger and then showed him his wide-breaking curve, but it missed its mark. With the count 1–2, Trout reared back and delivered a shoulder-high fast ball that crackled past the hitter and his bat for the third strike.[24] He had survived the threat. He had his shutout, a four-run lead, and he, the Dizzy one, was feeling great.

From that moment on this huge hulk of a man with the loud voice just got better. He gave up only two more hits. He laughed off the booing of 42,923 Chicago fans and turned in a superb performance. It was the game of his life.

The only run the Cubs could muster was unearned. Johnson tripled in the sixth. Lowrey hit a grounder to Outlaw at third, and Johnson was trapped between home and third, but Outlaw threw to first instead of running Johnson down. When York caught the ball for the out, Johnson was still off third. York threw back to Outlaw, who was out of position to catch the ball. Rudy uncorked a wild throw and Johnson trotted home with the unearned run. Dizzy shrugged it off. He knew he was still in charge of this game.

He strutted his stuff. When the sun burst forth in the fifth, his showboating became a serious matter for the rest of the afternoon. He deliberately irritated the fans with his stalling and halting of the game throughout the contest. If it wasn't his belt buckle it was his cap; if not the cap, it was the glasses; if not that, then the shoes. He practically dressed and redressed in one manner or the other the rest of the game. He would call time and bring his catcher, Richards, out to discuss, and when he was ready, and only then, he would resume pitching. And when he pitched, he pitched very well.[25] At one point Grimm wandered across the line from the coaches' box and onto the field during one of Dizzy's timeouts. He took off his cap and put his arms out in a pleading motion to the umpires as if to say, "Can't anyone do something about him?" In the ninth inning, Dizzy beat out an infield hit and took such joy with it that he grinned with merriment. The Chicago fans could hardly constrain themselves. Dizzy was in their faces. Trout most certainly threw exceptionally well on this day. The goat and the movie star gave way to Dizzy, who became the real show for this game. The Cubs had to dip deep into their bullpen to keep Detroit under control for the rest of the day. Derringer pitched through the fifth and then Secory pinch-hit for him. Trout struck him out. Hy Vandenburg pitched the sixth and seventh innings in relief effectively, putting Detroit down without a hit or a run. He was removed for pinch-hitter Paul Gillespie, who grounded out. Erickson finished up by flinging the last two innings for Chicago, giving up two hits but no runs.

Jimmy Outlaw remarked about Dizzy's work: "Dizzy did good that day. He was really throwing that ball. He was all business that day and he won us a ball game that put us back into contention."

Billy Pierce commented about Dizzy: "Dizzy was a great competitor. He was a fun guy without a doubt and I always thought he was underrated. He was a very good pitcher, a good, hard thrower and a great competitor. Yes, he had that red handkerchief that he would pull out and wave before he wiped his glass but he was just a real happy-go-lucky guy. We won that game and we still had Newhouser and Trucks ready, so that put us even with them."

After Nicholson fouled out to Richards for the third out in the ninth inning, the quaint Mr. Trout led the cheering and lifted his cap, bowing from the waist. He started off the field and decided to shake as many hands as he could reach. He started with Paul Richards, his catcher, and then thought he would shake hands with the opposition. The Cub players for some reason seem to ignore him. He then grabbed Jocko Conlan, the plate umpire, and left the ump speechless by saying, "I want to show my appreciation for your umpiring. You umpired a swell game today."[26] Mr. Conlan removed Dizzy's arm and hand from his person and excused himself. He had another honor beside Trout's appreciation to savor. He was the first umpire ever to officiate a World Series game in his home town.[27]

For the nine old men, this game was their best performance of the Series. They had pitching, hitting and superior defense despite York's wild throw. Rudy, although hitless, had been a big part of the solid defensive play, especially during the early part of the game. The fielding gem of the day, however, went to Webb, who made a sparkling pick-up from Johnson's hit into the hole, deep at short, in the eighth, and cut the speedy infielder down with a very strong throw to first base.

The Tigers preceded Trout into the locker area, and Newhouser broke the tension with a piercing yell the minute he stepped into the clubhouse door. "We certainly double-crossed those guys today," he screamed. "Boy, and how!"[28]

When Dizzy found the happy faces of players and reporters, he moved right into the mix. He was asked what he was pitching out there today and he said facetiously, "I was throwing my atom ball at the Cubs all afternoon, I stood up there and threw it at them and they swung and missed it."[29] Richards said that it was the best game Diz had pitched in three years and that the psychology O'Neill used on Trout was perfect: "Diz likes the limelight, he loves it. O'Neill keeps him out of action for two weeks and out of the Series for three games and Diz was hungry for competition and ready both physically and mentally. Diz had to win to get back in the limelight where he belongs—and he did."

In the Cubs' clubhouse, manager Grimm said, "Trout was very good but our pitching wasn't so bad, if we'd got some hits we'd been all right. So, we will get them tomorrow when they have to face Borowy again.... Trout was plenty fast, but I haven't seen anybody as swift as Trucks this season." He added that a couple of timely hits would have made the game a different story. Then he said, "We wondered if Diz was going to allow us the chance to swing at the ball as he took all day there, wiping his glasses, etc. He had us on the hook and he was thoroughly enjoying it."

Both teams had equal footing now, and tomorrow their top pitchers, Newhouser and Borowy, would bid for the series victory advantage.

Game Four, 10-06-1945, at Wrigley Field in Chicago

Detroit	0	0	0	4	0	0	0	0	0
Chicago	0	0	0	0	0	1	0	0	0

Detroit	POS	AB	R	H	RBI	PO	A	E
Webb	6	5	0	0	0	1	3	0
Mayo	4	3	1	0	0	1	1	0
Cramer	8	4	1	2	0	4	0	0
Greenberg	7	3	1	1	1	1	0	0
Cullenbine	9	3	1	1	1	1	0	0
York	3	3	0	0	0	10	3	0
Outlaw	5	4	0	1	1	0	3	1
Richards	2	4	0	1	1	7	0	0
Trout	1	4	0	1	0	2	2	0
Totals	33	4	7	4	27	12	1	

Chicago	POS	AB	R	H	RBI	PO	A	E
Hack	5	4	0	0	0	2	2	0
Johnson	4	4	1	2	0	1	3	0
Lowrey	7	4	0	1	0	3	0	0
Cavarretta	3	4	0	0	0	10	1	0
Pafko	8	4	0	0	0	1	0	0
Nicholson	9	4	0	0	0	1	0	1
Livingston	2	3	0	1	0	4	1	0
Hughes	6	1	0	0	0	3	3	0

Chicago	POS	AB	R	H	RBI	PO	A	E
b. Becker	PH	1	0	1	0	0	0	0
e. Merullo	PR — 6	0	0	0	0	1	0	0
Prim	1	0	0	0	0	0	1	0
Derringer	1	0	0	0	0	0	0	0
a. Secory	PH	1	0	0	0	0	0	0
Vandenberg	1	0	0	0	0	1	0	0
d. Gillespie	PH	1	0	0	0	0	0	0
Erickson	1	0	0	0	0	0	0	0
TOTALS		31	1	5	0	27	11	1

a. struck out (5th) for Derringer
b. singled (7th) for Hughes
e. ran for Becker (7th)
d. (7th) grounded out for Vandenberg

Pitching	IP	H	R	ERA	BB	SO
Det. Trout (W)	9	5	1	0	1	6
Chi Prime (L)	3⅓	3	4	4	1	1
Derringer	1⅔	0	0	0	0	0
Vandenberg	2	0	0	0	0	0
Erickson	2	2	0	0	1	2

UMPIRES: Conlan, Summers, Jorda, Passarella. ATTENDANCE: 42,923. TIME OF GAME: 2:00. DOUBLE: Cullenbine. TRIPLE: Johnson. SAC HIT: Prim. PASSED BALL: Livingston left on base. Det 6 — Chi 5.

18

Game Five

"Andy Pafko had a great arm.... I would have loved to have him on my team, but I am going to tell you something. Doc Cramer was as good a defensive outfielder as you would want.... I believe he belongs in the Hall of Fame.... Doc Cramer was a great ball player."

Virgil Trucks

The pride of American League pitching, Hal Newhouser, was faced with an intriguing question. Could he beat the Cubs after suffering the embarrassing loss he absorbed in game one? The Tigers' nemesis, Hank Borowy, would once again oppose him. Newhouser was eager to overcome the cloud that covered him as a Series loser. He was rested. O'Neill had made sure by not allowing him to be used in relief or in a starting assignment until now. He had only pitched 2⅔ innings of game one. There was no doubt his arm was weary from the season and then there was that lump on his shoulder, but his competitive nature told him if they would back him the way they backed Trucks and Trout with some good fielding and timely hitting, that would propel him to a win.

Time was running out in the knotted series for both teams, and this was to be another pivotal contest that could be a key to winning the championship. A one-game lead with two games left in hostile territory was practically a must for the Tigers. The ace pitcher just couldn't afford to flop again with the stakes this high. The Prince was Detroit's money pitcher, and there was a lot on the line today.

The Cubs had another capacity crowd of 43,463, and it marked the 15th million-dollar series to have been played in Series history. The receipts of this game would pass the record of $1,322,328 set at the 1940 Series between the Reds and the Tigers. The 1945 Series would produce the richest gate in World Series history.[1]

It was an unusually warm and sunny day for the spectators swarming into Chicago's picturesque Wrigley Field. They had hopes of watching the Cubs contain the bats of the beasts from Detroit and drive the ace lefty off the mound early as they had done in Detroit for game one. But things didn't start out well even before the game started.[2]

Today was the first time in three days the Cubs and Tigers were permitted to take batting practice.[3] The weather was good for a change, but the batting practice turned out to be a negative factor for the Cubs. The Cubs' starting shortstop, Roy Hughes, was crossing the diamond just as Rudy York started his batting practice. The Big Chief drove a line shot towards Hughes, who was unable to skip fast enough to avoid being hit. The ball cracked Hughes on the ankle and dropped him to the ground.[4] Getting up was a problem, but walking was even more difficult, and running was out of the question. The injury was so painful that Grimm had to scratch him from the lineup and insert the good-fielding but light-hitting Len Merullo in his place.

Inside the Detroit dugout, Dizzy Trout wasn't finished talking just yet. Like royalty, he started to speak to a crowd of reporters of what was to come and what was to be. "There's nothing to it," he said, "Newhouser will win today, Trucks tomorrow and we're all on our way home." The more realistic Newhouser was standing close by and replied in his humble and conservative manner, "I dunno. Those Cubs are a better ball club than I expected." Trout glared at him. "Nuts!" he bellowed. "We're a cinch," and then the loquacious one changed the topic by saying, "That game yesterday was a disappointment to me. I'll tell you why. Some bird offered a dozen nylon stockings to anyone hitting a home run. Before I came here, I told my wife, 'Honey, every time I get to bat I'll take one full swing for you and the nylons. After that you'll be on your own.' I almost got a-holt of one, but didn't get it solid." If his predictions held, he wouldn't need to pitch again, as there would be no more opportunities to swing for nylons.[5]

No matter what concerns Newhouser had, O'Neill's explosive wires were hooked up and starting to detonate in an orderly fashion. The T.N.T. charge was exploding on time with accuracy and consequences. The "T" loads had done their damage and now the "N" package was expected to discharge at Wrigley Field this afternoon for the Tigers.[6]

Newhouser tossed a bit of dirt into the air, and the lively breeze moved it, twisting and swirling, directly out towards center field.[7] Wrigley Field was known for tricky winds and the breeze left no doubt that it would have an effect and might cause more damage than the opposing batsmen.

For whatever doubts Hal might have had, he knew the warmer weather would affect him for the better. Physically he was feeling strong, and he was sure the heat of the day would be good for his arm. If the boys were hitting, Hal felt he would have no worries.

Richards wasn't sure whether the Prince or Hurricane Hal was ready to pitch a 2-hitter or a 20-hitter. The catcher was having a conversation with a reporter from the *Washington Post* while he was waiting to hit in batting practice. "I don't warm the starting pitcher so I can't tell what he has or doesn't have. Even if you warm a pitcher up there are times you don't know what to expect. They think their curve is working but their fast ball isn't. When they get out there to play the tension grips them and it's just the other way around." The reporter mentioned that in yesterday's game he noticed Richards would creep up behind the batter and give Trout a target he couldn't miss. It seemed like he hypnotized the ball to bring it to his glove at the exact spot. Richards said, "You noticed that? I've had others tell me the same thing. I do crowd up close in tight spots. The umpires, especially McGowan, seem to get nervous about it and they keep telling me to get back. They are afraid I will tip the bat or get hit by or interfere with the pitch." At 36 years old, Richards seemed agile and the reporter wondered how he lasted so long in the game as a catcher. Richards replied, "Catchers don't run around much. You're squatted back there and your legs don't take much punishment and as long as your arm holds out you're OK. Most catchers took the job because they were slow on their feet. If they could throw and run they went to the outfield; if they could just throw, they became catchers."

Richards had a lot to do with the success of the Detroit Tigers. If there ever was a savvy baseball player that could handle pitchers, Richards was that person.[8]

Borowy took his warmup tosses and Hank had no doubts about the outcome either. His confidence was imbedded in the rock-solid fact that he was facing a cousin he could beat. He had faced the Detroit squad fourteen times in his career and beaten them eleven times. This was, however, another day.

Borowy struggled from the beginning and it became obvious that he was no longer a puzzle. Newhouser wasn't as dominant as he had shown himself to be during the regular season, but he was nevertheless on his game.

He got his wish. The boys were hitting, but their inept fielding and the wind would keep him from feeling secure until the last Cub out. Game five was a loosely played game. In fact, mental errors tortured both sides, laying a foundation for the next outing, and the beginning of an epithet for the legend that this World Series was the worst ever played.

Webb led the first inning off by bouncing out to Hack, but Mayo popped a hit into left field for what should have been a double. Rounding first, Mayo slipped, stumbled, and took an unprofessional tumble, and the hit was but a single. Borowy looked over his shoulder. The bullpen had been activated, which raised the question in his mind whether the manager had all that much confidence in his outing for today. After Borowy fielded Cramer's hard hit back to the pitcher's box and threw him out, Mayo moved to second, but the Cubs had the all-important number two out. Hack then put Borowy in further difficulty when he butchered Greenberg's grounder for the second Cub error of the series, putting runners on the corners. Borowy, instead of retiring to the dugout, now faced Cullenbine. Batting from the left side against the righty, Roy sliced a shot along the line into left field that sent both runners across the plate and parked himself at second. Umpire Conlan had not been heard over the roar of the crowd, but he established his firm opinion that Cullenbine's hit had dropped just outside the foul line, and called the hit a foul ball. After a short but rather lively discussion, everyone was sent back to his original position, wiping out two would-be Tiger scores. Borowy bore down harder and Cullenbine fanned for the third out. The ace had escaped a snare.

In Newhouser's bottom of the inning he walked the first batter, and then after a strikeout he retired the order, thanks to a York-Webb-Mayo twin killing. The second inning flew by as both pitchers retired the side in order, and it looked like a pitching duel.

The Detroit nine drew first blood in the top of the third. Newhouser went down swinging, but Webb worked Borowy for a walk, and then Mayo drove another single deep enough into right to send Webb to third base. Cramer followed with a thunderous blow into left center. It had extra bases written all over it, but "Handy Andy" Pafko crossed over into left center and made a circus catch by snatching the drive out of the air for the second out. Webb, however, tagged up and the Tigers were on the board.

Then Greenberg connected. It was a long fly into right center and it was trouble. Once more the safety net, Pafko, appeared at the last moment for a great grab, ending the inning, and taking away what could have been a very productive opportunity for Detroit.

Pafko's play had been brilliant during these games and his magical play stood in stark contrast to the sloppy fielding that plagued Detroit's outfielders.

In the Cubs' third, Newhouser put the first two hitters away on grounders and a strikeout. Then, with two outs, he gave up his first hit, a double by Borowy. The hit went right by Outlaw at third. Jimmy had no jump at all on the ball. Hack proceeded to pick up his only hit of the day, a single, into center field. When Cramer fumbled the ball momentarily, there was no chance for a throw to the plate. Borowy scored the tying run. Newhouser, who had a solid move to first, picked Hack off first base for the third out. Cramer's inability to come up with the ball wasn't an error, but if had he fielded the ball smoother there was a chance Borowy would have had to stay at third and the Cubs wouldn't have scored.

The fourth was a three-up and three-down frame for both squads. Detroit wasted an opportunity in the fifth after Richards singled. Newhouser was allowed to hit instead of sacrificing the runner. He swung away and grounded into one of the Cubs' famous double plays, Johnson-Merullo-Cavarretta. Webb followed with a hit to center that could have scored a sacrificed runner if O'Neill had called for it. Mayo ended the inning by grounding out to Cavarretta.

Newhouser pitched well into the bottom half of the fifth. He struck out the pesky Pafko and then enticed Nicholson and Livingston to ground out.

Hal seemed to be hitting his stride and could, with a little luck, have been working on a two-hit shutout. Borowy, on the other hand, had been fortunate to escape disaster from the paws of the Tigers. He was being hit harder than the score showed.

The sixth inning became a decisive moment for the Cub pitcher. The dangerous bats of Detroit chose to find that unassailable number "4" in the sixth. Twice in the Series they posted that number in one inning, once for Trucks in the second game, and once for Trout in game four. That was all that those two needed to win their games.

Now they shelled the Cubs' ace for another four-run explosion. Cramer led with a single to center, but then an amazing incident took place. Pafko tried to field the ball from the side and the ball hopped past him for an error. Cramer sped into second standing

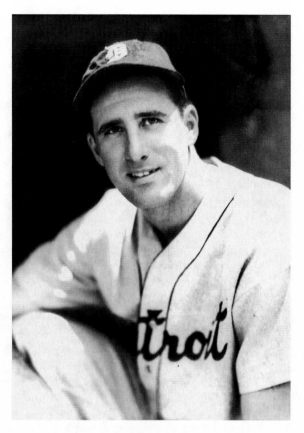

Hank Greenberg (Brace Photo).

up. The error by the fancy-fielding Cub shocked the crowd because Pafko didn't have many days in which he made an error.

Greenberg wasn't about to let this RBI opportunity pass by. He blasted a double right down the left field line and Cramer scored the go-ahead run. When Hank rounded first he stepped where Mayo had stepped before him in the first inning, and went airborne. A boisterous voice in the crowd cried out, "TIM-BER!"[9] as the 6'4" Greenberg descended, crashing in a heap. He had fallen flat on his face, but he lumbered into second with a noticeable limp. He had injured his ankle during the three-point landing, but otherwise was all right. He seemed more concerned about losing the chance to put a triple in the book instead of worrying about the injury.

Cullenbine continued the assault on Borowy by rifling a bullet between first and second, towards the open hole, but Cavarretta lunged to his right and with a diving grab, seized the ball before it reached the outfield. But he couldn't make the play at first, and Cullenbine beat it out for a hit, putting runners on first and third. Rudy York wasted no time in slugging the second pitch into center for a solid hit. Greenberg sprinted in from second base with the second run of the inning. The Tigers led 3–1 and Grimm waved "Tall" Hy Vandenburg into the game from the pen. "Vandy" had posted a 6–3 win-loss record, mostly in relief, and had a 3.63 ERA for the year. York and Cullenbine were sacrificed along with a nifty bunt from Outlaw, and Vandenburg intentionally passed Richards to load the bases for Newhouser.

The bases were full, and a fresh pitcher had been forced into a noisy and stressful situation. He searched for a plan of finding some way out of the inning. Cullenbine, on third base, then began some base-running antics to upset Vandenberg. He continually faked a steal of home on the lanky Vandenberg during his pitches to Newhouser, and shifted Hy's attention towards the runner instead of home plate. Vandenberg lost control and walked Newhouser, bringing in Cullenbine with the third run of the inning and fourth of the game. One of the commentators on the scene was Rogers Hornsby, who had a fondness for the horses, and he said, "They should pitch Vandenberg with blinkers."[10]

Webb grounded to Merullo, who forced Newhouser for the second out, but the play allowed York to score the fourth run in the inning and Detroit was up 5–1. Grimm decided it was time to play percentages and sent Hy on the long walk to the bench for a rest and brought in the southpaw Bob Chipman to face lefties Mayo and Cramer. Mayo walked to fill the bases again, but Cramer ended the Tiger attack with a tapped grounder to Johnson at second. Detroit had batted in four runs on four hits. Once again Detroit's hitters had given their pitcher the responsibility of holding a lead. With a 5–1 advantage, Newhouser was breathing easier, and delivering quite smoothly. He put the Cubs down in order in their sixth with a pair of ground balls and a strikeout.

Leading off the seventh, Greenberg faced another new pitcher, Derringer. He popped a little lazy fly ball to left that should have been an easy out for the speedy outfielder, Peanuts Lowrey, but Len Merullo, who had replaced Hughes at short, moved into Lowrey's territory, just when the wind caught the ball. That produced confusion in the outfield, and the ball dropped between them, giving Greenberg another double.

Cullenbine sacrificed, but his bunt went straight back to Derringer on the mound. Derringer had the choice of throwing to third or first, but took too long to decide. He chose to get Greenberg at third, but his throw was late and both runners were safe. York followed by hitting a short pop-up to center field. Greenberg stayed at third. He wasn't about to test the arm of Pafko. Outlaw took charge and drove a pitch deep into center field. Hank felt safe in coming home. Richards went out, Hack to Cavarretta, to end the inning. Newhouser had another run to work with. The score now stood 6–1, Detroit.

The Cubs finally got to Newhouser in the bottom of the seventh. He put Johnson down on strikes, but Lowrey singled to center on a pop fly that Cramer couldn't reach, and then Cavarretta walked. When Pafko hit straight back to

Hal Newhouser (AP Photo).

the mound Hal went to second with it, forcing Cavarretta for an out, but the Cubs had runners on the corners.

Nicholson then hit a grounder to Outlaw at third and Jimmy opened the gate for the Cubs. With two outs, Outlaw threw to second instead of first, and Mayo, who had been moved to his left by O'Neill, was playing deep as usual and thought Jimmy was going for the sure third out at first. He was tardy in arriving at second base. Pafko slid safely into second, and Lowrey scored on the miscue. Then the home crowd sat up and started to get back into the act. They gave out a genuine roar when the wind affected the next play. Livingston lifted a high fly down the right field line into foul territory. The Chicago wind did its duty and whisked the ball back onto the playing field, and before any player could catch up with it the wind dropped the ball just out of everyone's reach in fair territory. Then the ball took a strange, freakish twist upon landing, bouncing into the stands for a ground-rule double. Pafko scored, Nicholson was on third and Livingston on second. The score was 6–3 and Dewey Williams, a .280 hitter on the season, stepped up to bat for the shortstop Merullo. He represented the tying run. Newhouser's irritation was obvious. He reared back and blazed three strikes past Williams, who took all three pitches without swinging, and might as well have forgotten to bring the lumber to the plate. That ended the threat and the crowd noise subsided.

The Tigers went down in order in the eighth, but the Cubs, in their half, had opportunity. Secory, batting for Derringer, led off with a fly that the wind blew away from second baseman Mayo into short right field. The breeze became the 10th player for the home team and a potent weapon against Newhouser. It was hard to tell if Detroit should fear the Cub hitters or the annoying wind more.

Newhouser wasn't about to be denied. Hack grounded out to Hal, who threw to Webb for the force at second, and then Johnson dropped down a bunt that Outlaw fielded beautifully and disposed of with a quick toss to first. Lowrey followed by hitting a pop-up near home plate. Richards believed it would be a simple catch in foul territory near home plate, but the ball got caught up in that Chicago wind and began to move out towards the pitching mound with Richards in hot pursuit of the troublesome blown missile. Doing a little dance back and forth as the ball moved about, Richards wound up collaring it far behind the pitcher's mound for the third out, while everyone else in the park watched in utter astonishment.[11]

In the Tigers' ninth inning Cramer began by getting hit on the ankle with a pitch from new pitcher, Erickson. Greenberg belted his third double of the day, a long liner into deep left, sending Cramer to third. Cullenbine clubbed an Erickson pitch so far into center that it lodged in the shrubs on the center field wall. Pafko, insanely trying to locate the ball, began throwing leaves and pieces of shrubbery off the wall. When he couldn't produce it, the umpires invoked the ground-rule double decision.

The Tigers had two more runs, and Cullenbine was perched on second. Erickson retired York on a sharp liner to Hack, Outlaw grounded out to a new shortstop, Bill Schuster, and Richards hit a come-backer to Erickson who threw him out at first. With eight and a half innings played the Tigers had extended their lead to 8–3.

The Cubs had one more shot and Cavarretta started the ninth with a double between Cramer and Cullenbine. The two-base knock was another strange event in a weird game. It wasn't much more than an easy fly ball, but as Cramer started running over to catch it, Cullenbine yelled: "All right, all right!" Cramer stopped and Cullenbine, who had hardly begun to run, watched with Cramer as the ball fell to earth untouched. Cullenbine immediately fielded the ball and threw it back to the infield, but it was too late. Cramer then angrily turned to Cullenbine and said, "What the hell did you mean by that 'all right'?" "I meant it was all right for you to take it!" replied Cullenbine.[12]

Somehow Newhouser was able to overcome the Cub hitters, the fans, the wind, and the inept confusion of his own teammates, but it wasn't easy. He struck Pafko out, but Nicholson singled Cavarretta home for the Cubs' last run. Livingston flied to Cullenbine, who caught this one, and Schuster fouled out to Richards to end a weird contest. The final was Detroit 8, Cubs 4. The Tigers now had a 3–2 advantage in the Series.

Newhouser pitched a better game than the score showed. The writers had a field day and the headlines read: "Detroit's Batting Balances Slip-Ups," "Newhouser says Confusion Cost Him Shut-Out," and "Wind-Blown Hits Harass Both Teams."

Mr. Povich emphasized the poor base-running by calling the Tigers stumble-bum base runners and saying that two Detroit players fell flat on their faces as if tripped by an invisible wire."[13] Daniel reported, "With good fielding and throwing," the Tigers could have had a shutout rather than an 8–4 victory.[14] Joe Williams wrote, "It was easy for him [Newhouser] to handle the Cubs. Handling his Tigers was something else. What he did was beat two teams in one game."[15] Williams recognized Newhouser had to reach back and pitch over bad breaks and did a great job of overcoming the adversity that compounded his situation. "Actually, it should have been 8–1. And that one honest run came in the ninth when the meal was over, and the maid was clearing the table." He continued to comment, "Probably no pitcher ever had to work so laboriously to win a series game for his side. To put it bluntly, the Tigers played the most slovenly game I've ever seen a winning team play in a world series. One press box veteran of the 1919 Black Sox series started to look around for the astral body of Arnold Rothstein."[16]

Bloodgood of *Baseball Magazine* described it as "A comedy of errors— loosely played but good entertainment. The official box score can never come close to revealing the true story. One veteran reporter was heard to murmur, 'Barnum and Bailey have started rehearsing early.' That was the type of shindig it was. Newhouser hurled a far better game than is shown in the records and could sue his colleagues for non-support."[17]

Regardless of the comments, the spirit of the Tigers was high as they reached their clubhouse. "It's in the bag!" was the most common phrase circulating around the lockers after the game. They had all the confidence in the world that they would end the Series on the morrow. Their confidence amounted almost to conviction that the next day would see them established as baseball's top team.

They made no pretense that they had played a good game; they knew they hadn't. Above the commotion in the clubhouse, the reporters trying to interview, and photographers snapping away, the voice of O'Neill said:

> We won, even though we looked bad, because we finally started hitting. We scrambled a couple of plays, but Newhouser was strong all the way. You can't beat that combination, pitching and hitting. I recall two plays that were breaks for us. In the seventh they had two runs in and the tying run at the plate, when Newhouser struck out Williams. Confusion in the infield set up the situation. Outlaw, handling Nicholson's rap with Lowrey on third and Pafko on first, overlooked the fact I had Mayo playing way over on the right side of the infield. There was an easy play at first but Jimmy heaved it to second, and because Mayo was so late getting over Pafko, beat the throw.
>
> In the eighth, Outlaw came up with a marvelous play on Johnson's bunt. It was a bunt that could only be overcome by a barehanded grab and a quick, accurate throw. That's what Jimmy gave us. For the rest, it was easy.
>
> They'll finish it tomorrow if Grimm pitches Passeau. I thought he'd go with Wyse. Passeau needs more rest. I'm going with Trucks. He's ready and strong.[18]

Newhouser was overjoyed. "What a different feeling from the other day! I felt strong all the way, but I never worried because the boys were hitting behind me. I think the change in the weather helped me, it was warmer today and I felt better pitching."[19]

Greenberg wasn't satisfied with his three doubles. He wanted another home run. He had played in four World Series and had hit only one homer in each one. He pledged to hit one the next game, as he wanted a series where he had hit multiple homers.[20]

One of the unsung heroes of the series, reporters noticed, had been Skeeter Webb, whose fielding for Detroit had been exceptional compared to some of that of his teammates. O'Neill had been second guessed from the start of the season about starting his son-in-law instead of the better-hitting Hoover, but as of now Webb had been making plays, some of which had been quite difficult.[21]

Richards thought Newhouser lacked the sharpness of which he was capable, like the "kind of stuff with which he overpowered the Yankees through the season," commented Richards. Even so, Richards believed Hal pitched an outstanding game.[22]

Les Mueller commented on Hal's long season: "I don't remember too much about that game, but in my mind it doesn't seem to me that Newhouser was quite as sharp as he had been. I think Newhouser was about to run out of gas because he had pitched so many innings, and I think he was getting tired."

Cullenbine was happy about his hitting that day. He explained the reason the ball dropped between him and Cramer, saying that it was a lack of communication.[23]

Mayo complained of the wind and his loss of Secory's short fly in the eighth inning.[24]

The spills by Mayo and Greenberg were attributed to the softness of that particular bit of ground around the corner at first base.[25]

Borowy had the blues in the Chicago locker area and said, "I just couldn't put the ball where I wanted it, Cramer smacked a high pitch, and when I got it down, Greenberg and York whacked me. The one Cramer hit took a bad hop away from Pafko, which is the one pitch I would like to have taken back."[26]

Grimm stayed optimistic and said, "We'll still beat them tomorrow, but I see now it will take seven games. I'll throw Passeau at them tomorrow, and he'll even it up again. He had an easy game last time and is ready." Passeau nodded in agreement and repeated the part of having it easy beating them in game three.[27]

Grimm announced Hughes would miss the rest of the series and Merullo would be at short.[28] There was no information whether Hughes had a fracture or not, but the viciously-hit ball by York did enough damage to keep him out of the game.

This was Borowy's first defeat since August 24, when he lost a 1–0 decision, after giving up but three hits, to Harry Brecheen of the Cardinals.[29]

When pressed for a specific answer on why the Cubs lost this day Grimm said, "We got the hell kicked out of us. It was just boom, boom, boom — that's all." He praised the pitching of Newhouser and said that he threw the best change of pace he had ever seen. Cavarretta attributed Newhouser's success to his control of his curve ball. "He was getting them over today for strikes and he wasn't Wednesday," he said.[30]

The play execution at times might have been embarrassing, but the game itself was not boring. Newhouser had his strikeout pitch and very good control. He struck out nine Cubs when he needed to, due to his lack of support. He walked only two and scattered seven hits. Many of the hits dropped in where capable fielding would have made them outs.

Doc Cramer had been taking a lot of heat for his outfield play. Things happened to him that shouldn't have taken place. That Cramer was one of the great outfielders of the game there really was no question, and if his glove was giving him a problem, his bat most certainly was making up for it. He would be Detroit's top average hitter in this Series. The writers, however, began to question his fielding ability, citing his age as the problem. Trucks, who had seen Cramer before and during wartime, said: "Andy Pafko had a great arm. He had a shotgun. He was a very good defensive outfielder. I would have loved to have him on my team, but I am going to tell you something. Doc Cramer was as good a defensive outfielder as you would want. He is the one that came up with those sliding catches. Yes sir, I saw him make many of them and with some of the other statistics of some of the guys in the Hall of Fame, I believe he belongs in the Hall of Fame. Yes, I would say so. Doc Cramer was a great ball player. He was really a great guy and I really liked Doc Cramer."

A news revelation that was brought out into the open showed the political and business part of baseball. New Commissioner A.B. "Happy" Chandler's pre–World Series meetings with the rival managers, league officials and umpires the previous Tuesday in Detroit took a nasty turn for those involved. The power lines between Commissioner Chandler and the two league executives, as well as the umpire-league relationships between the parties involved, clashed at the close of the meeting. The league officials, Ford Frick and Will Harridge, took the rookie commissioner to task for bringing up the subject of salaries in front of the umpires. The new man on the block wanted good relationships with the men in blue and publicly announced at this meeting that he was in favor of a raise from $2500 a series to $4000 a series for the umpires. Both league officials nixed the proposal and then the fur started to fly. When the name of Ernie Stewart, a former American League umpire, found its way into the conversation, the discussion, which had been heated, rose to a boiling point. Harridge had fired Stewart for discussing salary conditions with all the league's umpires at the instigation of the commissioner, who since then had refused to make a public statement about the subject. Harridge minced no words and told the new man that the engaging and discharging of umpires was wholly a league affair and none of the commissioner's business. The former senator from Kentucky started to understand a little more about the subtleties of the game. The disagreement would lead to future changes as Chandler made the adjustment from government politics to baseball politics.[31]

As far as the series was concerned, Detroit was in the driver's seat now. But if game five was an adventure, game six would be a wild episode.

Game Five, 10-07-1945, at Wrigley Field in Chicago

Detroit	AB	R	H	RBI
Webb-6	4	1	1	1
Mayo-4	4	0	2	0
Cramer-8	4	2	1	1
Greenberg-7	5	3	3	1
Cullenbine-9	4	1	2	2
York-3	5	1	1	1
Outlaw-5	4	0	0	1
Richards-2	4	0	1	0
Newhouser-1	3	0	0	1
Totals	37	8	11	8

Chicago	AB	R	H	RBI
Hack-5	3	0	1	1
Johnson-4	3	0	0	0
Lowrey-7	4	1	1	0
Cavarretta-3	3	1	1	0
Pafko-8	4	1	0	0
Nicholson-9	4	0	1	2
Livingston-2	4	0	1	1
Merullo-6	2	0	0	0
b. Williams PH	1	0	0	0
Schuster-6	1	0	0	0

Chicago	*AB*	*R*	*H*	*RBI*
Borowy-1	1	1	1	0
Vandenberg-1	0	0	0	0
Chipman-1	0	0	0	0
a. Sauer PH	1	0	0	0
Derringer-1	0	0	0	0
c. Secory PH	1	0	1	0
Erickson-1	0	0	0	0
Totals	32	4	7	4

a. struck out for Chipman in 8th
b. struck out for Merullo in 7th
c. singled for Derringer in 8th

Detroit line score	0	0	1	0	0	4	1	0	2
Chicago line score	0	0	1	0	0	0	2	0	1

Doubles: Borowy, Cavaretta, Cullenbine, Greenberg(3), Livingston. Sac: Cullenbine; Johnson, Outlaw. Double Plays: Det. 4–3–6–4, Chi. 4–6–3. HPB: Cramer (Erickson). LOB: Det 9, Chi 4. Umpires: Summers; Jorda, Passarella, Conlan. Attendance: 43,463. Time of Game: 2:18.

Pitching
IP: Newhouser 9, Borowy 5, Vandenberg ⅔, Chipman ⅓, Derringer 2, Erickson 1
H: Newhouser 7, Borowy 8, Derringer 1, Erickson 2
ER: Newhouser 4, Borowy 5,Derringer 1, Erickson 2
BB: Newhouser 2, Borowy 1, Vandenberg 2, Chipman 1
S0: Newhouser 9, Borowy 4,
Winner: Newhouser (1–1)
Loser: Borowy (1–1)

19

Game Six

"Game six was when Hostetler did his flop. He was in his 40s and they made a big joke out of him. While we were playing the sixth game he fell between home and third base. Everybody blamed it on him because of his age and the war year. But it wasn't his age or the war year. Steve O'Neill was coaching at third and he had Chuck coming and going ... and he just fell. Even a young man would have fallen that day. Steve had his arms going in both directions and it was confusing."

Ed Mierkowicz

The Cubs had thought they would be able to win the Series easily after leaving Detroit the previous Saturday. Now they found themselves on the verge of blowing a home-field advantage. The Tigers took back-to-back games in Chicago behind the pitching tandem of Trout and Newhouser. O'Neill, looking to close the series, started "Fire" Trucks, who had won game two, for this sixth game at Wrigley Field, hoping to finish off the Cubs with another pitching gem. O'Neill's T.N. T. explosions were right on schedule.

The bats of Greenberg, York, Mayo, Cullenbine, and Cramer were contributing timely hitting, and Detroit had now emerged once more as the favorite. The Tiger power was convincing and the pitching staff was doing an A-one job.

The one favorable possibility the Chicago team could cling to was the recent history of the Tigers in the World Series. In 1934 against the Cardinals, and in 1940 against the Reds, Detroit had 3–2 advantages, and lost the last two games in each of those series.[1]

Across the street from Wrigley Field, in a third-story apartment building, Earl Marsh, an unemployed worker, put his ingenuity to work beginning with game five. He rented out his bedroom suite. The window had a perfect view of Wrigley Field just above the right field wall. Twenty fans pitched in $7.50 each to watch their beloved Cubs. Marsh served coffee and believed that if the series went seven games, he could clear $450.[2]

Besides Marsh and his apartment, Chicago had a world-infamous gatecrasher named One-Eyed Connelly. Seldom was One-Eyed stopped or caught because he was slippery as an eel, crafty as a leprechaun and bold as a bull in a china shop. Andy Frain, the Cubs' security administrator, lost so many confrontations to Connelly that he decided instead of wasting time catching him on a day he knew he would appear, he decided to offer Connelly an opportunity to be a gate attendant. One-Eyed quickly accepted the job, but it was a brief career. As the crowd milled through the gates, Connolly halted a man hurrying through the gate. "Where do you think you're going, buddy?" One-eyed said. "To my office. I'm Phil Wrigley, the owner," replied the man. "Baloney," Connolly snapped, "they all give me that line." When Frain confirmed that this indeed was Mr. Wrigley, Connolly's last word on the job was, "Nuts!" He was ushered out of the park. With that pre-game scene, Chicago opened up to one of baseball's strangest World Series games.[3]

The weather was cloudy. Although there was no threat of rain, there was a wintry dip in temperature. A number of people in the crowd were wrapped up in blankets.

In the dugout, Trucks, the former sailor, learned about the frost that would be there by the evening and said, "This Alabama boy isn't waiting for frost. We're getting out of here tonight." But it wouldn't work out that way.[4]

As Trucks blew on his hands to warm them for the cool weather, Claude Passeau, flaunting the number 13, started throwing his warmups. He still hadn't been scored on. After giving up just one hit and one walk in game three, the Tigers felt he would be just as tough as he had been before.

In the top of the first, Webb grounded out to second, Mayo flied out to Nicholson, and Cramer grounded out to second. As he left the mound, Passeau heard a vigorous cheer from the crowd. He had just added another inning to his scoreless string.

Trucks went out and retired the Cubs without a score in the bottom of the first. Hack picked up a walk and Johnson sacrificed him to second, York to Mayo, but Lowrey lined a drive straight into the glove of Cullenbine, and Cavarretta grounded out to Webb.

Detroit broke Passeau's mastery in the top of the second. After Greenberg flied to Lowrey, Cullenbine worked Passeau for a walk. York, who had the only hit off Passeau in game three, then got the first one for this game by clouting a long, sweeping hit into right center for a double. He thundered around first with unusual speed, and runners were now on second and third with only one out. Passeau intentionally walked Outlaw to fill the bases and get to the bottom of the batting order. The strategy backfired. He lost control, walking Richards and forcing Cullenbine home with the first run. But "Cool" Claude let the threat go no farther. Trucks popped up to shortstop Hughes, who had returned to play after his injury from York's batting practice. Then Webb's grounder to Hughes forced Richards at second for the third out.

The Cubs' half of the inning produced their first hit when Pafko singled

Stan Hack and Charley Grimm (Brace Photo).

up the middle. Nicholson fouled out to York, and Livingston grounded to Mayo, who forced Pafko with a toss to Webb. Webb, in his haste to complete a twin killing, overthrew the base, and Livingston headed for second. Richards, however, had backed up first, fielded the overthrow, and threw a perfect strike to Mayo at second for the third out. Enraged by being called out at second base, Livingston rebounded off the ground and went after the umpire. Jocko Conlan had retreated away from the base after calling him out, but within seconds Livingston ripped open the umpire's coat, put his hands on Conlon, and shoved him hard. The umpire responded by shoving the misguided player away. There was a series rule that prohibited an umpire from ejecting a player, otherwise Livingston's action of putting his hands on an umpire would have been an automatic ejection. The Cubs were fortunate to have such a rule because Livingston, later in the game, started a four-run rally with a hit. Manager Grimm trotted out to offer apologies on behalf of the Cubs, calming things down. Livingston's actions would allow Commissioner Chandler the opportunity to issue his first fine. Before the series started, the new commissioner had cautioned both managers and made it a point to say that players must keep their hands off umpires. After the World Series was over, Livingston received a letter from Chandler at the end of the month that said:

> As you well know, it is the most serious offense to attack an umpire in this manner. Ordinarily, it would require a very severe penalty in the way of a minimum of thirty days' suspension.
>
> However, I do not like to impose penalties upon players. In view of the fact that this misconduct did not result in any further consequences, I am, in this instance, merely imposing a fine of $250.[5]

It was Chandler's first, but far from his last fine.

Passeau dropped the Tiger hitters in 1-2-3 order in the third, and Trucks shut out the Cubs in their half of the inning by striking out the first two hitters. After allowing a hit to Hack, he induced Johnson to fly to Cramer for the last out.

Detroit mounted a small threat in the top of the fourth when Johnson misplayed Cullenbine's grounder at second. York popped up. Outlaw's groundout sent Cullenbine to second. Passeau walked Richards to get at Trucks and Virgil worked him for a base-on-balls to load the bases, but Webb's high fly ball into center ended the Tigers' hopes.

Trucks appeared to be on top of his pitching game as he struck out Lowrey in the Cubs' bottom half of the inning, but then Cavarretta singled. When the next hitter, Pafko, nailed a Trucks pitch flush on the sweet spot and drove it deep into left center, there was trouble brewing for the Tigers. The ball flew towards the gap with the ancient Greenberg galloping with great travail after it. Big Hank somehow caught up with the drive, reached out as far as his 6' 4" frame would allow, and in a state of exertion he desperately managed to haul the ball into his glove, thereby saving Trucks from a very sticky situation. This unexpected fielding gem from the Detroit outfielder was a most welcome relief for Tiger fans. When Nicholson popped up to Webb, the Tigers trotted into the dugout with a 1–0 lead still intact.

In the top of the fifth, Passeau again wove his magic. Mayo grounded to Hack and both Cramer and Greenberg hit fly outs to Lowrey.

In the bottom of the fifth, Trucks ran into a tempest that he couldn't control. Livingston started the storm with a single. Hughes bunted to sacrifice the runner to second. York moved over to field the ball, and waving Trucks off, he tried to make the play unassisted. But he slipped and fell. In desperation he threw from a prone position to Mayo, who had hustled over from second to cover the open base. The throw was high and off line. Mayo got a glove on the ball, but dropped it. Both runners were safe.

A pealing roar cut loose from the stands, encouraging the Cubs to take advantage of this gift. Passeau was the hitter, and twice he tried to bunt the runners along, but fouled off both pitches. On his third attempt he took a half swing and dropped a bouncer back to Trucks's left side. Virgil bounced off the mound and fielded the ball cleanly. He had seen the runner advancing to third out of the corner of his eye, and he pivoted to throw him out, but in his attempt to catch that lead runner he threw wide and just a little late. Outlaw had the ball, but the throw pulled him to his left, and Livingston slid to Jimmy's right, hooking the bag away from Jimmy's attempted tag. The bases were loaded.

Virgil Trucks commented:

> Yes, I started that 6th game and I may have been able to go further but Rudy York had a bad habit of when he got the ball he wouldn't throw it to you, and then he would say he had it, he had it, and you would back off, and the runner would beat him to the base. That's what happened in my case in that 6th game, which turned out to be a pretty good inning for the Cubs. But if he hadn't done that, and I cover first, and he throws the ball to me, the runner is out, and I get out of the inning. That didn't happen.
>
> He had done that on several occasions to other pitchers. I wasn't the only one he [had] done it to and he thought he could beat the runner. Rudy was no speed demon. He weighed about 230 lbs., and was about 6'1". He was as broad as he was tall.
>
> On the throw to third I was trying to lead the fielder to the bag, but Jimmy, of course, was playing away from the bag, and was just late getting there. The throw should have been an error on me even though it probably should have been caught. That was another of those earned runs that should have been unearned.

Virgil was in trouble and the stands clamored for blood. Smiling Stan turned up the pressure with a clean base hit, bringing two Cubbies across the plate. When Richards neglected to spy the unattended bat left by Hack next to Richards's right foot, he muffed Cramer's throw from center. He stepped on or over the bat, and was distracted. The scorers gave him the error. The score was 2–1, and the Cubs had the lead with runners on second and third and no one out.

The two runners held fast as Johnson grounded to Mayo for the first out.

Trucks walked Lowrey, loading the bases again. O'Neill then brought the Tiger infield in for a play at the plate. Cavaretta, the NL batting champion, drove a pitch over second base for a hit and the rally continued. That single scored a pair of runs, and put Trucks out of the game. If Mayo had been back in his usual deep position instead of drawn in, he could have made a play on the ball and gotten at least one out if not a double play. O'Neill's decision opened him to second-guessing by the fans and writers.[6]

O'Neill waved in Caster for much-needed relief. After warming up for 12 World Series games, six with the Browns the previous year, and six with the 1945 Tigers, Caster finally got his opportunity to actually pitch in a World Series game.[7] George filled the bill by getting Pafko to pop out to third and then

Doc Cramer (Brace Photo).

struck out Nicholson. But when the inning was over the Cubs had four hits, four runs, a 4–1 lead, and a solid grip on the game.

In the top of the sixth a serious situation for Chicago occurred. Passeau was now in control, and pitching well. Cullenbine, however, opened with a clean hit up the middle, only the second hit off the Cubs' veteran right-hander. When York popped out for the first out, it looked like lucky 13 would handle this small situation. But Outlaw slammed a rough comebacker to Passeau. Passeau blocked it with his bare hand and recovered in time to throw out the hitter at first. He then immediately called a time out and started to dance very delicately around the infield while holding his damaged middle finger.[8] Outlaw's hit had torn the nail off the middle finger of his pitching hand and split the finger. Passeau sweated and stewed for a few minutes but then decided to carry on. O'Neill sent Bobby Maier up to pinch-hit for Richards. Maier clipped another line-shot right back at Passeau, who this time threw up his glove, but the ball bounced off the glove hand for a hit. With runners on the corners, McHale pinch-hit for Caster, and whiffed to end the inning. The damage, however, had been done. Passeau's injury would affect the Series.

The Tigers brought in a new battery of Swift and Bridges for the end of the sixth. Bridges immediately found himself in trouble. Livingston dropped a short-popper into left, and the gale blew the ball back toward the diamond. Although Greenberg got a glove on it he couldn't complete the catch, and it fell for a double. Hughes followed with a solid double, scoring Livingston. Swift then whipped a throw to Webb, catching the inattentive Hughes off second for the first out. Bridges settled down, retiring Passeau on a liner to Mayo, and Hack on a grounder to Webb. The inning ended with the Cubs up 5–1.

As Passeau started the top of the seventh he turned to Grimm and said, "Watch me, Skipper."[9] Then he showed Grimm the finger, which was swelling badly and turning black and blue. It was the first of four unanticipated factors in this contest. It's impossible to anticipate such factors as injuries; they make baseball the interesting game that it is.

Hostetler started the inning by pinch-hitting for Webb. He slapped a pitch toward third. Hack's error at third allowed him to reach the bag safely. Cavarretta handled Mayo's bouncer unassisted, but Hostetler advanced to second.

The incident that happened next highlighted the entire Series and unfortunately tagged it, arguably, as the worst example of sloppy play. It helped to earn the unwanted legacy as the worst World Series played in the history of the game, and it hung a set of sportswriter's horns on Hostetler.

Hostetler played hard, and so when Cramer drilled a hit into left field, Hostetler felt he could score. Chuck, at 41, could outrun all of his teammates and he was one of the fastest men to play the game.[10] He became the second unanticipated factor that raised its ugly head in this series.

As Cramer's hit safely carried to the outfield, Chuck put his head down, kicked his legs into gear, and roared into third base like an express train. His intention was to go all the way home and score. O'Neill, coaching third, must have been astonished at the speed and drive of the man who was headed in his direction, and within a split second he pulled away from the coaching box, waving his arms and moving in the direction of home plate, quite a ways out of the coaching box. He waved vigorously at Hostetler. It looked like he was sending him home, but then, as he later remarked, he waved at him to pull up at third. But Chuck had turned loose the jets, and with his head down he was focused on crossing the plate safely. He ran straight through the stop sign, stubbed the bag while turning the corner wide in his sprint, and headed for the plate. The startled O'Neill's loud Irish voice yelled at him to cease and desist immediately. Chuck was about 15–20 feet down the line when the skipper's voice registered in his brain. He stumbled, trying to right himself, and took a header with his hands completely outstretched, like a diver in a free fall going off a high board. It happened so fast that everyone gasped at the sight of him hitting the ground. Amid the bellowing and howling of some 40,000 fans, Chuck pulled himself up, only to find he was in a rundown between third and home thanks to a Lowrey-Livingston-Hughes relay. Hughes put him out. Cramer took second. Greenberg then walked, Cullenbine singled, Cramer scored, and Greenberg moved to third.

After watching the two hits and a walk, Grimm felt it was time for Passeau to go. "I knew he couldn't go any further because he was suffering terrible pain," Grimm said.[11] Wyse came in to relieve. York greeted him with a solid hit to left field that knocked in Greenberg. Outlaw grounded out, ending the inning. Detroit had scored two runs on three hits and a Cub error, and the score was now 5–3 in favor of Chicago.

The question became how many more runs the Tigers could have had if the flop hadn't occurred. As for Hostetler, perhaps it would have been better if

Charles "Chuck" Hostetler (National Baseball Hall of Fame Library, Cooperstown, New York).

he hadn't been called upon to stop. He had a great jump and a good shot at making it home safely. To say that he felt bad would be a gross understatement. This one play would haunt him to his grave. In later life Chuck said, "I'll never forget it. I played only two years in the majors with the Tigers but this is what anyone ever talked about." Hostetler's teammate Johnny McHale remembered his misfortune. "Well, I remember Hostetler's comment after it was over. He had a real deep voice and when they asked him what happened about falling down between third and home he said, 'I tripped over a cigarette butt.' He tried to make a joke out of it."

Bill Pierce: "Well, he tripped over that cigarette butt. Things do happen and it's tough on a person when it happens. He came around third and fell. It's a shame because that's what he will be remembered for. Chuck, however, got some hits for us during the year and helped us out, but that one thing was what he called that cigarette butt he tripped over."

Les Mueller: "Oh well, it was kind of shocking and it was humorous too. You can't imagine how much. Hostetler was the kind of a fellow who, quite frankly, didn't have a lot of ability, but he played real hard. He would really bow his neck and try to give it everything he had. When he came around third and all at once you looked up, and there he was sprawled on the ground. You didn't dare laugh at the time, but you were thinking, 'Oh, my goodness!' It was one of those things, you know, and nobody felt worse than he did."

Ed Mierkowicz: "Game six was when Hostetler did his flop. He was in his 40s and they made a big joke out of him. While we were playing the sixth game he fell between home and third base. Everybody blamed it on him because of his age and the war year. But really it wasn't his age or the war year. Steve O'Neill was coaching at third and he had Chuck coming and going, and he didn't know what to do, and he just fell. Even a young man would have fallen that day. Steve had his arms going in both directions and it was confusing."

Red Borom: "Cramer didn't always have a fondness for O'Neill's decisions and he believed he shouldn't have stopped Chuck from going home."

The Cubs extended the lead in the bottom half of the inning. Bridges struck out Johnson, but Hoover had replaced Webb at shortstop, and when Lowrey hit a ball into the hole, Hoover mishandled the ball, which resulted in a late throw to first. Lowrey beat it out for a hit. Bridges walked Cavarretta, and Pafko flied to Greenberg in deep left. Bridges then lost control. He issued back-to-back walks to Nicholson and Livingston, forcing in a run. O'Neill dismissed him, and Benton limped up to the hill. Hughes greeted him with a hard liner that caromed of the big pitcher's leg, scoring Cavarretta. Benton then struck out Wyse, but the damage was done, and the Cubs had a 7–3 spread.

It looked like Chicago had a lock on the game, but the Tigers came snarling, clawing and roaring back, much to the dismay of some 40,000 Cub fans. The Tigers, at the top of the eighth, found that famous four spot.

Swift picked up a walk and then pinch hitter Walker doubled down the right field line. With men on second and third, Hack, who was having a hard day in the field, booted Hoover's grounder, and Swift scored. Mayo continued the assault with a base hit that knocked in Walker, but Mayo provided the third unanticipated factor. He tested Pafko's arm again and tried for a double. It was a decision that once again proved costly. Pafko's rifle arm threw him out for the second time in the series. Mayo's run was just as important as Hostetler's and that piece of base running, often overlooked due to the sensational fall of Hostetler, hurt the Tigers just as badly as Hostetler's flop.

Mayo's hit, however, ended Wyse's performance, and Pop Prim entered the game in relief to pitch to the left-handed hitter Doc Cramer. Cramer greeted him by blasting a long drive to left, Lowrey came up with a sensational diving catch, but Hoover tagged and scored. Detroit was within one run of tying the game.

Up stepped Greenberg with no one on base. Prim worked him carefully. The count ran to 3–2. Then the ex-Army Captain connected on the next pitch and drove the ball into a strong gale, through a crosswind, over the left field wall, onto the catwalk beyond, where it hit a railing and bounced back harmlessly onto the playing field.[12] The Tiger slugger had tied the game, 7–7. The Detroit bench exploded. The players were yelling, slapping each other and doing little dances. "That's it," yelled O'Neill from the third base box, "that's the payoff."[13] Cullenbine's grounder to short ended the inning.

This was becoming far from a routine World Series game. It was a combination of tragedy and farce, a mixture of good-great and bad-worse play with the highest of stakes at risk for both teams. The tension was high but the fans were enjoying a very interesting game, wondering what would happen next. Both teams now bent their backs, going for the win, the Tigers for the championship, and the Cubs for survival to play again.

With Passeau and Trucks gone, the second big-time duel of the game took center stage. O'Neill had the upper hand. He had Trout and Newhouser to bring home the bacon. Because Newhouser had pitched all of game five, it was Trout who heeded the call. Newhouser would stay as the ace in the hole in case of a seventh game. Both teams were running out of players. This contest set records for the number of players used. Thirty-eight players were inserted into the game, nineteen for each team; nine of them were pitchers. There were ninety-four at-bats for both teams, and twenty-four runners left on base.[14] Trout, as confident as ever, toed the rubber for the bottom of the eighth, and after walking Hack, he retired the Cubs in order.

In the top of the ninth the question for Chicago was who was going to pitch. Grimm felt he had no choice. He had to go with his ace. There would be no tomorrow if there wasn't a win today. Borowy went to the hill with very little rest.

After York grounded out, Outlaw singled. Swift sent him to third with another hit. When Hughes fielded Trout's grounder, Outlaw found himself trapped off third, which was another costly mistake. A rundown put him out, then Hoover flied to Cavarretta, and the Tigers' opportunity faded away.

Pafko started the ninth with a double. Trout went to work and struck out Nicholson, and then grabbed Gillespie's grounder for the second out. He walked Becker intentionally, and got Borowy to fly to Cramer. The potential winning run was wasted.

The teams headed for extra innings. In the tenth Merullo replaced Hughes at short. Williams replaced Livingston as the catcher. Mayo, in Detroit's tenth, lined to Hack and then Cramer singled, but Greenberg hit into a double play, and the score stayed tied.

The Cubs' Hack singled to left in the bottom of the inning, but Johnson went down on strikes, and Lowrey hit into a 4–6–3 double play.

The game continued into the eleventh inning, and Borowy put out Cullenbine, York and Outlaw in order. Trout returned the favor by retiring Cavar-retta, Pafko and Nicholson.

The twelfth opened with Swift flying out to Lowrey and Trout fouling out to Williams, but then Hoover stroked a hit. O'Neill sent Hoover on an attempted steal to get him into scoring position. As the Cubs' shortstop, Merullo, attempted the tag, Hoover flew into a slide with spikes high enough to cut Merullo in two places on the arm, but Merullo hung onto the ball and Hoover was out.[15]

The last factor now went into play during the Cubs half of the infamous twelfth inning. Trout started out well by retiring Williams on a grounder to Mayo, but then Secory, batting for the injured Merullo, startled Trout by clipping a single into left center. Grimm sent in speedster Billy Schuster to run for Secory. Trout went back to work and struck out Borowy. With two outs and a runner on first, Trout pitched to Hack, who had three hits in this strange contest. Trout threw a wide curve ball that missed, and then followed up by pumping two hard strikes past Hack. On the next pitch Hack sliced out his fourth hit, a liner, into left field. But no one was ready for what happened next. Greenberg came running in to field the ball on the first hop and hold Schuster at second. When the ball hit the ground, Hank bent down on one knee to field it, but it jumped as if an electric shock had hit it, and it bounced so quickly over his shoulder that it narrowly missed his face. With the big fellow in hot pursuit, the ball rolled all the way to the left-field wall as if it had a mind of its own. Grimm, coaching at third, saw Greenberg's large number 5 heading to the wall and yelled, "Come on, Schuster!"

The hard-running Schuster scored the Cubs' winning run. The entire Cub team blasted out of the dugout to hug Hack and lift him back to their Cub-cave with great delight.[16]

After a record-setting 3 hours and 28 minutes of one of the daffiest games played, the Cubs' 8–7 victory had forced a seventh and final game.

Jimmy Outlaw reflected: "That game is the one that the ball hopped over Greenberg's head. Oh, that looked bad. You know it hit the sprinkle head that they used to wet the field down with in the outfield. That's what the ball hit and it bounced over his head. When it hit that sprinkle head it just went everywhere. I said, 'Oh, there goes the ball game.'"

Ed Mierkowicz:

Yes, Hack hit a double on that play. Hank misplayed the ball. You got to remember Henry didn't always play the outfield. He was a first baseman. He wasn't the fastest man in the world, either. Hack was a left-handed hitter. When Hack hit the ball it hit that pipe and bounced over Hank's head. I went into play for Hank defensively in the seventh game. I know I was a better outfielder than Greenberg. Hank had good hands, but he could never move. I'm not taking anything away from Hank. He just was the type that wasn't as agile as the average player. He worked hard on his hitting and he made himself into a good hitter. It was a typical wartime ball game.

The ruling on Hack's hit became controversial. It was ruled a single and an error for Greenberg. Greenberg was not happy about the ruling.[17]

Strangely enough, it was the famous sportswriter Harry Salsinger of the *Detroit News* who felt Greenberg deserved the error. He accused Hank of "playing Hack's single poorly." He, in fact, insisted upon the error, and Ed Burns of Chicago and Marty Haley of St. Louis finally agreed to go along his request. Salsinger, however, admitted Greenberg never touched the ball.[18]

The ruling started a firestorm. Never in the history of the World Series had an error ruling been changed. The argument took five hours to resolve, and the papers by that time had filed the story that Greenberg had committed a crucial error.

Writer Fred Lieb was the alternate scorer. He disagreed with the ruling, and said he never would have given Greenberg an error. At the Palmer House enough pressure was put on Burns and Haley to make them decide to reverse their ruling. After the reversal was pronounced, Salsinger made it unanimous. Hack had a double and Greenberg didn't receive the error. It was the first time a reversal was made on a given error.[19]

In the Detroit locker room the atmosphere was dark, and hardly a word was spoken. It was hushed and subdued. The Tigers couldn't understand how they had lost. There was a feeling of resentment at the manner of their loss. Dizzy Trout, who usually had to be led away talking, just slumped down on his chair dejectedly in front of his locker and said nothing.[20] Cullenbine was the first to speak, and he said of Greenberg's fielding, "Hell, I could see it better than the official scorer in the press box. He never touched it at all. The ball went over his shoulder." Then O'Neill and Hank's teammates opened up about scoring the play as an error. "How in hell could anyone give an error on such a play?" demanded the skipper. Rudy York and others chimed in with similar views and Cullenbine punctuated the incident by standing up and throwing his glove against the wall and shouting, "I've seen everything now. Now the outfielders are supposed to catch a bad hop? Let me out of this business."[21] Greenberg was so upset he could hardly talk. The one person who did ask him what happened was roughly brushed off. No one approached him. He borrowed Tobin's shaving cream, grabbed a razor, and went off to shave alone. Some thought it was good that it was a safety razor and not a straight razor in his hand. After he cooled off he said, "I never had a chance on the ball. It just bounded over my shoulder." He was furious that they charged him with an error.[22]

Trucks took the blame on himself for the Cub's four-run fifth inning. "I didn't field Hughes' bunt after Livingston singled, and didn't make a play to third that I should have made," he said.[23]

O'Neill wasn't bitter about the play that gave the Cubs the game, but he was quite cutting of Hostetler and Mayo's base running. He said:

I tried to wave Hostetler back at third after he fell, but he was caught. He'd have scored on Cullenbine's single if he had stopped at third.[24]

In the eighth, Mayo tried to stretch his single into a double and was out. Then Greenberg hit his homer. That would have been the game if Mayo had been on base.[25]

It was a tough one to lose. We should have won it in regulation time. We had plenty of chances, but nothing went right. We made a lot of bad plays, and we did a lot of bad base running. There'll be no workout tomorrow. I think a day off will do the fellows more good. I'll pitch Newhouser Wednesday. I don't know who they'll pitch. They just about ran out of pitchers taking this one.[26]

Despite the dejection, there were no gripes, even though Detroit had been so confident of winning that they had made train reservations to head home for a victory celebration.

The Cubs' locker room was brimming with confidence, and it was a happy lot that celebrated. "How about Hank, I mean Borowy?" yelled Grimm when he finally got to be heard over all the noise. "How about him? With seven and one-half hours rest he went in and put it in there. Boy, that's working, that's my boy." Then he addressed Hack's hit: "What a way to win it! What a beautiful hop. No ball ever took such a beautiful hop that I know of. That hop and Borowy's pitching. There's the story in a nutshell. No, I won't tell you who'll pitch. I can't as a matter of fact. The boys will have a day off tomorrow. There'll be no workout. We'll come back strong for the finisher."[27]

Passeau lamented that fate had spoiled his chance for a second victory because of injury. He displayed the injured finger on his pitching hand, exposing the torn nail on his third finger, still covered with blood. "I just couldn't grip the ball," he said.[28]

Fondling a group of telegrams scattered about his locker, Grimm opened one and read, "Don't pitch to Greenberg. Base on balls. No team without him. (Signed) Paul Murphy." Grimm shook with laughter and said, "That arrived a little too late for me."[29]

Joyous turmoil reigned in the Cubs' locker room with Grimm right in the middle of it as if this were just a normal work day. Players ran back and forth, throwing gloves into lockers, kicking trunks, and running into and hugging each other. They were the exact opposite of their opponents. Shouting, smiling and happy, the players romped and took part in good-natured kidding as they complimented each other and ridiculed the Tigers individually and as a ball club. The clubhouse spirit was as if they had won the Series.[30]

It was just a crazy bounce of a baseball in a crazy game that gave the Cubs the win. But the huge elephant in the room was a question: Who would pitch the seventh game? The Cubs had to use four of their regulars, Wyse, Prim, Passeau, and Borowy to win the sixth game. That one question had the lobby bookies laying 2–3 for Detroit.

Two other incidents were reported at this time that played into the future of the game.

The morning of the sixth game the future of baseball's new $50,000 a year commissioner, A.B. "Happy" Chandler, was decided. Chandler had rubbed some of the reporters, owners and baseball administrators the wrong way and there was a big discussion about buying his contract out. Representatives of all the clubs were in attendance with the exception of the Giants, Yankees, Indians and Senators. The friction seems to have been about the salaries of umpires for the World Series and Harridge's dismissal of Umpire Ernie Stewart due to a salary dispute. The other question connected with the buyout was the matter of who had the final authority to make decisions. Reports had been hovering around Chandler concerning his relationship with his two top league officials, Ford Frick and Will Harridge. Frick had contacted the absent Giant representatives and, having the answer from seven of the clubs, he made the statement on behalf of the baseball magnates that there was no basis for published reports that an effort would be made to buy off the commissioner's seven-year contract. As newsmen pressed Chandler for details, he simply mentioned that he had a seven-year contract locked in his safe and that this was not his maiden venture in business. He laughed off the thought of resignation and with a smile he answered the questions about who initiated the anti–Chandler movement by saying, "I prefer not to think that any of my 16 employers are involved." That meeting cemented Chandler's future as commissioner for the time being.[31]

The other incident concerned the Tiger team. Jack Zeller submitted his resignation to owner Walter O. Briggs. Zeller confirmed the resignation and said on Monday evening, "I really think I need a rest, and with the Tigers in the World Series now is a good time to drop out." He said he was tired and wanted to go to his Texas home for a rest. Briggs refused to accept the resignation, but this time Zeller was firm and said he would take leave of the club on December 31 of that year.[32]

These two events ushered out something old and ushered in something new. Zeller represented the prewar era and the old-style business dealings of baseball teams.[33] Chandler represented the postwar atmosphere and the beginning of change. The cultural transition bridge had just been crossed. There was, however, one more game to play to complete the bridge.

The reporters of the day scorched both teams for the display publicly presented during the sixth game. Povich of the *Washington Post* wrote, "Actually, the game was won and lost a half dozen times by the two clubs on stupid base running, ineffective pitching, unpardonably bad coaching and damaging errors. Only five errors were charged against the teams, but there were other misplays."[34]

Arthur Daley of the *New York Times* described the sixth game as a mixture of good and bad baseball by writing:

> After yesterday's game no one knows what is likely to happen. That one had about everything — brilliant baseball, stupid baseball, timely hitting, futile hitting, plays made backward, runs thrown away, runs handed out as gifts and as the crowning

touch, the official scorers reversing themselves for the first time in the annals of the sport five hours after the contest had gone into the records.

This has been a series that almost defies description. So many incredible things have happened that a spectator hardly can believe his eyes.[35]

The *Washington Post*, in an article titled "Armageddon," printed these words: "What the last and decisive game tomorrow afternoon will be like is apparently beyond any prediction. In the effort to win yesterday both clubs threw into the struggle virtually everything they possessed, including all the pitching reserves. Meantime, all else has been, for the time being, crowded out of the public consciousness. Please don't talk to us about atomic bombs, or the Russian impasse, or the strike crisis, or full employment, or such matters, until the issue of this hair-raising 1945 World Series is settled one way or the other.[36] It was one of those things that stopped all traffic, and until the final out and the crowning of a champion could take place, the world would be on hold.

There was one player who was eagerly waiting for this last seventh game. Hal Newhouser might have an ailing back and shoulder and a tired arm, but he possessed a very willing spirit.

Game Six, 10-08-1945, at Wrigley Field in Chicago

Detroit	POS	AB	R	H	RBI	PO	A	E
Webb-	6	3	0	0	0	3	3	0
c. Hostetler	PH	1	0	0	0	0	0	0
Hoover	6	3	1	1	1	1	1	0
Mayo	4	6	0	1	1	4	5	0
Cramer	8	6	1	2	1	2	0	0
Greenberg	7	5	2	1	1	4	0	0
Cullenbine	9	5	1	2	1	1	0	0
York	3	6	0	2	1	9	1	0
Outlaw	5	5	0	1	0	2	0	0
Richards	2	0	0	0	1	4	1	1
a. Maier	PH	1	0	1	0	0	0	0
Swift	2	2	1	1	0	5	1	0
Trucks	1	1	0	0	0	0	0	0
Caster	1	0	0	0	0	0	0	0
b. McHale	PH	1	0	0	0	0	0	0
Bridges	1	0	0	0	0	0	0	0
Benton	1	0	0	0	0	0	0	0
d. Walker	PH	1	1	1	0	0	0	0
Trout	1	2	0	0	0	0	3	0
TOTALS	48	48	7	13	7	35	15	1

Chicago	POS	AB	R	H	RBI	PO	A	E
Hack	5	5	1	4	3	3	3	2
Johnson	4	4	0	0	0	2	6	1
Lowrey	7	5	1	1	0	6	1	0
Cavarretta	3	5	1	2	2	15	0	0

Chicago	POS	AB	R	H	RBI	PO	A	E
Pafko	8	6	0	2	0	1	1	0
Nicholson	9	5	0	0	0	1	0	0
Livingston	2	3	2	2	1	2	2	0
e. Gillespie	PH	1	0	0	0	0	0	0
Williams	2	1	0	0	0	1	1	0
Hughes	6	4	1	3	2	4	3	0
f. Becker	PH	0	0	0	0	0	0	0
g. Block	PR	0	0	0	0	0	0	0
Merullo	6	0	0	0	0	1	1	0
h. Secory	PH	1	0	1	0	0	0	0
i. Schuster	PR	0	1	0	0	0	0	0
Passeau	1	3	1	0	0	0	1	0
Wyse	1	1	0	0	0	0	0	0
Prim	1	0	0	0	0	0	0	0
Borowy	1	2	0	0	0	0	0	0
TOTALS		46	8	15	8	36	10	3

a. singled for Richards in 6th
b. struck out for Caster 6th
c. safe on error
d. 2BH 7th
e. 1–3 7th
f. BB 9th
g. ran 8th
h. singled 12th
i. ran for h. 12th

Pitching	IP	H	R	ER	W	SO
DETROIT						
Trucks	4⅓	7	4	4	2	3
Caster	⅔	0	0	0	0	1
Bridges	1⅔	3	3	3	3	1
Benton	⅓	1	0	0	0	1
Trout (L)	4⅔	4	1	1	2	3
CHICAGO						
Passeau	6⅔	5	3	3	6	2
Wyse	⅔	3	3	2	1	0
Prim	⅔	1	1	0	0	0
Borowy (W)	4	4	0	0	0	0

Line Score:

DETROIT	0	1	0	0	0	0	2	4
CHICAGO	0	0	0	0	4	1	2	0

DOUBLES: Hack, Hughes, Livingston, Pafko, Walker, York. SACRIFICE HITS: Johnson 2. HOME RUN: Greenberg. DOUBLE PLAYS: Chic 6–4–3, Det 4–6–2–6, 4–63. LOB: Det 12 — Chi 12. ATTENDANCE: 41,708. TIME OF GAME: 3:28. UMPIRES: Jorda, Passarella, Conlan, Summers.

20

Game Seven

"I'm gonna be all right. I can't for the life of me, however, figure how Borowy can hold up. Wait and see. We'll have him out of there in a hurry."

Hal Newhouser

"We won for Steve O'Neill. There was no man on the club who didn't want to win for Steve." Raising his glass, he toasted his manager: "To Steve, a man who never second-guessed a ball player, and always understood."

Hank Greenberg

History was about to prove the scribe Warren Brown wrong when he said, "I don't believe either one of them can win." On October 10, 1945, the winner of the seventh contest between Detroit and Chicago would be crowned the 1945 world champion.

It finally came down to one more game of baseball. It would bring an end this wonderful but weird season that had survived through a historical and difficult war. The game would be the ninth seven-game classic in baseball history, and the series would be one of the most discussed and controversial of all time.

After losing the sixth game with poor base running and bad breaks, the Tigers were forced into a seventh contest. Would it be another cliffhanger with another fairy tale ending, or would they blow their opportunity as they did in 1934 and 1940? Both teams had a much-deserved rest on October 9, and ticket sales flourished for tomorrow's final game.

Some Detroit players went to see a New York show on Tuesday evening. They picked an Olsen and Johnson comedy production. One New York reporter said, "It is doubtful if they found it as funny as the World Series has been."[1]

Also on Tuesday evening, comedians Bud Abbott and Lou Costello started their fourth year on the radio. Almost 20 million people tuned in for their famous routines, including that great baseball skit, "Who's On First?"[2] The Cubs, getting ready for the final game, were working on a routine called, "Who Will Pitch Game Seven?"

Grimm had chosen to use Borowy in relief for that sixth game and he stayed in to the end. Grimm would sink or swim with Borowy, so great was his confidence in him.

Borowy should have been scratched from pitching game seven. Grimm had Wyse, a 20-game winner, who had pitched six innings in the second game, and only ⅔ of an inning in game six. Derringer was a potential starter. The big hurler had thrown but 3⅔ innings. Then there was Paul Erickson, who had a 3.32 ERA. He had pitched but a total of five innings. The last choice for Grimm was Hy Vandenberg. Tall Hy had thrown 2⅔ innings in games four and five and hadn't allowed any earned runs.

Grimm's indecision showed in the locker room after game six. He told Vandenberg he was his choice for game seven, but then when Borowy, who should have known better, said he was ready to go again, Grimm decided to give him another opportunity.

Almost everyone knew that this was a bad decision. Some tried to change Grimm's mind. But Charlie went with what he thought was his best based on Borowy's knowledge of Detroit and his past record. Borowy, however, had crossed the line of being effective, and needed rest. Peter Golenbock in his book *Wrigleyville* described that locker-room decision: "Merullo said: Borowy never should have pitched in that last game. Never should have.... Borowy came in and said, 'Skip, I'll go right to bed tonight, we have a day off tomorrow, and I'll be ready for that seventh game.' Charley went with his best. But it didn't work out. He should have stuck with Vandenberg, who was rested." Hank Wyse, in the same book, said: "It was Grimm's fault. He didn't pitch the pitchers right. I don't know why he couldn't have pitched Erickson or why he couldn't pitch Vandenberg in that seventh game. They were furious, and so was I. Oh yeah, Erickson even went up to the office and asked to pitch. We knew to be effective, Borowy had to have four days' rest."[3]

The good news for the Cubs was that their shortstop, Hughes, would start the final game. He had been held out of game five, when he suffered the ankle injury due to a batting practice blow from Rudy York, but Grimm started him in game six. Roy, who lived with ice packs throughout the night, rewarded him with three hits in the extra-inning contest. Even though he had the misery of a sprained thumb, as well as a puffed ankle that he had been icing, the Cubs announced he was ready to play in the final contest. Chicago, like Detroit, was a tired and injured group of players at this point.[4]

Along Chicago's Lake Shore Drive in the Hotel Stevens, Hal Newhouser went to bed early. He put a Do Not Disturb sign on his door and pulled the phone cord out of its box. Two days' rest wasn't a lot, but it was one more day than Borowy would have, and Prince Hal's competitive juices were flowing hard. The next morning he had breakfast in bed and was as confident as any pitcher could be with a championship in the balance.[5]

When the scorekeepers reversed themselves and decided not to give Greenberg an error, the horns of the goat from game six were withdrawn from the head of the "Great" Greenberg. No one really wanted Hank to wear that head-dress, but they weren't about to dispose of the horns when there were others who could wear them. Chuck Hostetler and his spectacular spill had the honor of inheriting those horns.

The writers were unmerciful in their description of his bad fortune. To this day the 1945 World Series brings to memory "The Hostetler Flop," the title they tagged him with for life. Ira Kupcinet, a *Chicago Sun-Times* columnist, wrote that a friend told him that he had taken his elderly father to watch the sixth game and Ira replied, "I know. I saw him fall between third and home."[6] That was but one of the many cuts Hostetler suffered.

Hostetler was a 41-year-old man who played semi-pro and professional baseball for a number of years on some very good teams, and two of those years had been in the major league war years on pennant-contending teams. He hit .298 and played 90 games in 1944, his first year in the majors, and although a bench-player his second year, he was a certified member of this World Series team. He made contributions to Detroit's success during the season. Now he felt he would be blamed for losing the whole series, a difficult load for anyone to handle, but especially for a man of Chuck's pride. It was to be a long night for Hostetler knowing he might be held responsible for losing the series. It perhaps was the longest night of his life.

Red Borom recalls the situation: "Some of us returned late that night to the hotel and as we entered our floor and walked down the hallway we found Chuck. He was struggling to get up and his blood-shot eyes told the story. He kept saying over and over, 'I blew it, I blew it.' We got him to his bed and assured him it wasn't his fault, and that he shouldn't worry because we were going to beat the Cubs in game seven, and no one could blame him for anything."

Before batting practice for this last encounter, Hank Greenberg walked into Steve O'Neill's office and told him that he was hurting. Hank had aches and pains in his ankle, back and legs, but he could play through those ailments. In game six, however, he had tried to hit to the opposite field and injured his wrist. When he woke up in the morning the wrist was quite painful, and it didn't seem to be healing. He didn't think he could throw or even grip the bat correctly. He thought it might be better if he didn't start. There was a lot at stake. If he weren't up to par and able to give it his best, it wouldn't be fair to the others. O'Neill didn't say anything for a moment. Then he questioned what Hank's absence from the lineup did for the morale of the squad. There was a moment of silence as Greenberg immediately understood how important this game was to the skipper. He finally said he would try to do his best, but if anything went wrong he would appreciate being replaced. Only Hank and O'Neill knew of the injury. Greenberg held back from his regular pregame batting practice and took but one round at the plate, just so no one would detect that something might be wrong.[7] When the slugger finished his short practice session and returned to the dugout a reporter sarcastically inquired of him, "Hank, do you think the series will come to an end today?" Greenberg good-naturedly smiled at the question and replied, "I doubt it. That would be much too commonplace."[8]

Edward Prell reported for the *Tribune* that tickets went on sale at 8 A.M. and would continue until all 36,000 were sold. The price was $7.20 for box seats and $6 for the grandstand seats. The streets and corners around Addison Street the previous night were alive with people. At midnight the place harbored over 200 cold and shivering baseball fans of all ages. P.K. Wrigley, ticket manager George Doyle, and a squad of clerks were getting ready for a rush for the tickets and were prepared to spend the evening getting things in order. Wrigley, always proud to be of service to his customers, said he was attending to the wants of his own personal customers and rooters. Those fans would be the ones that were regulars during the bad times as well as the Cubs' pennant years.

In the absence of a police squad, Wrigley pulled Frain and all the ushers of his organization that he could get on short notice in to help. They were stationed outside the gates late into the evening and would go into early morning. Frain sent a hurry-up call to his uniformed men who were working at the Marigold Garden fights and at the ice revue in the Coliseum. Frain was busy all night answering questions of all kinds from fans who strolled by the ticket windows. He and his team were ready to spend the night and continue until the sale ended. The estimation was that by 8 A.M., 35,000 to 40,000 fans would be storming the Cubs' park. The temperature dropped into the low 40s before midnight and many brought blankets, newspapers and wooden boxes, and established position rights at each window by being labeled on the backs of their coats with chalk numerals. It was an orderly crowd and the distribution of tickets went well.

During pre-game batting practice Newhouser discovered something important. "It was a bright sunny day in Chicago, and they had a full house. While I was practicing some bunts before the game I noticed the ball was tough to see. Then I saw the reason. The fans in the centerfield bleachers had taken off their coats because it was getting to be a hot day, and most of them were wearing white shirts. It made the ball hard to pick up." Newhouser decided to adjust his arm angle on his pitching deliveries and throw more overhand. This would make his fast ball hop a little more, and when it hopped with a sea of white spread out behind it as a background, it would be difficult for the hitter to follow the pitch.[9]

When asked how he felt before the game Newhouser said, "I'm gonna be all right. I can't for the life of me, however, figure how Borowy can hold up. Wait and see. We'll have him out of there in a hurry."[10] He also commented on the playing field and said the mound at Wrigley Field is the best he ever worked from because the soil around the mound is solid and compact and has no give to it.[11]

Paul Richards (National Baseball Hall of Fame Library, Cooperstown, New York).

The umpire shouted "Play ball!" Webb, the leadoff hitter for the Tigers, opened the final game of the year by battling Borowy to a 3–2 count, and then clouted the next pitch into right field for a base hit. O'Neill flashed the hit and run sign for the next hitter, and Mayo jumped on the first pitch, lining it into right for another single. Webb scurried over to third. Cramer, the next hitter, was jammed on the second pitch, but he muscled a handle hit over third for the third straight hit, and Webb scored the first run of the game.

Grimm now understood Borowy wasn't up to the task, and after just nine pitches, six to Webb, one to Mayo, and two to Cramer, no outs, and one run in, he hurried to rectify his decision to start Borowy. Borowy, shattered, departed, and in came Derringer.

With Cramer and Mayo on first and second, Greenberg stepped up to the plate to face Derringer with no one out. The infield was back for a double play, and the outfield was deep, expecting the possibility of a long drive. Hank's wrist was still lame, and he felt that he couldn't swing effectively, so he surprised everyone and laid down a sacrifice bunt that advanced the runners. Cavarretta took the bunt for the out, and the managerial wheels began to rotate. The switch-hitting Cullenbine was batting left-handed against Derringer, so the Cubs gave him an intentional pass to fill the bases and allow for a force play to be made at any base. This brought up the dangerous but slow-footed York. A double-play ball would salvage the inning, and Chicago would only be down by one run. A frightening tremor flowed through the 41,590 fans when York clubbed a long, high-fly ball deep towards the right field wall very close to the foul line. Right-fielder Nicholson had no way of reaching it. The ball dropped to the ground just an inch or two foul. The anxious fans sat down, settled back, and watched Rudy pop the next pitch up to Hack at third. Now there were two outs with the bases still jammed.

One more out and Derringer would have the Cubs out of a sticky situation. Mayo began to annoy Derringer with his antics on the base path between third and home. Eddie's feints to steal home were a real threat because the Cub hurler was noted for using a big, long windup. Eddie might have stolen a score, but was satisfied to just keep getting on Oom Paul's nerves.[12] Outlaw stepped into the batter's box and made himself very small. The 5'8" infielder walked on four pitches as Derringer missed the plate with each pitch. Mayo trotted in with the gift run and Detroit was up 2–0. Many thought this walk decided the game. Derringer's lack of control would hurt the Cubs' chances.

Richards entered the batter's box. After three pitches Derringer had a 1–2 ball-strike advantage, and decided to put Richards away with his next pitch. But the catcher cracked a line drive into the left field corner very, very close to the foul line. It hit chalk, and as Lowrey tried to field it, the ball caromed off the wall and shot back towards Wrigley Field's left-center field. Richards's double unloaded all three runners. Now the game became anticlimactic. Newhouser had five runs in a game he was ready to pitch his heart out to win. The Tigers' bench leaped joyously from the dugout after Richards's double. The first one up was Hostetler, who almost hit his head on the dugout as he jumped in delight. It appeared he was off the hook. His boisterous, joyous voice filled the stadium. If he ever wanted the Tigers to win a game, this would be the one. All Newhouser had to do was to pitch well, as he almost always did, and the championship flag would fly over Briggs Stadium. Perhaps the scribes would forget that "Hostetler Flop." Newhouser then grounded to Johnson for the third out, but Detroit had batted around for five runs on four hits, and the game had barely begun.

Newhouser struck out the leadoff hitter Hack on three pitches in the bottom half of the inning. Then he ran into a little difficulty. Johnson hit his second pitch and doubled to left center. Peanuts Lowrey dropped down a bunt, and Newhouser, in his haste to field it, committed an error. The Tigers now had some concerns. Chicago had one out and runners on first and second. The question of enough rest was running through the minds of the crowd. Would Newhouser falter as Borowy did?

Cavarretta worked the count to 2–2 and then singled, knocking in Johnson, which moved Lowrey to third base. As Newhouser approached the rubber to pitch to Pafko he heard the familiar popping noise. It was baseball hitting leather. He turned to look and the whole bullpen staff was up and throwing. Trout, Trucks, Overmire, Benton and Bridges were heating up in a hurry. O'Neill wasn't about to make the same mistake as Grimm. Newhouser bore down and the Cubs' rally came to a sudden end when Pafko grounded to Webb for a 6–4–3 double play, ending the Cubs' hopes to get back in the game. The Cubs, however, were on the board with one run on two hits and an error. But Newhouser had survived the inning. The bullpen staff took their seats.

In the second Derringer put away Webb and Mayo on fly outs. It looked like he had settled down, but Cramer banged out his second hit into right field, and Derringer then lost control. It became ugly. He walked Greenberg, Cullenbine, and York, forcing in another run, and the score went up to 6–1. Grimm sprinted out to the mound and brought in Vandenburg, who immediately retired Outlaw on a comebacker for the third out.

Newhouser and Vandenberg both began to put opposing hitters down in order. Hy would straighten out the Cubs' pitching, but the score still stood 6–1 in favor of Detroit.

In the bottom of the fourth the Cubs started a breakthrough. After Lowrey flied to Cullenbine, Cavarretta singled. Pafko then sent the ball into deep straightaway center. When Cramer misplayed it, Pafko was credited with a triple, and Cavarretta scored. Dan Daniel, the sportswriter, shook his head in the press box and commented that he couldn't understand how quickly Doc Cramer had aged before their very eyes in this series and how the writers had missed seeing his deterioration during the season.[13] Yet Cramer recovered quickly and threw a hard strike to Webb on the relay. Webb in turn pegged a perfect throw to Richards at home, but Richards couldn't hold the ball. If he had, Cavarretta would have been cut down at the plate. Newhouser bore down and Nicholson and Livingston both bounced out, 1–3, to end the inning.

Vandenberg continued to subdue the Tigers by inducing York to ground out to Hack for the first out. Outlaw legged out a hit to deep short, and immediately stole second, but Hy forced Richards to ground out to Hack, and Newhouser to fly out to left. Vandenburg had shut Detroit out and compared to his predecessors was looking like an ace.

In the bottom of the fifth Newhouser faced Hughes, who was called out on strikes. Then Grimm pinch-hit Ed Sauer for Vandenburg. "Jolly Cholly" had finally found a stopper, and now he removed him. His pinch hitter struck out swinging, and there was some booing in the stands about the decision.[14] It was Tall Hy's last work ever as a Cub, but he left looking like a champ. He had held Detroit to one infield hit by Outlaw and gave Chicago 3½ quality innings of pitching. Hack ended the inning with a grounder to Webb.

Erickson, the new Cubs pitcher, started the sixth. Webb and Mayo flied out; the aged Cramer, however, not only singled for the third time, but also stole second, putting a possible run in scoring position. Greenberg, still hampered with his bad wrist, couldn't deliver, and struck out to end the fifth.

Newhouser was throwing hard and pitching smart. He struck out Johnson for his fifth strikeout. With one out, Lowrey singled to left, but Cramer hauled in Cavarretta's fly ball for out two, and Pafko ended the inning by striking out.

The Tigers picked up another run in the top of the seventh when Erickson walked Cullenbine. York watched the third strike go past him for the first out, and Erickson put Outlaw away on a fly ball to center; however, Richards stepped up and crushed the hopes of Chicago by slicing out another double, this time into right-center. Cullenbine scored the Tiger's 7th run. Newhouser's fly to Pafko ended the inning.

Prince Hal started the seventh by getting Nicholson on a grounder to York, but after Livingston singled, Newhouser wild-pitched him to second. Newhouser continued to falter by walking Hughes. But Secory, pinch-hitting for Erickson, watched a third strike whiz by and struck out looking. It was Hal's seventh strikeout, and his fifth in the last three innings. He was coming up with the strike out pitch at the right time.

Chicago began to complain bitterly about the ball-strike calls from Art Passarella, who was an American League umpire.[15] Their outrage fell upon deaf ears. Outlaw ended the inning by scooping up Hack's grounder and forcing Livingston at third.

The Tigers added a final touch to Detroit's score in the top of the eighth inning. The Cubs put Passeau back into the pitching box, and he opened the inning by walking Webb. Passeau's finger injury was far from being healed. Mayo pushed the count to 3–2, and then the clutch-hitting Tiger infielder lined a double over third base, scoring Webb. When Johnson threw Cramer out on a grounder, Mayo ended up on third. Greenberg managed to make contact, in spite of his ailing wrist, and lined the ball deep enough to Lowrey in left to score Mayo with Detroit's last run, pushing the score up to 9–2. Cullenbine's pop fly to Johnson ended the inning.

In the bottom of the eighth Newhouser continued to keep the leadoff man off base by inducing Johnson to ground out to Webb at short. But Lowrey singled to left and moved to third on Cavarretta's third hit of the game. Once again a furor of Tiger bullpen pitchers rose to loosen up their arms. Newhouser was becoming uncomfortable with the shoulder pain, but focused hard on Pafko and struck him out.

After that last strike it was Richards who stood up in pain. The pitch had broken his right pinky finger. Unable to grip the ball, he had to give way to Swift. Nicholson, who hadn't been able to get the ball out of the infield, then lifted the hopes of Cubs fans with a double to left, scoring Lowrey and moving Captain Phil to third base. But Newhouser wouldn't be denied. He fanned Livingston for his ninth strikeout to end the inning. It seemed he kept something extra back for these situations, and would reach back for that something special on his strikeout pitch.

Richards had been ushered into the locker area to treat his broken finger with ice packs. When the cameramen who were waiting for the Tigers to arrive started to snap pictures he showed his angst by cautioning them that the game was far from over. "You guys are premature, there's two innings to go yet." He kept showing his apprehension of not being able to see or hear the game from the locker area, and as time passed by he continued asking questions of those who would relay answers down from the field: "What's the score? Who's up? Is anybody out? Has Hughes hit? Is McCullough out yet? Are you sure?"[16]

Hank Wyse, the Cubs' twenty-game winner, finally made an appearance. In the top of the ninth he put Detroit down in order. York flied to right, Outlaw flied to center and Swift grounded to third. One wonders if Grimm was second-guessing himself about starting Borowy after watching Vandenburg and Wyse pitch well.

For defensive purposes, in the bottom of the ninth O'Neill pulled Greenberg and inserted the speedy rookie Ed Mierkowicz into left field. For the first time in the game, Newhouser allowed the leadoff hitter to get on base when Hughes opened with a single. Newhouser, however, was just too much for Chicago on this day, and he wasted no time in completing his assignment. Clyde McCullough pinch-hit for Wyse. McCullough became the first player ever to play in a World Series without playing in a regular season game that same year. Like Virgil Trucks, McCullough was allowed under the war rules to rejoin his team after being discharged from the service. He was in time for the Series, but, unlike Trucks, he didn't have the time to play in any games before the Series.[17]

Newhouser made him his tenth and last strikeout victim. That strikeout was Newhouser's 22nd for the Series and set a Series record for strikeouts by one pitcher.[18] Hack followed with a harmless fly to Cramer for the second out. Webb then fielded Johnson's grounder and flipped it to Mayo covering second, forcing Hughes for the last out, ending not only the 1945 World Series but also the last of baseball's war-year seasons. The Tigers were the first postwar world champions.

It was 4:01 P.M., October 10, 1945, at Wrigley Field when Mayo stepped on the bag to record the last out of the series, and after he stuck the souvenir ball in his hip pocket, he joined the elated Tigers in hurrying over to the box seat where the owner was sitting.[19] Briggs sat in his wheelchair accepting congratulations and being showered with good wishes. It was one of the proudest moments of his life and everyone thought that it couldn't have happened to a finer guy. Goodwill and happiness flowed like an aged smooth wine from a bunch of very elderly players.

This was the moment that the 54-year-old Stephen Francis O'Neill called the greatest day in his career. As soon as the last out was recorded, the skipper trotted over to Briggs's box seat and offered his personal congratulations to the Tigers' owner.[20]

The players yipped and yelled their way into the dressing room and turned the clubhouse into a jungle of ecstatic Tigers, raising the noise level every time another player filed through the narrow locker room door. Coach Art Mills led the parade, followed by Greenberg, Overmire, Benton, Tobin, Trucks and York. As each player hustled through the passageway to the clubhouse, the noise accelerated to a raucous level.[21]

John McHale recalls the enthusiastic scene: "The players who were factors in the game were celebrating, I mean everybody, the newspaper and media wanted to talk about it. We, the rookies, were spear carriers and we were just happy and delighted to be on the club that had won."

O'Neill fought his way through a swarm of fans and arrived 15 minutes later behind the stomping players. When he arrived a victory cheer was sent up as a welcome. A gang of 30 photographers practically blinded all of them with one flash after another. Facing a cadre of reporters for interviews, O'Neill replied to their questions by saying:

> It's a great thrill for me coming up to the highest baseball can offer you. It's a marvelous thing to be up in the majors, and then go down to the minors, come back up again and win a World Series. My boys did that for me.
> As baseball goes, of course, it wasn't much of a series, but it must have been great for the fans. They saw it all, including a lot of things we managers never like to see.[22]

Newhouser sat for questioning and expressed his appreciation for the early lead that his teammates accumulated for him in the first inning. "I never felt tired," he said. "I felt about the same as always, except that my back...." The lump on his back indicated that he had pushed his limits. He wouldn't say anything more about the obvious deformity and no one pushed him to comment about it.[23] He was handicapped through the last part of the American League season with this growth on his left shoulder blade. No one wished to discuss the question of the use of Novocain. It looked like he may need surgery in the off-season. The pain was considerable, and for now he was given Novocain that would deaden it.[24] His performance was a tribute to his competitive nature.

Commissioner Albert B. Chandler managed somehow to work his way through the crowded clubhouse and into the ear-splitting den of the Tigers to offer congratulations. Ford C. Frick, National League president, practically had his overcoat torn off him as the usually professional and cool-responding Tigers took over the clubhouse. Will Harridge, the American League president, decided to stay on the rim of the jam-up after watching Frick being bounced around.[25]

Richards was all smiles as he delicately held his right hand in an iced Turkish towel nursing the pain of his split finger. "For three or four innings Newhouser had his stuff," he said, "but I thought he changed then, although he always held the upper hand. Hal is the kind of pitcher who must have his three days of rest to be himself. There were three or four pitches when he faced danger, particularly in the sixth inning on Cavarretta. After Lowrey singled, Hal came in with a change of pace to Cavarretta that was a beauty."

Greenberg declined to talk about his injury, but seemed to enjoy surprising the Cubs' infield with his bunt.[26]

O'Neill was warm in his admiration of his players. When asked to single out his best Series player, he laid out a number of names beginning with Newhouser and Greenberg, and then adding a number of others until he blurted out: "Take your pick, they all did a helluva job!" He also named a number of Cubs as standouts. Amongst them were Cavarretta, Hughes, Pafko, Passeau, Lowrey and Borowy.[27]

Then suddenly the locker-room victory celebration ended just as quickly as it had started. The sweaty, soaked uniforms were thrown into trunks and everyone was hurrying up so they could catch the victory train leaving in two hours for Detroit. Webb pleaded with the players to hurry. "Come on, gang, let's go get that bus. I'm scared my wife ain't packed yet. It always takes her a month of Sundays." A loud, joyous voice of a half-dressed Greenberg roared back, "To hell with the bus. I'll walk downtown."[28]

As the last of the Tiger remnant departed the dressing room, leaving it to an eerie silence, a smiling Roy Cullenbine strolled towards the exit door and, then like Porky Pig at the end of a Merry Melodies cartoon, he pivoted back to the almost deserted room and shouted out, "That's all there is, brother!"[29]

Wartime baseball sprinted to its exits, and with the end of the 1945 World Series it moved into the record books. At the finish it was the hitting and slugging of Greenberg, Cramer, Cullenbine, Richards and Mayo, combined with the strong-armed pitching trio of Trout, Newhouser and Trucks, that overcame the stumbling base running and obnoxious outfield play. It wasn't pretty, but it was highly suspenseful and entertaining, and at the finish Detroit wore the crown for the last and perhaps most difficult year of wartime baseball. It was a unique historical era not to be seen again in the history of the game.

In the Cubs' locker room Manager Grimm tried to put the best construction on a difficult situation, and admitted that good pitching had stopped Chicago's attempt to win its first championship since 1908. He said that the Cubs had been beat by a good team, but not a better team.[30] Grimm believed that if Passeau hadn't been injured in the sixth game that he wouldn't have had to deplete his pitching staff and Chicago would have had the ring. The Cub players believed to a man that they should have won that series.

Sometime afterwards the Cubs' owner P.K. Wrigley received the infamous short telegram that read, "Who smells now?"[31] The signature below the message was that of tavern owner Billy Sianis. Murphy, the goat, had the last laugh and the curse had started. As of this writing, the 2010 season is about to get underway, and the Cubs still haven't appeared in World Series play since. They own the longest dry spell without a league pennant and the longest World Series drought in baseball history.

Outlaw vividly remembers the day: "I will never forget when we won that last game in Chicago I got up in the bus and said, 'THIS IS TRULY THE DAY!' Oh, we had a good time drinking beer [on the train to Detroit]. We drank a little. I'm not a drinker, but I'll tell you I drank some that day."

Les Mueller: "I can remember the train ride home. That was quite a train ride. Everybody was drinking champagne, and in those days they didn't just throw it on people's heads, they drank it. I will never forget that scene in Detroit when we arrived there, never in my life had I seen so many people. You couldn't see the curbs. It was just mass humanity."

Bob Maier related his memories to nephew Ben Benwell: "There was a special train to take us back to Detroit, with one car filled with champagne, all packed in ice. You could go in and drink all you wanted. There were just two of us, Les Mueller, a pitcher, and me who didn't drink. But we went down and watched the others enjoying themselves. My salary that season was around $4,500, but my World Series check came to $6,445."[32]

Detroit voted to split their reward into 31 shares for $6,445 for each man. The Cubs split their loser's earnings into 33½ shares or some $4,000 apiece. All told, the shares were $475,714.50, which was the greatest amount divided up for any World Series.[33]

Red Borom remembers:

Oh, we had a train ride. We got back into Detroit about 12:30 that night. They had it all roped out, and the train station wasn't about maybe 4 or 5 blocks from the hotel in downtown Detroit. Of course it was cool and most of them in Chicago had carried topcoats. Greenberg didn't get off with us, he went over the back end of the train, got off, and walked back the other way to avoid the crowd. When we got off I was getting off right in front of Richards. He had a bunch of stuff he was carrying. We all carried our own bags. They had cabs out there, two in a cab, so we could go to the hotel. So, Richards hollers at me, 'Hey Red, would you hold this for me?' He hands me a bottle of Scotch and I stuck it in my coat pocket. I started through, and I had bags in my hand when some lady there said, 'Hey Red, what have you got in your pocket?' She grabbed that bottle and I haven't seen it or her since. Every time I would see Richards after that, he would holler, 'Where's my bottle?'"

Virgil Trucks recalls:

When we got off the train in Detroit there was 10,000 people that lined up on both sides of where the train pulled in. Of course the team always had the rear end of the train; they put our cars back there for safety because if there was a wreck those two cars usually stayed on the rail. We had to walk all the way to the front of the station, usually 10 or 15 cars, and that is quite a walk. When you get off that tail-end car and walk to the depot it's a long ways. But there were all these people and they were just noisy that was all. They never tried to touch you or get in the way, but just cheered you, and were happy you were back and had won the World Series.

Mr. Briggs wasn't about to let his team out of town without a celebration feast. He made those nine old men and the rest of the squad the toast of the city the following evening at the Book-Cadillac Hotel. Detroit's City of Commerce hosted the party. Food was eaten, drinks were consumed, speeches were made and honors bestowed. *The Sporting News* gave Eddie Mayo its American League's 1945 MVP award, and Hal Newhouser received its American League best pitching award. Each player was given a beautiful silver trophy. Hank Greenberg rose to speak and said, "We won for Steve O'Neill. There was no man on the club who didn't want to win for Steve." Raising his glass, he toasted his manager: "To Steve, a man who never second-guessed a ball player, and always understood."[34]

Ed Mierkowicz remembered the gathering:

Detroit was a great sports town. They would really back you. When we won the Series all the business people gave us gift certificates from big companies. We could get shirts and all that. We could get tons of things and the products were good. When we won the World Series, the Chamber of Commerce threw a dinner for us. They honored all of us. Newhouser and Mayo won awards. They raffled a car at the dinner and I won it. I was just a rookie and didn't play at

Walter Owen Briggs (National Baseball Hall of Fame Library, Cooperstown, New York).

all and some of the veterans resented me winning the car. Greenberg, however, talked up for me. 'Hey, he is a rookie and he can use it more than we can. Don't begrudge the kid his good luck.' Greenberg was hard not to like. He was so polite and so courteous that it was hard not to like him.

Red Borom: "The fans gave each one of us a silver bowl. They had a long table in a big hall there and they had presents on that table. I spent three days in Detroit going around to the stores picking up hats, suits, hunting jackets and everything you can think of. The fans of Detroit presented that to us. It was quite an affair."

Virgil Trucks: "They also had a banquet in 1935 when they won their first World Series and I wasn't there but I knew about it. Gehringer was about the only one that showed up for that 1935 banquet and they gave them cars. This time everyone showed up and you know what? They called out a number and gave away a car. They called out my number first, but they were going to give it to the fifth ball player, and my number comes up first. Mierkowicz won the car. They gave us all a silver trophy and I still got it. The people of Detroit were the ones that donated the money to buy those trophies. It was a great banquet."

John McHale adds:

A city banquet was given which was wonderful. They gave us many wonderful gifts. Ed Mierkowicz won a Chevrolet car. In 1935 when they won their first World Series— Schoolboy Rowe told me the story a lot of times when he was my pitching coach in the minor leagues— he said he was designated as the guy to get players to come to this dinner put on by the top people at Chevrolet and he invited everybody and about six or seven showed up. I believe "Salty" Parker, a rookie, won the car. Rowe said, "You know, these guys were angry with me and the next time I went back, they said, 'Why didn't you tell me they were going to give away a car?' I said, 'I didn't know they were going to give away a car.'" Parker had just arrived from the minor leagues and he walks over to Rowe, and Schoolboy said, "Are we going to dinner?" He says, "OK." And then he walks out with the keys to a new car. The 1945 dinner was a civic dinner. I have a picture of that somewhere. Pierce, Mierkowicz and I were all together at one table that night."

Red Borom recollects:

Yes, and there is a little story behind that, too. In 1935 when they had the banquet only six players showed up. One was a rookie, "Salty" Parker, who later managed for years in the Texas League. When he turned his plate over at the 1935 banquet there was an order slip for a new car. In 1945 everybody on that ball club, including the bat boy, showed for the banquet. They had all heard the 1935 story. They suspended the making of cars during the war and didn't make them again until 1946. We turned over our plates and there wasn't anything there but the tablecloth. So they had a drawing. They put our uniform numbers in a hat. The seventh number drawn out of the hat would win the car. They couldn't give them a car so they were going to present them with a hubcap, and then when the cars were back in, the hubcap holder would get the car. Would you believe that my number was one of the first drawn? The seventh one, and I was glad to see it, was a rookie, Ed Mierkowicz. When we went to Detroit for that reunion I said to him, "Ed, do you

Commissioner Chandler, security person, O'Neill, Newhouser and Richards, with towel around his split broken finger, celebrate Detroit's championship after game seven (Richards collection: Waxahachie Museum, Waxahachie, Texas).

still have that hubcap?" He said, "You bet." I think he framed it and put it on the wall, but he did get the car.

For many of those players it was the last time they would play major league ball. The wave of youthful players returning from the military would bump most of them out.

The pundits couldn't figure out why everyone enjoyed such a sub-par series. Joe Williams wrote: "Pitching was the tell in the final game, as it usually is, and Newhouser was the teller, winning his second game in three starts. It was a wild daffy series, what with one ordinary club trying to outstumble another ordinary club. For the most part the baseball was shocking to the critical gentry, but the customers who came out in record numbers seemed to love it, indicating that the press should not take themselves too seriously."[35]

The 1945 Series set 21 records and tied 18 others. It became the richest World Series in baseball history up to that time. It broke, amongst other records, all the old attendance marks. Newhouser set a record for total strikeouts with 22 and it was 18 years before Sandy Koufax broke it. If the Series had been sloppy, and not as artistic as the baseball aficionados would have liked, there were moments in that Series that produced very good pitching, excellent hitting and outstanding fielding. It was baseball's contribution to the wartime home front. The quality of games at this time declined, but they lifted the spirits of folks who were immersed in a horrid war. People should have tipped their caps to these players for contributing to the continuance of the game in midst of difficult times.

Jimmy Outlaw: "It was down to the wire, let's put it that way. Every game meant something, and I guess every time at bat meant something. There were a couple of wide-open games, but then the rest of them were tough."

Bill Pierce agrees:

There have been critical statements about that Series, but I tell you, when I look at our Detroit ball club, Trout, Newhouser, Trucks, Greenberg and York at that time, they played ball before the war and they played after the war. They were good ball players, there was no doubt about that. There were some players that were wartime ball players on both teams. But it was still a World Series. To me baseball is the team that is put out there on the field. The Cubs went seven games. They put good competition out there. I don't like the idea of knocking something when you are not in it yourself. I have watched the media over a period of years and it seems like the thing is to talk negative about everything instead of positive. I just don't like that. I like to speak positive and if you have a team that wins the pennant, wonderful. If you have a team that represents our city, that's our team. I don't care if it's wartime. Stan Hack was a good ball player for a long time, Phil Cavarretta was a good ball player, and Hank Borowy was a good pitcher too. There's no question there were some that wouldn't have been there if it wasn't for the war. We found that out next year after the war ended. Man alive, there wasn't too many of them fellows left. Of course a lot of them were older too. So I mean it is hard to say Detroit is a wartime team; it wasn't. A lot of those players were good, very good. You can look through a lot of World Series and see good quality of play and then you will see some World Series way after the war that there were a lot of errors and a lot of bad plays. The players were there during the war, but they were decent players. I can't say the quality of that Series was bad."

The Series of 1945 mirrored its times just as the Series of every era had, and this was the team that proved to be the best in that time of our history.

I remember I had to wait until Saturday to celebrate in my own way. Later on in the week I made my way into town and walked into Chandler's News Store and bought a copy of *The Sporting News*. Afterwards I crossed the street and turned left down Main Street to Fox's Ice Cream Emporium for a tin-roof sundae. I sat there turning the pages of the *TSN* paper, reading baseball articles, and tasting the rich chocolate and the salty Spanish peanuts that mixed with the sweet vanilla ice cream. I searched diligently, and savored carefully not only the sundae, but those magic names of the nine old men and the one young arm that had won the 1945 World Series. At that moment, while reading about my new heroes and enjoying the sundae, I felt a rare happiness and pride in the championship accomplishments of others.

The season fled into history, and that team became a part of it. I walked home, took my baseball glove, oiled it, put a baseball in it, and tied it up to form a comfortable pocket. Afterward I picked up my cracked, taped hickory Jimmy Foxx Louisville Slugger bat from the kitchen corner, and put it and the other items into the old toy box along with my ball cap. I couldn't wait for the winter to vanish and pass quickly. I prayed that the springtime would arrive early, so I could get back to the sandlots and play the all–American game. I was hooked. I never would read a paper in the summer again without first turning to the box scores.

A couple of weeks later, after the Tigers had finished their celebrations, a new dynamic ushered itself into American society. On October 23, 1945, the Dodgers signed Jackie Robinson, an African American player. It was a seed that had needed planting for a long time. Branch Rickey, the Brooklyn Dodgers' executive, and the new baseball commissioner Happy Chandler introduced this dynamic into, not only baseball, but also American society and its civil rights history. The winds of change blew strongly through our country, but there were few at the time that realized the immense strength of that wind.

Game Seven, 10-10-1945, at Wrigley Field in Chicago

Detroit	POS	AB	R	H	RBI.	PO	A	E
Webb	6	4	2	1	0	0	5	0
Mayo	4	5	2	2	1	2	1	0
Cramer	8	5	2	3	1	2	0	0
Greenberg	7	2	0	0	1	0	0	0
Mierkowicz	7	0	0	0	0	0	0	0
Cullenbine	9	2	2	0	0	2	0	0
York	3	4	0	0	1	8	1	0
Outlaw	5	4	1	1	1	1	2	0
Richards	2	4	0	2	4	9	0	0
Swift	2	1	0	0	0	2	0	0
Newhouser	1	4	0	0	0	1	2	1
TOTALS		35	9	9	9	27	11	1

Chicago	POS	AB	R	H	RBI	PO	A	E
Hack	5	5	0	0	0	1	3	0
Johnson	4	5	1	1	0	1	3	0
Lowrey	7	4	1	2	0	3	0	0
Cavarretta	3	4	1	3	1	10	0	0
Pafko	8	4	0	1	1	6	0	0
Nicholson	9	4	0	1	1	1	0	0
Livingston	2	4	0	1	0	4	1	0
Hughes	6	3	0	1	0	1	1	0
Borowy	1	0	0	0	0	0	0	0
Derringer	1	0	0	0	0	0	0	0
Vandenberg	1	1	0	0	0	0	1	0

Chicago	POS	AB	R	H	RBI	PO	A	E
a. Sauer	PH	1	0	0	0	0	0	0
Erickson	1	0	0	0	0	0	0	0
b. Secory	PH	1	0	0	0	0	0	0
Passeau	1	0	0	0	0	0	0	0
Wyse	1	0	0	0	0	0	0	0
c. McCullough	PH	1	0	0	0	0	0	0
TOTALS		37	3	10	3	27	9	0

a. Struck out for Vandenberg in 5th
b. Struck out for Erickson in 7th
c. Struck out for Wyse in 9th

Pitching	IP	H	R	ER	W	SO
DETROIT						
Newhouser (W)	9	10	3	3	1	10
CHICAGO						
Borowy (L)	0	3	3	3	0	0
Derringer	1⅔	2	3	3	5	0
Vandenberg	3⅓	1	0	0	1	3
Erickson	2	2	1	1	1	2
Passeau	1	1	2	2	1	0
Wyse	1	0	0	0	0	0

Line Score

Detroit	5	1	0	0	0	0	1	2	0	(9)
Chicago	1	0	0	1	0	0	0	1	0	(3)

DOUBLES: Johnson, Mayo, Nicholson, Richards (2). TRIPLES: Pafko; STOLEN BASES: Cramer, Outlaw. SACRIFICE HITS: Greenberg. DOUBLE PLAYS: Detroit—Webb-Mayo-York. WILD PITCH: Newhouser. UMPIRES: Passarella, Conlan, Summers, Jorda. ATTENDANCE: 41,590. TIME OF GAME: 2:31.

Epilogue: Where Did They Go?

> "I was in the dugout for the opening day in Detroit and the ball game was just about ready to start when Richards came up to me and said, 'Les, they want to talk to you in the office." I said oh-oh, maybe I got traded. I went up there and the general manager, Trautman — I believe Jack had retired — said, 'You are going over to Buffalo.'"
>
> Les Mueller

And then 1945 became 1946 and things changed quickly. Everyone wondered when Detroit would sign an African American player, but that would be a long time in coming.

The Tigers returned to their regular training site in Lakeland, Florida. Many of the 1945 team had moved on, or out, and many others had been reduced to bench roles. The competition was fierce for positions with the return of the veterans from the service, and with the new young talented rookies that were being signed.

Les Mueller was arduously trying to gain a starting position in the rotation of Detroit's 1946 pitching staff. He had labored hard in spring training and seemed to be having a good spring. The Tigers were considered serious contenders. But the front office had changed and George Trautman, the former president of the American Association, had succeeded Zeller. He was trying to organize his job and pull things together in a hurry. All the new changes rushed him into getting the team set for the coming season. His decisions were to affect a number of lives.

Les Mueller remembers:

The pitching coach had talked with me and said, "Well, Les, I think you are set for a very good year." This was just before the season started. I had pitched pretty well in spring training. In fact, coming north just before the season started, I pitched either four or five innings against the Boston Braves at that time and shut them out. So the last two times I pitched for Detroit I pitched two shutout innings in the World Series, and I pitched four or five innings of shutout ball in spring training coming north.

I was in the dugout for opening day in Detroit and the ball game was just about ready to start when Richards came up to me and said, "Les, they want to talk to you in the office." I said oh-oh, maybe I got traded. I went up there and the general manager, Trautman — I believe Jack had retired — said, "You are going over to Buffalo." I was really shocked. In fact, another right-hander, Hal Manders, was there and he was also assigned to report to Buffalo, New York. We both said we weren't going to go. I don't know how many days I waited, but after a few days I gave in and said I might as well go. Manders, however, didn't, and continued to say he wasn't going. You know, he ended up going to the Red Sox and then to the Cubs.

I was traded from Buffalo to the Yankee system in 1947. Richards was managing Buffalo then. They really needed a third baseman quite badly and Richards came up to me and said, "We've traded you to Newark and that might be a break for you because the Yankees like you." I ended my career there. I pitched for three years in Newark, and was 26–25 for my efforts. When I was 29 I thought it was time to quit. They wanted me to stay and sent me a real good contract. In fact, a better contract than I ever had in baseball, and they were disappointed I didn't play.

When I went to spring training in 1946 I think the Tigers had about 18 pitchers in spring training. All of these fellows coming out of service, plus the ones that were already there, allowed for a lot of fellows to get lost in the shuffle. Some, however, got a break and stayed there for one reason or the other.

I recall that on my way up to the office that day I ran into, I'm not going to mention his name, another Detroit pitcher, and he said, "Well, Les, if anybody would have got sent out, I would," but he didn't. In fact, he pitched there for quite a few more years. A lot of the pitchers that stayed there practically did very little as far as their record was concerned over the next few years. I don't know if it's one of those things but it was a shocker for me. I thought in coming back after being in the service I had pitched pretty well, everything considered. I remembered that Ed Rommel, one of the league's umpires, told me he thought I was set for a good year.

Unfortunately O'Neill wasn't there at that time. He was having one of his sick spells, and I didn't get to talk to him. Richards told me that if I wanted to get back to the majors I needed to develop a slider. It was a popular pitch. I never did.

Mueller spent the rest of his pitching career at Newark and then retired and took over the family furniture business back in Belleville, Illinois.

Mueller was just one case of the disappearing champions of 1945. Others from that 1945 team didn't even get to spring training. Red Borom, Chuck Hostetler, Hub Walker, Jim Tobin, Walt Wilson, Joe Orrell, and Joe Hoover were either released or picked up with semi-pro or minor league teams without the hope of seeing the majors again.

Zeb Eaton was assigned to the minors as an outfielder. Detroit thought he had good possibilities as a hitter. He was hitting a league-leading .359 with the Tigers' affiliate in Birmingham, Alabama, in 1947 when he was hit in the head with a pitch that ended his career.

Bob Maier believed he should have received a raise but Detroit didn't. They sent him a contract for the same amount as the previous year. Maier said, "I had no idea what I should get for the 1946 season, so I talked to a couple of the guys and they said to ask for $10–12,000. The Tigers wanted to pay me the same as they did in 1945, so when they sent me a contract I sent it back. I sent

Paul Richards a playing manager at Buffalo, New York (Paul Richards collection, Waxahachie Museum, Waxahachie, Texas).

it back two or three times, and when it got to be the start of the season, I was a holdout. Detroit sent me to Buffalo. I wasn't about to go to Buffalo, so they finally let me go."[1]

George Caster pitched 41.1 innings for Detroit in 1946, winning 2 and losing 1 before being released. Tommy Bridges, listed as a pitching coach, pitched 21 innings and posted a 1–1 record in 1946, and then he was let go as a player. Bridges caught on with a minor league west-coast team for a while, and later turned up as a coach with Toledo and did some scouting for a while. Then he disappeared.

Richards became manager of the Chicago White Sox in 1951. He joined Billy Pierce, who had been traded to the White Sox by Detroit in November of 1948. Pierce turned into a winning pitcher for the Sox. His career 211 victories included two 20-game-winning seasons. *Left to right:* Pitcher Harry Dorish, Manager Paul Richards, Coach Ray Berres and Pitcher Bill Pierce.

John McHale bounced around as a player between Buffalo and Detroit until 1948. He left the player part of the game and went to the executive side of baseball, and became a successful general manager and president with several major league teams. He finished a fine administrative career working in Major League Baseball's Commissioner's Office. He also was part of the Hall of Fame's veterans committee.

Eddie Mayo's injuries in 1946 put him in a secondary role to Jimmy Bloodworth that year. He never had another year like 1945. His last year was 1948. He did a stint as manager in Toledo, and also held a coaching job with the Philadelphia Phillies. When he left baseball he applied himself to the business world and became quite successful.

Jimmy Outlaw stayed on as a full-time utility player and continued in that capacity until he moved on in 1949. He managed a little in the minor leagues before calling it a career.

Doc Cramer spent the next three years as a utility outfielder, coach, and pinch hitter for Detroit, and then moved to a coaching position with the White Sox and their new manager Paul Richards. He taught a number of outfielders in Detroit and at Chicago how to make that sliding catch, and he was a good batting instructor. Perhaps his most famous pupil was Hall of Fame infielder Nellie Fox from the White Sox.

Ed Mierkowicz bounced around Buffalo and Detroit before ending up in the Cardinal system, where he spent time in the Triple A league with Rochester and other minor league clubs.

Bill Pierce and Art Houtteman turned into top-notch, front-line pitchers for the White Sox and the Tigers. Pierce mastered his pitches, and his control, and posted over 200 major league wins. Detroit made the worst trade in its baseball history when they traded him to the White Sox after the 1948 season for a Yankee/White Sox catcher named Aaron Robinson.

Houtteman had tragedy strike him several times during his career that involved his family and his health. But he was considered an excellent pitcher when healthy and had a 19-win season for Detroit in 1950. Later in his career he won 15 games for the 1954 Indians in their successful race for the AL pennant.

Roy Cullenbine hit .335 in 1946 with 15 homers and 56 RBIs. But Detroit wanted him to fill the empty job at first base after Greenberg was traded and felt he should contribute more home runs for the team. They encouraged him to swing more for the fences and not to worry about his average so much. In 1947 he led the league in walks, hit 24 homers and knocked in 78 runs, but his average fell to .224. The Tigers released him and he retired.

Frank "Stubby" Overmire, who was one of O'Neill's favorites, stayed in the majors until 1952. His best year was 1947, when he posted an 11–5 record. He was traded to St. Louis in 1950, and pitched some of the 1951 season with the Yankees. Stubby finished his pitching career with the Browns in 1952. His career record was 58–67.

"Skeeter" Webb became a utility player for two more years in Detroit, before he was sold to the A's and ended his major league career there in 1948.

Al Benton continued on as a relief pitcher with the Tigers for the next three years. In 1945 Benton was second to Newhouser as the most effective ERA pitcher in the American League. He had a 2.02 earned run average.[2] After his leg injury he seldom finished a game but he continued as a very good relief pitcher. He put in a couple of years with Cleveland after he left Detroit, and by 1952 he ended up in Boston, where he finished his career. "Big Al" had a career 98–88 win-loss record for fourteen major league seasons. He also had the distinction of being the only pitcher who pitched to both Babe Ruth and Mickey Mantle during his career.

Paul Richards ended his playing career after the 1946 season as a utility catcher and a coach. He still caught Newhouser some in 1946, and continued to mentor him during Hal's third straight 20-game-winning season. Paul became manager of Buffalo in 1947, and moved on to a twelve-year major league managing career in Chicago and Baltimore. He also worked as an administrator in the Baltimore, Houston, and Atlanta organizations. His ability to handle players and create modern innovations, along with his managerial skills and teaching abilities, brought him the respect of both players and management.

Rudy York was traded after the 1945 season to Boston for shortstop Eddie

Lake. This allowed Greenberg to move back to first base for the Tigers in 1946, and return some young blood to the Detroit outfield. It also let the Tigers insert a young Eddie Lake at shortstop. York, however, became instrumental in helping Boston capture the pennant in 1946. He batted .276, hit 17 home runs, and knocked in 119 runs with the Red Sox. It was his last productive year. After spending time with the White Sox he finished his career with the A's in 1948. He managed and coached in the minors before retiring.

Newhouser continued his brilliant career in 1946 by posting a 26–9 win-loss season and a 1.94 ERA record. He shared the major league pitching spotlight with Bobby Feller that year as each put 26 victories in his win column. His wins and ERA statistics were the league's best and he almost won his third straight American League MVP award but finished second to Ted Williams, whose hitting led the Red Sox to the pennant. He had one more 20-game season in 1948, before his arm broke down and he was let go in 1953. He finished with 200 career wins as a Tiger, then played a year for Cleveland. He was an effective relief pitcher for the Indians in their 1954 pennant-winning season. Later he worked as a scout for the Houston club and also had a career in the banking business.

Bob Swift continued as a regular catcher for the Tigers until 1953, and then became a coach and manager within the Detroit farm system until his death. He will always be remembered for two special games. He was the catcher who bore the burden of catching the long game for Les Mueller, and he was the receiver for Detroit on August 19, 1951, when Bill Veeck, the Browns' owner, sent a 3'7", 65 lb., midget named Eddie Gaedel to bat in one of the his promotion stunts. The classic photograph of a laughing Swift on his knees behind Gaedel, trying to set a target for his pitcher, is a classic gem.

Dizzy Trout played with Detroit until June of 1952, when he became part of a blockbuster trade with Boston. As a Tiger, Trout won 17 games in 1946, but had losing seasons in 1947 through 1949, and worked mostly in relief until he managed his last winning year, a 13–5 record, in 1950. After the trade in 1952 he finished the year with Boston, appearing in 36 games, and retired at the end of the year. But then, after a five-year layoff, in 1957 he tried to come back and had a very short two-game stint in Baltimore which convinced him he was finished with pitching. His record is 170–161 over a 15-year career. He worked afterwards in Chicago for Bill Veeck as an announcer and a public relations person. He was an entertaining after-dinner speaker. Dizzy was always one of the most quoted players. Paul Dickson's book *Baseball's Greatest Quotations* quotes Dizzy's answer when he was asked about his retirement as a player. He said, "One day I was pitching against Washington and the catcher called for a fast ball. When it got to the plate, it was so slow that two pigeons were roosting on it. I decided to quit." He went out the way he came in, talking baseball and spinning stories for the press.

Virgil "Fire" Trucks had an excellent pitching career and posted a 177–135

The 1945 champs get a golf tune-up before getting ready to defend their title. Over the next few years Trucks improved his score to the mid–60s. The 1946 pennant race, however, went to the Red Sox as Detroit finished a distant second that year. *Left to right:* Unknown golfer, rookie catcher Joe Ginsberg, Hal Newhouser, Virgil Trucks, Paul Trout; kneeling, Art Houtteman (courtesy Virgil Trucks).

mark during a 17-year career. Without the two lost years in the service and the one year he lost because of injury, he would have easily registered over 200 career victories. In 1949 he won 19 games, was the American League strikeout leader with 153, and had a fine 2.81 ERA while logging 275 innings for the Tigers. He also was the AL winning pitcher in the annual All-Star Game in 1949. Unfortunately the only year he had an arm problem was in 1950, when the Tigers almost won another flag. If he had been healthy that year, Detroit probably would have had another series opportunity.

In 1952, Detroit's worst season in their baseball history at that time, Trucks threw two no-hitters. He was traded to the Browns in 1953 and then split the season with St. Louis and the White Sox. He won a total of 20 games against only 10 losses for both teams and picked up 19 more wins for Chicago the next year. Then he bounced between Kansas City, Detroit and New York, ending his career as a coach and batting practice pitcher with the Pirates and later the Orioles.

Hank Greenberg returned a married man in 1946, but started slow and took a lot of criticism. He, however, finished with a torrid hitting streak in September, and for the fourth time in his career topped the AL in home runs and runs batted in. After a salary dispute, and a misunderstanding about a newspaper article which pictured him in a Yankee uniform, Mr. Briggs traded him to Pittsburgh in 1947, where he hit 25 home runs, batted in 74 runs, and led the league with 104 walks. His biggest contribution to the Pirates was the tutoring of Ralph Kiner, who went on to be a great National League home-run hitter. Kiner, who ended up in the Hall of Fame, gives Greenberg credit for improving the skills that made him so productive. After that year Hank retired as a player. Later on he formed a partnership with Bill Veeck and helped administer Veeck's winning clubs in Cleveland and Chicago before retiring.

Steve O'Neill lasted as a manager in Detroit until the end of the 1948 season. He was fired amidst rumors that accused him of running a country-club team after a fifth-place finish. Usually a players' favorite, he was condemned for being too soft on his players. The Detroit newspapers believed O'Neill's inability to control Dick Wakefield and deal with the problems Wakefield caused had a lot to do with his being let go. He was replaced with ex-Yankee third baseman Red Rolfe. O'Neill's teams finished 2nd to Boston in 1946 and 2nd again in 1947 to the Yankees. But in 1948 Detroit fell into the second division and Briggs felt a change was needed. Steve ended up managing Boston in 1950 and 1951, finishing third both years, and then moved to the National League and managed the Phillies from 1952 through 1954, finishing fourth twice and third once in Philadelphia. He had a 14-year career as a manager and never had a losing season. He had a career record of 1,039 victories against 819 defeats.[3]

Walter O. Briggs, the owner of the Detroit Tigers, never won another pennant or a World Series. His teams played and competed well until 1951. Briggs was a man who wanted a team that would make him and the city proud. He was demanding in performance and loyalty, but he could be very generous as well. Detroit set a number of attendance records during the next five years after winning it all in 1945.

In 1950 Detroit had a great team, but lost the pennant to New York right at the end of the year after being in first place for most of the year. From that time on they took a headlong dive that dropped them into the cellar of the American League in 1952. It was the first time in their history that they finished in last place. It took a long time to rebuild the team and return it to its 1945 winning ways and a championship. Twenty-three years later, in 1968, the Tigers finally won another World Series flag.

Mr. Briggs passed away at his Florida winter home in January of 1952 and never witnessed the final collapse of his beloved Tigers. He was a product of his times, well respected throughout the country and in baseball for a number of years as an owner, industrialist, sportsman and philanthropist. His public reputation reversed itself after his death and a new era painted a negative picture of the industrialist. Pictured as a racist and as a robber baron by many of the historical writers and critics of the 1960s and 1970s, he faded into history as a person who held minorities down and should have promoted the welfare of the laborer and the common person much more than he did.

He was the target of a number of activists. His stubborn insistence concerning African Americans participating as players in Major League Baseball were well known. The labor unrest and the racial riots during the 1930s and 1940s made him even more cautious about his relationships with activist groups and minorities. William Allan, a writer for the *Daily Worker*, a Communist newspaper published in New York City, in 1941 wrote demandingly that Briggs and the city should have the brilliant play of the Negro players showcased on Brigg's Tigers teams. Mr. Briggs had been watching a game from his field box between the Chicago Negro Giants and the Kansas City Monarchs at Briggs Stadium. 35,000 fans of all races cheered the talents of the immortal Satchel Paige. Allan decided to push his agenda in the paper.[4] Despite the article and local community pressure, the writer's demands fell upon deaf ears.

It's always easy to look back and point a finger without the light of history. Our society was altogether a different culture and its people looked at its values in a far different light. W.O. Briggs was an industrialist in the mid–20th century with the cultural foundation of a person who grew up within a late 19th-century community. He was typical of the rugged individualist stereotype and he strove to pull himself up by his bootstraps because, although he wasn't born poor, he was not born into wealth, either. Whatever one might think of him and his ilk, it might be good to take a look at him through the eyes of his contemporaries. One such person would be H.G. Salsinger, the popular sportswriter of his day, a member of Baseball's Hall of Fame who was inducted for his writing and promotion of the game, its players, and its owners. On January 18, 1952, Salsinger's column, *The Umpire*, mentioned what he knew and believed about Mr. Briggs: "Walter O. Briggs was more than a great industrialist; he was a great personage. His name was known across the nation, but comparatively few knew the man. His charities were many and nearly all anonymous. He was a deeply sentimental person. He was direct and straightforward, a man of quick decisions. He was faithful to his principles, honest with himself. No man was ever more loyal to his friends, none ever more concerned with their welfare." Salsinger wrote on about the good deeds and love of baseball that Briggs had. He considered Briggs a man who made his baseball decision based on the welfare of the game and its fans.[5]

Walter O. Briggs believed in making the best of what opportunity his freedoms would allow him to pursue in the era he lived in, and he was part of that era's American dream of living free and working hard. He was also a baseball man. His kind passed away a long time ago as our country took on new wars and new social issues and a number of new regulations. Whatever one might believe about Mr. Briggs, he believed deeply in the country and in this game and its fans. He gave much to the city of Detroit, but the Tigers and their stadium might have been his best gift.

The 1945 Tiger team had two players who have been inducted into Baseball's Hall of Fame: Hal Newhouser, the dominant, competitive pitcher of his time, and Hank Greenberg, truly one of the game's greatest sluggers. Both had outstanding careers and deserve their plaques. It might be possible to consider several other players from that 1945 team for the Hall.

Doc Cramer, in spite of his poor fielding in the 1945 Series, was considered one of the best fielders of his day, and he had one of the strongest throwing arms in the game. Although not known as a slugger, he was one of the most consistent contact hitters in the game's history. He logged 2,705 hits over a 20-year career. He hit over .300 eight times in his career, led the league in at-bats seven times, and led the league in hits once. He posted 200 hits in one season three times. His sliding catches were his innovated contribution to the game. He most certainly should be worthy of serious consideration.[6]

Bill Pierce, a Tiger rookie in 1945, was a dominant left-hander in the 1950s with the White Sox. He won twenty games twice, led the league in wins once, led the league in earned runs once, topped the league in complete games three times and in strikeouts once. He recorded 211 victories, struck out 1999 hitters, pitched 3306.2 innings, and had a fine 3.27 ERA in a stellar 18-year career with three pennant-winning teams.[7]

A borderline case could be made for Virgil Trucks's 17-year career statistics, with his two no-hitters in one year, 177 victories, 1534 strikeouts, and 2682.1 innings pitched. He had one of the best fast balls in the history of baseball, and is overlooked when one considers the real flamethrowers of the game.[8]

There are those that would also give credence to admitting Steve O'Neill, the Tiger manager, into the HOF. O'Neill had an excellent record as a manager in the majors and worked well with the players, especially the veterans of the 1945 season.

The author admits to prejudice, but these aren't bad numbers. Those numbers and their longevity attest to endurance and consistency, as well as fine statistics and talent.

The 1945 season was extraordinary not just for baseball, but because World War II ended and the servicemen returned. The music of the big swing bands, highlighted by the Glenn Miller Orchestra and later the Count Bassie Band, still had a few more years in them before giving way to the new rock-and-roll sound of the early '50s. The job market was productive, contractors were building whole new communities called suburbs, postponed marriages were now being sanctified, and America's population was growing by leaps and bounds. Building construction, the development of a whole new system of superhighways, the marketing of TV, and the beginning of computers, work-saving appliances, stylish new autos, the appearance of frozen foods on the market, and so much more were all paving the way for a brand-new American way of life. Wartime baseball came to an end, but it contributed to the value of recreational leisure in the midst of war, and allowed it to continue to be a strong part of a happy, optimistic attitude that America projected for the game and the country's future. The surge of patriotism and the spirit of America's great pride in being the greatest nation on earth forcibly moved through the whole population of America at this time. It was 1945, a good time to be an American, and it was a wonderful era for baseball fans, especially those who respected and loved the old English D.

Series Leaders: Hitting, Fielding

AB: 30 Hack — Chi; Det 29 — Cramer
R: 7 Greenberg, Cramer — Det; Chi 7 — Cavarretta
H: 11 Cramer — Det; Chi 11— Hack, Cavarretta
RBI: 8 Nicholson — Chi; Det 7 — Greenberg
2BH: 3 Greenberg — Det; Chi 3 — Hack, Livingston
3BH: 1 Johnson, Nicholson, Pafko— Chi; Det 0
HR: 2 Greenberg — Det; Chi 1— Cavarretta
BB: 8 Cullenbine — Det; Chi 4 — Hughes, Hack
SO: 8 Johnson — Chi; Det 4 — York
SB: 1 Outlaw, Cullenbine, Cramer — Det; Chi 1— Johnson, Pafko
BA: .423 Cavarretta — Chi; Det .379 — Cramer
SA: .696 Greenberg — Det; Chi .615 — Cavarretta
PO: 71 Cavarretta — Chi; Det 67 — York
A: 24 Webb — Det; Chi 24 — Johnson
E: 3 Hack — Chi; Det 1— York, Mayo, Webb, Richards, Newhouser

Series Leaders: Pitching

G: 4 Borowy, Erickson — Chi; Det 3 — Newhouser, Benton
CG: 2 Newhouser — Det; Chi 1— Borowy, Passeau
IP: 20⅔ Newhouser — Det; Chi 18 — Borowy
H: 25 Newhouser — Det; Chi 21— Borowy
R: 14 Newhouser — Det; Chi 8 — Borowy
ER: 14 Newhouser — Det; Chi 8 — Borowy
BB: 8 Passeau — Chi; Det 5 — Trucks
SO: 22 Newhouser — Det; Chi 8 — Borowy
W: 2 Newhouser — Det; Chi 2 — Borowy
L: 2 Borowy — Chi; Det 1— Newhouser, Overmire, Trout
ERA: 0.66 Trout — Det; Chi 2.70 — Passeau

TOTAL ATTENDANCE: 333,457
WINNER'S SHARE: $6,443
LOSER'S SHARE: $3,930

Chapter Notes

Chapter 1

1. Fred Lieb, "Browns Again Shape History...," *The Sporting News*, October 4, 1945.
2. *Ibid.*, 27.
3. Lyall Smith, "Hank's Bat Wins Flag," *Detroit Free Press*, October 1, 1945.
4. Earl Rickard, "Wartime Baseball," *US History 1929–1945*, Suite 101.com., April 1, 2002.
5. "Greenberg Hailed by Joyous Tigers," *The New York Times*, October 1, 1945.
6. "Tigers Annex...," *The New York Times*, October 1, 1945.
7. "Tigers Whoop It Up After Taking Flag," *Chicago Daily Tribune*, October 1, 1945.
8. Shirley Povich, "Greenberg's Homer...," *The Washington Post*, October 1, 1945.
9. "Newhouser Pitches for 25th Victory," *Adrian Daily Telegram*, p. 5, October 1, 1945.
10. *Ibid.*
11. *Ibid.*
12. Joe Falls, "The World of Dizzy Trout," Cooperstown, Baseball Hall of Fame Library, Newspaper Clipping Files, Detroit, MI, 3–18, 1972.

Chapter 2

1. David Pietrusza, *Judge and Jury: The Life and Times of Judge Kenesaw Mountain Landis* (South Bend, IN: Diamond, 1998), 1–2.
2. Frederick G. Lieb, *The Detroit Tigers* (New York: Putnam's, 1946), 40.
3. Richard Bak, *Cobb Would Have Caught It* (Detroit: Wayne State University Press, 1991), 50–51.
4. Patrick Harrigan, *The Detroit Tigers: Club and Community 1945–1995* (Toronto: University of Toronto Press, 1997), 43–47.
5. Bak, 113–114.
6. Harrigan, 29–31, 127, 182–187; Pietrusza, 153, 372, 506.
7. *Ibid.*, 405–430.

8. Bak, 92–107.
9. Henry Ford Sr., *The International Jew* (Dearborn, MI: Dearborn Independent, 1922).
10. Brian Lamb, *Booknotes* interview with Donald Warren, author of *Radio Priest: Charles Coughlin, the Father of Hate Radio* (New York: Free Press, 1996), September 8, 1996; Harry T. Williams, *Huey Long* (New York: Knopf, 1969), 696, 800–802.
11. P.R. Karieff, "Detroit's Infamous Purple Gang," *Detroit News*, January 16, 1999.
12. Pietrusza, 347–370.
13. Charles C. Alexander, *Breaking the Slump: Baseball in the Depression Era* (New York: Columbia University Press, 2002), 243–244.
14. H.G. Salsinger, "Landis Declares Ninety-one Tigers Free Agents" and "The Umpire," in Dean A. Sullivan, ed., *Middle Innings: A Documentary History of Baseball, 1900–1948* (Lincoln: University of Nebraska Press, 1998), 178–179.
15. William Marshall, *Baseball's Pivotal Era: 1945–1951*, Chapter 1, "Winds of Change," 1 (Lexington: University Press of Kentucky), 1999.
16. *Ibid.*, Chapter 2, "No One Is Qualified," 18–27.
17. *Ibid.*, Chapter 8, "Jackie Robinson's America," 129.

Chapter 3

1. Alexander, 9.
2. David Finoli, *For the Good of the Country* (Jefferson, NC: McFarland, 2002), 11.
3. *Ibid.*, 25, 39, 41, 104, 134, 204.
4. Marshall, 7.
5. *Ibid.*
6. Pietrusza, 372.
7. *Ibid.*, Chapter 26, "Pieces Were Dropping Off of Me," photo section featuring Hartnett and Capone.
8. *Ibid.*, 440–444.
9. Hank Greenberg, *The Story of My Life*,

edited by Ira Berkow (Chicago: Triumph, 1989), 140–141.

Chapter 4

1. Pietrusza, 433.
2. Pietrusza, 435.
3. Sam Greene, "Zeller Steps Up Training Plans...," *The Sporting News*, March 1, 1945, 18.
4. "Home Town Product," *The Sporting News*, March 15, 1945, 17.
5. Lieb, 235–238.
6. "Tigers Well Set," *The Sporting News*, March 1, 1945, 18.
7. "WMC Checks on Status of Ball Players," *Chicago Daily Tribune*, March 17, 1945, 20.
8. Sam Greene, "Zeller Steps Up Training Plans...," *The Sporting News*, March 1, 1945, 18.
9. Sam Greene, "Hub Walker...," *The Sporting News*, March 15, 1945, 17.
10. Sam Greene, "McHale Claims...," *The Sporting News*, March 8, 1945, 17.
11. *Ibid.*
12. Lieb, 260.
13. Sam Greene, "Benton, Ex-Sailor, Ready...," *The Sporting News*, February 8, 1945, 5.
14. Lieb, 260.
15. Harrigan, 52.
16. Red Smith, "Doghouse to Let: Apply Newhouser & Trout," *The Saturday Evening Post*, March 31, 1945, 22.
17. David M. Jordan, *A Tiger in His Time* (South Bend, IN: Diamond, 1990), 59–60; Bill Gilbert, *They Also Served: Baseball and the Home Front* (New York: Crown, 1992), 232–233.
18. J.G. Taylor Spink and Paul A. Rickart, *Baseball Register* (C.C. Spink & Son, The Sporting News Publishers, 1946), 5–20.
19. Red Borom, Scrapbook.
20. "Bosse Field, Home of the Evansville Otters," http://www.digital ballparks.com.
21. "Giants to Play 1st Intra-Squad...," *Chicago Daily Tribune*, March 18, 1945, A!.
22. Walter Haight, "Flyer, One Leg Off...," *The Sporting News*, March 22, 1945, 3; Frederick G. Lieb, "One-Armed Gray Is...," *The Sporting News*, March 22, 1945, 6.
23. Walter Haight, "War Veteran to Pitch...," *The Washington Post*, March 18, 1945, M6; Walter Haight, "Denies Pact with N.Y....," *The Washington Post*, March 19, 1945, 10.
24. "Hero Amputee Almost Causes...," *Chicago Daily Tribune*, March 19, 1945, 20; "MacPhail Accused of 'Piracy,'" *The Washington Post*, March 19, 1945, 1; James P. Dawson, "Lieut. Shepard...," *The New York Times*, March 19, 1945, 15.
25. "Baseball Hails WMC Ruling...," *Chicago Daily Tribune*, March 22, 1945, 29; "Baseball Leaders ... Elated," *The New York Times*, March 22, 1945, 18.
26. Ben Benwell, *Bobby Maier: A Baseball Memoir*, National Baseball Hall of Fame Library, Cooperstown, New York, September, 1992, 6–7.
27. Borom, Scrapbook.
28. "McPhail Argues for Baseball," *Los Angeles Times*, March 23, 1945, A8; "Basic Training in Baseball," *Chicago Tribune*, March 22, 1945, 20.
29. Arthur Daley, "The Latest Green Light," *The New York Times*, March 23, 1945, 16; Oscar Fraley, "The Sports Patrol...,"*The Washington Post*, March 23, 1945, 8.
30. Charley Cherokee, "National Grapevine," *The Chicago Defender*, March 24, 1945, 11.
31. Irving Vaughan, "Sox, Tigers Schedule...," *Chicago Daily Tribune*, March 23, 1945, 25.
32. Borom, Scrapbook; "On the Baseball Front: Pete Gray...," *The Washington Post*, March 25, 1945, M6.
33. "Luck of Draft Held Key...," *The Washington Post*, March 26, 1945, 8.
34. "On the Baseball Front: Giants Bow to..." *The Washington Post*, March 26, 1945, 8; Borom, Scrapbook.
35. Benwell, 1.
36. *Ibid.*
37. *Ibid.*
38. "Tigers Get Exercise," *Chicago Daily Tribune*, March 31, 1945, 18.
39. "Phillies Defeated By...," *The New York Times*, April 5, 1945, 17.
40. Irving Vaughan, "Thornton Lee Yields 2 Hits...," *Chicago Daily Tribune*, April 8, 1945.
41. Sam Greene, "Trout First Tiger to Win," *Detroit Free Press*, April 9, 1945; Irving Vaughan, "Cubs Whip...; Tigers Rout Sox...," *Chicago Tribune*, April 9, 1945.
42. Arch Ward, "In the Wake of the News," *Chicago Daily Tribune*, March 23, 1945, 25.
43. "Tigers Turn Back White Sox...," *The New York Times*, April 10, 1945, 23; Irving Vaughan, "7 Run Detroit Rally...," *Chicago Daily Tribune*, April 10, 1945, 17.
44. "Newhouser Stops White Sox," *The New York Times*, April 11, 1945, 26.

Chapter 5

1. Arthur Krock, *The New York Times*, "End Comes Suddenly at Warm Springs," April 13, 1945, 1.
2. "Griffith Calls President Best...," *Chicago Daily Tribune*, April 13, 1945, 25.
3. "Baseball Cancels Activities Today," *The New York Times*, April 14, 1945, 20.
4. Gilbert, 177–178.

5. Jordan, 129.

6. Ted Williams with John Underwood, *My Turn at Bat: The Story of My Life* (Simon & Schuster, 1969), 69.

7. Jordan, 91.

8. John P. Carmichael, "He Pitched Against Death!" *Baseball Digest*, April 1947, 13–14 (condensed from *Chicago Daily News*).

9. Jack Hand, "All-St. Louis Series Seen by Writers," *The Washington Post*, April 16, 1945, 8.

10. "Jakucki Halts Tigers...," *The Washington Post*, April 18, 1945, 8.

11. "Browns Rout Tigers' Newhouser...," *The New York Times*, April 18, 1945, 28.

12. "Dizzy Trout Shuts Out...," *Los Angeles Times*, April 19, 1945, A8.

13. "Tigers Defeat Browns, 1 to 0...," *Chicago Daily Tribune*, April 20, 1945, 26.

14. "Indians Trim Tigers...," *The Washington Post*, April 21, 1945, 6.

15. "Tigers Edge Indians...," *The Washington Post*, April 22, 1945, M6; "Newhouser Hurls Victory," *Los Angeles Times*, April 22, 1945, A6.

16. "Tribe Errors Factor...," *Los Angeles Times*, April 23, 1945, A7.

17. "O'Neill Hears Tigers Win...," *Chicago Daily Tribune*, April 27, 1945, 24.

18. Marshall, 17–27.

19. Finoli, 228.

20. "Benton Hurls Two-Hit Ball...," *Los Angeles Times*, April 29, 1945, B6.

21. "Indians Defeat Detroit ...Vice Versa," *Chicago Daily Tribune*, April 30, 1945, 24.

22. "Tigers Obtain Cullenbine...," *Chicago Daily Tribune*, April 30, 1945, 23.

Chapter 6

1. "Tigers' Don Ross May Not Report," *The Washington Post*, May 1, 1945, 12.

2. "Haynes Hurls One-Hitter...," *Los Angeles Times*, May 2, 1945, A9.

3. "Tigers Beat Chisox, 2–1...," *The Washington Post*, May 3, 1945, 8; "Benton Hurls Tigers to 2–1 Win...," *Los Angeles Times*, May 3, 1945, A8.

4. Oscar Fraley, "The Sports Patrol: Mack Rates Tigers...," *The Washington Post*, May 4, 1945, 10.

5. "Kramer Blanks Tigers...," *Los Angeles Times*, May 6, 1945, A6; "Browns Beat Tigers...," *The Washington Post*, May 6, 1945, M6.

6. "39,482 Watch Detroit...," *Chicago Daily Tribune*, May 7, 1945, 24; "Tigers Blank Browns Twice," *Los Angeles Times*, May 7, 1945, 8.

7. "Trout Hangs Up Fourth Victory...," *Los Angeles Times*, May 10, 1945, 10; "Trout Ties 8th Knot...," *The Sporting News*, May 17, 1945, 7.

8. "Yankees Win, 7–3...," *The Washington Post*, May 12, 1945, 6; "Yankees Defeat Detroit...," *Chicago Daily Tribune*, May 12, 1945, 16.

9. "Trout Ties..., That Deal Sending Don Ross...," *The Sporting News*, May 17, 1945, 7; "American League Highlights," *The Sporting News*, Box Scores, May 24, 1945, 15.

10. "Boos and Cheers...," *The Sporting News*, Major Flashes, May 24, 1945, 12.

11. H.G. Salsinger, "Why Do Fans Ride York?" *The Sporting News*, September 2, 1943, Baseball Hall of Fame Library, Cooperstown, NY; "Big Rudy...," Red Smith, *Syracuse Herald-American*, February 3, 1970, Baseball Hall of Fame Library, Cooperstown, NY; "Obituaries: Rudy York...," Baseball Hall of Fame Library, Cooperstown, NY, February 21, 1970.

12. "Tigers Blank Red Sox...," *Chicago Daily Tribune*, May 14, 1945, 26.

13. "Trout Loses a Mole," *The Sporting News*, Major Flashes, May 24, 1945, 12.

14. Sam Greene, "Twin-Bill Pileup Doubles Load...," *The Sporting News*, May 24, 1945, 9.

15. Joe Williams, "Dizzy Trout...," Baseball Hall of Fame Library, Cooperstown, NY, January 22, 1946.

16. "Newhouser Stops the Senators...," *The New York Times*, May 20, 1945, S3; "Detroit, Senators Split," *Chicago Daily Tribune*, May 20, 1945, A3.

17. "Pieretti Ends Benton String," *Los Angeles Times*, May 21, 1945, A7.

18. "Browns Defeat Yankees...," *Chicago Daily Tribune*, May 21, 1945, 22; "Browns Wreck Yanks...," *Los Angeles Times*, May 21, 1945, A7.

19. "Tigers Prevail, 7–1...," *The Washington Post*, May 24, 1945, 10.

20. "Tigers Take 2d Place," *Chicago Daily Tribune*, May 24, 1945, 26.

21. "Tigers Beaten ... Benton Injured," *Chicago Daily Tribune*, May 25, 1945, 25.

22. "Tigers Tie for 2d...," *Chicago Daily Tribune*, May 26, 1945, 16.

23. "Tigers Defeat A's, 5–4," *Chicago Daily Tribune*, May 27, 1945, A2.

24. "Tigers, Senators Split," *Chicago Daily Tribune*, May 28, 1945, 24.

25. "Yankees, Tigers Divide...," *Chicago Daily Tribune*, May 31, 1945, 21; "67,816 Watch Tigers, Yankees...," *The Washington Post*, May 31, 1945, 8.

26. "Mueller in Two-Hitter...," *Los Angeles Times*, June 1, 1945, 10; Louis Effrat, "Mueller of Tigers Stops Yankees, 2–0," *The New York Times*, June 1, 1945, 18.

Chapter 7

1. "Bosox Score by 6–4 on Hurlers'...," *The Washington Post*, June 2, 1945.

2. "Buys Shoes—Takes Walk," *The Sporting News*, June 7, 1945.

3. "Johnny Lazor's Home Run...," *Chicago Daily Tribune*, June 3, 1945.

4. "Bosox, Tigers Split...," *The Washington Post*, June 4, 1945.

5. "Red Sox, Tigers Divide Pair...," *Chicago Daily Tribune*, June 4, 1945.

6. "Tigers, Red Sox Divide...," *New York Times*, June 4, 1945.

7. "Hal Newhouser Saves Last One...," *Los Angeles Times*, June 4, 1945.

8. "Tigers Tail Off...," *The Sporting News*, June 7, 1945.

9. "Embree Blanks Detroit, 9–0," *Los Angeles Times*, June 6, 1945.

10. "Overmire in...," *Los Angeles Times*, June 7, 1945; "Tribe checked by Overmire...," *The Washington Post*, June 7, 1945.

11. "Doc Cramer smashed...," *Ibid.*, 10.

12. "Tigers Defeat Indians," *Chicago Daily Tribune*, June 8, 1945; "Newhouser Takes Seventh...," *The Washington Post*, June 8, 1945

13. "Tiger Punchers...," *The Sporting News*, June 14, 1945.

14. "Tigers Beat White Sox, 2–1," *Chicago Daily Tribune*, June 9, 1945.

15. "Tigers' 4 Run...," *Chicago Daily Tribune*, June 10, 1945.

16. "Leo Durocher Assault Case...," *Chicago Daily Tribune*, June 12, 1945.

17. "'I Didn't Hit Anybody'...," *The Sporting News*, June 14, 1945.

18. "Tigers, White Sox Split...," *New York Times*, June 11, 1945.

19. "Tigers Win in 11th...," *New York Times*, June 13, 1945.

20. "Rudy York's Bat Booms..." *Los Angeles Times*, June 14, 1945.

21. "Rudy York Hit His First...," *The Sporting News, Major Flashes*, June 21, 1945.

22. "Hank Greenberg Gets....," *The Washington Post*, June 14, 1945.

23. "Stephens' Homers Subdue...," *New York Times*, June 15, 1945.

24. "Champs' Ace Gets...," *The Washington Post*, June 15, 1945.

25. "Greenberg Out of Army; ...," *Chicago Daily Tribune*, June 15, 1945.

26. "Greenberg Out...," *New York Times*, June 15, 1945.

27. "Greenberg's Return Provides...," *The Sporting News*, June 21, 1945.

28. Irving Vaughan, "Tigers...," *Chicago Daily Tribune*, June 17, 1945.

29. "O'Neill Plays....," *The Sporting News*, June 21, 1945.

30. "Cubs Win, 3–1; Sox Whip...," *Chicago Daily Tribune*, June 18, 1945.

31. "White Sox Triumph...," *New York Times*, June 19, 1945.

32. "Detroit Sees Tough..." *The Washington Post*, June 19, 1945; "Detroit Pennant Fever Isn't...," *Los Angeles Times*, June 19, 1945.

33. "Greenberg to Enter Tiger Line-Up...," *New York Times*, June 21, 1945.

34. "Tigers Nose Out Tribe..." *Los Angeles Times*, June 20, 1945.

35. "Sewell, Three Browns Fined...," *Chicago Daily Tribune*, June 24, 1945; "Barnes Calls Browns' Brawl...," *The Sporting News*, June 28, 1945.

36. "Hal Allows Five Hits...," *The Washington Post*, June 21, 1945.

37. "Greenberg Is Getting Set for...," *Chicago Daily Tribune*, June 21, 1945; "Hank Has First...," *The Washington Post*, June 22, 1945.

38. "Hank in A-1 Shape...," Sam Greene, *The Sporting News*, June 28, 1945.

39. "Tigers Cuff....," *Los Angeles Times*, June 22, 1945; "Tigers Defeat...," *The Washington Post*, June 22, 1945.

40. "Browns Stop Tigers, 8–4." *New York Times*, June 23, 1945.

41. "Tigers Add to Lead; ...," *Chicago Daily Tribune*, June 24, 1945.

42. "Tigers Annex...," *Los Angeles Times*, June 25, 1945.

43. Arthur Daley, "Sports of the Times: The Passing Baseball Scene," *New York Times*, June 26, 1945.

44. "ODT Bans Benefit Game," *New York Times*, June 27, 1945.

45. "Nats Wallop...," *Los Angeles Times*, June 28, 1945; "Dutch Grants Four...," *The Washington Post*, June 28, 1945.

46. "Bengal Hurler Shades...," *The Washington Post*, June 29, 1945; "Nats Bumped by...," *Los Angeles Times*, June 29, 1945.

47. "Senators Club...," *Los Angeles Times*, June 30, 1945.

48. "Pieretti Tops...," *The Washington Post*, June 30, 1945; "Little Men Big On...," *The Sporting News*, June 21, 1945.

49. "Tiger's Defeat A's...," *Chicago Daily Tribune*, July 1, 1945, A2.

50. "Player of the Week; Hal...," *The Sporting News*, June 28, 1945.

Chapter 8

1. "47,729 See Bengals Top...," *The Washington Post*, July 2, 1945, 10; "Hank Greenberg Comes Back....," *Chicago Daily Tribune*, July 2, 1945, 19; "Hank Breads in Again with a Bang," *The Sporting News*, July 5, 1945.

2. "Al Benton Also Back on Job," *Ibid.*

3. Obituaries, Baseball Hall of Fame Library, Cooperstown, NY, Rudy York, February 21, 1970.

4. Bak, 202.

5. Rudy York, as told to Furman Bisher, "A Letter to My Son," in *The Fireside Book of Base-*

ball, ed. Charles Einstein (New York: Simon & Schuster, 1956), 385.

6. *Ibid.*, 383.

7. "Red Sox Blank Tigers," *Chicago Daily Tribune*, July 4, 1945, 24.

8. "Benton Back, Trips Boston...," *The Washington Post*, July 5, 1945, 8; "Ferris Nabs 13th but Benton Wins...," *Los Angeles Times*, July 5, 1945, A7.

9. "Tigers Victors, 9–8, On Greenberg's Hit," *The New York Times*, July 6, 1945, 15.

10. James P. Dawson, "31,288 See Grimes Pace Yanks...," *The New York Times*, July 7, 1945, 8.

11. James P. Dawson, "Yanks Lose, 3–2 in Tenth Inning: Cramer's Triple Scores York...," *The New York Times*, July 8, 1945, 23; "Rog Cramer's Triple Wins...," *The Washington Post*, July 8, 1945, M6.

12. James P. Dawson, "56,164 See Yanks Split with Tigers," *The New York Times*, July 9, 1945, 8.

13. "Cards and Tigers Dominate...," *The Sporting News*, July 12, 1945.

14. "Tiger Twilight Games Going Over...," *The Sporting News*, July 12, 1945, 10; "Greenberg with Tigers Draw Top...," *The Sporting News*, July 19, 1945, 10.

15. Sam Greene, "Reserves Leave Tigers Weak...," *ibid.*

16. *Ibid.*

17. "Trout, 2 Other Tigers Ailing...," *The Washington Post*, July 12, 1945, 8.

18. "Bosox Trip Tigers, 2–1...," *The Washington Post*, July 13, 1945, 8.

19. Willard Mullin, "Starts Bridging Big Gap...," *The Sporting News*, July 5, 1945, 1.

20. "Ferris Records 15th...," *Los Angeles Times*, July 14, 1945, 6.

21. "Bosox Take 3rd Straight...," *The Washington Post*, July 15, 1945, M6.

22. Sam Greene, "Tigers' Double-Duty Eaton...," *The Sporting News*, August 16, 1945, 9; James P. Dawson, "Yanks' 3 in Sixth...," *The New York Times*, July 16, 1945, 6.

23. "Tigers Club Yanks...," *Los Angeles Times*, July 17, 1945, 10.

24. "Tigers Turn Back Senators...," *The New York Times*, July 19, 1945, 16.

25. "Senators Conquer Tigers...," *The New York Times*, July 21, 1945, 14.

26. "Tigers Execute Triple Play but...," *Chicago Daily Tribune*, July 21, 1945, 14.

27. "Athletics Battle Tigers 24...," *The New York Times*, July 22, 1945, 49.

28. "Tigers Score, 9–1, Then Lose...," *The New York Times*, July 23, 1945, 22.

29. "Newsom's Arm and Bat Defeat...," *Chicago Daily Tribune*, July 24, 1945, 15.

30. "Mayo's Homer Nets Tigers...," *Los Angeles Times*, July 28, 1945, 7.

31. Irving Vaughan, "Trout, Tigers...," *Chicago Daily Tribune*, July 29, 1945, A1.

32. Jonathan Goldman, *The Empire State Building Book* (New York: St. Martin's Press, 1980), 66.

33. Irving Vaughan, "13 Hits Provide No Luck...," *Chicago Daily Tribune*, July 30, 1945, 17.

34. "Newhouser Beats Browns...," *The New York Times*, August 1, 1945, 22.

Chapter 9

1. H.G. Salsinger, "Hal Calls It Yank 'Luck,'" *The Sporting News*, August 9, 1945, 12.

2. "Cullenbine's Double...," *The Washington Post*, August 2, 1945, 8.

3. "Benton of Tigers...," *The New York Times*, August 3, 1945, 20.

4. Sam Greene, "Eddie Helps to Steady...," *The Sporting News*, August 9, 1945, 4.

5. Irving Vaughan, "Caldwell Shuts Out...," *Chicago Daily Tribune*, August 4, 1945, 13.

6. Irving Vaughan, "Grove Whips Newhouser...," *Chicago Daily Tribune*, August 5, 1945, A1; "White Sox Make It...," *Los Angeles Times*, August 5, 1945, A6.

7. Rob Neyer, *A Last Great Season: The Senators in 1945, Saturday, August 4: A Firestarting Reliever and...*, ESPN.com, May 13, 2004, 3; Gilbert, 213.

8. "Tigers Drop Two...," *The New York Times*, August 6, 1945, 19.

9. "Detroit Holds Fraction Lead...," *The Washington Post*, August 7, 1945, 10; Shirley Povich, "Nats Defeat Boston...," *The Washington Post*, August 6, 1945, 1; "Tigers Split...," *Los Angeles Times*, August 7, 1945, A8.

10. Austin Bay, "Thank God for the Atom Bomb...," www.creators.com; "Hiroshima remembers...," *USA TODAY*, pg 8A, August 6, 2002; "R. Nelson, Operator of 'Enola...," *Los Angeles Times*, February 7, 2003, 7B.

11. "Case Injuries Leg...," *The Washington Post*, August 9, 1945, 1; "Tigers, Red Sox Split," *Chicago Daily Tribune*, August 9, 1945, 24.

12. *Ibid.*

13. Ben Benwell, "Bobby Maier: A Baseball Memoir," National Baseball Hall of Fame Library (Cooperstown, New York, September, 1992), 8.

14. "Caster Pinch Pitcher...," *The Old Scout*, Newspaper Clippings, Baseball Hall of Fame, Cooperstown, NY, September 17, 1945; "Tigers Obtain...," *Chicago Daily Tribune*, August 10, 1945, 20.

15. "Tigers' 15 Blows Rout...," *The New York Times*, August 10, 1945, 20.

16. "Heflin of Red Sox...," *The New York Times*, August 11, 1945, 16.

17. "Tigers Defeat...," *Chicago Daily Tribune*, August 12, 1945, A2.

18. "Tigers Take 2...," *Chicago Daily Tribune*, August 13, 1945, 22.

19. "Hank Greenberg Figures...," *The Washington Post*, August 14, 1945, 10.

20. James P. Dawson, "41,956 See Tigers...," *The New York Times*, August 14, 1945, 24; "Tigers Defeat Yankees...," *Chicago Daily Tribune*, August 14, 1945, 16.

21. "Nats Defeat...," *The Washington Post*, August 16, 1945, 1; "Leonard and Senators Beat...," *Chicago Daily Tribune*, August 16, 1945, 24.

22. "Newhouser Beats...," *The New York Times*, August 17, 1945, 13.

23. "Senators Triumph...," *The New York Times*, August 18, 1945, 14; "Haefner Gets 7-Hitter...," *The Washington Post*, August 18, 1945, 6; "Tiger's Lead Is Cut...," *Chicago Daily Tribune*, August 18, 1945, 16.

24. Shirley Povich, "Nats Trounce Tigers...," *The Washington Post*, August 19, 1945, M1.

25. "Tigers Bow in 11th After 6-1 Triumph...," *The New York Times*, August 20, 1945, 15.

26. "Cullenbine and Cramer Hit Homers...," *The Washington Post*, August 21, 1945, 10; "Tigers Overcome Athletics...," *The New York Times*, August 21, 1945, 24; "Newhouser Captures 20th...," *Los Angeles Times*, August 21, 1945, 10.

27. "Athletics, Tigers Divide...," *The New York Times*, August 22, 1945, 18; "Tigers Split with Macks, 'Bobo' Fails...," *The Washington Post*, August 22, 1945, 8.

28. "Trout Wins...," *The Washington Post*, August 23, 1945, 10.

29. "Tigers, with Tobin...," *The New York Times*, August 24, 1945, 12; "Tigers Swell League Lead...," *Los Angeles Times*, August 24, 1945, 10.

30. "Feller, Indian Ace, Released...," *The New York Times*, August 23, 1945, 19; "Bob Feller Doffs...," *The Washington Post*, August 23, 1945, 10; Frank Mastro, "When a Sailor...," *Chicago Daily Tribune*, August 23, 1945; Bus Ham, "Return of Feller...," *The Washington Post*, August 24, 1945, 12.

31. "Feller Comes Back!" *Chicago Daily Tribune*, August 25, 1945, 15; "Feller, Fanning 12...," *The New York Times*, August 25, 1945, 14.

32. "Tigers Get Bridges...,"*The New York Times*, August 26, 1945, 59.

33. "Tigers Lose Twice...," *The New York Times*, August 27, 1945, 13; "Indians Deal Tigers Double Setback...," *Chicago Daily Tribune*, August 27, 1945, 20.

34. "Newhouser Victor...," *The New York Times*, August 29, 1945, 20.

35. "Browns Top Tigers...," *The New York Times*, August 30, 1945, 17.

36. "3-Run Indian Blow...," *The New York Times*, September 1, 1945, 14.

Chapter 10

1. Frederick G. Lieb, "Jakucki Put Off Browns' Train...," *The Sporting News*, September 6, 1945, 4; Peter Golenbock, *The Spirit of St. Louis: A History of the St. Louis Cardinals and Browns* (New York: Avon, 2000), 317–318,.

2. "Tigers Top Indians...," *The New York Times*, September 2, 1945, 61.

3. "Bagby of Indians...," *The New York Times*, September 3, 1945, 19.

4. Benwell, 9.

5. "Tigers Turn Back...," *The New York Times*, September 4, 1945, 18.

6. Joe Falls, "The World of Dizzy Trout," Newspaper Clippings, National Baseball Hall of Fame Library, Cooperstown, New York, March 18, 1972.

7. James P. Dawson, "Trout of Tigers...," *The New York Times*, September 5, 1945, 26.

8. Joe Williams, Yankees' Warm-up...," *The Sporting News*, September 13, 1945, 5.

9. "Hank to Wed...," *Ibid.*

10. "This Morning with Shirley Povich," *The Washington Post*, September 5, 1945, 8.

11. Arch Ward, "In the Wake of the News," *Chicago Daily Tribune*, September 8, 1945, 15.

12. James P. Dawson, "51,511, See Yanks...," *The New York Times*, September 6, 1945, 18.

13. *Ibid.*

14. Sid Feder, "McCarthy's Club...," *The Washington Post*, September 7, 1945, 12.

15. *Ibid*; James P. Dawson, "Yanks...," *The New York Times*, September 7, 1945, 26.

16. James Zerilli, "Beating Yanks on One Curve," *Baseball Digest*, July 1950, 19.

17. James P. Dawson, "Yankees Defeated...," *The New York Times*, September 8, 1945, 19.

18. "Hank Clouts...," *The Washington Post*, September 9, 1945, M6; James P. Dawson, "Yankees Battered..." *The New York Times*, September 9, 1945, 79.

19. "Tigers Victors...," *The New York Times*, September 19, 1945, 13.

20. "American League...," *The Sporting News*, September 13, 1945, 15.

21. "Tigers Top...," *The New York Times*, September 11, 1945, 29.

22. "Trout Yields 2 Hits...," *Chicago Daily Tribune*, September 12, 1945, 26; "Trout 2-Hitter Tops...," *The New York Times*, September 12, 1945, 28.

23. Povich, September 10, 1945, 10.

24. "Tigers Bow in 16th...," *The New York Times*, September 13, 1945, 29; "Bob Estalella

Doubles...," *The Washington Post*, September 13, 1945, 10.

25. "Tigers Lose in 9th...," *The New York Times*, September 14, 1945, 26.

26. Benwell, 9–10; "Maier Steals Home...," Newspaper Clippings, National Baseball Hall of Fame Library, Cooperstown, New York, September 14, 1945; "Tigers Down A's...," *The Washington Post*, September 14, 1945, 1.

27. Conversations with Red Borom.

28. *Ibid.*

29. Arch Ward, "In the Wake of the News," *Chicago Daily Tribune*, September 15, 1945, 15.

30. Conversations with Red Borom.

31. Arthur Daley, "Sports of the Times: Short Shots...," *The New York Times*, September 15, 1945, 20.

32. "Nats, Tigers Lead with Aces...," *The Washington Post*, September 15, 1945, 6.

33. Irving Vaughan, "Tigers Wipe...," *Chicago Daily Tribune*, September 16, 1945, A1; Louis Effrat, "Tigers Twice Beat...," *The New York Times*, September 16, 1945, 81.

34. Povich, September 16, 1945, M6.

35. "Diz Out-Dizzed," *The Sporting News*, September 27, 1945, 2.

36. Louis Effrat, "Tigers Win...," *The New York Times*, September 17, 1945, 13.

37. Louis Effrat, "Tigers Will..." *The New York Times*, September 18, 1945, 17.

38. Louis Effrat, "Senators' 16...," *The New York Times*, September 19, 1945, 29; Gayle Talbot, "Lead Bulge Cut...," *Los Angeles Times*, September 19, 1945, A7.

39. Sam Greene, "Schedule Seen as...," *The Sporting News*, September 20, 1945, 5; "Player of the Week Dizzy Trout," *Ibid.*, 13.

40. "Feller's 1-Hitter...," *The New York Times*, September 20, 1945, 27.

41. "Nightmare of Errors...," *The Washington Post*, September 21, 1945, 12.

42. Irving Vaughan, "Tigers Given...," *Chicago Daily Tribune*, September 23, 1945, 16.

43. "Newhouser Blanks Browns...," *The New York Times*, September 23, 1945, 79.

44. "Potter of Browns Blanks...," *The New York Times*, September 24, 1945, 13.

45. "Tigers Shut Out...," *Los Angeles Times*, September 24, 1945, 10.

46. "Senators Triumph After...," *The New York Times*, September 24, 1945, 13; Povich, September 24, 1945, 10.

47. "Tigers Split, Need One...," *The New York Times*, 1945, 27; "Tigers Split...," *Adrian Daily Telegram*, September 27, 1945, 12.

48. Povich, September 30, 1945, M6.

49. Povich, September 29, 1945, 8.

50. "Bengals to Face...," *Adrian Daily Telegram*, September 29, 1945.

51. "Greenberg's Home Run..." *Los Angeles Times*, October 1, 1945, 10.

52. Povich, October 1, 1945, 10.

53. *Ibid.*

54. Povich, October 2, 1945, 12.

55. Daley, October 3, 1945, 23.

56. Shirley Povich, "Newhouser Choice...," *The Washington Post*, October 3, 1945, 11.

Chapter 11

1. Bak, 319.

2. Bak, 318.

3. "Dizzy Trout Dies...," Newspaper Clippings, National Baseball Hall of Fame Library, Cooperstown, New York., February 29, 1972.

Chapter 12

1. "1945 American League Expanded Leader Boards," baseball-reference.com, May 20, 2003, 1–5.

2. Statistics from baseball-reference.com, 1945 Detroit Tigers Statistics, September 24, 2003; baseball-reference.com, 1945 Detroit Tigers Team Statistics, October 10, 2001; BaseballLibrary.com, 1945 Detroit Tigers, February 03, 2003.

Chapter 13

1. James P. Dawson, "Detroit Is...," *The New York Times*, October 2, 1945, 17.

2. "Crowded Detroit...," *The New York Times*, October 3, 1945, 23.

3. "Louis Discharged...," *The New York Times*, October 2, 1945, 18.

4. "Blind Veterans at Series," *The New York Times*, October 3, 1945, 23.

5. Arch Ward, "In the Wake of the News," *Chicago Daily Tribune*, October 2, 1945.

6. Dawson, October 2, 1945.

7. "Crowded Detroit."

8. Peter Golenbock, *Wrigleyville: A Magical History Tour of the Chicago Cubs* (New York: St. Martin's Griffin, 1999), 309; Ward, October 3, 1945.

9. Shirley Povich, "Newhouser Faces...," *The Washington Post*, October 2, 1945, 12.

10. Golenbock, *Wrigleyville*, 305.

11. Arthur Daley, "Sports of the Times," *The New York Times*, October 3, 1945, 23.

12. James Dawson, "O'Neill, Grimm See 6...," *The New York Times*, October 3, 1945, 23.

13. Jordan, 157.

14. "Crowded Detroit..."; "Line-Up of Series...," *The New York Times*, October 3, 1945, 23.

15. "Line-Up of Series...," *The New York Times*, October 3, 1945, 23.

16. Charles Segar, "Cub, Tiger Work...," *New York Daily Mirror*, October 3, 1945, 82.

17. Shirley Povich, "Newhouser Choice...," *The Washington Post*, October 3, 1945, 11.

18. John Drebinger, "Series Will Open...," *The New York Times*, October 3, 1945, 23.

19. "The 1945 World Series Swing by Swing," *The Sporting News*, October 11, 1945.

Chapter 14

1. Red Smith, "Newhouser...," *New York Herald Tribune*, October 4, 1945, 26.

2. "Borowy's Arm..." *New York Herald Tribune*, October 4, 1945, 26.

3. Arch Ward, "In the Wake of the News," *Chicago Daily Tribune*, October 4, 1945, 29.

4. Red Smith.

5. *Ibid.*

6. Joe Williams, "Newhouser's...," Newspaper Clippings, National Baseball Hall of Fame Library, Cooperstown, New York, October 4, 1945.

7. "This Morning with Shirley Povich," *The Washington Post*, October 4, 1945, 12.

8. *Ibid.*

9. John C. Skipper, *The Cubs Win the Pennant!* (Jefferson, NC: McFarland, 2004), 132.

10. Arthur Daley, "Sports of the Times," *The New York Times*, October 4, 1945, 19.

11. Povich, 12.

12. *Ibid.*

13. *Ibid.*

14. *Ibid.*

15. *Ibid.*

16. *Ibid.*

17. *Ibid.*

18. *Ibid.*

19. James P. Dawson, "Margin of...," *The New York Times*, October 4, 1945, 13.

20. *Ibid.*

21. *Ibid.*

22. *Ibid.*

23. *Ibid.*

24. *Ibid.*

25. *Ibid.*

26. *Ibid.*

27. *Ibid.*

28. *Ibid.*

29. Joe Williams, "Tigers Played Bad Baseball."

30. Red Smith, "No Last-Minute Changes."

31. *Ibid.*

32. *Ibid.*

33. Arthur Daley, "A Distinct Improvement."

34. Shirley Povich, "Cubs Blank...," *The Washington Post*, October 4, 1945, 1.

Chapter 15

1. Arch Ward, "In the Wake of the News," *Chicago Daily Tribune*, October 4, 1945, 29.

2. Dan Parker, "Virgil, 'Homer' Teach...," *Daily Mirror*, October 5, 1945, 27.

3. Arch Ward.

4. Arch Ward, "In the Wake of the News," *Chicago Daily Tribune*, October 5, 1945, 25.

5. *Ibid.*

6. Golenbock, *Wrigleyville*, 309.

7. Arthur Daley, "Sports of the Times: Cubs Collide with Trucks," *The New York Times*, October 5, 1945, 19.

8. "This Morning with Shirley Povich," *The Washington Post*, October 8, 1945, 11.

9. Arthur Daley.

10. *Ibid.*

11. Dan Parker.

12. Arthur Daley.

13. Charles Segar, "Overmire 5–6 Over...," *Daily Mirror*, October 5, 1945, 28.

14. James P. Dawson, "Tigers Show...," *The New York Times*, October 5, 1945, 18; Charles Segar.

15. Charles Dunkley, "Greenberg...," *The Washington Post*, October 5, 1945, 14.

16. James P. Dawson.

17. *Ibid.*

18. *Ibid.*

19. *Ibid.*

20. *Ibid.*

21. Golenbock, *Wrigleyville*, 310.

22. James P. Dawson.

23. *Ibid.*

24. *Ibid.*

25. Clifford Bloodgood, "The Tigers—in Seven Games," *Baseball Magazine*, December 12, 1945, 223.

26. Arthur Daley.

27. "This Morning with Shirley Povich," *The Washington Post*, October 5, 1945, 14.

28. Andrew Herrmann, "What Was It Like...," *Chicago Sun-Times*, October 8, 2003.

29. "To Detroit Club...," Distribution Letter, A.B. Chandler, Baseball Office of the Commissioner, 1945.

Chapter 16

1. Greenberg, 78–79.

2. "Empty Tank...," *The Sporting News*, October 11, 1945, 6; Arch Ward, "In the Wake of the News," *Chicago Daily Tribune*, October 6, 1945, 19.

3. "History of the World Series—1906," *TSN*, SportingNews.com, 2002; "Passeau Knots...," *The Sporting News*, October 11, 1945, 6; *The Baseball Encyclopedia*, 9th ed. (New York: Macmillan, 1993), 2687.

4. Arthur Daley, "Sports of the Times," *The New York Times*, October 6, 1945, 21.

5. "Chicago Now Leads...," *Adrian Daily Telegram*, October 6, 1945, 8.

6. "Claude Passeau," Biography, BaseballLibrary.com, September 18, 2008.

7. Arch Ward.

8. Arthur Daley.

9. James P. Dawson, "Both Teams...," *The New York Times*, October 6, 1945, 17.

10. Arthur Daley.

11. *Ibid*; *The Sporting News*, 6.

12. *Ibid*.

13. *Ibid*.

14. Andrew Herrmann, "What Was It Like...," *Chicago Sun-Times*, October 8, 2003.

15. *The Sporting News*, 6.

16. Ken Smith, "A.L. Hopes on Trout...," *Daily Mirror*, October 6, 1945, 14.

17. "Passeau Keeps Calm...," *The Chicago Daily Tribune*, October 6, 1945, 21; James P. Dawson.

18. Ken Smith.

19. *The Chicago Daily Tribune*.

20. *Ibid*.

21. Bak, 320.

22. Ken Smith.

23. Arch Ward.

24. Arthur Daley.

Chapter 17

1. Edward Burns, "At Home to...," *Chicago Daily Tribune*, October 6, 1945, 19; Lieb, *Tigers*, 267.

2. *By Joe Williams*, "O'Neill...," Newspaper Clippings, National Baseball Hall of Fame Library, Cooperstown, New York, Oct. 6, 1945.

3. Golenbock, *Wrigleyville*, 265–280.

4. "This Morning with Shirley Povich," *The Washington Post*, October 6, 1945, 10.

5. "Fourth Game Gossip," *The Sporting News*, October 11, 1945, 6.

6. Arthur Daley, "Sports of the Times," *The New York Times*, October 7, 1945, 82.

7. *The Sporting News*, October 7, 1945; Arch Ward, "In the Wake of the News," *Chicago Daily Tribune*, October 7, 1945, A1.

8. "The History of the Billy...," 1, *Wise Guys Corner*, tribads.com, December 11, 2002.

9. Arch Ward.

10. Golenbock, *Wrigleyville*, 202–203.

11. Arch Ward; *The Sporting News*, October 7, 1945.

12. *ESPN The Magazine*, May 9, 2005, 60.

13. "Curse of the...," *Wikipedia*, 1; Answers.com, February 17, 2007.

14. *ESPN The Magazine*.

15. *Ibid*.

16. Lieb, *Tigers*, 268.

17. *Ibid*.

18. Zipp Newman, "Jackson was well...," *The Birmingham News*, September 14, 1975.

19. Edward Burns.

20. Arthur Daley.

21. *Ibid*.

22. *Ibid*.

23. Arch Ward.

24. John Drebinger, "Trout Wins in Box," *The New York Times*, October 7, 1945, S1.

25. Shirley Povich, "Trout Beats Cubs...," *The Washington Post*, October 7, 1945, M!.

26. Daley.

27. "This Morning with Shirley Povich," *The Washington Post*, October 7, 1945, M6.

28. Charles Dunkley, "Series Clubhouse Notes," *Los Angeles Times*, October 7, 1945, A6.

29. James Dawson, "Trout Gives Credit to His 'Atom Ball,'" *The New York Times*, October 7, 1945, S1.

Chapter 18

1. Arch Ward, "In the Wake of the News," *Chicago Daily Tribune*, October 8, 1945, 21.

2. John Drebinger, "43,463 See Tigers...," *The New York Times*, October 8, 1945, 1.

3. Arch Ward.

4. *Ibid*.

5. Arthur Daley, "Sports of the Times," *The New York Times*, October 8, 1945, 23.

6. *Ibid*.

7. John Drebinger.

8. W. Martin, "Richards' Handling...," *Washington Post*, October 8, 1945, 12.

9. Arthur Daley.

10. "This Morning with Shirley Povich," *The Washington Post*, October 8, 1945, 11.

11. Arthur Daley.

12. Lieb, *Tigers*, 269.

13. Shirley Povich, "Tigers Beat Cubs...," *The Washington Post*, October 8, 1945, 1.

14. Jordan, 161.

15. *Ibid*.

16. Joe Williams, "To Beat...," Newspaper Clippings, National Baseball Hall of Fame Library, Cooperstown, New York, October 8, 1945.

17. Clifford Bloodgood, "The Tigers—in Seven...," *Baseball Magazine*, December 12, 1945, 226.

18. James P. Dawson, "Detroit's...," *The New York Times*, October 8, 1945, 22.

19. *Ibid*.

20. *Ibid*.

21. Shirley Povich.

22. James P. Dawson.

23. *Ibid*.

24. *Ibid*.

25. *Ibid*.

26. *Ibid*.

27. *Ibid*.

28. Arch Ward.

29. *Ibid*.

30. *Ibid*.

31. "Chandler Angers...," *The New York Times*, October 8, 1945, 22.

Chapter 19

1. "This Morning with Shirley Povich," *The Washington Post*, October 8, 1945, 11.
2. *Ibid.*
3. Arch Ward, "In the Wake of the News," *Chicago Daily Tribune*, October 8, 1945, 21; Jerry Liska, "World Series Notes: Greenberg from Hero to Goat...," *The Washington Post*, October 9, 1945, 10.
4. Arthur Daley, "Sports of the Times," *New York Times*, October 9, 1945, 17.
5. Jerry Liska, "World Series Notes"; "Sixth Game Gossip," *The Sporting News*, October 11, 1945, 7; "Cubs' Catcher Fined $250," *The New York Times*, October 31, 1945, 27; Charles Segar, "Cubs Tie Series...," *Daily Mirror*, October 9, 1945, 26.
6. Dan Parker, "Chicago Burns Again...," *Daily Mirror*, October 9, 1945, 27.
7. *The Sporting News*.
8. John Drebinger, "Cubs Beat Tigers," *The New York Times*, October 9, 1945, 16.
9. Charles Dunkley, "Grimm High in Praise...," *The Washington Post*, October 9, 1945, 10.
10. "Charles Hostetler," Obituary, Newspaper Clippings, National Baseball Hall of Fame Library, Cooperstown, New York, 3–6-71.
11. "Grimm Takes Out...," Charles Dunkley, *Los Angeles Times*, October 9, 1945, A6.
12. Shirley Povich, "Cubs Defeat Tigers...," *The Washington Post*, October 9, 1945, 1; Edward Burns, "Cubs Win...," *Chicago Daily Tribune*, October 9, 1945, 21.
13. Lieb, *Tigers*, 271.
14. Arch Ward, "In the Wake of the News," *Chicago Daily Tribune*, October 9, 1945, 21; Dan Parker, "38 Players...," *Daily Mirror*, October 9, 1945, 26.
15. Ken Smith, "Jolly Cholly...," *Daily Mirror*, October 9, 1945, 27; Edward Burns; Golenbock, *Wrigleyville*, 310–311.
16. "Hack's Freak Double...," *Adrian Daily Telegram*, October 9, 1945, 10, C4.
17. Lieb, 272.
18. Edward Burns.
19. "Sixth Game Gossip," *The Sporting News*, October 11, 1945, 3; Greenberg, 150.
20. Charles Dunkley.
21. Lieb, *Tigers*, 272; "This Morning with Shirley Povich," *The Washington Post*, October 10, 1945, 14.
22. Arch Ward; Greenberg, 150; Joe Trimble, "Hostetler...," Newspaper Clippings, National Baseball Hall of Fame Library, Cooperstown, New York, October 10, 1945.
23. Charles Dunkley, "Grimm High...," *The Washington Post*, October 9, 1945, 10.
24. *Ibid.*
25. *Ibid.*
26. John Drebinger.
27. James P. Dawson, "Scorers Reverse...," *The New York Times*, October 9, 1945, 16.
28. *Ibid.*
29. *Ibid.*
30. *Ibid.*
31. Irving Vaughan, "Big Leaguers Rally...," *Chicago Daily Tribune*, October 9, 1945, 21; "Rumor of Move...," *The New York Times*, October 9, 1945, 16.
32. "Zeller Sends Resignation...," *Adrian Daily Telegram*, October 9, 1945, 10; Arch Ward.
33. "Sixth Game Gossip: Zeller to Quit Tigers," *The Sporting News*, October 11, 1945, 3.
34. Shirley Povich.
35. Arthur Daley, "Sports of the Times," *The New York Times*, October 10, 1945, 17.
36. "Armageddon," *The Washington Post*, October 9, 1945, 6.

Chapter 20

1. Arthur Daley, "Sports of the Times," *The New York Times*, October 11, 1945, 19.
2. Robert Burtt and Bill Main, "1945 Commemorative Yearbook," *Time Passages*, 1999.
3. Golenbock, *Wrigleyville*, 310–312.
4. Al Wolf, "Sportraits," *Los Angeles Times*, October 11, 1945, 11.
5. Jordan, 162; Dan Parker, "Ailing Owner Gets...," *Daily Mirror*, October 11, 1945, 36.
6. Gilbert, 256.
7. Greenberg, 150.
8. Arthur Daley.
9. Gene Guidi, *Detroit Free Press*, Newspaper Clippings, National Baseball Hall of Fame Library, Cooperstown, New York.
10. Arthur Daley.
11. Dan Parker.
12. Al Wolf.
13. Dan Daniel, "Over the Fence," *The Sporting News*, October 11, 1945, 12.
14. Dan Parker.
15. Al Wolf.
16. Ken Smith, "Bengals Celebrate...," *Daily Mirror*, October 11, 1945, 86.
17. Jerry Liska, "Tigers Even Series Victories...," *The Washington Post*, October 11, 1945, 10.
18. Edgar G. Brands, "21 Records Set...," *The Sporting News*, October 11, 1945, 3.
19. Jerry Liska; Dan Parker.
20. Charles Dunkley, "Steve O'Neill Gets...," *The Washington Post*, October 11, 1945, 10; Charles Dunkley, "O'Neill, Happy...," *Los Angeles Times*, October 11, 1945, 10.
21. James P. Dawson, "Six Tigers Called...," *The New York Times*, October 11, 1945, 18.
22. *Ibid.*
23. *Ibid.*
24. John Drebinger, "Tigers Rated Edge...," *The New York Times*, October 10, 1945, K.

25. James P. Dawson.
26. *Ibid.*
27. Charles Dunkley.
28. Charles Dunkley, "Sidelights," *The Washington Post*, October 11, 1945, 11.
29. *Ibid.*
30. *Ibid.*
31. *ESPN The Magazine*, May 9, 2005, 60.
32. Benwell, September, 1992.
33. "Each Tiger's Share...," *The New York Times*, October 11, 1945, 19.
34. Lieb, *Tigers*, 273–274; "Tigers Are Honored...," *The New York Times*, October 12, 1945, 28.
35. Joe Williams, "Son-in-Law...," Newspaper Clippings, National Baseball Hall of Fame Library, Cooperstown, New York, October 11, 1945.

Epilogue

1. Benwell, 13.
2. Lyall Smith, "Benton's Average Survives," *Baseball Digest*, February 1946, 7.
3. John C. Skipper, *A Biographical Dictionary of Major League Baseball Managers* (Jefferson, NC: McFarland, 2003), 244.
4. William Allan, "Tiger Owner Briggs Watched...," *Daily Worker*, 1941 (date unknown).
5. H.G. Salsinger, "The Umpire," *The Detroit News*, January 18, 1952.
6. *Baseball Encyclopedia*, 795.
7. *Ibid*, 2163.
8. *Ibid*, 2302.

Bibliography

Books

Alexander, Charles C. *Breaking the Slump: Baseball in the Depression Era.* New York: Columbia University Press, 2002.

Anderson, William M. *The Detroit Tigers: A Pictorial Celebration of the Greatest Players and Moments in Tigers History.* Detroit: Wayne State University Press, 1999.

Bak, Richard. *Cobb Would Have Caught It.* Detroit: Wayne State University Press, 1991.

Barber, Red. *1947: When All Hell Broke Loose in Baseball.* New York: Da Capo Press, 1982.

The Baseball Encyclopedia, 9th ed. New York: Macmillan, 1993.

Bjarkman, Peter C. *Warren Spahn: Baseball Legends.* Philadelphia: Chelsea House, 1995.

Brown, Warren. *The Chicago Cubs.* Carbondale: Southern Illinois University Press, 2001.

Carmichael John P. *Who's Who in the Major Leagues.* 12th ed. Chicago: B.E. Callahan, 1944.

Deveaux, Tom. *The Washington Senators 1901–1971.* Jefferson, NC: McFarland, 2001.

Dickson, Paul. *The New Dickson Baseball Dictionary.* New York: Harcourt Brace, 1999.

Finoli, David. *For the Good of the Country.* Jefferson, NC: McFarland, 2002.

Ford, Henry. *The International Jew: The World's Foremost Problem.* Dearborn, MI: Dearborn Independent, 1922.

Gilbert, Bill. *They Also Served: Baseball and the Home Front.* New York: Crown, 1992.

Goldman, Jonathan. *The Empire State Building Book.* New York: St. Martin's Press, 1980.

Golenbock, Peter. *The Spirit of St. Louis: A History of the St. Louis Cardinals and Browns.* New York: Avon, 2000.

_____. *Wrigleyville: A Magical History Tour of the Chicago Cubs.* New York: St. Martin's Griffin, 1999.

Greenberg, Hank. *The Story of My Life.* Edited by Ira Berkow. Chicago: Triumph, 1989.

Harrigan, Patrick. *The Detroit Tigers: Club and Community 1945–1995.* Toronto: University of Toronto Press, 1997.

Jordan, David M. *A Tiger in His Time.* South Bend, IN: Diamond, 1990.

Lieb, Frederick G. *The Detroit Tigers.* New York: Putnam's, 1946.

Marshall, William. *Baseball's Pivotal Era: 1945–1951.* Lexington: University Press of Kentucky, 1999.

Phillips, John. *The Tigers vs. the Cubs: The 4-F World Series of 1945.* N.p.: Capital Publishing, 1997.

Pietrusza, David. *Judge and Jury: The Life and Times of Judge Kenesaw Mountain Landis.* South Bend, IN: Diamond, 1998.

287

Ritter, Lawrence S. *The Glory of Their Times*. New York: Vintage Books, 1985.

Skipper, John C. *A Biographical Dictionary of Major League Baseball Managers*. Jefferson, NC: McFarland, 2003.

_____. *The Cubs Win the Pennant!* Jefferson, NC: McFarland, 2004.

Spink, J.G. Taylor, and Paul A. Rickart. *Baseball Register*. C.C. Spink & Son, The Sporting News Publishers, 1946.

Sullivan, Dean A., ed. *Middle Innings: A Documentary History of Baseball, 1900–1948*. Lincoln: University of Nebraska Press, 1998.

Trimble, Vance. *Heroes, Plain Folks and Skunks: The Life and Times of Happy Chandler*. Chicago: Bonus Books, 1989.

Warren, Donald. *Radio Priest: Charles Coughlin, the Father of Hate Radio*. New York: Free Press, 1996.

Williams, T. Harry. *Huey Long*. New York: Knopf, 1969.

Williams, Ted, with John Underwood. *My Turn at Bat: The Story of My Life, a Fireside Book*. New York: Simon & Schuster, 1969.

York, Rudy, as told to Furman Bisher. "A Letter to My Son." In *The Fireside Book of Baseball*. Edited by Charles Einstein. New York: Simon & Schuster, 1956.

Personal Interviews

Baker, Del Jr. 15 March 2004, Boerne, TX, oral taped interview.

Borom, E.J. "Red." 26 May 2002, Richardson, TX, oral taped interview.

Kell, George Clyde. 29 November 2002, Hollywood, FL, oral taped interview.

McHale, John J. 21 July 2002, Palm Garden, FL, oral taped interview.

Mierkowicz, Ed. 14 June 2003, Grosse Isle, MI, oral taped interview.

Mueller, Les. 16 August 2003, Millstadt, IL, oral taped interview.

Outlaw, Jimmy. 19 June 2002, Jackson, AL, oral taped interview.

Pierce, Bill. 17 May 2003, Lemont, IL, oral taped interview.

Trucks, Virgil. 09 June 2002, Leeds, AL, oral taped interview.

Various Media

1997, player illustrations, John Phillips, Perry, GA.

Associated Press (AP), New York, NY.

Corbis Photo, Chicago, IL.

George Brace Photo Co., Chicago, IL.

Major League Baseball, Home Video, *The 1945 World Series*, 1992.

Newspaper Clippings, National Baseball Hall of Fame Library, Cooperstown, New York.

Newspapers

Adrian Daily Telegram: 1945 January–December

The Chicago Daily Tribune: 1945-December.

The Chicago Defender: 1945, January–December.

The Daily Mirror: 1945.

The Daily Worker: 1941.

The Detroit Free Press: 1945.

Los Angeles Times: 1945, January–December.

New York Herald Tribune

The New York Times: 1945, January–December.

The Sporting News: 1945, January–December.

The Washington Post: 1945, January–December.

Periodical and Internet Articles

Bay, Austin. "Thank God for the Atom Bomb...," www.creators.com.

Benwell, Ben. "Bobby Maier: A Baseball Memoir." The Baseball Hall of Fame, Cooperstown, New York, September 1992.

"Billy Goat Curse." *ESPN The Magazine*, 60. March 09, 2005.

Bloodgood, Clifford. "The Tigers—in Seven Games." *Baseball Magazine* (December 1945).

Borom, E.J. "Red." Scrapbook.

"Bosse Field, Home of the Evansville Otters." http://www.digital ballparks.com.

Burtt, Robert, and Bill Main. "1945 Commemorative Yearbook." *Time Passages*, 1999.

Carmichael, John P. "He Pitched Against Death!" *Baseball Digest*, April 1947, 13–14 (condensed from *Chicago Daily News*).

Cherokee, Charley. "National Grapevine." *The Chicago Defender*, March 24, 1945.

"Curse of the Billy Goat." http://www. answers.com/topic/curse-of-the-billy-goat?print = true. February 17, 2007.

"Curses." July 03, 2002. http:// www. hepcat.come/goodman/doormat.html.

Dorsey, Tommy. "They're Either Too Young or Too Old." CompleteAlbumLyrics.com, 2002–2008.

Falls, Joe. "The Old Ballpark: 1945 Series featured the Hostetler flop." *The Detroit News*, September 20, 1999.

Herrmann, Andrew. "What Was It Like..." *Chicago Sun-Times*, October 8, 2003.

"Hiroshima remembers...," *USA TODAY*, August 6, 2002.

Hollingsworth, Harry H. *The Best and Worst Baseball Teams of All Time: From the '16 A's to the '27 Yanks to the Present*. New York City: SPI Books, 1994. http://members.aol.com/tomho13/tops30.html.

K., John. "That Memorable Year—1945." Warren Spahn informal discussion. Beverly Hills Café, Hollywood, FL, 2002. http://www.newlifestyles.com/storyteller/text-page.cfm.

Karieff, P.R. "Detroit's Infamous Purple Gang." *Detroit News*, January 16, 1999.

Neyer, Rob. *A Last Great Season: The Senators in 1945, Saturday, August 4*. ESPN.com, May 13, 2004.

1945 Detroit Tigers. www. Baseballlibrary.com, 2003.

1945 New York Yankees. www. Baseballlibrary.com, 2003.

"A Place for Summer: A Narrative History of Tiger Stadium," www.metrotimes.com.

"The Plane That Crashed Into the Empire State Building," The History Net: 20th Century History, http://history 1900s. about, 2004.

The Presidential Colloquium, Clemson University Web site.

Rickard, Earl. "Wartime Baseball." Suite 101.com.

Sargent, Jim. "Edward Red Borom: From Semipro Ball to the Big Leagues." *Baseball Almanac*, February 23, 2002. Baseball History Site, Sylvan Learning Center, http:// www. Baseball. Almanac.com/, May 2002.

"Sloppiest World Series Confrontations." <http://www.encyclopedia.com/doc/1G1-121537238.html. March 13, 2007.

Smith, Red. "Doghouse to Let: Apply Newhouser & Trout." *The Saturday Evening Post*, March 31, 1945.

"What Did You Do in the War, Grandma?" Timeline, file://A\1945%20timelines.htm.

Index

Numbers in **bold italics** indicate pages with photographs.